Loch Vennachar

Farewell Beautiful Lady.

Paul W Simpson

Clippership Press

Also by the same author.

Fleurieu Shipwrecks
Gosport - An American Tragedy
The Missing
Star of Greece - For Profit and Glory
The Last Captain
Neptune's Car - An American Legend
Windjammer
Around Cape Horn Once More

All books available at
these online retail outlets.
www.lulu.com/spotlight/clippership_press

Clippership Press
Adelaide, South Australia
paulsimo2010@yahoo.com.au

© Paul W Simpson 2026

National Library of Australia CiP entry upon request.

Author: Simpson, Paul W.,(1969 -) author.
Title: Loch Vennachar – Farewell Beautiful Lady./ Paul W Simpson.
ISBN: 978-1-7646836-0-9
New Printed Edition.

Notes: Includes index, bibliography, cartography,
b/w photographs.
A minimal amount of AI has been used to restore old, faded, out of focus, and damaged photographs.
Subjects: Loch Vennachar (ship), Shipwrecks—Victoria Melbourne, Geelong, South Australia--Kangaroo Island. Sailing ships--Scotland--History.

Dedication.

To Fon, my guiding star on a smooth and mirrored sea, and to Bruce Stevens, modeller maestro and truest friend.

Foreword

When Loch Vennachar slid from the slipway, and into the River Clyde, on August 4th1875, she entered service at the height of the great iron-hulled clipper era. Built by the renowned yard of James & George Thomson, she was one of a growing fleet of fast, purpose-built sailing ships designed to carry Scottish manufactured goods to Australia and return laden with wool. Owned by a consortium that included James Aitken, James Lilburn, John P. Kidston and other members of the Kidston family, along with Partick businessmen James Galbraith and brothers Thomas and John Henderson, Loch Vennachar represented both commercial ambition and confidence in sail at a time when steam was beginning to challenge its dominance.

Operating under the flag of the Glasgow Shipping Company, she sailed regularly from Broomielaw, Glasgow, to Hobson's Bay, Melbourne, later extending her southern voyages to Port Adelaide as competition from steamships began to erode profits on the traditional clipper routes. Between 1875 and 1905, Loch Vennachar completed more than twenty-five successful round voyages, earning a reputation as a strong and capable ship.

Her career, however, was not without drama. In 1892 she was dismasted by a cyclone in the Indian Ocean, necessitating months of repair in Mauritius. In 1901 she was sunk following a collision in the River Thames, only to be raised and repaired at considerable expense to her owners and insurers. Despite surviving these ordeals, and remarkably losing only one life during her dismasting, with none lost in the Thames collision, Loch Vennachar came to be regarded as an 'unlucky' ship.

Ironically, it was only after the retirement of her long-time master, Captain William Bennett, that Loch Vennachar's story reached its tragic conclusion, ending against the rugged and isolated cliffs of Kangaroo Island's western coast.

This book tells her story in words and pictures, the result of fifty years of interest and research, finally brought together to illuminate the life of a ship that embodied the final great age of commercial sail. It is a story of enterprise, endurance, and the sea's enduring power to humble even the strongest vessels.

P. W. Simpson

2026

Thankyou.

Thanks must go to Gifford Chapman for his research and book on the shipwrecks of Kangaroo Island; Richard Boon for permission to use his family photographs; Terry Drew for permission to use his photographs and diagrams from the Society for Underwater Research survey report; Amer Khan, former archaeologist with the South Australian Department of Environment and Heritage, for allowing access to Loch Vennachar artefacts once stored at Netley; and Peter Christopher for posting the SUR videos of the Loch Vennachar expeditions to the wreck site in 1977 and 1980. Finally, thanks to Steve Reynolds for posting his 2011 dive video of the wreck of the Loch Vennachar, confirming the location of the larger stern section of the ship.

Contents

I

The Dreams of Ordinary Men

Born of copper-clad timbers in the 1840s, clipper ships, as is well known, grew out of the need to transport relatively small but highly valuable cargoes vast distances quickly. Whether it was tea or migrants, the early American and later British clippers were built for speed, not comfort, and being small could carry but a limited amount of cargo.

The early wooden hulls could withstand the rigours of rounding the two capes for but a few years before needing to be replaced. This and economies of scale began to see composite clipper designs begin to appear in the late 1850s and early 1860s. Yes, the hulls of these sleek racers were still copper-clad timbers of Oregon, oak, cedar, and pine, but their skeletal frames were iron. This gave ships such as the legendary Cutty Sark the structural soundness to push hard through the Roaring Forties and frequently beyond in the tea races of the mid-19th century.

Timber eventually gave way to iron as the first iron clippers began to appear from British yards in the late 1860s. Averaging 1,200 tons, thousands of these fast, rugged, and relatively economical clippers were built over the next 30 years. Some of them clocked up sailing times to rival the best of their lighter wooden and composite forebears, but with the age of steam, these vessels lost the tea runs from China.

From there, the focus shifted to the wool and wheat runs from Australia to Britain. For the next few decades, composite former tea clippers and purpose-built wool and wheat clippers plied the sea lanes, bringing migrants and much-needed wares to Australia and New Zealand, and returned to Britain and Europe with much-needed wheat and wool. Such exports made both young nations and the clippers' owners very wealthy. Riding upon the sheep's back kept the age of the clipper alive for many years.

James Lilburn.

James Aitken.

As shipbuilding methods improved, so did the size of the clipper ships. Large 1,500-ton and 1,600-ton fully iron clippers began to appear in the 1870s. More slab-sided than their smaller, sleeker predecessors, they nevertheless managed to attain speeds close to or exceeding the ageing wooden and composite clippers. The larger iron ships were the forerunners of even larger four-masted clipper barques. Painted as floating bins, these ungainly ships carried large cargoes from ports not serviced by coal-guzzling steamships.

Thus was born the age of the windjammers. Large 2,000-ton iron barques were replacing the smaller 1,200-ton clippers of the 1860s and 70s. At the same time, the smaller 1,500-ton iron clippers were being superseded by 2,000-ton steel-hulled ships, which in turn were complemented by the last great square-riggers to sail the oceans: the 2,500-ton and 3,000-ton steel-hulled windjammers of the 1890s and early years of the 20th century.

Vessels such as the Loch Vennachar and her sisters, the Loch Ard and Loch Garry, represented a transition from clipper to windjammer. In the design of the 1,600-ton Loch Ard, they perhaps got it quite wrong, but with the slightly smaller 1,500-ton Loch Garry, the designers of the iron clipper perfected their art.

It was inevitable that when James Aitken and James Lilburn met at the offices of Patrick Henderson & Co, great things would happen. Employed as shipping clerks in the ship brokerage firm, the two ambitious men every day witnessed fortunes being made and lost by others no less ambitious or better than themselves. Drawn to the sea by a love of sail, yet finding themselves unwilling or, due to poor health, unable to follow, Aitken and Lilburn set out to establish themselves as shipping magnates in their own right.

The risks were great, but the potential rewards much greater. Slowly and surely during the early 1860s, the two men cultivated contacts, searched out potential financial backers and dreamed of the ultimate line of the fastest, most luxurious passenger and cargo carrying clippers on the Clyde.

James Aitken was born in 1826 in the town of Dundee, Scotland. His father was Alexander Aitken, a well-known merchant and businessman with connections to the shipowners and financiers of Glasgow. James attended the Trades School in Glasgow, where he met many of his future contacts. He had a sister, Margaret, who later married and moved to San Francisco, California.

James began his career working as a clerk for Kidston and Co., shipowners of Glasgow, and later became a partner in Aitken & Birrell, shipping managers and marine insurance brokers. Driven to succeed, he followed his dream of going to sea and pursued a career as a merchant heading to Constantinople and the Aegean ports. In Turkey, James acted as a shipping agent and buyer for a variety of business interests.

On his return to Scotland, James again found work as a shipping clerk working in the firm of Patrick Henderson, well-known shipowners and agents with interests in the colonial clipper trade to New Zealand and Australia. In early 1869, James Aitken, a widower with a daughter Edith Louise from his first marriage, married Emily Hill, the daughter of a wealthy merchant. With this marriage came money and financial opportunities that James made good use of. James Aitken was a man of prospects, and his marriage to Emily was of mutual benefit to both families.

For much of his life, James did not enjoy good health, yet despite this, he and his wife Emily had six children together: James, Arthur, Lionel, Florence, and Reginald. Arthur died as a youngster of T.B. and Reginald was locked away and forgotten by the family. The last child, Alice, was born in Mentone on the Italian Riviera where the family kept a holiday villa.

As a result of his failing health, James and Emily spent much of their time in Italy where they retired, with James handing over his half of the business to James Lilburn and his son. He remained a silent partner until his death in 1900, aged 74. When he died, great tribute was paid to him by his fellow merchants, agents, and peers of the realm.

In the Glasgow Herald of May 2 1900, tribute was paid to him as a Trustee from 1881-7 by Lord Provost Sir Samuel

19th century Buchanan Street in Glasgow where Aitken, Lilburn & Co, had their office at number 80.

'Ben Nevis' launched 1868
State Library of Victoria

Clan Ranald launched 1868, later bought by the Glasgow Shipping Co
& renamed Loch Rannoch.
State Library of Victoria

Chisholm. He said that former colleagues of Mr Aitken looked back on their friendship with him with very pleasant memories, and added:

"He was a most courteous and obliging colleague and all who had intercourse with him reported the happiest recollections of him."

Another colleague said of him: "Most gentlemanly and courteous in manners, he was very highly esteemed amongst us, and our remembrance of him is of the pleasantest kind."

Donald Fullarton - helensburgh-heritage.co.uk

James Lilburn was born in 1830 in Barony, Glasgow, to James and Hannah Lilburn. James's father worked in the shipping industry, and it was from sailing yachts as a lad and travelling with his father that James developed his love for the sea. The family moved around a lot, from Glasgow to Lochgilphead, and then back to Glasgow in 1861 when James began his career as a shipping clerk.

James's early career took him to Tradston where he met and fell in love with Isabella Binnie. In 1871 James moved into Cathcart, a well-to-do suburb of Glasgow filled with fellow merchants and shipping agents, situated on Govanhill above the River Clyde and the Govan docks. It was whilst working and living in this area that he married Isabella and together they moved into a two-storey home called Park Villa at Crosshill, Cathcart. As the family grew they moved frequently, but continued to inhabit the Govan and Rothesay districts, staying close to James's place of business. The couple had four children: James, Jane, Edwin and William.

James began his career as a shipping clerk, establishing contacts and his reputation in a variety of commercial ventures that saw increasing returns. He began working for Patrick Henderson in the early 1860s, and it was whilst here that he struck up an erstwhile friendship with the older and more experienced James Aitken. The two made an unlikely partnership, but their personalities, interests and work-a-day habits perfectly complemented each other.

James Lilburn fell in love with the sea from an early age and indulged his passions for sail by first learning to sail small skiffs and then moving on to larger craft. For many years he was an active member of the Royal Northern Yacht Club, and later became the club's Commodore for a number of years. James maintained close ties with the company he and James founded way back in 1867. It was not until 1900, with the death of his close friend and partner, that James Lilburn began thinking of retirement.

At first, his eldest son James took over most of his ageing father's duties overseeing the loading of the company's various sailing vessels, with James Snr taking on a managerial role. Even still, he would often travel down to the Govan and Queen's Dock to oversee the loading of the last of the Loch Liners. But from 1901 onwards, after a meeting with the principal ship owners, it was agreed that the company would begin to wind down its investment in vessel ownership and move to the more economically viable areas of shipping management, brokerage and marine insurance.

With the advent of steam and fewer and fewer paying passengers, James Lilburn slowly withdrew from his daily involvement with the company. By 1912 the last of the Loch Liners had been sold off, and on the 13th of March of that year James Lilburn Snr and his son James Jnr met at the chambers of James R. Hamilton & Cuthbert Gemmill, Law Clerks, and signed over the ownership of the company Aitken, Lilburn and Co to their business partners William Hepburn, Samuel Macfarlane, and William M'Kenzie Hepburn, who would continue the company under its previous operating name. With the final sale of the company, James withdrew from public life. He died quietly at his home, Glenlora, Lochwinnoch, Renfrewshire, on the 30th of August 1914, aged 74.

The genesis of the Glasgow Shipping Company was born in the offices of Patrick Henderson & Co in the mid-1860s. Both James and James dreamed of one day becoming shipping magnates, owners and managers in their own right. They both knew that there was little money in going to sea as ships' officers, and becoming a senior sailing master would take years and was fraught with risk to life and limb. The men, James aged 40 and James aged 37, gathered together a group of backers , financial speculators, ships' captains, sailing masters and owner-investors, and carefully planned their first commercial venture in 1866.

One of the keys to their securing financial backing was finding suitable captains who were willing to join them and take a risk with a new company. The first to sign on board was Sailing Master William 'Bully' Martin, a widely respected, methodical and hard-driving captain with an almost faultless record. James Lilburn used his contacts to find shipbuilders and backers who were willing to allow Aitken, Lilburn and Co to manage their ships, organise the finding and loading of the cargoes, and also to act as brokers for the underwriting of the ships and cargoes.

James Lilburn and James Aitken incorporated their company in 1867, leaving their employ at Patrick Henderson's and setting up their new offices at 80 Buchanan Street in the heart of Glasgow's mercantile district. The Hendersons, interestingly enough, provided some of the start-up capital for the fledgling business. Working with financial backers, the first two ships to be contracted by Lilburn & Aitken were the yet-to-be-built full-rigged ships Clan Ranald and Ben Nevis.

As part of the deal that attracted Bully Martin to their employ, this curmudgeonly captain personally supervised the building of the Clan Ranald to his personal specifications and commanded her for the first few years. The Ben Nevis was owned and built for the Watson Brothers, who were financial backers of the new company. With their growing success, the Watsons contracted Aitken, Lilburn & Co to manage many of their ships of the 'Ben Line' on the colonial runs to Australia. Launched in June 1868 from the yards of Barclay, Curle and Co of Glasgow, the Ben Nevis was chartered along with the Loch Awe by Aitken and Lilburn and Co for the Australian trade. This business arrangement of leasing the Clan Ranald, Loch Awe and Ben Nevis lasted until the completion of the first six ships of the Glasgow Shipping Company.

The brand new ship Clan Ranald, under the command of Captain William 'Bully' Martin, departed Glasgow on the 5th of July 1868 bound for Melbourne with a load of general cargo. After an eventless trip of light winds to the line and then fast westerlies to Cape Otway, the ship dropped anchor in Hobson's Bay on the 30th of September. She lay at anchor whilst her load of gunpowder was lightered off, then was towed to Sandridge Railway Pier to discharge her maiden cargo. Onlookers were much impressed at the fresh, clean lines of this new clipper, which featured all that Captain Martin thought necessary for a safe and speedy trip across the seas.

After a short stay in which most cargo space had been pre-sold, the Clan Ranald departed for London on the 14th of November 1868 from Hobson's Bay with a load of wool destined for the February wool sales in London. Also on board was a large quantity of gold destined for the bank vaults of London. Expectant of a clean run home, the Clan Ranald arrived in London on March 5th after a harrowing return journey, in time for the March sales. Despite this minor setback, the financial return on the trip was enough to prove to her backers that they stood to make a small fortune, proving that with the right ships and the right captains, good returns were possible for Aitken, Lilburn and their subscribers.

Departing just after the Clan Ranald was James Lilburn's and James Aitken's second great gamble, one in which they had invested much of their savings and reputations. The new and untested clipper Ben Nevis, built using similar demanding specifications as laid out by William Martin, departed Glasgow on the 21st of August 1868 bound for Melbourne. The brand new clipper was under the command of Captain Alex McPetrie. After a quick trip, with one day making over 300 nautical miles, the Ben Nevis beat to windward in challenging easterlies to arrive in Hobson's Bay on the 12th of November 1868 with 10 passengers, including one Mr Strachan in first class and nine others in steerage.

The ship tied up at Sandridge Pier loaded to the gunnels with a veritable cornucopia of goods, all of which were in great demand in the colonies. Amongst the merchandise unloaded from her hold were: boxes of galvanised iron, barrels of linseed oil, cases of wine and fine whisky, boxes of beer, camp ovens and furnaces, pig iron, fine China, barrels of soda and soda ash, barrels of nails, oil and other hardware, corks, sulphuric acid, casks of paint, grease, bales of leather, iron and copper tubes and piping, packets of sash weights, stationery, ginger and dry spices, boxes of girdles, ovens, kitchen sinks, tobacco and tobacco pipes, and her most dangerous consignment, 900 kegs of gunpowder.

After a lengthy delay waiting for cargo to be consigned and loaded, the Ben Nevis sailed for London with a load of wool and wheat. It was towed out to the Hobson's Bay anchorage on the evening of the 11th of January 1869 and set sail on the morning of the 12th at 8 am. Even after a longer than usual round trip, her cargo still fetched a good price at the grain and wool sales back in London. This second financial windfall was more than enough to convince Aitken, Lilburn and Co to go ahead with their grand scheme to build a line of clippers second to none.

A third ship, the Loch Awe, finished in 1869, was leased by the company and sailed forth to Australia, bringing further financial rewards to this blossoming company. With the backing of the Watsons and other subscribers, Aitken and Lilburn placed orders for six brand new hulls, four to be built by Lawrie of Glasgow and the others by Barclay, Curle & Co. Each was built to specific and demanding standards not seen before on the Clyde. The lessons learned from 'Bully' Martin were applied vigorously by the company to these new ships. Each was 1,200 tons and classed A1 by Lloyd's of London when surveyed.

The Loch Katrine, Loch Earn, Loch Lomond and Loch Leven, all built by Lawrie of Glasgow, and the Loch Ness and Loch Tay, built by Barclay, Curle & Co, were considered state-of-the-art when they were floated out of the docks. The six ships, along with the Clan Ranald, were to form the nucleus of a new company called the Glasgow Shipping Company. Each ship was going to be named after a famous Scottish clan, but another company registered the idea first, so Aitken, Lilburn and Co settled on the idea of naming each of their ships after famous lochs in Scotland.

In line with this system of nomenclature, the Clan Ranald, when purchased in 1875 from Kidston, Ferrier-Kerr and Black, was renamed the Loch Rannoch.

The managing owners of the Loch Line, James Aitken and James Lilburn, did business in a way that was fast becoming old-fashioned by other company bosses. Instead of employing others to hunt out freighting contracts and to oversee the loading and discharging of cargoes, the two men took a great personal interest in the goings-on of the ships and crews in their care. Basil Lubbock, in his book 'Colonial Clippers' published in 1921, stated:

"In the old days it was the custom for owners to make a daily visit to intending shippers; this was Aitken's part of the work and he continued to make a practice of it long after other owners had given it up. Lilburn superintended the loading and despatching of their ships, and so great was his practical knowledge and so keen his interest that it is no exaggeration to say that no ships were better kept up than the Loch liners. All over the world the Loch Line clippers were held up by seamen as examples of what well run and comfortable ships should be... Mr Lilburn was a man who not only thoroughly understood ships but loved them for their own sake. And it is under such owners that sailors consider themselves lucky to serve."

— Basil Lubbock, 1921.

Four of the six ships, plus a number leased by the company, performed above and beyond what was expected for many years and brought great financial rewards for their owners and investors. Things, however, did not always go so smoothly. As often happens, disaster was just a navigational error or hurricane away.

The Loch Leven ended her career on just her second voyage. Whilst sailing from Melbourne with a load of wool and wheat valued at £154,000, she ran aground on the shores of King Island in Bass Strait on the 22nd of October 1871. The crew were all saved, except for Captain Branscombe, who went back to the wreck to rescue the ship's papers. His small boat capsized, spilling the crew into the surf; Captain Branscombe was drowned. Most of the cargo was salvaged and then transferred back to Melbourne, and after insurance claims were settled, the remainder of the cargo and most of the crew transferred to other Loch Liners for the trip back to London.

The Loch Earn was the second of the Loch Liners to come to grief when, on the 21st of November 1873, she collided with the French Trans-Atlantic mail steamer Ville du Havre. The steamer sank, taking 226 passengers and crew to the bottom. Two days later the Loch Earn, with her bow crushed and her watertight collision bulkhead breached, began to founder. The pumps were unable to keep up and the crew took to the ship's boats as the Loch Earn sank, Captain Robertson and his crew being rescued by a passing ship.

Such was the initial success of the company, despite a few financial setbacks, that James and James decided to set up a second company with a second set of shareholders, William Hepburn and Samuel Macfarlane amongst others. Orders were placed for two more hulls to be laid down and, in 1873, the General Shipping Company was formed. Thus the ships Loch Laggan (purchased from J. H. Watt, Glasgow, in 1875), Loch Maree and the Loch Ard were the nucleus of the new company, also managed by the firm Aitken, Lilburn & Co.

The company was also responsible for managing the 'Ben Line' of ships that were operated by the Watson brothers; these included the famous Ben Nevis, Ben Cruachan, Ben Ledi, Ben Venue and the Ben Voirlich. Of the ships of the General Shipping Company, the Loch Maree disappeared with all hands in 1893, the Loch Laggan (originally named America) disappeared with all hands in 1875, and the Loch Ard came to grief on the wild coast of Victoria in 1878, from which there were only two survivors, one of which was Thomas Pearce Snr, father of one of the apprentices on the Loch Vennachar when she too disappeared.

Whilst James Aitken handled the onshore business of generating income, it was James Lilburn who directly influenced the design of the ships that were to enter service with the Glasgow and General Shipping Companies.

Loch Garry

State Library of Victoria

James did not act alone; he listened with great interest to his captains, men such as William Martin, Bill Bennet, Robert Pattman, Andrew Black and James Horne.

In 1873, discussions turned to creating the ultimate iron-hulled clipper. The average tonnage of the Loch Line clippers was 1,200 tons; James Lilburn dreamed of something bigger, faster and more luxurious than anything currently under sail. However, with this would have to come greater crew comfort and safety, so the Loch Line sailing masters were heavily consulted and contributed greatly to the design specifications. Armed with the design requirements that would ensure that the Loch Line would retain its competitive edge in the colonial trade, James Lilburn headed down to Clydebank to look for a firm of shipbuilders who could meet his demands within time and on budget.

Eventually, James Lilburn settled upon the firm of J & G Thomson. This renowned shipbuilding company was founded by James and George Thomson, engineers with works in Finnieston Street, in 1847. After the brothers had both died, the firm was taken over by the sons of the elder brother, also called James and George Thomson.

The firm moved to Clydebank in 1871 where they established the Clyde Bank Iron Shipyard and developed a reputation for the outstanding quality and standards of their engineering and for innovation in design and manufacture of ships, both sail and steam. Aitken, Lilburn & Co commissioned the design and production of two identical ships, sisters in every sense of the word. These ships were to be the state-of-the-art clippers of their day in both comfort, safety, durability, reliability and speed.

Most sailing masters in 1875 were of the agreement that the twin sisters Loch Vennachar and Loch Garry were the finest clipper ships in the world at the times they were launched. The Loch Garry weighed in at 1565 tons and the Loch Vennachar a touch under at 1552 tons; there was almost nothing to separate the ships in length, beam or draft.

Both were equipped with the latest safety gear, ships' boats, navigational instruments and rigging. Each had the latest in donkey boilers and steam-powered winches for the anchors, main mast rigging and main hold crane. Both ships were fitted with waterproof collision bulkheads and the finest quality rigging and steering gear. At the time of their launching, the sisters' staterooms were unsurpassed in luxury and appointment, with each able to carry up to 24 saloon and second-class passengers in their spacious mid-deck houses.

Basil Lubbock summed up several of their unique features thus:

"A new feature was adopted in the placing of her masts. Her mainmast was stepped right amidships, with the fore and mizzen masts at equal distances from it. Loch Garry and her sister ship Loch Vennachar... were rigged in a manner peculiar to themselves. They had short topgallant masts with fidded royal and skysail masts, on which they crossed royals and skysails above double topgallant yards. When in port their upper topsail and upper topgallant yards would be half mast-headed, and with the seven yards on each mast, all squared to perfection, they presented a magnificent appearance."

Basil Lubbock 1921 – The Colonial Clippers, p. 261.

The Loch Garry had a long and distinguished career but was not free of incidents. In 1880, while sailing off the Crozets in stormy conditions, the Loch Garry lost her weather forebrace, fore-topmast and the main topgallant mast. It took the ship a month to get to Melbourne under a jury rig.

She was almost completely dismasted again in 1889 off the coast of Africa and had to limp into Mauritius; once there, she waited almost five months for new masts, spars and sails. The Loch Vennachar was a similarly tough and durable ship, but the sisters' fates were very different.

SAIL PLAN OF "LOCH MOIDART" AND "LOCH TORRIDON."

The Loch Garry had just three captains during her time with the Loch Line and finished her time with the company being sold to Italian interests in 1911 as scrap iron for the princely sum of £1800. Her final fate, however, was somewhat unexpected. The ship was enlisted into the Italian navy and disappeared sometime before 1918; her fate and that of her crew are unknown.

With the construction and launch of the twin 1,500-ton ships, Aitken, Lilburn and Co. also ordered more hulls to fill the expanding needs of their clients. In just three years, seven more ships were commissioned and launched from various yards about the Clyde.

The Loch Long, Loch Fyne, Loch Ryan, Loch Sloy, Loch Shiel, Loch Etive, and the Loch Sunart, all 1,200-tonners, were launched into service, all built to the exacting standards of the Loch Line sailing masters and owners. Each ship had a varied and chequered career.

- The **Loch Long** disappeared with all hands in 1903, just before she was due to be sold.
- The **Loch Fyne** disappeared in 1883 somewhere in the English Channel.
- The **Loch Ryan** served faultlessly until 1909, when she was sold to the Australian Government.
- The **Loch Sloy** was wrecked in 1899 off Kangaroo Island; there were just three survivors.
- Of the remaining ships:
- The **Loch Shiel** ran aground in 1894 and then sank; all aboard were saved.
- The **Loch Etive** was sold at the same time as the Loch Garry to an Italian firm for scrap metal in 1911; it is not clear if she ever joined the Loch Garry as a wartime vessel.
- Lastly, the **Loch Sunart** ran aground and sank on just her second voyage in 1879. All were saved and the Captain had his extra-master's ticket suspended.

Captain Robert Pattman

By the end of the nineteenth century, the Loch Line owners moved away from building three-masted 1,200-ton clippers as freight prices dropped and steam became the preferred method by many to travel and move cargo. In order to stay competitive, Aitken, Lilburn and Co., instead of moving to steam, continued to persevere with sail, but did make several fundamental changes to the way they operated their businesses.

To cut costs, all the Loch Line 1,200-ton ships had their mizzen spars removed and were from then on barque-rigged with double gaff sails on the mizzen and larger staysails in a fore and aft configuration. The company also upped the ante in 1881 by ordering from Barclay, Curle & Co. two four-mast barques of 2,000 tons. These windjammers were the sister ships Loch Moidart and Loch Torridon; Loch Moidart was launched in September and Loch Torridon in November of that same year.

These ships proved to be both economical and fast, and before long James Lilburn had more 2,000-ton hulls on order. The Loch Moidart lasted but nine years before running aground on the north coast of Holland; from this wreck there were just two survivors. Her sister ship, the Loch Torridon, had a much longer and more successful career. The ship eventually came under the command of Robert Pattman, one of the best trainers of men upon the colonial trade routes at the time. It was seen by many at the time a privilege to sail with either Captain James Horne or Captain Robert Pattman. Both were considered true masters of their craft, and many an apprentice felt fortunate that they had had the advantage of being trained by one of these captains.

The career of Robert Pattman and the Loch Torridon was a long and financially successful one. He and the ship made its owners a small fortune. In 1908, Robert Pattman retired from command of one of the most successful clippers of all time. He switched over to steam but never really felt comfortable in his new role. It seemed that the Captain and his ship were like an old married couple, for in 1912, when the Loch Torridon was sold to Russian interests, Captain Pattman badly broke his leg whilst at sea. He died that same year ashore at Falmouth Hospital. The Old

Lady did not last much longer, for she sank in the English Channel in early 1915.

Loch Garry dismasted off Mauritius, c. 1889.
State Library of Victoria.

Such was the initial success of the giant four-masted barques that two more were ordered from the yards of Barclay, Curle & Co. These next two ships, the Loch Carron and Loch Broom, were as pretty and powerful as their predecessors and continued to bring in good returns for their owners. The Loch Carron, under the command of Captain Stainton Clarke (the best friend of Robert Pattman), made many successful voyages to and from Australia in the colossal barque.

Yet her career was not without moments, for In 1889, whilst trying to round the Cape of Good Hope, the Loch Carron was struck by a storm and broached, injuring many of her crew.

Again in 1904, she was again in heavy weather when she collided with the clipper Inverkip just off of the Fastnet light. The Inverkip sank in minutes, the only survivors being the steward and a carpenter who jumped aboard the Loch Carron just as the two ships separated.

The Loch Carron had her bow holed (but the collision bulkhead held), her fore-topgallant mast and all headgear, including the bowsprit and figurehead, were gone. The ship managed to limp into Queenstown, Ireland, where she was repaired for £1,500. Aitken, Lilburn and Co. were made liable by Lloyd's and a Marine Board enquiry and forced to hand over more than £30,000 in damages. The Loch Carron was eventually sold in 1912 as the company was being wound up.

The largest three-master and the last full-rigged ship employed by the Loch Line was the anomalously named 2,062-ton Brabloch, built in 1889 by Barclay, Curle & Co. In contrast to the earlier iron-hulled ships of the line, the Brabloch was the first of a larger, steel-hulled design. She had a short career under the command of Captain William Hawkins before sitting idle for many months. The ship's long career with the company ended in 1912 when she was sold to Norwegian interests and renamed the Vinga.

Her one great misadventure came when she was transporting a load of coal from Newcastle to San Francisco. Almost to port, the load caught fire, repeatedly blowing off the cargo hatches. The ship was eventually towed into harbour, beached, and allowed to burn out. The Brabloch was completely gutted, but rather than sell her as a hulk, James Lilburn had her refitted and put back into service.

The last and largest vessel to be employed by the company was the 2,400-ton, four-masted barque, the Loch Nevis. Launched in 1889 from the yards of Barclay, Curle & Co., she was the company's last great attempt to stay competitive with the growing fleet of fast and reliable steamers. The ship performed admirably, managing to maintain a small profit for much of its career.

However, by 1895, the writing was on the wall. The smaller ships, the 1,200-tonners, were consistently losing money. Only the 1,500-ton ships and the four-masted barques really stood any chance of turning a profit. However, three key events spelled the slow and inevitable end of the dreams of ordinary men in the days under sail: a lack of apprentices, a lack of experienced crews, and the vast improvements in steam-driven ships and technology.

The Loch Nevis was sold in 1900, just after the death of James Aitken. From this time onwards, the surviving windjammers were gradually disposed of until in 1912, at the age of 72, James Lilburn signed over his share of the firm to his business partners, thus bringing to an end the golden age of sail in the colonial trade. The Loch Line was the last great company still exclusively under sail. The entity continued as a managing agency, ships' brokerage, and marine insurance agent, but the era of the great wool and wheat clippers was all but over.

<u>The last four masted barque 'Loch Nevis'</u>
State Library of Victoria

II

A Most Extraordinary Lady

When the Loch Vennachar was first ordered, her prospective owners were looking for something new. They had already decided that 1,200 tons was not big enough, and that 1,600 tons was too unwieldy. They wanted a premier liner and freight carrier that would be the flagship of their growing fleet of wool clippers.

James Lilburn and James Aitken consulted far and wide before settling upon the advice of experienced shipbuilders J & G Thompson and Sons, and master mariners like William Martin. The new vessels had to be the best that money could buy: fast, sleek, strong, and capable of carrying a variety of cargo and passengers in speed and relative comfort from Britain to Australia.

When she was loosed down the slipway of yard 139, the Loch Vennachar was the most modern clipper afloat. Larger, longer, and more spacious than her 1,200-ton predecessors, stronger, more stable, and just as swift as her composite cousins, with greater keel length and area of sail, she was a ship to be envied and admired.

Along with her sister ship, the Loch Garry, the Loch Vennachar was the pride of the fleet and set a standard that would only be superseded by the later triple-masted steel ships and the larger windjammers of the late 19th century.

Loch Vennachar running her easting down under original rig of skysails over royals.
Painting by A.V. Gregory.
State Library of Victoria.

Construction profile of the Loch Vennachar

**Built by J & G Thomson Clydebank, Yard No 139.
Surveyed & Rated AA1 100% by Lloyds of London on the 1st
September 1875.**

Ordered: 1873
Keel Laid: 1874
Propulsion: Sail. 3 masts
Sails: Fully ship rigged
Launched: Wednesday, 4th August 1875
Built: 1874 - 1875
Ship Type: Iron ship
Construction: Iron ribs & frames, ½ inch thick, 36 inch x 12 foot ,
iron hull plates riveted every 6 inches, two wooden decks,
foc's'le, mid-deck house and poop deck/saloon cabin.
Keel dimensions 9 ½ "x2 ½", Stem 9 ½ "x2 ½", Stern Post 9' x 2
½" Frames – angle iron 3/5 amidships
Do. 1/5 each end 5 ½" x 3 1/2 ".
Frames extend from keel to gunnels riveted to plates with ¾
inch rivets, 6 inches apart. Rudder diameter 6 ½ " at head, 3 1/2
" at foot.
Two cemented waterproof collision bulkheads 1' 6" thick,
behind which is a water-tight compartment forward and aft.
 15045 iron rivets used in her construction.
Rigging: masts iron, mainmast was stepped right amidships,
with the fore and mizzen masts at equal distances from it.
Foremast – 85'6" x 31"
Mainmast – 89' x 31"
Mizzenmast – 81' x 29"
Bowsprit – 36' x 31"
Topmasts - fore & main 52' x 19"
Mizzen top 44' x 16 3/4 "
Lower yards – fore & main 84'6" x 21"
Mizzen yard – 70' x 17"
Steel lower topsail yards – fore & main, 72' x 18"

Sails: two full suits, best extra flax canvas, except royals, mainstay sails, sky sails, mizzens staysails, fly jibs, 1 each, boat covers, mast covers.

Cables: Wire & hemp.

Chain: 270 fathoms

Sails: topsail and top-gallant yards are carried on the fore and mainmasts, topsail and patent reefing top-gallant sail on the mizenmast, carries courses, topsails, top-gallant sails, and royals only, the top-gallant sails having a great hoist, supplied with topmast backstays on each side, port and starboard.

Rigging changes: Originally was rigged in a manner peculiar to just a few ships. She had short topgallant masts with fidded royal and skysail masts, on which were crossed royals and skysails above double topgallant yards. When in port the upper topsail and upper topgallant yards would be half mast-headed, and with the seven yards on each mast, but this proved to interfere with her stability as there was too much weight aloft. She was then given topgallant and royal masts in one with crossed royal yards over double-topgallants.

Winches: 1 Harfields Patent steam windlass & 3 capstans.

Pumps: Adair Bilge Pumps.

Boiler: Donkey boiler for winches in foredeck, and for main hold and rigging. Boiler covered in a coating of non-conducting cement.

Water Condenser : Attached to boiler leading to two below deck water storage tanks.

Hatches: Plate & angle iron; Main Cargo hatch 16' x 10' x 6", Fore hatch 6'3" x 6', Quarter hatch 6'6" x 6', a shifting beam secures main hatch in place.

Anchors: 7 – 3 bowers, 2 stream, 2 kedges. The anchors are weighed by *Harfield patent steam windlass* which works with its own engine by steam supplied from the donkey boiler located beneath middeck.

Boats: 4 – 2 life boats, 1 cutter & 1 gig, (gig fitted with mast and sails).

Compasses: 3 binnacles – steering binnacles & compass, standard in poop front & board compass, 1 suspended compass, azimuth on skids.

Logs: Patent and Hand Log

Safety Equipment: Six Life Preservers, lifebelts for everyone on board, signal rockets.

Figurehead: carved wooden maiden draped in flowing gown, right hand across lower chest, painted white with gold tinting.

Deck cabins: Forecastle: 36'6" long, Deckhouse 45'x20', Poop 46' long. The forecastle is a roomy house situated in the eye of the vessel and fitted up for the accommodation of 20 plus seamen. The deck-house has berths for 20 passengers, oil lockers, a galley, and engine room, and is situated between the main hatch and foremast. All the lower deck under the engine-house and galley is iron, cemented and bricked, and the centre of the main deck, from the main to the after hatch, is of teak planking. The cabin accommodation is under the poop deck, which is of a rounded form, with an iron bulkhead at the fore-end. The accommodation consists of captain's and officers' rooms, saloon pantry, and a few staterooms. The idlers, mates and apprentices are berthed in a commodious house, built on the main deck amidships.

Surfaces Protection: Cement & paint. Vessel cemented to limber holes amidships, thence to bilges to cover boltheads, all inaccessible parts are filled with cement, upper deck water way flushed with cement, painted iron scuppers & pipes. Small rust holes in strakes to filled with wooden pegs covered in cement.

Inspections: First one ordered 12th December 1874, last carried out 1st September 1875.

Ship's Role: Worldwide tramping voyages.

Tonnage: 1557 grt | 1492 nrt

Length: 250.1 feet

Breadth: 38.3 feet

Draught: 22.45 feet

Recorded regular top speed: 14 knots under full sail, average speed of 10-12 knots.

Owner History: Glasgow Shipping Company - James Aitken, manager, Glasgow. 1892 James Lilburn appointed manager after the forced retirement of James Aitken due to poor health.
Captains:
Captain Francis 'Frank' Wagstaff (1875-1876)
Captain William Robertson (1876 – 1878)
Captain James 'Jimmie' Ozanne (1878 – 1884)
Captain William 'Fighting Bill' Bennett (1884 – 1904)
Captain William 'Bill' Hawkins (1904 – 1905)
Crew Berths: 30 – 38 (30 + up to 8 apprentices)
1 Master, 3 mates, 1 ships doctor, 1 donkeyman, 1-2 stewards,
1 carpenter, 1 sailmaker, 1-2 cooks, 17 - 20 plus able & ordinary seamen, up to 8 apprentices.
Status: Went Missing After - 06/09/1905
Remarks: O.N. 71748. 1875: Registered at Glasgow 23 October.
Description: A fine sharp lined vessel, a black walled frigate style clipper, with painted 'gun' ports upon the side, a Trompe-l'oeil, originally designed to fool pirates into believing that the ship was an armed merchant frigate. Later it became a characteristic of many clippers giving observers the illusion of spaciousness below decks. The fittings are all of the latest and most improved description, and include donkey boiler, steam winch, patent main pumps, and also a steam pump for use in the event of fire occurring on board. The windlass is Harfield's patent, and is driven by a capstan placed on the forecastle head, and is also geared to suit, being worked from the steam winch.

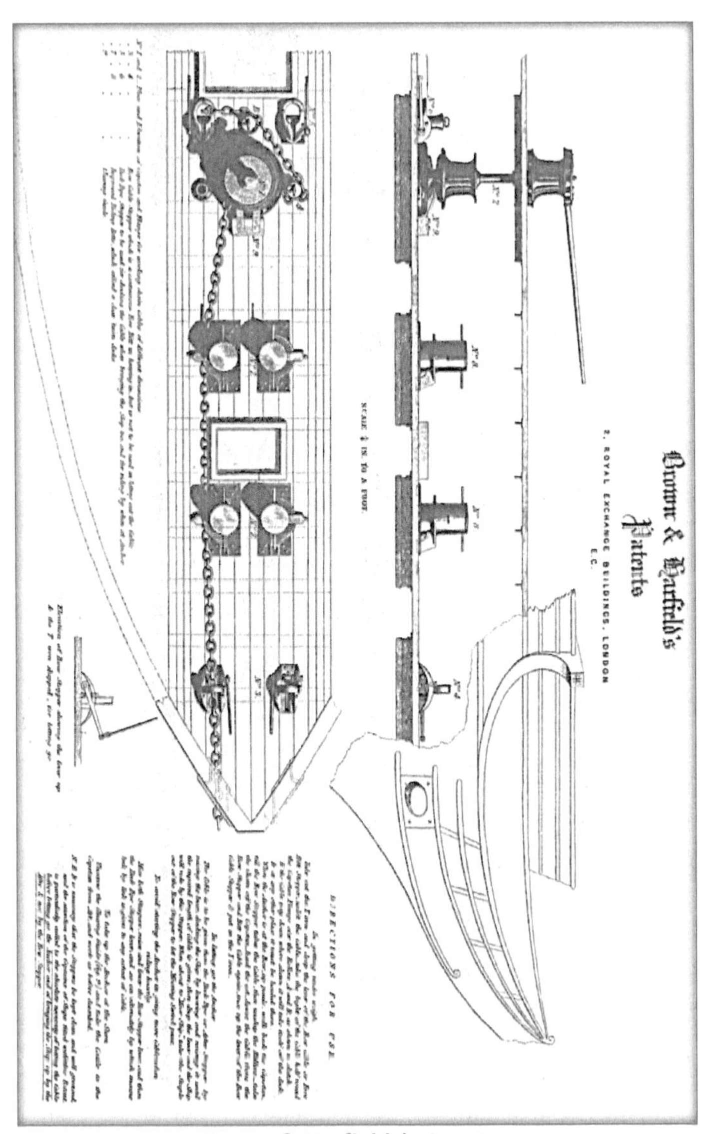

Brown & Harfields's Capstan

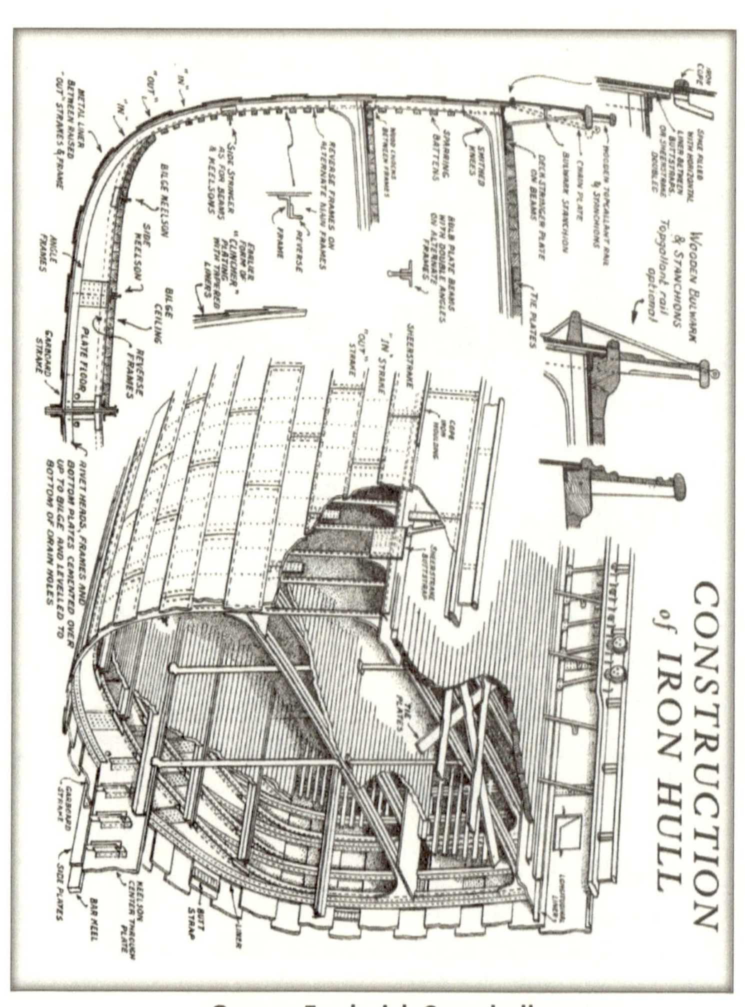

George Frederick Campbell

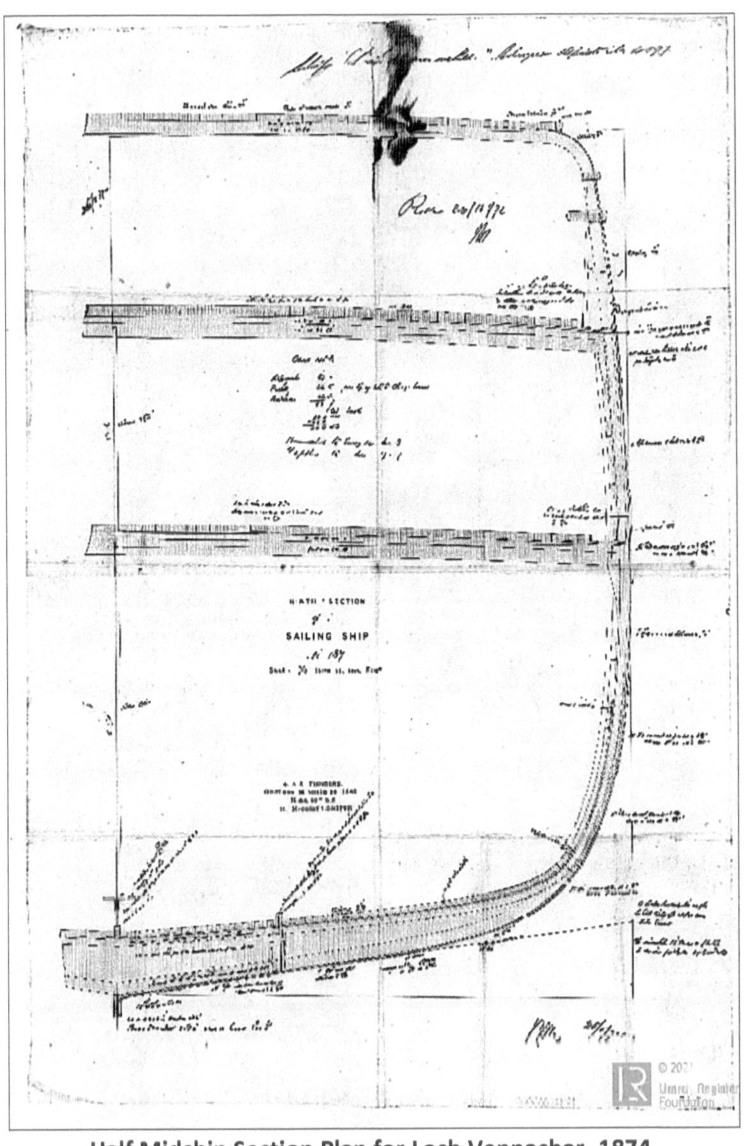

Half Midship Section Plan for Loch Vennachar, 1874.
Lloyds Archive.

J & G Thomson Shipyards on the Clyde River. (Later known as the John brown & Co Shipyards.)

When the 1500-ton clipper Loch Vennachar slid out of her flooded dry dock and into the Clyde River little did her owners realise the fame and fortune she would bring them. For James Lilburn the ship was a dream made real, for James Aitken she represented the ultimate statement in utility and luxury. The ship itself was fitted with the latest loading, navigation and safety devices. Her design made the Loch Vennachar fast yet flexible, designed to be driven hard yet able to stand up the rigours of extended ocean voyages. At 1500 tons she was the largest three master in the Loch Line fleet at the time of her launch. Whilst James Lilburn oversaw her design specifications, it was James Aitken who applied the finishing touches to the passenger accommodation and cargo handling and carrying capabilities.

Lloyd's final survey of the ship took place on the 1st of September 1875. The Loch Vennachar was rated 100A1, the highest standards in terms of design, maritime efficiency and crew safety. Much of the credit was due to Thompson's design engineers and shipwrights; however, the luxurious interior of the saloon, and the finely appointed staterooms, the quality of the China, linen, and the menu were all the work of William and James who had paid very close attention to even the smallest details.

The interior of the saloon was finished in polished teak, maple and rosewood. Fine carved wooden mouldings lined the cornices, whilst individual wooden panels had tiles painted with unique floral designs at their hearts. The large and spacious saloon had a high arched tinted glass skylight that allowed a softened light to filter onto the large dining table. The table itself was fixed to the floor with wrought iron brackets, its legs ornately carved.

The walls were hung with fine landscapes from the collections of the owners and each stateroom was similarly decorated. There were several plush, velvet-covered lounging chairs for the comfort of the passengers, as well as a sideboard filled with fine bone China tableware monogrammed with the Loch Line insignia. High up on the walls hung gimbled brass lamps and candleholders, their filigree chosen to enhance the wooden scrollwork carved into the sideboard, doors, tables and chairs.

She had a handsome and well-ventilated saloon, with large cabins fitted with every convenience. Bed and bedding and towels marked with the Loch Line monogram were provided to each saloon passenger. The eight staterooms each accommodated two people (though they could be fitted to carry two children and two adults, at greater cost to the passengers). Each room came with two bunks, a washbasin fixed to the wall, a wash set, a small wardrobe and chest for belongings, a wall-mounted mirror above the washstand, towels, soap, gimbled lamps and lamp oil, and candles; each stateroom had its own toilet.

The saloon deck was equipped with men's and women's bathrooms, a sizeable galley and pantry. Bolted to the back wall of the saloon lounge was an upright piano for the guests and a carefully selected library for use by the passengers. Within the cupboards were the latest magazines, and cards and games for the amusement of the guests. The saloon passengers were attended to by at least two stewards who worked in four-hour shifts like the rest of the crew.

At the time of the Loch Vennachar's launch, the menu for first-class passengers included an abundance of fresh and canned foods. The ship's cook was employed to produce regular fresh bread and rolls for the guests and the ship's officers; he was assisted by the ship's steward and ship's cabin boy when times were busy.

The steward was also in attendance on the second-class passengers who were quartered in the teak and iron mid-deck house. The four mid-deck cabins each accommodated up to eight passengers who were provided with bedding, towels, candles and a communal bathroom. The second-class passengers were supplied with all table requisites, including linen and steward's attendance. The cabins were fitted up in a superior manner, and for health, comfort, and convenience that was unsurpassed by any other vessel in the trade at the time.

On her maiden voyage, the steerage passengers had to supply their own bedding and linen, were expected to put up with communal bathing and toilet facilities, and were supplied with a basic fare without regular steward's attendance. Often when weather was rough, the steerage quarters were battened down for days at a time and the poor passengers' only crew contact was the cook and his assistants who brought them food and fresh water. In such conditions, only first and second-class passengers were allowed the run of the deck.

Also carried aboard the Loch Vennachar in her hey day as a migrant vessel was a ships doctor. The doctor was responsible for the health and safety of everyone on board, including both passengers and crew. They treated illnesses and injuries, managed the spread of infectious diseases in crowded conditions, and oversaw hygiene and sanitation to prevent outbreaks. On long migrant voyages, they also handled emergencies such as childbirth or serious medical cases, and kept records of health issues during the journey. Both the doctor and captain were paid a bonus for every migrant they brought out who survived the voyage.

At first, Aitken Lilburn and Co worked hard to provide for every need and comfort of their passengers by providing a cow for milking, live chickens, pigs, goats and other stock animals to be killed en route. The paying guests were further looked after by the ship's surgeon, a fully qualified doctor who attended the guests' every health need and saved many lives that would have otherwise been lost without his services. Amongst those saved were several badly injured crew members who were injured during onboard accidents during stormy conditions.

III
The Maidens First Run
Captain Francis Wagstaff
1875 – 1876

The ship was launched on the 4th of August by Mrs Isabella Aitken to much ceremony and fanfare. Upon receiving her final certification on the 1st of September 1875, the Loch Vennachar's first master, Captain Francis Wagstaff, immediately set the ship to loading at the Govan docks. Taken onboard was a variety of merchandise desperately needed in the colonies; included in her cargo were bales of corks, quarts of acetic acid, Singer sewing machines, bales of pig iron and barrels of olive oil.

Loading was completed in less than 14 days as the task of finding customers willing to risk their wares in the new ship had already been taken care of by the ever vigilant James Aitken, who personally knew all of those shipping goods to Australia in his vessels.

The ship set sail from the Tail o' the Bank anchorage on September 4th. with a full hold, including a full saloon and mid-deck house, as well as 50 steerage passengers crammed into the 'tween decks. The ship and her tug passed Inishtrahull which was left on September 6th, with light southerly and variable winds, which continued to the equator. The lightest airs, as well as the longest spells of calm weather, were found between the 10th parallel of north latitude and the line, which was not crossed until October 10, in long. 19° west. The weather in the Southeast trades was in favourable contrast to that experienced in northern latitudes, and strong fair breezes were carried to latitude 22° south, where the prevailing westerly winds were fallen in with.

The meridian of the Cape of Good Hope was crossed on October 28th , as the Loch Vennachar began her to run her easting down along the 44th degree of latitude, Cape Otway being passed during the night of November 18th. The ship sailed through Port Phillip Heads on the morning of the 19th , after a cracking run of just 76 days at sea

The run eastwards was met by steady westerly winds, which on only one occasion increased to a gale. During the voyage, one of the second-cabin passengers a 38 year old man named Thompson, died from liver cancer. He was buried at sea. On leaving the ship the passengers, who were conveyed on shore by steamer, gave three cheers for the Loch Vennachar.

Captain Wagstaff was a well-respected and experienced sailing master who had previously commanded the Loch Lomond for a number of years. Under his direction, the Loch Vennachar's average daily run was 253 nautical miles, and Captain Wagstaff considered the new clipper a fine blue-water ship capable of handling the worst weather with dry decks. Her sister ship, the Loch Garry, was under construction and would sail sometime in mid-November.

Steam-Tug 'Warhawk' in Hobson's Bay.
State Library of Victoria.

Her best week of sailing was 2,065 miles with successive daily runs of 285, 290, 320, 320, 312, 268 and 270 miles. The new Loch Liner reached Hobson's Bay 74 days out from Greenock. Captain Wagstaff had been hand-picked from amongst the Loch Line captains as the one most capable of handling the new, faster ship. He had learned his trade on the smaller 1,200-ton ships, having previously commanded the clipper Commissary for a number of years and then the Loch Lomond.

Passengers on the maiden voyage were booked through to Melbourne or Sydney; each was charged according to their accommodation. First Class passengers residing in the state rooms of the poop deck paid £45, those in second class berthed in the mid-deck house paid £25, and those third class souls in steerage paid £17 for adults, and small children travelled for half that.

The 'La Hogue' at Sydney
State Library of South Australia.

The Loch Vennachar stayed tied to the Railway Pier at Sandridge for almost two months whilst she waited for the wheat harvest to be shipped to Port Melbourne and the wool bales to be loaded into her hold. Paying passengers were eager to be away but had to wait upon the vagaries of the wheat and wool markets.

Captain Wagstaff was anxious to be away in time to meet the wool sales in London; the highest prices were commanded by the first to arrive, and being second or third meant that owners' profits and the captain's commission were likely to be much, much lower.

Finally, on the morning tide of the 12th of January 1876 at 10 am, the Loch Vennachar slipped away from the Sandridge Pier to the mooring buoys where she hung whilst her compasses and clocks were adjusted. On the morning of Thursday the 13th of January, she dropped her moorings at the Hobson's Bay anchorage and was towed into the bay by a steam tug, Warhawk. From there, she set sail for London on the return leg of her maiden voyage to Australia, clearing the Heads of Port Phillip Bay at 8:10 am.

The return leg to London was not long by the standards of the time, just 88 days, but the owners of the Loch Vennachar were looking for something more and had hoped that a record run might attract the desired publicity like that associated with more famous clippers like the Cutty Sark and Thermopylae.

The ship dropped anchor off Gravesend on Tuesday, April 11th, 1876, having completed her maiden round trip and successful commercial trial. The returns on investments were more than enough to justify the expense of building a 1,500-ton ship. The late return of the Loch Vennachar meant that she missed the monthly wool sales, and thus the profits were not all that was expected.

Captain Francis Wagstaff was not engaged to skipper the ship on her next journey south, and he handed over the ship's logs and command to Captain William Robertson, a former master of the Loch Earn. This was seen by some as a controversial decision and hinted at Captain Robertson's well-connected backers.

The removal of Captain Francis Wagstaff from the *Loch Vennachar* in 1876 was the result of a high-profile Court of Marine Inquiry held in Melbourne. Despite the glowing reports often found in contemporary newspapers, the official investigation painted a significantly different picture of his conduct during the voyage from Glasgow. Following the ship's arrival in Melbourne in early 1876, serious allegations were brought against Wagstaff by several passengers and members of the crew. They claimed that he had been intoxicated and incapacitated for a significant portion of the passage. The testimony suggested that his drinking rendered him unable to effectively command the vessel during critical periods of the voyage.

The inquiry, conducted by the Victoria Steam Navigation Board, scrutinized his management of the ship. While the Loch Vennachar made a smart passage, the board found that Wagstaff's personal habits had jeopardised the safety of the vessel and those on board. The board ultimately found the charges of intemperance proven. Wagstaff's master's certificate was suspended for a period of three to six months. Following the legal ruling, the owners of the Loch Line, Aitken, Lilburn & Co., dismissed him from their service to maintain the reputation of their fleet.

The popular and well-known Captain Wagstaff was quickly snapped up by rivals and given command of the clipper La Hogue after she had undergone a complete overhaul. It would be upon this ship he would go on to forge a long and distinguished career.

IV
The Famine Years
Captain William Robertson
1876 – 1878.

The Spafford daughters, Annie, Maggie, Bessie, and Tanetta
drowned when the S.S. Ville du Havre sank.

The departure of Francis Wagstaff was not without its critics, but the Loch Vennachar's owners and managers felt that his cautious approach was not going to be profitable enough. Taking his place was William Robertson, a captain who had been with the Loch Line for some time as former master of the Loch Earn. He was a man with an unfortunate blot on his logbook. In the early hours of Sunday 22nd November 1873, the transatlantic steamer Ville du Havre collided with the Loch Earn and sank in 12 minutes with the loss of 226 lives. Only 61 passengers and 26 crew members survived, rescued by Loch Earn and, subsequently, an American vessel, the Tremountain. The Loch Earn subsequently sank and Captain Robertson was held partly responsible.

At the Board of Trade Enquiry, Captain William Robertson of the Loch Earn stated that when he first saw the Ville du Havre, he realised the two ships were on a collision course and he took appropriate actions, including sounding a warning with the ship's bell and porting his helm. He also stated that the Ville du Havre turned to starboard, causing the ship to cross the bow of the Loch Earn and causing the collision.

A summary of both the French and British investigations was prepared by the Bar Society of New York:

"It clearly appeared in the subsequent investigations as to the cause of the accident, ordered by the French and English authorities respectively, that each vessel saw the other plainly from ten to fifteen minutes prior to the collision! Is it not most extraordinary that thus in mid-ocean, on a clear starlight night, two vessels in plain sight of each other should nevertheless come crashing together? The accident must have been the result of carelessness, but as the authorities of each nation after a full investigation relieve the ship of their own nation from blame and charge it to that of the other, the question as to where the responsibility for the accident properly rests is one that will probably forever remain open. The sad consequences of that

The collision of the Loch Earn with the Ville du Havre, c.1873.
http://en.wikipedia.org/wiki/SS_Ville_du_Havre

Steam Tug Warhawk and the dismasted ship Loch Ard, circa 1874.

State Library of Victoria.

The removal of Captain Francis Wagstaff in 1876 was triggered by a high-profile Court of Marine Inquiry in Melbourne, which shattered the image of the "smart passage" reported in the press. Despite public testimonials from some passengers, the inquiry found Wagstaff guilty of habitual drunkenness and incapacity during the voyage from Glasgow. His master's certificate was suspended, and the Loch Line dismissed him immediately to protect their commercial reputation and the safety of their fleet.

Captain William Robertson was chosen as his successor because he had been legally exonerated for the 1873 collision between the Loch Earn and the Ville du Havre. A Board of Trade inquiry ruled that the steamship was at fault for failing to yield to Robertson's vessel, which was under sail. Furthermore, his reputation was bolstered by his heroic conduct during the disaster; he successfully rescued 87 survivors and stayed with his mortally damaged ship until the last possible moment, proving his resilience under extreme duress.

For the owners, Aitken, Lilburn & Co., Robertson represented a disciplined and sober alternative to the disgraced Wagstaff. The Loch Line relied on "hard-driving" masters who could maintain competitive speeds in the Australian wool trade, and they viewed Robertson as a technically superior mariner who had been a victim of circumstance rather than negligence. By placing him in command of the Loch Vennachar, the owners signalled their continued confidence in his skill while ensuring the vessel remained under the control of a reliable, proven commander.

He was known for his cool head under pressure, and this was demonstrated when he skippered the Loch Ard on her maiden voyage to Australia, a voyage in which the ship was allowed to slip her mooring whilst at anchor in the Clyde River, and was almost totally dismasted on her way to Australia.

His intrepidness and seamanship in an emergency were unchallenged; after all, he had managed to bring the Loch Ard 4,500 miles to Melbourne under a jury rig, yet many were the questions raised about his general judgement in avoiding such situations in the first place. In the end, it did not matter much as Captain Robertson was in command of the greatest and most luxurious clipper in the Loch Line fleet.

William Ellis Robertson took command of the Loch Vennachar as she left the Tail of the Bank anchorage on Wednesday the 31st of May 1876, with a hold packed with general hardware and a full complement of passengers and crew.

For 12 days the ship was beset by hard gales and high head seas, and at the end of that period had only made Tuskar. The foul weather was followed by light variable winds to the northeast trades, and these lasted just three days, petering out by 15° north. The passage to the equator was hot, sultry and tedious, the line not being crossed until the 39th day out.

The weather, south of the equator, was equally contrary, and instead of carrying fair winds through the southeast trades, the ship had almost a dead beat of it against southerly and south, by sou'west winds, until reaching the 35th parallel, where westerly winds were found. The meridian of the Cape of Good Hope was crossed on August 9th as the ship began her easting run. This was done between latitudes 44°and 45°degrees south, with moderate westerly breezes all the way to Cape Otway.

Although having a weighty cargo of pig iron and pipes and heavy machinery on board, the ship made some good running in crossing the Southern Ocean, and the distance from the Cape to Port Phillip was performed in ?? days. On the 31st August, the Loch Vennachar was sighted off Cape Otway under full sail, making for Port Phillip Heads.

After her passengers were taken ashore by steam launch, the Loch Vennachar sat at anchor for nearly 10 days at the outer moorings until her load of gunpowder had been lightered off. Captain Robertson had his ship towed to the Railway Pier at Sandridge and began to discharge the cargo within the hold.

Passengers alighting from the Loch Vennachar were, in first class: Mr and Mrs Lewis, Mr Weir and the Misses Weir (two), Mr and Mrs Archdeacon Colquhoun and the Misses Colquhoun (three), Mrs Flett and Miss Flett, Mr and Mrs D. Smart, Miss A. Wilson, Dr Watson L. King, Messrs Charles Bell, William S. Soutar, Charles Menzies, and James H. Thomas; and 50 people in the second and third class cabins.

The Loch Vennachar stayed dockside until her hold was crammed full of wheat and wool. Australia was once again falling into the grip of drought, so the quality and quantity of both commodities were down this year. The ship was towed away from the wharf by the steamer Warhawk and, on the morning of the 8th November 1876, Captain Robertson gave orders to drop the mooring lines as she left Hobson's Bay bound for London, arriving on the 8th February at Gravesend in time for the February wool sales. The quality of the clip was down, but such was the demand for this currently scarce resource that Captain Robertson was able to secure excellent prices for his cargo, thus rewarding the faith his employers placed in him.

Reports continued to filter in from returning Loch and Ben liners that the season's clip was not good and, with the worsening drought, conditions were only going to worsen, so alternative cargoes and ports would have to be considered.

Saturday 7th April 1877 found the Loch Vennachar headed for Melbourne, having sailed from London in late February for the Govan docks, where the ship had her hull careened and painted to prevent fouling. Captain Robertson was again in charge but knew before he left that the chances of filling his hold were slim, so he had signed on a crew at £6 each on the understanding that the ship may have to head to a third or fourth port in order to fill her hold. Thus, the clipper sailed into uncertain economic times with 54 passengers and a cargo that included gunpowder and a large consignment of whisky and beer.

The clipper passed through Port Philip Heads on the afternoon of June 22nd, 76 days from Greenock.

"The Loch Vennachar has done very well on her present voyage, although at times she had to contend against baffling weather, especially after losing the S.E. trades. In spite of this, however, she has pulled through in 76 days from Glasgow to Port Phillip, with a heavy deadweight cargo. The ship, as usual, is in first-rate order, although the deck is lumbered up with quite a houseful of draught stock, which has arrived in admirable condition. Captain Robertson reports leaving on April 7, and meeting with strong southerly winds for seven days, followed by light northerly airs, which continued until falling in with the N.E. trades. Moderate breezes were carried through the trades to the equator, which was crossed on the 25th day out in lon. 25deg. W. Very good work was done across the S.E. trades, the breezes being fresh and favourable, but after parting with them variable contrary winds set in for several days and these were followed by moderate and strong winds from N.W. and N.N.W. until nearing this coast, there being no southing in the winds whatever until then. The meridian of the Cape of Good Hope was passed on the 52nd day out, in lat. 44deg., and the longitude was run down between that and the parallel of 45. A number of passengers have arrived by the ship. The voyage throughout was devoid of incident, and on Saturday she was berthed alongside the Sandridge railway pier to discharge cargo." **The Argus 25 June 1877.**

The Loch Vennachar arrived in Hobson's Bay at the height of the drought and Captain Robertson knew almost immediately that cargo was scarce and margins tight. After unloading his passengers and cargo at the Sandridge Pier, he anchored the Loch Vennachar at its usual mooring in Hobson's Bay and waited for a cargo of wool to arrive. It would be a long wait.

It quickly became apparent to all concerned that, because of the drought, there would be no cargo to fill the Loch Vennachar's hold. Rumours were rife about the docks that the clipper would be ordered to Calcutta in ballast to receive orders. By the beginning of August, word from Glasgow arrived confirming the rumours and Captain Robertson ordered sails set

Shipping in Calcutta Harbour 1870's
Columbia University.

on the 8th of August. The Loch Vennachar sailed out of Hobson's Bay, in ballast, bound for Diamond Harbour, Calcutta.

After a steamy two-month journey north, the Loch Vennachar arrived off of the mouth of the River Hooghly on September 26th, after a 49 day voyage. After another two days being towed up river behind a wheezing paddle-wheeler, they Loch Vennachar arrived at her destination, Calcutta's Garden reach. Calcutta's riverside ghats at the end of the monsoon season were filled with ships, all eagerly awaiting cargo to fill their empty holds. October in Calcutta was the most humid time of the monsoon season, but this year, due in large part to the effects of an El Niño-like weather pattern, the rains failed.

Captain Robertson and the ship's surgeon, Dr Phillip Alexander, did their best to keep the rates of infection from the city's many brothels from overtaking the crew whilst the ship's hold was filled with bales of jute, barrels of castor oil, and sacks of wheat and corn. As the cool season lengthened, food and water shortages began to bite. At first only the outlying towns and villages were affected, but before long, shortages became famine, and with the famine came diseases as the poor flooded into the city desperate for food.

The Great Famine of 1876–1878 in colonial India killed between 6 and 10 million people and affected 58.5 million others. Even at the height of the famine, grain merchants exported 640 million pounds of grain to Europe rather than relieve starvation in India.

The Loch Vennachar lay at anchor on the Hooghly off Calcutta for three months waiting for cargo, and in that time tragedy struck not only the crew of the Loch Vennachar but just about every ship in the harbour. In Calcutta, thousands of people succumbed to plagues of typhoid, cholera, and dysentery. Amongst the many victims were hundreds of sailors and dock workers.

Included in the growing list of victims were members of the crew of the Loch Vennachar. Many well-known deep-sea

Bags of Indian grain awaiting export at the height of the
Great Famine of 1877-8.

captains, including Captain William Robertson, died of typhoid and on the 5th of December 1877 and had to be replaced. Captain Robertson was just 35 and his loss was keenly felt. The first officer, James S. Ozanne of Newton, Geelong, took command of the ship and, along with the ship's surgeon, Dr Alexander, fought to save the ship and her crew from the plagues ravaging crews of ships anchored in Calcutta's harbour. Every man on board knew how close they had come to being buried in the Bhowanipore Cemetery alongside Robertson.

Bhowanipore Cemetery, Calcutta, late 19th century.

V
Finally Making Money
James S Ozanne
1878 - 1884

After a tumultuous time in India, the Loch Vennachar finally dropped anchor at Gravesend in early 1878, her crew saddened and much reduced by disease and death. James Aitken and James Lilburn are happy just to see the ship and its crew again.

Eva Carmichael & Thomas Pearce, survivors of the Loch Ard.
State Library of Victoria.

The jute and corn were unloaded in London, and the ship sailed around Land's End, through the Irish Sea, and up the Channel to her anchorage off Govan. There was much sadness as the full implications of the disaster in Calcutta were realised.

With a severe shortage of suitable sailing masters with the knowledge required to drive a ship like the Loch Vennachar,

James Ozanne was confirmed as her Captain as a reward for bringing back the ship, her cargo, and crew safely to Glasgow.

Again, disaster seemed to follow William Robertson even unto death, when on the 3rd of June 1878 word was received that the ship, the Loch Ard, Captain Robertson's old command, had been wrecked one day's sailing from Port Phillip Heads with the loss of all but two lives.

The two survivors were Thomas Pearce, a young midshipman of the Loch Line, and a female passenger he rescued, Evelyn Carmichael, 19 years of age, from Ireland. Amongst the dead were 17 passengers (including Evelyn's father, mother, two sisters and brothers) and 25 crew members. The Loch Ard, under Captain Nicholls, was pushed ashore in a violent storm, dragged her anchors, and struck rocks beneath towering cliffs. The vessel was holed amidships and sank within 10 minutes as her spars crashed into the sea and her decks were swept clean.

Tom Pearce would go on to serve with the Loch Line for a number of years before becoming a ship's master in his own right. Later he would send his own sons to sea to serve their apprenticeships aboard other Loch Line clippers, his eldest, Tom Pearce Jnr, serving his time aboard the Loch Vennachar beginning in 1901.

Freshly painted, rigged and repaired, the glimmering black-walled form of the Loch Vennachar dropped anchor in Hobson's Bay on the 24th of September 1878. James Ozanne took the Loch Vennachar out to Melbourne in 77 days. He beat this passage in 1880, arriving in only 72 days. Her best sailing was 5,850 miles in 21 days, and 2,080 miles in 7 days.

The new captain quickly established himself as a calm, efficient sail master. His runs to and from Melbourne were fast and he took few risks when running his easting down through the roaring 40s or when rounding the Horn. He was seen as urbane, sociable and a careful seaman who took no risks with the lives of his passengers and crew. Others described him as a cautious, wise and forward-thinking captain.

TESTIMONIAL
To
Dr. ALEXANDER PHILIP,
Of Ship LOCH VENNACHAR.

Dear Sir,—The ship Loch Vennachar's company beg to present you with the following address as a kindly remembrance of the high respect in which they hold you ; especially would we, as a company, return to you thanks for the unremitting and humane treatment which they experienced at your hands in all cases.

Judging from the skill shown in the above cases, we feel astured that you shall excel in your profession, and that your kindly, affable, and gentlemanly address will gather sround you a circle of well-wishers and sincere friends ; with which wishes, we beg to bid you a kindly farewell.

J. S. Ozanne	Daniel Sutherland
George Munro	James Morrison
John Turnbull	Sam. Morrison
A. E. Oppenheim	Mr. John Wright
John R, Yuill	Mrs. Wright
Elissbeth Yuill	Mrs. M'Callurn
Willlam J. Maxwell	Henry Burton
Isabelia Maxwell	W. G. Armstrong
Jno. Munro	Wm. Gilchrist
Marjorie P. Munro	Margaret Gilchrist
Hughina Munro	Potur Crawford
George Munro	Hugh Jamieson
Isabelia M. Munro	John Campbell
Alice Stearne	Margaret Campbell
Andrew G. Logan	Andrew M'Kerron
James Miller	Edward Mullally
James Lang	Jane Blakly
John M'Millen	James Hume
James M'Nellage	Wm. Berry
David M'Kay	Willlam Love
John M. Edwarda	Fcancis M'Gtuty
Denis M'Neill	Kelman D. M'Gsw
James Mathason	Alox. M'Lasn
David M'Donald	James A. Phillips
James Boyle	Henry Ciolland
Wm. Wallace	Roderick M'Leod
David Laing	David Gionsa
James Jamieson	Malcolm N. Bethune
Simon Train	Willlam Wood
George Watson	Sasnusl Letty
Daniel Dally	Jas. White
John Gibson	Wm. Montgomerie
Allan Stevenson	David Mason.

Hobson's Bay, September 23, 1878.

The Argus
Wednesday 25 September 1878.

Again, with the ship's arrival in Melbourne on the 24th of September 1878, the Loch Vennachar's resident surgeon, Dr Alexander Phillip, decided to leave the ship and the service of the Loch Line. After his experiences in Calcutta, he was more than ready to begin life ashore. The passengers and crew of the ship paid great tribute to his services, and Captain Ozanne in particular was sad to see his friend depart after all they had been through together.

Tied to the pier at Sandridge, the Loch Vennachar quickly discharged her cargo, but then began the long wait for cargo. The Loch Vennachar had left Glasgow via Greenock on July 6th and passed The Smalls light on the 10th, having been delayed by light winds and fog in the Channel. Light northerlies and easterlies prevailed until the vessel passed over the 10th parallel when a sudden southerly change took hold and Captain Ozanne piled on the sails to make up for lost time.

The ship crossed the equator on the 4th of August and soon picked up fresh south-easterly trades until the 28th latitude was crossed. Strong easterlies continued for a week before winds lightened from the north-west as the Loch Vennachar ran her southing into the Roaring Forties to catch the westerly trade winds. The best two days' runs were 325 miles and 311 miles as she ran her easting down along the 45th parallel. Approaching Cape Leeuwin, winds became light and variable from the north-west so that the last three weeks of the trip were undertaken in variable winds and unsettled conditions. All the way across the Southern Ocean, the temperature never rose above 29 degrees Fahrenheit. Port Phillip Heads was passed through on Monday the 23rd of September and she passed up the South Channel into Hobson's Bay at 5 pm, finally anchoring late that evening.

Aboard were six first-cabin passengers, the Williams family and Mr and Mrs Yuill; with them were 34 second and third-cabin passengers. At the end of the voyage, Dr Alexander Phillip, who had been aboard during the terrible days in Calcutta, decided to sign off from the Loch Vennachar. All the passengers and crew of the clipper wrote a letter and published it in the Argus, publicly praising Dr Phillip for all his work aboard the ship.

The drought had only recently broken and sheep numbers were well down and grain yields small. In early January, an industrial dispute between deep-sea sailors and clipper ship captains came to a head. Before coming to Australia, deep-sea able seamen were able to demand £7 a month for a return trip. With the drought affecting Australian freight rates, wages being offered by ships' captains for sailors leaving from Australia were just £5 a month.

The sailors refused to sign on and many a ship was picketed. The sailors themselves had the backing of the boarding-house owners of Williamstown and Sandridge who provided bed and board for the striking sailors. They did this not through any sense of altruism but because they could then charge the sailors more later, and they could then demand more money from the ships' captains when it came to organising crews for the ships. The crimpers and the boarding-house masters stood to make a small fortune on the backs of the poor unfortunate sailors.

Fortunately for Captain Ozanne, the Loch Vennachar's crew had signed on and contracted for £5 a month, and because they had done this before the strike had been called, they were left alone. Other seamen who tried to get work at this lower rate were labelled scabs and treated accordingly by the striking deep-sea sailors and their supporters. It was only after languishing at anchor for more than three months in the stifling summer heat that Captain Ozanne had the ship towed into the bay from her moorings. Then on the morning of the 6th of January 1879, the Loch Vennachar cleared the heads bound for the London wool sales.

In addition to their legal servitude and the brutality of bucko officers, the seamen had to contend with *"land sharks"*, the crimps and boarding masters, parasites feeding on "blood money" and experts in shanghaiing.

The crimp, a middleman between the shipping employer and the seaman, was usually a shipping or boarding master who extorted payment for arranging a job. The system was simple: in many cases, the crimp collected *"blood money"* from the master of the ship which was then deducted from the seaman's pay as a spurious allotment. Payments to crimps, who swindled seamen *"on the beach"* (ashore) into accumulating large debts, could virtually wipe out a seaman's pay.

The Dead Horse Chantey
A poor old man came riding by
And we say so, and we hope so
A poor old man came riding by
Oh, poor old horse.
Says I, "Old man, your horse will die."
And we say so, and we hope so
Says I, "Old man, your horse will die."
Oh, poor old horse.
And if he dies we'll tan his skin
And we say so, and we hope so
And if he don't we'll ride him again.
Oh, poor old horse.
For one long month I rode him hard
And we say so, and we hope so
For one long month we all rode him hard.
Oh, poor old horse.
But now your month is up, old Turk
And we say so, and we hope so
Get up, you swine, and look for work
Oh, poor old horse.
Get up you swine and look for graft
And we say so, and we hope so
While we lays on and drags ye aft
Oh, poor old horse.
He's as dead as a nail in the lamp-room door
And we say so, and we hope so
And he won't come worrying us no more
Oh, poor old horse.
We'll use the hair of his tail to sew our sails
And we say so, and we hope so
And the iron of his shoe to make deck nails
Oh, poor old horse.
We'll hoist him up to the fore yard-arm
And we say so, and we hope so
Where he won't do sailors any harm
Oh, poor old horse.
We'll drop him down with a long, long roll
And we say so, and we hope so

Where the sharks will have his body and the
Devil take his soul.

– The Lookout of the Labour Movement - Sailors' Union of the Pacific

The crimps were assisted by runners who went aboard newly arrived ships to hustle men into saloons and boarding houses; a common incident was the pulling of men off ships during a swarming attack on the vessel and its officers by crimps and runners. Once in the crimps' hands ashore, the sailor often found himself shanghaied onto a new vessel by the next day.

The day aboard a vessel when the seaman celebrated the final working-off of an allotment to a crimp might feature an elaborate ceremony with the destruction of a dummy, the "dead horse", symbolising the burden that had been imposed on the mariner's income, and the singing of a traditional chantey, "The Dead Horse."

The Loch Vennachar passed out The Heads on January 7th. Captain Ozanne set his ship's course to run south of new Zealand. After 101 days, the Loch Vennachar arrived in London on the 18th of April 1879 behind the sidewheeler, India, just as the wool sales were getting underway. Stocks of wool were desperately low after the two-year drought in Australia, and cotton stocks were similarly depleted. After a short stopover, the ship set sail again for the Clydebank docks to have her hull cleaned and painted.

Upon arrival, Captain Ozanne had the ship towed into Govan Graving Dock and then discharged his officers and crew. James then headed into Glasgow to report to the head office to settle accounts and collect his mail. The Loch Vennachar was cleaned and any worn or damaged equipment repaired or replaced.

Towards the end of June, James Ozanne was once again onboard supervising the resupply of the ship. Tins of fish and barrels of flour, along with other dry rations, were loaded by the ship's steward into the mid-deck galley. Fresh linens and other creature comforts for the guests were also loaded aboard.

Loch Vennachar berthed at Geelong Pier alongside the Romanoff, and Ben Cruachin.
State Library of South Australia.

Sailors signing on were offered £5 a month if they signed on for the round trip. Thus, by the end of June, the Loch Vennachar had been fully provisioned and most of her cargo space and cabin berths filled. At dawn on the morning of Saturday the 5th of July, the ship weighed anchor, drifting slowly down the Clyde on her way to Melbourne. Captain Ozanne was hoping for a safe and speedy voyage, for aboard the ship was his father, Dr Frederic Newell Ozanne, a stern man and resident medical officer in Geelong.

The journey across the deep Southern Ocean was not without risk as, in early September, the Loch Vennachar passed through an ice field, within 20 miles of the icecap. The sailors aboard prayed for good fortune as they passed more than 30 large icebergs on their way around the Cape of Good Hope. The ship sped across the Roaring Forties, arriving in Melbourne on the 18th of September 1879 at the height of a raging storm. When the passengers disembarked, they were glad to once again be on dry land.

Dr Ozanne travelled to Geelong to see his family, while James stayed to supervise the unloading of the cargo of hardware and cut timber. Passengers alighting from the *Loch Vennachar* included Mr and Mrs John Capper and Master Ernest Capper, Mr James Bennie, Dr F. N. Ozanne, as well as 35 passengers in the second cabin and steerage. Dr Ozanne was a respected member of the community in Newtown, Geelong. He later worked in Yorkshire at Harrogate Hospital, first as an honorary medical officer and subsequently as a leading expert in mental illness and a member of the Royal College of Surgeons.

On the 14th of October, still with part of the cargo aboard, the Loch Vennachar sailed for Geelong to unload many of his father's personal effects and exhibitor's cargo for the upcoming Geelong Exhibition. To make the detour worthwhile, James Ozanne planned to pick up a cargo of wheat, which at this time was commanding a much higher freight price than the current wool clip. Whilst in Geelong, one of the ship's crew slipped off the wharf when drunk and drowned. A court of enquiry was held at which members of the crew were called to testify.

The Loch Vennachar stayed anchored in Corio Bay for a further three months waiting for cargo. This gave James and his father time to catch up with each other at the family home. The ship finally weighed anchor on the 14th of January 1880, her hold filled with 5,808 bales of wool, 147 pipes of tallow, 105 cases of meat, 40 cases of wine, 17 bales of hair, 174 bales of leather, 1,133 bags of wheat, and 2,367 bags of flour. It had taken longer than was necessary to fill the hold, but with the value of the cargo, it did not seem to bother the owners terribly much. After a voyage of 96 days , the Loch Vennachar reached Gravesend safely on the 19th of April 1880. James said farewell to his father and, after discharging his vessel's cargo, sailed once more for Glasgow.

The year was young enough that the owners of the Loch Vennachar had most of her cargo space consigned even before she tied up alongside the newly built Queen's Wharf in Glasgow. So it was that less than a month after her arrival in Glasgow, James Ozanne once more slid his ship down the Clyde with a full hold, leaving on the 29th of May 1880. After just 72 days at sea, the Loch Vennachar entered Port Phillip Heads on the 12th of August. Under full sail, including skysails, and with a large crew, this was a near record for the ship and its crew.

The Loch Vennachar had been towed from her Greenock mooring on the 29th of May and, once outside the Firth of Clyde, ran head-on into a fierce south-westerly gale that forced Captain Ozanne to seek shelter in Lamlash Bay. Once the storms had passed, the Loch Vennachar ran quickly down St George's Channel, passing Tuskar on the 1st of June. Once out into the open ocean, light and variable north-westerly winds were encountered all the way to the equator; this slow portion of the passage south was punctuated by periods where the clipper was becalmed for days at a time in hot and sultry conditions.

The line was crossed on the 26th day at sea, and eventually, the freshening south-east trades were picked up, taking the vessel in smart time to the 16th parallel. Following these, more favourable winds were encountered as the Loch

Vennachar passed beneath the line of the Cape of Good Hope on the 48th day.

Captain Ozanne then headed deeper into the Southern Ocean, starting out on the 44th parallel as he began his easting run. Deep into the Roaring Forties, Captain Ozanne ordered every piece of canvas raised as the clipper raced along the 45th parallel. She then covered 5,850 miles in just three weeks. Her best run was 2,080 nautical miles in just 7 days. For much of this time, the decks were constantly awash with green water and the third-cabin passengers were confined below decks. Relief finally came for all aboard as the Loch Vennachar approached Cape Leeuwin.

The winds dropped as the ship sailed northeast, becoming light and variable from the north-north-east for three days. These gave way to a few more days of very light and variable breezes as she passed through Bass Strait and into Port Phillip Bay on the 13th of August 1880. After unloading her cargo of gunpowder, she was towed into her berth alongside the Sandridge Railway Pier to discharge the rest of her cargo.

The ship arrived in Melbourne having sailed up the South Channel with a load of gunpowder, floorboards and weatherboards, wines and whisky, two thoroughbred draught horses, and 32 passengers, amongst whom was Robert Robertson, the brother of the late Captain William Robertson. The passengers and then the gunpowder were lightered off whilst the ship sat at the outer anchorage in Hobson's Bay. It was only after this that she was towed up alongside the Government Pier at Williamstown so the crew could discharge her cargo. Whilst in port, James Ozanne was asked to defend his friend and fellow ship's master, Captain William Thomson of the barque Trochrague.

Captain Thomson of the Trochrague was accused by several members of his crew of committing a serious crime while serving as master of the vessel. The allegation was that he had committed an indecent assault against one of the seamen. On the strength of testimony from what were described as disgruntled crew members, he was convicted, imprisoned for

Naval Illumination Hobson's Bay 1880.
State library of Victoria.

three months, and had his master's certificate suspended indefinitely.

However, the case did not end there. Further investigation cast serious doubt on the credibility of the accusations, with indications that the charges had been motivated by discontent among the crew. The conviction was subsequently regarded as unsafe, and Thomson was ultimately exonerated. His master's certificate was restored, allowing him to resume his career at sea.

In October 1880, the opening of the Melbourne Exhibition was cause for great celebration amongst the city's inhabitants. A spectacular display of flags and bunting was put on

The iron barque 'Arthurstone', 1288 tons.
State Library of Victoria.

by visiting naval ships from Britain and Germany. Also participating were dozens of merchant vessels anchored in Hobson's Bay and tied up at Sandridge and Williamstown.

Many of the ships' crews, including the Loch Vennachar's, participated by decorating their ships' masts and rigging with bunting, lights and flags in honour of the Exhibition opening. The ship's officers, apprentices and those crew members who had signed on for the return journey spent time enjoying the sights of the Exhibition whilst the ship was in the Alfred Graving Dock being cleaned and having her hull repainted with anti-fouling agents.

By the 19th of October 1880, the Loch Vennachar had been floated out of the graving dock and sailed to the Sandridge Pier to finish loading her cargo of wool. While docked, many people came to admire the famous lines of the ship. Many were the immigrants who had travelled on the ship, and many others came to inspect the commodious cabin accommodations whose luxurious reputation almost guaranteed full cabin and second cabin bookings for the return run to London on October 29th.

After an eventful year which included spending Christmas becalmed in the tropics, Saint Nicholas looking more like King Neptune, the Loch Vennachar arrived back in London on January 31st after 94 days on the water.

Back in the Clyde and fully loaded, Glasgow was hit by a violent spring storm on the morning of 12th March 1881. Much damage was done to ships and ashore, but Captain Ozanne, fiercely confident in his ship's ability to weather such things, gamely set forth on his next voyage to Australia. Eager to repeat the successes of the previous season, the Loch Vennachar and her brave crew were amongst the first to set forth to gain the profits available with the reportedly bumper wool and wheat crop currently being gathered in Victoria and South Australia.

The ship set forth with a small number of passengers in cabin and second cabin and many more in steerage. Buried within her hold were hundreds of barrels of gunpowder that Captain Ozanne had conveniently forgotten to mention to his passengers.

"The Loch Vennachar on her present voyage from the Clyde has had heavy weather, both at start and finish. She sailed from Greenock on March 12, passed Tory Island on March 19, and Cape Clear on March 21. Madeira was passed on April 2, and Palmas on April 6, and up to this date the log is an almost unbroken record of southerly and S.W. gales, and generally tempestuous weather. The equator was crossed on April 19, and after carrying moderate breezes through the latitude of the S.E. trades, the meridian of the Cape of Good Hope was crossed on May 15. A stretch was made away to the southward in search of westerly winds, and the longitude was run down between the parallels of 46deg. and 48deg. Some good work was done in crossing the Southern Ocean. Cape Otway was passed on Tuesday last, and the Heads were entered yesterday morning, 87 days from Greenock, or 80 days from Tory Island. The ship has a quantity of gunpowder on board, and had to bring up at the outer anchorage. There was a rough sea when she came up, and it was not until well on in the afternoon that the customs and health officers could board her." **The Argus 9th June 1881.**

The clipper arrived on the 8th of June 1881. After passing through the Heads, she was towed to Hobson's Bay with her load of gunpowder; however, the ship, along with her anxious passengers and crew, was forced to wait out the storm at the outer anchorage. There she remained for several days before the passengers, and then the gunpowder, were lightered off. Only then did Captain Ozanne guide the ship into Sandridge Pier.

By the 20th of October 1881, with her hold nearly full of wheat, skins, leather and wool, the fleet of waiting merchant ships was struck by the fiercest storm in living memory. Whilst anchored at the Sandridge Pier, the Loch Vennachar was beset by troubles when she and the barque Arthurstone collided heavily, causing much damage. Both vessels were anchored on the east side of the town pier and the bow chain of the Loch Vennachar came free from the pile-head. The ship then swung on her anchor chain and came crashing down upon the barque, snapping off her bowsprit.

The bowsprit, figurehead, and head gear were snapped clean off and carried away in the storm. The barque then drifted away, grounding her keel; subsequently, the wheel was torn off and the rudder loosened from its gudgeons. The Loch Vennachar did not escape unscathed: her taffrail, wheel and steering gear were destroyed and also carried away in the gale.

In the aftermath of the storm, it took Captain Ozanne some days to recall his shore-bound crew and organise for repairs to be made. Many were the ships that were equally damaged in the storm, and the owners of the Arthurstone were planning to recover their losses from the owners of the Loch Vennachar.

After more than two weeks of repairs and at great expense, the Loch Vennachar passed through The Heads on the 9th of December making her way to London, the hold filled with 7,113 bales of wool, 1,500 cases of preserved meat, 16 casks of paint, 1,120 bags of flour, 156 casks of tallow, 1 bale of cotton and 34 bales of sheep skins. She arrived safely at her Gravesend berth on the 9th of March 1882.

After a speedy resupply and reloading in Glasgow, the Loch Vennachar was once more despatched to Melbourne, her hold filled to capacity. She weighed anchor on the 6th of May and was frustrated by light and variable winds that saw her not pass the Scilly Islands until the 14th of May. Aboard was the usual cargo of pig-iron, pipes, hardware, distilled spirits and beer. From there, light easterlies were encountered all the way to the equator, which was crossed on the 8th of June.

Light and squally easterlies continued to follow the Loch Vennachar as she journeyed south into the sou'east trades. As the ship passed under the 22nd parallel, the weather closed. What followed was a series of storms that pushed the clipper along by gale force west-southwest and west-nor'west winds. High trailing seas pushed the vessel deeper into the Southern Ocean. Captain Ozanne piled on the canvas, and most passengers were obliged to stay below decks as they were regularly awash.

The Cape of Good Hope was passed along the 46th parallel, and vicious northerly squalls accompanied by snow, sleet and hail lashed the ship as she raced east. On the 13th of July, a hurricane struck the ship with a high beam sea and powerful winds from the southwest.

Loch Vennachar coming through the Rip.
(Port Phillip Heads)
State Library of Victoria

Almost taken aback, the Loch Vennachar floundered in the high crosswinds and beam seas as waves smashed upon the deck, sweeping away the poop ladders and ventilators.

Waters flooded the deckhouses and galleys, washing away anything loose upon the decks. Unfortunately, this would have included much of the livestock kept beneath the break of the poop. It was as she was running her easting down that she recorded three consecutive days of near-record runs: 328, 314 and 310 nautical miles before the hurricane struck.

Once past Cape Leeuwin, winds began to moderate as the Loch Vennachar veered northeast across the Great Australian

Bight. For three days' work, she covered nearly a thousand nautical miles as freshening sou'westerlies hurried her along.

The Loch Vennachar passed through the Heads on the night of Thursday the 27th of July and anchored just short of the south channel, 82 days out from Glasgow.

She sought to get under way on the 28th, but light winds prevented her making any progress. Refusing the offer of a tow to save money, Captain Ozanne waited until winds freshened on the 29th to sail into Hobson's Bay. Reaching the outer anchorage, the Loch Vennachar's passengers were taken aboard by steamer and then her 1,000 kegs of gunpowder were unloaded. Once finished, the clipper was towed to her berth at the Sandridge Pier to discharge the rest of her cargo.

Once ashore, it soon became apparent that there was going to be some trouble filling the ship's hold in a timely manner. There was discussion with the clipper's agents that she would be towed to Corio Bay, Geelong, to load wheat, but the Loch Garry got there first. There was a fierce if friendly rivalry between the two ships, and such a setback greatly annoyed James Ozanne, who wanted to be first away to London. Eventually, with her deck furniture replaced and her hold filled almost to capacity with wool and wheat, the Loch Vennachar was hauled out into the Bay on the 5th of September 1882.

She was towed over to the Williamstown Breakwater to finish loading some late-arriving bales of wool. She lay alongside the breakwater until the 4th of November when loading was finished, and freshly painted and rigged, the Loch Vennachar was hauled out into Hobson's Bay; aboard were 7,681 bales of wool.

The clipper cleared out on the 8th of November, entering the south channel on her way to The Heads. The clearing out of the wool ships bound for London was on in earnest as the race to gain the greatest prices at the upcoming season's wool sales began. As the various vessels passed through The Rip, they were met by freshening sou'westerlies and rising seas that soon smoothed out to rolling swells out in the Tasman Sea. Racing to London alongside the Loch Vennachar were the clippers

MacDuff, Horndale, Ben Cruachan, Loch Garry, Ben Voirlich, and Miltiades.

The return to London was satisfyingly free of major drama for the Loch Vennachar, her owners, captain, and crew. Her load of 7,600 bales of washed wool was brought to London for the sales and realised a tidy profit. With each trip, the reputation of the ship and her captain grew. James, however, was looking for greater challenges. He had come onto the Loch Vennachar as her first officer and as such he really wanted a ship of his own, to establish a financial base from which to invest in his own ship and build his fortune.

Whilst in Glasgow, waiting for stevedores to finish loading her cargo, James Ozanne met the young, affable, and ambitious master of the clipper Blairhoyle, William S. Hawkins. The two were contracted to take their ships together to Melbourne carrying important machinery for the colony of Victoria. Both ships sailed London on the 8th of November and raced down the Channel; the Loch Vennachar kept company with the clippers Ben Voirlich and the Lord Warden. Out in the channel, the vessels were hit and separated by a fierce snowstorm that left snow and ice upon the yards and deck. The winds were then unsteady from the north-west.

The race with the Blairhoyle was won on the 6th July 1883 when the Loch Vennachar dropped anchor in Hobson's Bay just ahead of Captain Hawkins' vessel. The ship had made the run south in just 79 days, with 50 saloon and intermediate passengers aboard. Within her hold were the parts of two new tug boats that were to be assembled in Melbourne. The other parts were being brought out in the Blairhoyle.

Whilst on the voyage, John Gray, the ship's engineer, had fallen overboard during rough weather. Captain Ozanne shortened sail and prepared to come about. Lifelines, ship's buoys, and life rings were thrown to him in the heaving seas, but he sank before the ship's boat could reach him. There was one other death aboard the ship; an apprentice, William Mackechan, died on board from gastritis and was buried at sea.

The crew were not the only ones affected by the weather conditions. One of the passengers, nervous about his safety during the stormy conditions and a very heavy drinker, fell and developed a mental illness and had to be cared for, but was not a threat to other passengers or crew. He was locked in the hold and kept restrained for much of the journey. On the 17th of July 1883, Captain Ozanne was called to appear in the Williamstown Magistrates Court to sign over the mentally impaired passenger, a Mr John McCallan, who had injured himself on the voyage out, suffering a serious head wound which caused him to become deranged.

The magistrate ordered Captain Ozanne to pay a £100 bond for the man's care in the Kew Asylum until he could be taken back to his family in England. Captain Ozanne paid the bond and immediately wired Glasgow with the details of the voyage and the inordinate number of casualties incurred. He was told he would be reimbursed upon his arrival back in Glasgow and that the families of the dead and deranged would be contacted as soon as possible.

The Loch Vennachar's time at anchor in Hobson's Bay dragged on for many months; James chose to discharge most of the crew, keeping the ship's idlers and apprentices about to help with ship's maintenance. By late September, the Loch Vennachar, tied up alongside the Loch Tay, was once again back at the Government Pier in Williamstown preparing to take on cargo.

James Ozanne and William Bennett, captain of the Loch Tay, were forced to wait as south-east Australia was again in the grip of a terrible drought; thus, the quality and quantity of the wool clip available forced freight prices way down. As a result, the Loch Vennachar and Loch Tay were delayed in port for some months until their holds could be filled with other general, less valuable cargo.

Loch Vennachar & Loch Tay, Williamstown Pier 1883.
State Library of South Australia.

The two ships finally left Port Melbourne in the first week of November 1883, on the 3rd of November, and arrived in London with a much-reduced cargo of wool the following February. The Loch Vennachar's passage was particularly slow as she struck strong head winds trying to make her way through Drake Passage. She arrived home after 114 days at sea.

Once in port, Captains Ozanne and Bennett met ashore and were summoned to the offices of Aitken, Lilburn & Co. at 80 Buchanan Street in Glasgow. Once there, James Ozanne learned that he was to be replaced as master of the Loch Vennachar by his good friend Bill Bennett, whilst he was to take command of the Loch Line clipper, Loch Ryan.

VI
A Man With Promise
William H Bennett
1884 - 1904

Captain William Henry Bennett
Commodore of the Glasgow Shipping Company Fleet
State Library of Victoria

William Henry Bennett began his career at 14 sailing as a ship's boy aboard a 300-ton barque, Hilton, in 1860, bound for Jamaica. Upon his return, he was apprenticed to W. H. Tindall, serving his time as an apprentice aboard the barque Albemarle travelling between Britain and the Antipodes. The ship would take migrants to Australia and New Zealand and then return with wheat and wool.

Bennett continued his indentured time aboard the 1,000-ton ship Nimroud. Commanded by Captain Oughton, she would haul coal from Cardiff as well as migrants to New Zealand. It was while the Nimroud was anchored in Auckland Harbour, New Zealand, that William Bennett joined the local militia as a soldier at the height of the Maori Wars. Almost as soon as he had enlisted, William was sent to the fighting in the hills and forests outside of the town.

Within two weeks of leaving the Nimroud, William Bennett was badly wounded and had to be carried back to Auckland to recuperate in the Auckland Hospital. He spent some time in the hospital recovering from his wounds before being discovered by the local police who were looking for absconding sailors. He was apprehended and promptly returned to his ship, the Nimroud, before she sailed again for Britain.

From the Nimroud, the young apprentice sailed in the 410 ton barque Ravensbourne, under the command of Captain William Richardson, sailing from Hartlepool to Bangkok and Yokohama return. They then sailed out to Melbourne before crossing to Point de Galle, Ceylon, to load tea, spices, and indigo, and thence to Calcutta to complete loading for home. He spent 490 days in total aboard the barque, finishing his time as an acting third mate on November 14th, 1865.

It was while he was acting third mate aboard the Ravensbourne that the barque was involved in a nasty accident outward bound from Calcutta on the River Hooghly:

"The Nemesis left her moorings at Garden Beach on the morning of the 23rd of May and proceeded without meeting with any occurrence calling for remark until the morning of the 25th instant. On the morning of the 25th, at 9:15 a.m., the Nemesis was threading her way among a maze of ships in the dangerous locality of Silver Tree. At this part, the River Hooghly is somewhat over four miles in width and is almost filled with treacherous shoals and sandbanks; but the navigable channel is extremely narrow, being only about two hundred yards broad. Through this,

within the distance of a few hundred yards, some half dozen ships were struggling to find their way.

On the Nemesis' port bow was the Defiance, having the Andromeda in tow and endeavouring to make the best of what remained of the flood tide in her course up the river. On her starboard bow, pursuing the same course as herself, were those two splendid rivals in the eastern trade, the John Bright and the Arratoon Apcar, both racing under steam. Immediately ahead of her were the outward bound ships: the Red Jacket in tow of the Electric and the Ravensbourne in tow of the Rattler; while in her wake lay the Columbus steam tug, which afterward became so valuable a refuge for the shipwrecked passengers.

At this juncture, the Nemesis, to avoid the Ravensbourne, which was shearing across her course, put her helm a-port and stopped her engines. The ship's head consequently swung off to the westward, and it was while in this position that the pilot, presuming, probably, that he should clear the tail of the sand, gave the order to move ahead at full speed, an order which was immediately obeyed.

The consequence of this unfortunate manoeuvre was that the Nemesis rushed with such violence upon the sand as at once to deprive her of all floating support and to cause her to heel over to a dangerous extent. At this trying crisis, nothing could exceed the admirable behaviour of all on board. Captain Coleman, who has before now given proof of his courage and promptitude in danger, immediately gave orders for the hatches to be battened down and the cargo secured, a precaution to which the safety of the lives and property on board is certainly due.

When the ship heeled over, she fell on the starboard side, but recovered herself somewhat as the tide rose. An effort made to back her off the sand only resulted in sending her broadside on. She is now lying in a most dangerous position, in a place where a tug cannot get within two hundred yards of her and where, at low water, the sand under her bilge is four feet above low water mark. The water on the other side is only some three feet deep.

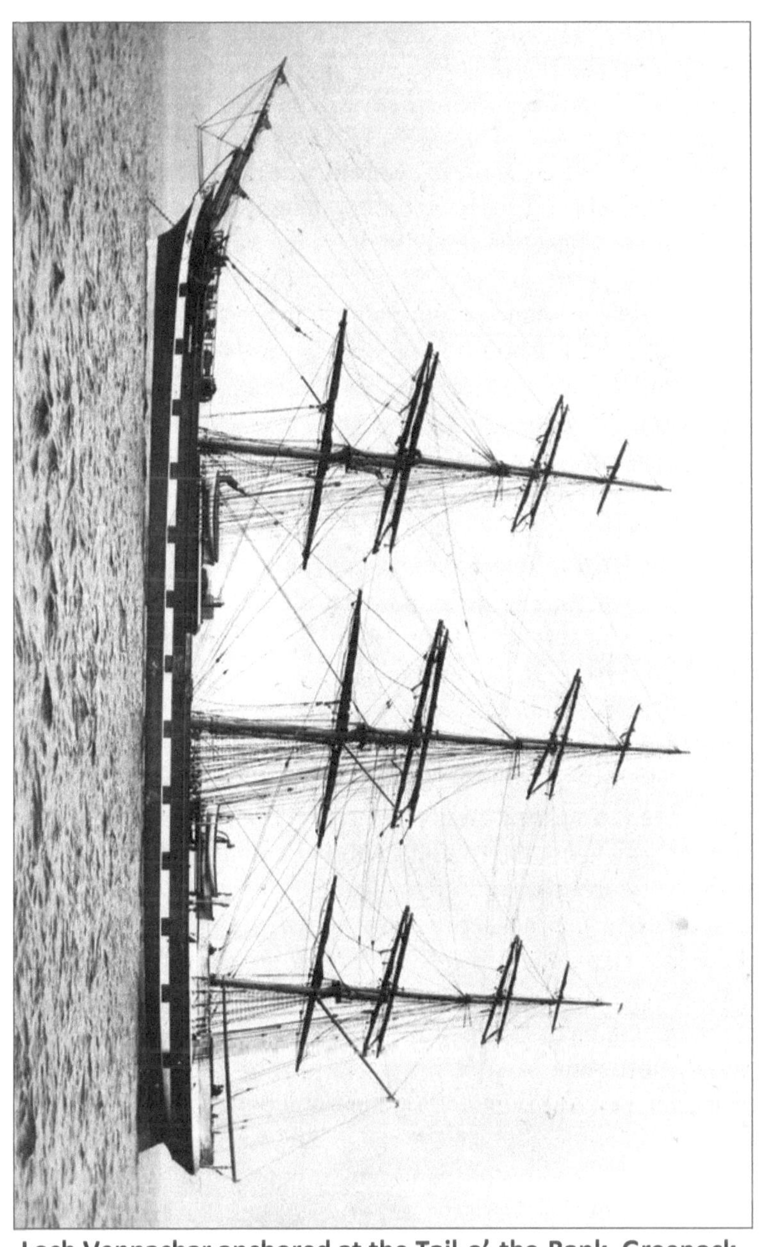

Loch Vennachar anchored at the Tail-o'-the-Bank, Greenock.
State Library of South Australia.

But to resume: the orders for the lowering of the boats were given and obeyed with perfect steadiness, and by 11:30 a.m. the last of the passengers had been transferred to the Columbus steamer, which was lying to at a respectful distance from the sand." – **The Sydney Morning Herald, Tue 18 Jul 1865.**

Upon his return to London, William sat for and gained his second mate's ticket on the 28th of November 1865, returning to the Ravensbourne as her official third mate. This time, he was getting paid for what his work was worth. William then stayed aboard the Ravensbourne, serving as both third and second mate, until the 20th of December 1867 as the barque lay at anchor in the Bremen Roads.

The previous day, the Ravensbourne had been in a collision with the barque Ceres as she was outward bound. The German vessel collided with the Ravensbourne, carrying away the British barque's jib-boom. It was Bill Bennett who had been on anchor watch, and he was signed off the next day. To avoid any uncomfortable questions from the upcoming enquiry, he shipped out from Bremen as an able seaman aboard a steamer, under a "*purser's name*," aboard a Canada-bound vessel. He did not return to England for almost three years.

He left the ship in St John's, New Brunswick, and was determined to start a new life away from the sea. During the next almost three years, he tried his hand at being a farmer, working on a cattle ranch, and then spent time working upon the steamers cruising the Great Lakes. However, he eventually tired of the cold climate and longed for a return to the sea. He boarded a steam packet at Halifax bound for London, arriving back home at the beginning of October 1870.

Returning to Kent to visit family, he found that he was anxious to return to sea and signed on aboard the barque Teviot as an Able Seaman, which set sail on November 11th bound for Colombo. She was accompanied by a barque called the Boyne. The master of the Teviot, Captain Thomas Mackwood, whilst keen to have William Bennett aboard, did not quite trust that the young man's skills as a sailor were quite up to scratch after three years away from square-riggers, so had signed him on as an ordinary sailor for the run out to Ceylon to load coffee from Colombo.

After arriving in Ceylon just ahead of the Boyne, Captain Mackwood was more than happy with Bennett's skills as a mariner and set him aboard the Boyne as second mate for the run back to London. Tom Mackwood was both master mariner and coffee merchant with shares in the Teviot and the Boyne. Captain Wheelan of the Boyne was happy to have a proven deep-sea mariner who came with Mackwood's approbation. The Teviot set sail from Colombo on May 8th 1871, the Boyne setting out four days later.

The Teviot rolled on home to London, arriving at Gravesend on September 3rd 1871, 118 days from Ceylon. The Boyne had a rougher voyage home and did not reach Gravesend until October 3rd, 148 days, a month after the Teviot's safe return.

After returning to Kent for a month, Captain Mackwood was keen to employ William Bennett as his second mate for another voyage. He signed papers on November 15th 1871 and boarded the Teviot for another voyage to Colombo, and the barque sailed from Gravesend on the 20th. The barque sailed also to Calcutta, thence to Mauritius and Reunion Islands, transporting indentured Indian labourers to the sugar plantations on both former French colonies.

The Teviot then sailed back to Calcutta to take on another charter of Indian labourers for Mauritius. Once at the island, the Teviot's hold was filled with sugar and molasses for the London markets. Unfortunately, as the barque was passing near Wolf Rock on December 30th 1872, the Teviot collided with the Scottish schooner Malvina on a foggy morning. The Teviot lost her headgear and her foretopmast and then limped into Bristol under jury rig, arriving on January 1st 1873. William Bennett signed off the very next day and travelled back to London by train.

After leaving the Teviot, William Bennett travelled home to Chatham and spent much time working along the docks. It was during this time ashore that he met and began courting a young

The Loch Rannoch (ex-Clan Ranald).
State Library of South Australia.

woman named Mary Ann Wilmott. She was the daughter of tailor and merchant George Wilmott and his wife Mary Ann. It was during his time ashore that William sat for and gained his First Mate ticket on March 17th 1873.

After a few months ashore, he firmly established a commitment to Mary Ann; William signed on as first mate of the clipper ship Bengal outward bound for Madras. Her master, Captain Paynter, is glad to have the eager young William Bennett aboard, familiar as he is with the waters of the sub-continent. The Bengal sailed out to India, Galle and Australia. William Bennett signed off from the vessel on January 27th 1874, as the ship departed Port Melbourne bound for Newcastle and then Madras.

Ashore in Australia once more, William took the opportunity to look up friends he had made last time he was there. After a month ashore and with funds again getting low, Bennett began looking for an officer's berth aboard an outward bound British vessel. He eventually found himself standing in the saloon of the Glasgow Shipping Co vessel, Clan Ranald. Seated at the vessel's central table with bills of lading, lists of victuals, bills for wages, and the like was Captain Jack Erskine.

The master of the Clan Ranald had a formidable reputation as a no-nonsense master who was famed for making fast passages and keeping strict discipline aboard ship. After inspecting William Bennett's paperwork and questioning him about his previous service, Jack Erskine had one question: was William a church-going Christian and a member of the Wee Free? In answering yes to both questions, the master of the Clan Ranald invited William to sign on as first mate for the run firstly to Newcastle to load coal and thence to Galle.

The Clan Ranald sailed on April 9th 1874 from Newcastle laden with 1,500 tons of coal destined for the steamships sailing to and from Colombo. From Ceylon, the Clan Ranald sailed on to Bombay to load cotton for New York. From New York, the Clan Ranald sailed home to Glasgow in just 16 days, and thus began William Bennett's almost thirty-year association with Aitken, Lilburn and Company. Upon return of the clipper, her owners changed the vessel's name to that of Loch Rannoch to match those of her sisters, Loch Carron, Loch Ness, Loch Lomond and Loch Tay.

OFFICIAL NOTICE. — PROPOSAL TO CHANGE A SHIP'S NAME.
I, JAMES ARTHUR, of Glasgow, hereby give NOTICE, that in consequence of the other ships in which I am interested being called after Scottish Lochs, it is my intention to apply to the Board of Trade, under Section 6 of the Merchant Shipping Act, 1871, in respect of my ship CLANRANALD, of Glasgow, Official Number 60,354, of gross tonnage 1,242 54-100 tons, of register tonnage 1,185 01-100 tons, heretofore owned by James Arthur, 78 Queen Street, John Pearson Kidston, 81 Great Clyde Street, Walter Birrell, 4 Royal Exchange Buildings, Henry James Watson, 62 Jamaica Street, all of Glasgow, for permission to change her name to LOCH RANNOCH, to be registered under the said new name at the Port of Glasgow, as owned by the individuals aforesaid.
Any objections to the proposed change of name must be sent to the Assistant Secretary, Marine Department, Board of Trade, within fifteen days from the appearance of this advertisement.
Dated at Glasgow, this 19th day of January, 1875.
[368]   JAMES ARTHUR.

Lloyd's List 1 February 1875

With his return to Britain, Bill Bennett had accrued enough sea-time to allow him to sit for his Ordinary Master's Certificate. He had been studying under the tutelage of Captain Erskine, who was keen for the young man to take the captain's exam upon their arrival in Scotland. He was soon on the train to London to report to the Board of Trade's examination hall at Tower Hill, London. He passed the three exams with flying colours and was awarded his master's certificate on March 18th 1875.

He then reported to the offices of Aitken & Lilburn in London looking for a posting, yet none was immediately forthcoming. He was told to head north to Edinburgh to make further enquiries with the agents in the company's headquarters. Upon arrival, all that was offered to Bill Bennett was the position as first mate of the Loch Tay, serving under Captain Alex Scott as a second captain. It was a tried-and-true method that James Lilburn used to test the mettle of potential masters of his ships.

The Loch Tay set sail from Broomielaw on April 3rd 1875, outward bound for Melbourne via Greenock to take on

St Paul's Church, Rochester where William Bennett married Mary Wilmott. Now demolished.

passengers and mail. On her way down river from Greenock, the Loch Tay ran aground whilst in tow and was delayed upon the mud for several hours until the next high tide. Eventually, the ship was refloated and proceeded on her way. They made their number off Port Phillip Heads on June 29th, 86 days from Greenock. The voyage, though relatively quick, was not without drama:

"the meridian of which was crossed on June 1, in lat 41deg S, and on June 4, the barometer, which had given previous indication of coming mischief, fell rapidly. On that date the storm burst forth in all its fury, the wind blowing a living gale from N and NW and giving rise to a tremendous sea, which threatened to engulf the ship. Beyond the flooding of the decks, however, there was no substantial damage done. Several days afterwards the ship met with even a severe visitation, the wind racing with hurricane force and sending a frightful sea, which smashed in the topgallant bulwarks on the starboard side, damaging the boats forward, bursting in the house on deck, breaking skylights, and disabling one of the crew, besides sweeping the decks of everything movable. The barometer was down to 28 22. The gale, which lasted for three days, was succeeded by very variable weather, the wind freshening suddenly into stiff gales, followed by flat calms, until the 25th instant."

– The Argus, Wed 30 Jun 1875.

There were several delays in loading the Loch Tay; however, she was finally cleared out, laden with thousands of bales of wool, on August 19th 1875. The ship set forth bound for London, having undergone an extensive refit prior to sailing. November 16th saw the Loch Tay pass Dover behind a steam-tug, inward bound for Gravesend. The ship reached her berth opposite Tilbury Fort the following day, 90 days out, there to await a river pilot to con the vessel upriver behind a paddle-tug.

It was during the five weeks at home that William Bennett returned to Chatham to visit his fiancée, Mary Wilmott. Short of time, after speaking with her father, George Wilmott, he kept his promise. Mary and William were married on December 5th 1875 at St Paul's Church in Chatham. Yet for Bill Bennett, it was but a brief time of happiness that came to an end all too quickly for the young couple. Mary Bennett continued to live with her father whilst her husband travelled back to London to prepare the Loch Tay for her departure.

A week later, the Loch Tay put back to sea behind a tug that was chartered to take the clipper down to the Lizard, from where she would make her own way to the River Clyde. They were on their way west on December 20th 1875 when a howling westerly gale forced tug and clipper to seek shelter off Deal, tucked in behind the Goodwin Sands. They tried again on the 21st without success, as the tempestuous weather forced the tug and Loch Tay to put back to Deal on December 22nd. Eventually, the weather abated enough for the ship and her tug to successfully make the passage down channel. It was not until the 27th that the winds shifted, allowing the Loch Tay and dozens of other vessels to make their way west and out into the North Atlantic.

The Loch Tay was back at her Broomielaw berth on January 1st 1876, awaiting a fresh cargo and passengers to take to Australia. They were once again underway on February 4t , heavily laden, with Alex Scott in command and Bill Bennett as first officer. However, once they arrived at the Tail-of-the-Bank anchorage off Greenock, Alex Scott fell ill and was forced to relinquish command. Rather than promoting Bennett to command the Loch Tay, Captain David B. Inglis was placed aboard and assumed command for the voyage. The tug Vanguard hauled the clipper down the Clyde on February 7th and left her off the Mull of Galloway at 8 a.m. the following morning, as Captain Inglis set his course to sail down the South Channel on the port tack across a freshening easterly wind.

The Loch Tay fell into the doldrums on February 29th at 4°north 22.5°west, 22 days from the Mull of Galloway, and crossed the equator the following afternoon. The ship passed through Port Phillip Heads on April 22nd 1876, 75 days from Greenock. It was a cracking run and cemented the reputation of her master, David Inglis.

The ship was soon after hauled into the Williamstown pier to discharge her cargo. As Captain Inglis was ashore taking care of company business, Bill Bennett had his hands full dealing with a rather fractious crew. Three sailors went on a drunken spree in Williamstown and failed to return to the ship when required; First Mate Bill Bennett had them rounded up and arrested. Appearing before the local magistrate, the men were placed into the less than tender mercies of Bennett when Captain Inglis refused to press charges. His leniency backfired spectacularly when another drunken sailor punched David Inglis. Bennett and some loyal sailors jumped on the enraged sailor and hauled him off to the police station. For his efforts, seaman Richard Davis spent four weeks in gaol.

Things did not improve for Inglis or Bennett as the crew of the Loch Tay continued to cause trouble. The next case involved the third mate, a seaman named Kelly, who raped one of the apprentices and later absconded from the ship. A warrant was issued for his arrest. Later in May, the ship's cook, Bill Lann, left the ship without permission, purchased some whisky, and then returned later; he and the ship's steward got rip-roaring drunk. The cook was hauled off to the police by Bill Bennett and was later given 14 days in gaol with hard labour for his troubles.

The Loch Tay at last set sail on June 22nd 1876, heavily laden with wool for the first sales of the season. Yet, due to foul weather, the clipper did not pass through the Heads until the 29th. Captain Inglis was a fine sea-going master and brought the *Loch Tay* home in 90 days, passing Deal behind the tug *Ben Nevis* on September 27th. The Ben Nevis left the ship off Tilbury Fort the following morning, and then a smaller tug and river pilot were engaged to haul the Loch Tay to London dock to discharge. Her cargo was offloaded in time for the pre-Christmas wool sales, and the ship was towed back down the Thames on October 11th and then set sail for Glasgow after being let go by her tug off Prawle Point at 1 p.m. on the 14th, having battled contrary winds and weather.

Expecting that he may have finally been given command of the Loch Tay after the way Captain David Inglis had dealt with the crew, leaving Bill Bennett frustrated at his "softness" when dealing with an ill-disciplined crew, Aitken & Lilburn were not yet ready to discipline one of their favourite masters. He remained as First Mate for the voyage to Melbourne, which began on November 4th as the tug hauled the clipper out from her Broomielaw berth and shifted the Loch Tay to Greenock. Then, with the last of her gunpowder and passengers aboard, the Loch Tay left her Tail-of-the-Bank mooring on November 7th. However, David Inglis was no longer in command. He had left the ship in Greenock, having been asked to take command of a newly purchased vessel, the 1,500 ton clipper America, currently off Birkenhead, near Liverpool.

VII

Master of the Loch Tay

The Loch Tay passed through Port Phillip Heads on February 1st 1877, 86 days from Greenock, and came to anchor in Hobson's Bay the following morning. The ship was towed into Hobson's Bay in pristine condition. In order to create a sense of pride and discipline in his crew, Bill Bennett had insisted that the vessel be cleaned from stem to stern, alow and aloft. Even when the clipper was moored at the outer marker to allow her passengers to disembark, the crew were kept busy stowing gear and overhauling the standing and running rigging, bringing the Loch Tay to harbour stow. The papers were effusive in their praise for Bennett's first run as captain, and the crew were equally proud.

"The Loch Tay has completed another, and, considering the light weather met with throughout, very successful passage from the Clyde. The ship on this voyage is commanded by Captain Bennett, formerly chief officer under Captain Scott, and the good name she acquired then for the excellent order in which she was kept, is evidently well maintained. She has been brought into port scrupulously clean and trim alow and aloft, and much scrubbing has been the order of the day in coming along.

Captain Bennett reports leaving the Tail-of-the-Bank, Greenock, on November 4, at 8 p.m. and passing Tuskar on November 8 with a light N.W. breeze, which shifted on the following day into S.W. and continued light from that point, with occasional calms and thick weather until falling in with the N.E. trades in lat. 18deg. N. and lon. 21deg. 20min. W. Madeira was passed on November 19, and a course was shaped to the eastward of the Cape de Verdes, which were passed on December 2. The N.E. trades were parted with in lat. 8deg. 50min. N. and lon. 23deg. W., and the S.E. trades were picked up on December 7, in lat. 6deg. N. and lon. 23deg. 30min. W. The equator was crossed on December 10, in lon. 23deg. 48min. W., and the S.E. trades were carried to lat. 31deg. 7min. S., and lon.

A heavily laden Loch Vennachar just arrived at her London
Dock berth with sails drying on the spars.
State Library of Victoria.

27deg. 8min. W. Off Tristan d'Acunha, which was passed on December 25, light S.E. winds prevailed for three days.

The ship crossed the meridian of the Cape of Good Hope on January 1, in lat. 43deg. S., and the easting was run down in the parallel of 45deg., with light northerly winds and thick weather until crossing the longitude of Cape Leeuwin on January 23, in lat. 42deg. 50min. S. Light easterly weather was met with afterwards for four days, and was followed by moderate winds from N.W. to S.W. until arrival. The run from the time of sighting Cape Otway to the anchorage was made in 10 hours. The passengers were highly pleased with their pleasant voyage, and presented an address to that effect to Captain Bennett before leaving the ship.

The Loch Tay brings a very large cargo of machinery and hardware, bulk and case whisky, beer, soft goods, etc., which she will discharge at the Williamstown railway pier."

— *The Argus* (Melbourne, Vic. : 1848 - 1957) Sat 3 Feb 1877.

The Loch Tay was moored alongside Williamstown Railway pier to discharge cargo, and it was whilst she was alongside the pier that the topmast was shivered by a lightning bolt during a nasty summer storm. The lightning shattered the truck, blew a lignite block apart, and then travelled down the mast and exited the ship, shattering the poop rail. Yet this was the most dramatic occurrence for the entire stay in Melbourne; Captain Bennett's efforts to keep his crew's behaviour in check had been handsomely rewarded, and most of the sailors who had arrived aboard the clipper set sail with her on March 25th 1877. She was heavily laden with 3,528 bales of wool stowed beneath her hatches.

The clipper passed Wilson's Promontory on the 27th and spoke to the schooner Alcandre that was on her way to Melbourne. The return journey was a fair-weather voyage across the South Pacific, passing Cape Horn on April 27th, 33 days from Melbourne. There they spoke to the barque Garland on her way to England, and a day later they passed the ship Aldborough, sailing from San Francisco to Queenstown for orders.

The run up through the South Atlantic was slow, the doldrums not being cleared until June 3rd, whilst in company with the barque Argo, on her way to Queenstown from Rangoon, filled with rice. The Loch Tay reached the western approaches on June 28th and she made her number off Prawle Point on July 3rd, 100 days from Port Phillip Heads. The clipper was towed on up the Thames and entered her London Dock berth on July 5th, her cargo eagerly awaited by her agents Skinner & Co.

Almost as soon as the ship's business was seen to, Bill Bennett was on his way home to Kent. By now Mary had moved into a home of their own, 30 Clover Street in Gillingham. There she lived with a maid named Harriett Gibson and William's new son, who had been born whilst he was away. His stay, as usual, was measured in weeks, and soon William was on his way back to his ship.

Berthed alongside the western quay, the Loch Tay's cargo was quickly discharged and, after taking on a load of cement as ballast, Captain Bennett was keen to have the ship get back to Glasgow. He did not have to wait long, and the clipper was headed back down the river, passing Tilbury Fort on July 30th behind a tug. The tow continued until they passed the Lizard; from there, Captain Bennett sailed the Loch Tay home, arriving back at Broomielaw on August 6th 1877.

There was little time to waste on niceties as the clipper's hatches were quickly opened and a cornucopia of wares was stowed in the hold: timber, flooring tiles, fire-clay goods, fire bricks and blocks, boiler plates and tubes, gutters, drain pipes, iron (pig, old, bars, pipes), castings, furnace grates, flue iron, earthenware, bleaching powder, acetic acid, chloride of zinc, cod oil, various paints and oils, rivets, brass castings, machinery parts, hardware, sash weights, tools, registers, frying pans, boxes, bales, packages, paper, stationery, photographic goods, leather, brushes, brooms, bottled beer, whisky, brandy, ginger wine, fishing nets, cordage, canvas, and wadding.

The Loch Tay was hauled out from her Broomielaw berth on September 4th behind the steam-tug Flying Dutchman. The steamer and a second smaller tug guided the clipper down to Greenock, where a load of gunpowder was taken aboard before her passengers were lightered out to the Loch Tay's Tail-of-the-

Bank moorings. The Flying Dutchman and her charge set sail down the Clyde on September 6th and stayed together until the tow line was dropped off Inishtrahull at 7 p.m. on the 8th.

"The ship Loch Tay, a well-known regular trader to this port, arrived during Sunday night from Glasgow, and having gunpowder on board brought up at the outer anchorage, where the powder will be lightened, and the vessel afterwards taken alongside the Williamstown Railway Pier. Captain Bennett reports as follows of the passage: — Left Greenock 6th September, Tory Island 9th September, and had fresh gales from S.W. to Madeira, and then calms; had no N.E. trades, the wind being light and from the S.W., passed the Cape de Verdes on the 29th September, and then encountered light airs and calms for a week, twenty-one ships being in company for four days; afterwards had strong S.W. winds which drove the ship down to the African coast.

The equator was crossed on 13th October in 22 west, and the S.E. trades were fallen in with the same day, and carried as far as 27 south. Tristan d'Acunha was passed on 31st October, where a strong N.E. gale was experienced. Passed the Cape of Good Hope on 8th November in 42 south. The easting thence was run down in 44.80 south, with fresh S.W. and N.W. winds. A very heavy gale was met with in 100 east and 44.30 south, the wind veering from N.W. to S.W., and blew with great violence for twelve hours, the sea having to be kept before the ship, filling the decks and aft, also the saloon passengers' cabins. Cape Leeuwin was passed on 26th October in 43 east, and Cape Otway on 2nd December at 6 a.m. Mrs Annie Buntin, a saloon passenger, died on 14th November, and a birth occurred on 26th November."

The Age Tue 4 Dec 1877.

Now a regular visitor to Melbourne, William Bennett was welcomed into the homes of old friends and spent more time ashore than onboard the Loch Tay. He often left his first mate in charge of the day-to-day maintenance of the ship, though the officer was perhaps a little too lax for Bill Bennett's liking. On January 16th 1878, two seamen from the Loch Tay were arrested for having deserted the ship without permission. They were the unlucky ones, as several others had gotten clear away from Bennett's hard, almost martial, shipboard discipline. The deserters were sentenced to four weeks' hard labour aboard the prison hulks anchored in Hobson's Bay and were to be escorted back to the clipper just before her departure. Luckily for the men, their sentences were cut short by the departure of the Loch Tay on January 31st 1878. Towed to sea behind the tug Resolute, the Loch Tay did not get far before being forced to anchor for the night just inside Port Phillip Heads. Due to a collision between nearby vessels and the call for witnesses to the Naval Board enquiry, the Loch Tay did not sail out through the heads until February 12th.

The run home was no record, the Loch Tay making her number off Dungeness on June 7th, 115 days from Port Phillip Heads. She was soon tied up alongside Pier 1 inside London Dock. Once her hatches were lifted, the eagerly sought cargo of wool was quickly discharged. The voyage had been slow, but the Loch Tay had arrived in good order and her owners were happy. The time spent unloading gave William time to head home to Mary and their son. It was the first mate who commanded the Loch Tay as she was towed downriver at the end of the month and who conned the ship as she sailed home, docking at Broomielaw in ballast on July 18th.

Bill Bennett was back in Glasgow at the start of August, taking over from the ship's husband who had been overseeing the loading of general cargo destined for Melbourne. The tug Vanguard was engaged to tow the Loch Tay back out to sea on August 5th from her Glasgow berth, and they sailed from Greenock the following afternoon. The clipper stayed with her tow until left off Tory Island at 10 p.m. on the 9th. The voyage out to Australia was such a rough and dramatic one that all aboard were glad to see the sight of Port Phillip Heads on November 8th, 94 days from Greenock. A battered clipper sailed through the Heads and dropped anchor off Queenscliff to await a tow up to Hobson's Bay.

"The ship Loch Tay arrived last evening from Glasgow/Greenock and anchored off the breakwater, displaying unmistakable signs of having encountered severe weather. While a large portion of the topgallant bulwarks was new and unpainted,

the quarter rail of the poop, the wheel, and parts of the front of the poop had only received temporary repair. Despite the vessel's severe ordeal, Captain Bennett brought her into port in creditable order, having done his utmost to mitigate the damage.

The Loch Tay left the Tail of the Bank (Greenock) on August 6th at 6 p.m., taking a departure from Tory Island on August 9th. Initially, she enjoyed a fresh breeze from the S.W. until August 15th or 16th, when a heavy gale set in from the W.N.W. The N.E. trades were subsequently met in 32°42' North and 20°50' West. They were light throughout and lost in 15°7' North and 28° West. Four days of light and variable weather followed before being succeeded by strong S.W. winds/breezes. The Equator was crossed on September 14th in 26° West. The S.E. trades were picked up the following day in 2° South and 28° West and lasted until 21° South.

On October 9th, the ship crossed the meridian of the Cape of Good Hope in 43° South (running her easting down between the parallels of 43° and 44° South), and immediately encountered heavy S.E. gales that lasted for three days.

The most perilous event occurred on October 19th, when the ship, on the meridian of 55° East, was caught in a dangerous cyclone. The wind veered violently from N.W. to S.S.W. and blew a "perfect drift" with great vehemence for about eighteen hours. Captain Bennett kept the ship running before the wind and sea, recording an incredible day's distance run of 420 miles. During the hurricane, the sea raged with ungovernable fury, keeping the decks and cabins in a state of chronic deluge. One towering sea broke over the poop, smashing the wheel and severely injuring the two men who were steering. It also carried away the poop rail, the after-part of the cabin skylight, and burst in the ventilator under the break of the poop, flooding the saloon and cabins. Further damage included the after-hatch being stove in, parts of the topgallant rail on both sides being carried away along with all the poop ladders, two boats on the starboard side being smashed, and the doors of the second cabin deck-house being burst in, alongside other minor damage.

During the voyage, the Loch Tay was involved in notable incidents beyond the weather. On August 14th, in 43° North and 15° West, the crew of the Portuguese brig Regina of 198 tons, from

Congo River to Liverpool, were taken off their vessel as it was in a sinking condition; she had eight feet of water in her hold and was going down by the head in rough conditions. Captain Bennett welcomed them aboard, and they remained until August 31st, when they were transferred to the homeward-bound ship Star of Erin, from Calcutta to London. Furthermore, a second cabin passenger, Mrs. Chalmers, gave birth to a male infant, who sadly survived only three days.

The ship spoke to several vessels en route: on September 3rd, in 12° North and 28° West, she spoke the ship Waikato, 85 days out from New Zealand for London; and on September 29th, in 36° South and 9°17' East, she signalled the German barque Hesperus, 67 days out from Sweden for this port (Port Phillip).

The meridian of Cape Leeuwin was crossed on October 30th in 43° South. From there, moderate northerly winds prevailed to Cape Otway, which was passed at noon on the 7th or 8th instant. The final leg to the Heads, entered at 11 a.m. yesterday, involved calm, fine weather. The total voyage time was 93 days from Greenock and 90 days from Tory Island."

The Argus & The Age, Sat 9 Nov 1878.

The Loch Tay was soon berthed alongside the Williamstown Railway Pier, her hatches lifted and the ship's carpenter sent ashore to order the requisite timbers and other materials to begin proper repairs to the clipper's upper works. Captain Bennett quickly learned that much of the wool clip was yet to arrive from inland and so there would be quite a wait before the Loch Tay's hold would be filled.

As such, most of the crew were paid off, leaving just the standing officers, carpenter, sailmaker and a few regular hands who always sailed aboard the clipper to maintain the Loch Tay during her extended stay in Melbourne. Cargo was slow in coming; the Loch Rannoch, Captain James Ross, and the larger clipper Loch Vennachar, commanded by James Ozanne, were tied up near the Loch Tay and their captains were frequent visitors to each other's shore-side accommodations.

There was a friendly wager made between the three master mariners as to whose vessel would make the best passage to Britain. The wager involved a fine bottle of whisky being provided to the captain with the quickest time. No unnecessary risks were to be taken.

The Loch Vennachar's hold was filled first and Captain Bennett could only look on in exasperation and envy as she was towed to sea on January 7th 1879. The waiting was starting to get to the crew, as was the summer heat and an excess of drink being smuggled aboard by the crew. At one point tempers boiled over into a violent brawl.

An argument erupted between two crewmates who had been drinking during an unusually hot evening of January 27th. Seaman James Houlstone pulled a knife on Joseph Feley and stabbed him, causing grievous injuries. The mate and other crew subdued both men and the police were called. Houlstone was taken into custody and charged with attempted murder. Morale aboard the Loch Tay was at an all-time low.

The time for departure came on February 8th when the hatches were sealed and battened down. The Loch Tay was hauled out from her Williamstown berth and into Hobson's Bay the following day. The tug Resolute towed her down to Port Phillip Heads on February 10th. The Loch Rannoch was the last to depart, being towed to sea on March 11th, the Loch Vennachar being just a month out from London.

The Loch Vennachar made her number off Deal on April 18th, 101 days from Port Phillip Heads, whilst the Loch Tay arrived off Prawle Point on May 11th, 90 days out, and the Loch Rannoch dropped anchor off Deal on June 20th, 101 days from Port Phillip. The Loch Tay's run, though, was as drama-filled as her run to Australia.

The Loch Tay hove off west of Dungeness and was approached by the tug Cambria that steamed up under the clipper's stern. When within hailing distance, the tug's master and Captain Bennett began to haggle over the price of a tow. It was beginning to become very foggy and William was in no mood to run the narrows in such hazardous conditions. Soon after, a tow line had been passed from the stern of the tug to the forebits of the Loch Tay.

The wooden ship 'Swiftsure', 1212 tons.
SLSA Collection.

It was well past dusk when, surrounded by fog, the Cambria and Loch Tay again got under way, making a steady 2.5 knots. Just after midnight, the fog and rain thickened to a regular pea-souper. It was just after 1:30 am, four miles off Sandgate, that the crew of the Cambria heard a deafening crash and the crunch and squeal of metal buckling. The tow line went bar-tight and the tug's stern tow-post was almost pulled from the deck.

The mate of the tug released the shackles connecting the tug to the Loch Tay and soon the sidewheeler had come about, her crew aghast at what emerged through the fog: the bright lights of two vessels locked together, yet perpendicular to each other. A heavily laden sailing vessel, in this case the coal-carrying Swiftsure, had sailed headlong into the Loch Tay, carrying away bulwarks, breaking coverboards of the forehatch, buckling deck plating, and stoving in hull plates to the waterline abaft the collision bulkhead.

The Swiftsure's jib-boom then tore through the fore rigging, bringing down the topmast and royal yard. In turn, the Swiftsure had her stem crushed in, her timber hull planks a shattered and splintered mess. She had also lost her jib-boom and headgear. Both ships were locked together for 90 minutes until a second tug came alongside to help extricate the collier from the Loch Tay.

The Swiftsure was taken in tow by the tug Bennachie, the collier's master Captain McLaren admitting no fault, blaming the Loch Tay for not displaying the correct lighting at her bow, with no sidelights being visible in the thick fog. The Cambria soon had the Loch Tay once more attached to a tow line and the pair soon steamed off under reduced speed, the iron clipper having several slow leaks.

They reached Gravesend at 1:15 pm on May 15th and, with a certain urgency, the Loch Tay was taken under tow of two smaller river tugs and guided up to her London Dock berth so her cargo could be discharged and a full survey begun. The Swiftsure, which had been sailing fully laden from Shields to Turkey, came into Gravesend behind the Bennachie at 4:30 pm the same day.

London Dock, circa 1880.
London Illustrated.

Upon the discharge of a portion of her cargo, the Loch Tay was shifted across to Green's Upper Dry Dock, Blackwall, for a full Lloyd's inspection on May 16th. The damage was extensive: two sheerstrake plates, six bulwark plates, stanchions, six chainplates, and pinrails from the forecastle to the main hatch were damaged. Deck planks, stringer plates, and port side rivets from the forecastle to the main hatch were replaced above the waterline, as was all the rigging of the foremast on the port side; the jib-boom and fore and backstays were also lost. It was going to be a lengthy and expensive repair.

The Loch Tay spent a month in dry dock before passing her reclassification survey on June 18th. The repairs came to almost £2000, and the master of the Swiftsure was found to be liable for the damage to both vessels by a Trinity Board of Enquiry. Captain McLaren's master's ticket was suspended by Justice Sir R. J. Phillimore.

"The facts of the case, as appeared upon the evidence for the plaintiffs (the Loch Tay), were that shortly before 1:20 am on the 14th of May last, the Loch Tay, with a crew of 29 hands all told, and laden with a cargo of wool and other colonial produce, was, whilst on a voyage from Melbourne to London, in charge of a duly licensed Trinity House Pilot, in the English Channel, between Dungeness and Folkestone. The wind at the time was a moderate breeze from the SW, the weather was thick with fog, and the tide was in the last quarter ebb, running about half a knot an hour. The Loch Tay, under topsails only, in tow of a tug called the Cambria, was steering ENE and making about 2.5 knots an hour, the vessel and her tug showing their proper lights and keeping a good look-out. Under these circumstances the green light of the Swiftsure was seen at a distance of about 200 yards, and bearing three points on the port bow, whereupon the helms of the Loch Tay and her tug were put hard a-port, the steam-whistle of the tug sounded, and the Swiftsure hailed to starboard her helm, but she, instead of doing so, sailing rapidly, struck the Loch Tay on her port side just before the fore-rigging, and did her so much damage that it was feared she would fill.

The defendants' version (the Swiftsure), was that the Swiftsure, at the time of the collision, was on a voyage from

Newcastle with a cargo of coals, and when in the English Channel, between Dungeness and Folkestone, the wind was a moderate breeze from the SW, the weather being a little hazy with passing showers, and the tide running westward at the rate of about two knots an hour. The Swiftsure was steering about S by E, close-hauled on the starboard tack, and making about four knots an hour, exhibiting her proper lights and keeping a good look-out. In these circumstances the lights of the Cambria, with the Loch Tay in tow, were seen on the starboard bow about a mile off, and shortly afterwards the red and green lights of the Loch Tay were seen on the starboard bow. The Swiftsure kept her course and blew her fog-horn, but the Cambria and the Loch Tay kept coming on, apparently heading to cross the bows of the Swiftsure, whose helm was ordered to be ported, as a collision seemed inevitable, but, notwithstanding, the Loch Tay, with her port bow near the fore rigging, came into contact with the jib-boom and stem of the Swiftsure, and sustained considerable damage." **— Shipping and Mercantile Gazette, 03 July 1879.**

The ill fortune of the Swiftsure continued when she was involved in another disastrous collision between the barque and another ship, the Cundell, whilst both were being towed along the River Tyne.

Upon discharge from the dry dock, the Loch Tay was sailed north under tow, commanded by her first officer John McCallum, arriving at Broomielaw on July 1st 1879. Her master, Bill Bennett, had been detained in London to attend the Trinity Masters Court of Enquiry.

Captain Bennett had spent his time between London and Chatham before returning to Glasgow in the third week of July. Her loading was well in hand, being overseen by John McCallum, and the clipper was slated to depart Glasgow on August 5th.

The Loch Tay was towed down to Greenock on August 4th and sailed from the Tail-o'-the-Bank, being towed out to sea by the steam-tug Flying Arrow. The tug was parted with the following evening off South Rock.

The Loch Tay hove to off Port Phillip Heads on October 28th 1879, 84 days out, having been outside the heads for more than a day, having rounded Cape Otway on the evening of the

27th. At 1:00 pm the following afternoon, as she was making for the Heads, the Loch Tay was hit by a nasty squall. Captain Bennett quickly ordered sails reduced to headsails and topsails, but these were quickly blown clean out of the bolt ropes, the shreds of canvas being quickly whipped away by the wind. Forced to bear away, the pilot took the Loch Tay out into deeper water until new sails were bent to the yards and set after the squalls had passed. The clipper then sailed on through the Heads without further incident and came to anchor just inside the south channel.

The clipper was towed up to her Hobson's Bay moorings whilst customs and pratique were cleared. The passengers and their baggage were then lightered ashore before the Loch Tay was then taken into berth alongside the Williamstown Pier to discharge. The Loch Garry was already tied up and well into discharging her cargo. Once it was emptied, the ship City of Agra came alongside and transshipped a quantity of manganese ore as ballast.

This was an unexpected and somewhat unwelcome cargo as it was prone to shifting and liquefaction during rough weather. Captain Bennett made sure that it was well stowed with shifting boards before being tamped down and canvas covered before deck boards were laid over the top in preparation for bales of wool to be taken aboard.

Whilst he had been away, an agent working for Captain Bennett had purchased land at Bittern on the Mornington Peninsula as part of a selection. Once the Loch Tay's paperwork had been dealt with, Bill Bennett took the time to travel down to Bittern to inspect the land he hoped to clear for sheep and cattle. He employed contractors to clear and improve the land for later development. Satisfied with progress, he returned to Port Melbourne and the home he rented.

While he had been away in the country, crew discipline had been allowed to slacken as her first mate, John McCallum, had left the Loch Tay in the care of the second and third mates. Several of the sailors had left the ship without permission; most had escaped into the city or left the colony.

The Clyde Shipping Co' tug Flying Arrow.

One sailor though, John Upton, the ship's cook, had been arrested having been away for two days, and was sentenced to seven days' gaol. Upon his return to the ship, an irate Captain Bennett upbraided his first mate and made sure that there were no more absconders.

The Loch cleared out on December 29th 1879, the crew having spent Christmas day at the Seamen's Mission Christmas dinner and concert. Loading was completed and she was towed out from the Williamstown Railway Pier on January 2nd 1880, heavily laden, behind the steam-tug Resolute. There, Captain Bennett brought the ship to anchor, waiting for the last of the passengers to be lightered out to the clipper. The following morning, with everyone safely aboard, the latest newspapers and last-minute mail were taken aboard with the pilot.

The clipper sailed out through the Heads on January 4th bound for London. The Loch Tay had doubled Cape Horn on February 10th in company with the American barque Gulf of California and crossed the Equator on March 11th, 68 days from Melbourne. Also due to sail for London, laden with wool, were the Loch Garry, commanded by Andrew Black, which sailed on January 23rd; the Loch Vennachar, under Captain James Ozanne, which sailed on January 14th; and the Loch Rannoch, under James Ross, which sailed on February 18t .

The first clipper to make her number was the Loch Tay, which passed the Isle of Wight on April 16th, 103 days from Port Phillip Bay. The Loch Vennachar passed the Isle of Wight on the 17th, 85 days out, and the Loch Garry passed Dover on the 18th, 95 days from the Heads. The Loch Tay and Loch Garry arrived in tow off Deal on the 17th of April 1880, and soon both were on the way up river to Gravesend.

The Loch Tay was taken up to London Dock to discharge and the following day, even as her cargo was being discharged, was placed on the berth for New York. Most of the same crew were kept aboard as they had signed articles that meant they would not be paid off until the Loch Tay returned to Glasgow. The ship was towed back to sea behind the tug Robert Bruce on May 28th with general merchandise aboard for Henderson Brothers.

William Bennett brought his ship safely into New York Bay on July 1st, reaching her Hudson River berth two days later behind a huffing paddle-wheeler. She was at New York for just a month before clearing out on August 2nd laden with general merchandise for Glasgow and set sail from Sandy Hook on the 5th.

The Loch Tay made a cracking run back to the Clyde, reaching her Tail-o'-the-Bank moorings on September 1st 1880. That evening the ship was back at Broomielaw, her cargo discharged the following day. The cargo was an eclectic mix of goods: thousands of bags of wheat, tobacco, soap, walnut logs, cases of tin toys, barrels of wheat and resin.

Once her cargo was discharged and the crew paid off, Captain Bennett stepped ashore and visited the offices of Aitken, Lilburn & Co., where James Lilburn waited to greet his friend. It was James who was always dockside when one of the vessels he and his partners managed arrived. Bill and James had become fast friends and the company had even allowed Captain Bennett to trade privately and to invest in the very cargoes being shipped to Australia. Whilst he and James were catching up on the latest news on the state of trade and shipping, 50 tons of pig iron were being loaded aboard the Loch Tay. Moored in front of the Loch Tay was the Loch Katrine, also on the berth for Melbourne. Her master, Captain Fred Burton, was well regarded and eager to test his ship against the well-known flyer Loch Tay.

Bill Bennett was given leave to return home to Kent, the Loch Tay not being scheduled to sail until the end of October. He caught the train home to London, then a second one to Chatham and his house in Clover Street. Mary was glad to see her husband and by now their first-born, Harry, was now two; yet to him Bill was a stranger. The maid, Harriet, was on hand to keep the toddler busy while Bill and Mary spent some much-needed alone time renewing their relationship that had been on hold for a year. Yet the time soon came for Captain Bennett to return to Greenock where he would meet the Loch Tay before she sailed for Melbourne.

The Loch Tay arrived at Greenock on November 3rd 1880 with a crew of 36 aboard. She was well down to her load marks and, as Captain Bennett travelled out to the clipper aboard the local steamer, Bill noticed the ship was down an inch or two by the stern, allowing for better bite of the rudder during rough weather. However, before they could allow passengers aboard, the Loch Tay had to be taken out to the outer moorings to take on 25,000 pounds of gunpowder. Later that day, with the hatches firmly sealed and battened, the passengers were welcomed aboard.

The ship set off down the Clyde behind a steam-tug that evening, outward bound for Melbourne. However, the winds were against them and the Loch Tay and her tug were forced to put in to Lamlash Bay for the remainder of the night. They set sail later the next morning and the clipper farewelled the tug Flying Meteor off South Rock at 6:00 pm on the 4th.

After another successful voyage, the Loch Tay made her number off Cape Otway on January 22nd and, due to contrary winds, rounded up off Port Phillip Heads in the early morning of the 23rd, unable to enter even after taking on her pilot. A favourable slant was made just after lunch and they sailed into Port Phillip Bay at 1:20 pm.

"She left the Tail of the Bank, Greenock, on the 3rd November, and put into Lamlash the same evening, as the weather was not favourable for sailing; left Lamlash on the 4th, and passed Tuskar on the evening of the 5th, with the wind light from W.N.W. and from that point occasional S.W. winds with light weather were met with until falling in with N.E. trades in 26 north and 22 west. San Antonio, one of the Cape Verde Islands, was sighted on the 23rd November, and the N.E. trades were lost in 6 north and 27 west; afterwards till falling in with S.E. trades strong southerly winds were met with and one day's calm until the equator was passed on the 2nd December in 29 west. The S.E. trades were picked up in 3 south and 26.10 west, and proved fresh throughout. The meridian of the Cape of Good Hope was passed on the 23rd December in 41.10 south forty-nine days out, and the easting ran down in between 42° and 43°

The paddle-tug Flying Meteor owned by the Clyde Shipping Company.

south, with the exception of four days light easterly weather in 100° east; the winds were moderate from north to south-west, with fine weather to the meridian of Cape Leeuwin, which was passed on 15th January, when a fresh gale from N.E. set in, and lasted for eighteen hours. Cape Otway was signalled at 2 p.m. on Saturday, the 22nd inst., and the ship entered the Heads on Sunday morning, seventy-nine days from Tuskar. The weather throughout was very fine." **The Age, Tue 25 Jan 1881.**

The clipper, upon discharging her cargo of gunpowder, was hauled into Sandridge Pier to unload the rest of the cargo and then load for home. Instead of wool, the clipper was contracted to load wheat along with the ship Zuleika. They were to sail to the English Channel for orders. After discharging her cargo, the Loch Tay was shifted across to Williamstown Pier to complete loading.

By February 23rd, the Loch Tay had completed loading and was hauled out into the bay waiting upon the boarding house runners ashore to round up enough sailors for the run home. However, just before she was towed out, two of the crew stole a number of items from the ship and absconded. Captain Bennett reported the desertion and theft to water-police and was eager for the men to be caught and punished. He had no time for thieves as aboard a vessel trust was everything, especially during stormy weather.

The clipper arrived in Port Phillip Bay on January 1st 1882, 88 days from Greenock. It had been a slow passage, yet the clipper was in fine trim, though one passenger short, the man having died of tuberculosis on the voyage out. The Loch Tay's lengthy passage was blamed on a succession of contrary and baffling winds and the fact that the ship had not been docked for over fifteen months, her bottom being extremely foul. On two or three occasions during calms, Captain Bennett had ordered the mate to get the boats out and, by means of sheets of iron and thrummed mats, have men scrape the marine growth and barnacles off as low down as could be reached.

Once her cargo of gunpowder was offloaded, the clipper was berthed alongside Williamstown Pier for the discharge of the remainder of her cargo. The discharge of cargo left the crew with little to do in the weeks before the first of the Loch Tay's wool arrived. One of her crew, John Frazer, a seaman, was charged with being absent without leave from the Loch Tay. The absconder was arrested as he returned to the ship extremely drunk. Captain Bennett called the water police and had the sailor arrested. Later, before the police magistrate, Bennett and the first mate appeared in court, with Bill wanting to make an example of the recalcitrant sailor to keep the other members of the crew in line. The local magistrate agreed and sentenced Fraser to seven days in gaol before being handed back to the first mate Mr. Stewart's less than tender care.

Upon the complete discharge of the cargo and the taking on of some ballast, the Loch Tay was hauled into the Alfred Graving Dock for a scrape, clean, and painting with anti-fouling agent. While she was on the blocks, the ship's hull underwent a full survey by a Lloyd's assessor, so encrusted had her hull been in weed and crustations. The ship was found to be perfectly sound and retained her A1 insurance rating. Then, once cleaned and painted, the Loch Tay was floated out of the dock and sent back to Williamstown Pier to complete loading.

As the time to depart drew closer, the Loch Tay's crew grew increasingly restless. While Captain Bennett was ashore attending to personal business and visiting his holdings on the Mornington Peninsula, several crew members went on a drunken spree and became involved in a violent brawl with police in Williamstown.

Donald McWatt, James Skinner, William Miller, Robert Grant, and James McClinchy were brought up on charges at the Williamstown Court on February 8th 1882. They had been arrested for insulting behaviour, resisting arrest, assaulting police, and disorderly conduct. The five had started a brawl with the local constabulary after they had been ejected from the Woolpack Hotel for using abusive language and fighting. They then stumbled on to the Oriental Hotel where they were met by police. Unwilling to go peacefully, the police had been forced to resort to billy-clubs and fists to bring the drunken sailors to account.

All were found guilty and heavily fined: McWatt, the key instigator of the violence and most mouthy of the men, was fined £4 10 shillings; Skinner £3 10s; Grant £1 10s; and the other two were fined 10 shillings each. Captain Bennett agreed to pay the fines on condition that the men were put on board the Loch Tay for the first mate to deal with. They were, and Mr. Stewart was none too gentle in reminding the men of their duties and the debt they owed their captain. Bill Bennett's reasons for paying the fines were twofold: the first was that, as it was so close to the sailing time of the Loch Tay, he did not want to have to find five more sailors; and second, the men would have the fines deducted from their wages upon being paid off in Glasgow. So, for the master of the Loch Tay, it made perfect sense to pay the fines.

The clipper was hauled off the wharf on February 8th just after the recalcitrant sailors were brought aboard in irons by the water police. However, it was low tide and the ship was forced to anchor at the outer edge of Hobson's Bay until the following morning when the tide was on the rise. The ship was towed to sea behind the steamer Hercules, and Port Phillip Heads was cleared at 9:30 am the following morning. Captain Bennett set course to sail east through Bass Strait bound for Cape Horn.

The Loch Tay passed the Lizard on May 5th 1882, 83 days from Port Phillip Bay, and was entered into customs on May 11th. They had doubled Cape Horn on March 10th, 29 days out. Running north along the coast of South America, the clipper fell in with the ship John Rennie and two Peruvian barques laden with guano from Valparaiso. The vessels stayed together until the doldrums, where the Loch Tay slowly crept away. The Loch Tay crossed the equator on April 12th, passing the ship Dunbritton, outward bound for Port Adelaide.

As the clipper was being shifted from Gravesend to London Dock, Captain Bennett was on the train to London to hand over the manifest, logs, and crew list to her agents Thomas Skinner & Co. Upon arrival at the London office of Aitken, Lilburn

& Co., Bill learned that the Loch Maree, now under the command of his old friend and mentor, Captain Alex Scott, had gone missing sailing from Geelong to Cape Horn. There had been plenty of icebergs on the run to Cape Horn and Bennett was sure that the Loch Maree, if missing, had met her end running into one of these. However, for the time being, all that anyone could do was wait and hope the ship had put into a port somewhere and was undergoing repairs.

Upon discharge of her cargo, the Loch Tay was hauled back down to Gravesend on June 1st and was towed out to Deal the following day. The clipper was kept under tow until June 6th, as contrary winds did not allow for a quick sail down the Channel. Instead, each night they put into a safe anchorage until the tug was kept all the way to Greenock, which was reached on June 9th 1882 with 11 tons of spelter, 270 tons of chrome ore, 2 tons of redwood, and 102 tons of cement aboard. Even before the last of her cargo had been discharged, James Lilburn had the Loch Tay placed on the berth for Melbourne, scheduled to sail on June 28th. This gave Captain Bennett almost no time to head home to Chatham, so his visit was brief.

Right on time, the ship was towed down to Greenock, where she was transferred to Gareloch to load gunpowder. Her captain and passengers joined the clipper upon her return to Greenock on the evening of June 29th, and the tug Flying Hurricane, towing the Loch Tay, set off down the Clyde that evening. Bill Bennett only had a crew of 32 officers and men for the run to Australia, and he was concerned about the low numbers of reliable seamen available at Glasgow.

After another lengthy journey, the Loch Tay made her number off Port Phillip Heads on the afternoon of September 25th, after 88 days at sea. The pilot then conned the clipper up through the South Channel to Hobson's Bay, where the anchor was let go. The twenty passengers aboard were sent ashore the following morning, and the Loch Tay was shifted across to Williamstown to discharge her very heavy cargo.

"The ship left the Tail of the Bank, Greenock, on June 28, and had almost calm weather in Channel, so that Scilly was not

passed until July 6. Strong S.W. winds were then encountered until falling in with the N.E. trades in lat. 32 deg. N. and lon. 28 deg. W. The trades were light throughout. Then passed the ship Cotopaxi on August 16th at 39 deg. S, 106 deg. E. and asked to be reported 'All well!' The prime meridian was crossed on August 26 in lat. 83 deg. S., and the easting was run down mostly in the parallel of 41 deg. Strong westerly gales, with a very high sea and showers of hail, prevailed across the Southern Ocean to the longitude of Cape Leeuwin, which was crossed on September 17. The ship made some capital running from that date until September 22, when light easterly weather set in for 21 hours. Cape Otway was made at 6 p.m. on Sunday last, the wind at the time blowing a gale from the westward, and the squalls being fierce and frequent. The Heads were reached on Monday morning, and Captain Bennett states that he had to wait five hours for a pilot. The voyage was completed in 83 days from Greenock, or in 81 days from Scilly."

The Argus, Fri 22 Sep 1882.

There were a number of Glasgow Shipping Company vessels in port: the Loch Tay, Loch Garry, Loch Sloy, and the fleet's flagship, the Loch Vennachar. Their crews were frequent visitors to each others' ships and occasionally would be absent from their berths without permission. So it happened to sailors Charles Moore and John King of the Loch Tay. Caught by the water police, the two men were sentenced to twelve days in prison; however, after a plea from Captain Bennett, they were released into his custody and he paid their fines. Thus he kept his sailors and docked their pay to recoup his expenses. Unwilling to control his urges, John Moore again absented himself from the Loch Tay and this time, when caught, spent the next seven days in Williamstown gaol.

January 1st 1883 saw Captain Bennett and a fellow master, Captain Matthias of the Hampshire, travel to Sandhurst at the invitation of Robert Clark, member of the Victorian Legislative Assembly for Sandhurst. The two captains stayed at Clark's palatial residence. They were guests at a gathering organised by the local Caledonian Society during the day and attended the society's dinner that evening.

The ship's bottom was badly fouled with weed and barnacles, and so upon discharge of her cargo the clipper was shifted across to Alfred Graving Dock for a scrape, clean, and painting with anti-fouling agents. There was not an inch of her hull below the water line that was not covered in a thick layer of green. After three days in dock, she was refloated and sent back to the Railway Pier to complete loading. The Loch Tay was cleared out from Williamstown before dawn on January 23rd 1883 and towed out through the heads by the tug Resolute at 9:10 am the same morning. Captain Bennett set his course to run east through Bass Strait heavily laden with 5461 bales of wool, 42 bales of leather, 1300 cans of preserved meat, 258 bags of antimony, and 5 packages of merchandise being shipped by Bill Bennett.

They were making excellent time, Cape Horn being doubled on February 28th and the equator crossed on March 20th 1883, passing the ship Scottish Wizard on her way to Townsville from Glasgow. The keepers of the Scilly lighthouse marked the Loch Tay's passing on April 17th, 81 days out. She passed the Lizard that afternoon and a pilot was picked up soon after off Plymouth. The tug Vizier was contracted west of Prawle Point, and the pair steamed up past Deal on the 18th headed for Gravesend. The Loch Tay, after clearing customs, was towed into her London Dock berth.

Discharge of her cargo was left to the supervision of the first mate as Captain Bennett left for London to visit the office of Skinner & Co. before travelling home to Chatham. William arrived to find another son, John Willmott Bennett, had arrived on October 10th the previous year. He had instantly been called Jack by the family, and Bill was filled with pride and love for his new son. He was greeted with enthusiasm by his other two children, Harry and Ettie.

The first mate took the Loch Tay from Gravesend on May 1st and she was towed all the way back to the Lizard, arriving at Greenock on May 11th and Broomielaw on the 14th, 1883. The turnaround for the Loch Tay was almost a record, her cargo discharged and the clipper back down at Greenock by May 25th.

That night, still in Chatham, Captain Bennett attended a farewell dinner at the Mitre Hotel, hosted by his Masonic lodge friends; he was on the overnight train straight after and was back at Greenock just in time to board the Loch Tay. A tug hauled the clipper off down the Clyde the following afternoon, with Bill Bennett once more in command. They passed Kildonan at 3:30 am on the 27th, the lights of Dublin shining brightly.

The ship made her number outside Port Phillip on August 23rd 1883, 89 days from Greenock. The clipper's appearance caused a stir dockside when she dropped anchor in Hobson's Bay. Her bulwarks were missing, as was one of her boats, whilst the other was badly damaged. The voyage report supplied by Captain Bennett made compelling reading:

"The Loch Tay left the Tail-of-the-Bank, Greenock, at 10 p.m. on May 26, and came out by way of the North Channel, Tory Island being passed at 11 p.m. on the following day. Then the trouble commenced. Strong gales set in from S.S.W., and held unchecked sway for five consecutive days. During this period there was a continuous high cross sea, which made clean breaches over all, and broke on board from all quarters, flooding the decks and washing everything movable adrift. The winds after this burst veered to the westward, and the weather moderated. In lat. 31 deg. N. the N.E. trades were taken. They proved light throughout, however. Madeira was passed and sighted on June 8, and the ship was on the equator on June 30 in lon. 24 deg. W., 34 days out. The S.E. trades were picked up in lat. 2 deg. N., and fresh breezes were carried to lat. 24 deg. S. They were accompanied with a high topping sea, which at times caused the ship to plunge heavily. Light variables and calms were next met with for two days, and these in turn were succeeded by a strong southerly gale, which lasted for three days. There was a heavy confused sea with it, and large bodies of water were shipped.

This weather was followed by light northerly and easterly winds until crossing the prime meridian on July 24, in lat. 39 deg. S. The longitude was run down mostly on the parallel of 41 deg., with generally light winds and moderate weather until crossing the meridian of 90 deg. E. Here the Loch Tay was called on again to contend with tempestuous weather. Strong gales from N.W. to

W., blowing at times with hurricane violence and attended with furious squalls and heavy hail showers, set in and continued until nearing lon. 124 deg. E. The gales sent along a fearful sea, which dashed over the ship with dangerous force, smashing one of the forward boats, bursting in the doors of the second cabin, carrying away a portion of the topgallant bulwarks and the after hatch, and tearing the tarpaulin off the main hatch. All stray or unsecured articles were also swept overboard. The ship afterwards had a sequence of fresh gales until making Cape Otway at 4 p.m."

The Argus, 25 Aug 1883.

Williamstown Railway Pier was a hive of activity as the Loch Tay was berthed alongside. Repairs were going to take longer than usual because the ship's carpenter, William Brady, had died from the effects of a stroke whilst at sea, and Bill Bennett had to find a replacement to oversee much-needed repairs to the Loch Tay's storm damage.

Most of the wool was yet to arrive, and the quiet time allowed the crew of the Loch Tay to get up to mischief. Three of her crew broke into the hold and stole several bottles of whisky and helped themselves to bottles of beer. The men were discovered drunk as lords in the hold and held in irons until the water police arrived to take the thieves into custody. They were later convicted of broaching the cargo and sentenced to three months in prison. Bill Bennett was happy to see them imprisoned and had no intention of employing the thieves for the run home.

The clipper was to be sent to Alfred Graving Dock for her regular clean and paint before the last of her cargo was stowed. This allowed one of her crew to skip out for a spree ashore. The unlucky sailor, Robert Sherman, was found 'three sheets to the wind' and, after being convicted, was sent to gaol until just before the Loch Tay was cleared to sail. If Captain Bennett thought that his crew troubles were over, then he was to be disappointed. As the Loch Tay was in dry dock, her sailmaker, Donald McMillan, helped himself to a pair of ducks that happened to belong to a local police constable. The benighted mariner was arrested and later convicted of larceny. For his efforts, McMillan was sentenced to two months' imprisonment.

Once clear of the dry dock, the Loch Tay was sent back to her Sandridge Pier berth to complete loading. This was well underway when, on Sunday November 4th, the captain and crew of the clipper noticed the schooner Gannet, moored near the pier, was on fire. Responding quickly, Captain Bennett dispatched a boat and several sailors to the schooner to help put out the fire. They were successful in saving the Gannet, but the cabin was gutted and the timbers around the hatch were badly charred.

The following Sunday was the annual regatta held by the Victoria Yacht Club. The racing took place off St Kilda. A number of different classes competed during the day, with the five-oared gig race held between crews belonging to the ships Aristides, Loch Tay, and the Greta. The crew of the Loch Tay acquitted themselves well but were beaten to the line by four lengths by the Aristides.

Against the background of the celebrations, there was an ongoing dispute between railway authorities, ship owners, and local stevedores. Captain Bennett had been given orders to complete loading by midnight of Wednesday November 21st 1883. The problem was that stevedores only worked until 6:00 pm and there was no way that the last bales could be loaded aboard without paying ruinous overtime to the stevedores. So, faced with no choice, Bill paid the fees and the clipper was cleared out just before the midnight deadline and was towed out to anchor in the bay.

The steamer Williams was engaged to tow the Loch Tay out to sea the next day, passing through The Rip at 9:10 am. They passed below Cape Horn on Christmas Day, 33 days from Melbourne, passing the barque Chiloe, and crossed the equator on January 25th. The run home was somewhat troubled; the Loch Tay having suffered storm damage rounding the Horn and suffering further damage during a series of storms on the run into the English Channel.

Captain Bennett dropped anchor in Falmouth Bay on February 27th after 97 days at sea. Several injured sailors were sent ashore to the hospital and the stop allowed Bill to send a telegram to Glasgow reporting their safe arrival. The ship set out from Falmouth the following day and soon after a pilot was picked up and a tug engaged to tow the clipper up to her Gravesend mooring. The tug was farewelled off Tilbury Fort on March 3rd and the Loch Tay was entered in through customs later that evening.

Bill Bennett left the clipper to his first mate to take into London dock to be berthed near to the Loch Vennachar. At the same instant Bennett, after visiting Skinner's office in London, was on the train to Chatham to visit Mary and the children. He also made time to become reacquainted with his fellow Freemasons of the Royal Kent Lodge of Antiquity, attending one of the regular meetings and banquets at the Mitre Inn and Clarence Hotel, and also visited other nearby lodges during his time ashore.

As Bill was at home enjoying the company of family and friends, the officers and standing crew of the Loch Tay and a team of runners were taking the clipper home to Glasgow, departing London on April 9th 1884, towed home behind the tug Flying Huntress. They safely reached Greenock on April 14th and Broomielaw the following morning. The clipper was brought up to Broomielaw with a ballast of cement aboard. The first mate signed over the ship to James Aitken, who passed responsibility to the ship's husband for her refit and Lloyd's survey.

Clyde Shipping Company tug, Flying Huntress.

VIII
A Lucky Ship and Master

William Bennett received some welcome news whilst at home in Chatham when a telegram from James Lilburn arrived, offering him command of the company's flagship, the Loch Vennachar. The previous master, James Ozanne, had returned to his home on Guernsey for a time and Bill Bennett was their first choice to replace him. It was an opportunity too good to refuse and came with many perks, including a substantial pay rise.

AT GLASGOW—FOR MELBOURNE,

The magnificent Clyde-built Iron Clipper Ship

LOCH VENNACHAR,

1480 Tons Register, 190 A 1 at Lloyd's

W. H. BENNETT, Commander,

Will receive Goods engaged for up to and all

WEDNESDAY, 23RD APRIL.

(If not previously full)

Has splendid Accommodation for Passengers.

CABIN ....£45 | SECOND CABIS...£22 and £25
INTERMEDIATE,....................£17.

Passengers are Booked at Through Rates to Sydney Adelaide, and all other Colonial Ports.

Cabin Passengers will be supplied with Bed, Bedding Toweis, and Tabie Linen, and Second Cabin Passengers will be supplied with all the table requisites.

For Freight or Passage, apply to
AITKEN, LILBURN & CO., Managers,
80 Buchanan Street.

The Fine Iron Ship ' LOCH TAY '' follows.

Loch Tay under barque rig at an unknown port.
SLSA Collection.

Loch Tay in original rig.
State Library of Victoria.

William 'Bill' Bennett's first run as master of the Loch Vennachar began when he sailed her out of the Clyde for Melbourne. Twin tugs hauled the clipper out from her Queens Dock berth, Broomielaw at 10:00 am on April 25th and she was hauled down river to the Tail-o'-the-Bank to collect her passengers and master. Housed on deck were a dozen Shetland ponies in stalls on deck.

When Will Bennett came aboard he was surprised at the size of the crew, 44 men and boys, a refreshingly able body of mariners who were all eager to serve aboard the company flagship. The Loch Vennachar departed Greenock on 26th April behind the tug Flying Huntress, and passed through the North Channel on the 27th, with fresh N.E. winds and dirty weather. The Flying Huntress was farewelled off Inishtrahull at 8:00 pm the same day.

On the fourth day out, during a thunderstorm from the west, the cap of the fore topsail yard carried away by the upper fore topsail yard falling on it. Captain Bennett was forced to have the Loch Vennachar hove to whilst the damage was repaired. The ship afterwards had southwest gales for three days. Madeira was passed on the 7th of May, and the northeast trades, which were light throughout, were picked up in 39½° north.

The equator was crossed on 29th May in 26° west, and the meridian of Greenwich on 18th May in 38° south. The easting was run down on the parallel of 41°, with gales from nor'west to sou'west, until passing Cape Leeuwin on the 9th of July. Light winds and fine weather continued all the way to Cape Otway, which was passed at 10 p.m. on July 15th. There was rough weather outside the Heads and Captain Bennett ordered the pouring of oil out through the scuppers which calmed the waters enough for the pilot to successfully board the ship.

The Heads were entered on July 16th, 81 days from Greenock. The barque River Nith, from Liverpool for Melbourne, was spoken to by the Loch Vennachar on 25th May in 2° south and 27° west and asked to be reported 'All well!'

After lightering off her cargo of gunpowder, she was tied up at the Williamstown Railway Pier and her passengers alighted. On board were First cabin passengers Mrs Soutter, Mr James Graham, Mr Claude Sturrock, Mr D Sutherland, Master Harold Bennett, and 35 in steerage. Stacked neatly into her hold were 20,000 floorboards, large bundles of sheet, hoop, angle and pig-iron, haberdashery, candles, hardware, stoves, twine, a fire engine, iron pipes, sewing machines, 1150 cases of beer and dozens of kegs, cases and casks of brandy, whisky, wine and beer.

The ship stayed tied to the pier for some months whilst the wool clip came in and other cargoes were arranged. Bill Bennett used the down time to catch up with friends and to attend to his own personal and company business. He was however called back early in September to attend a Coroner's Inquest.

On the 12th September 1884, the Loch Vennachar's boatswain James McLinhie met with an unfortunate accident whilst returning to the ship after a Saturday night out drinking with a fellow crew member. On crossing the Falls Bridge they turned onto the landing of the flight of steps leading down to the south bank of the Yarra, and drunk and stumbling McLinhie tripped and fell, tumbling to the bottom of the stairs.

Unconscious, the boatswain was found to have badly gashed his head. His mate moved him in a cab to Gladstone Place, where help was called. A doctor arriving at the scene examined the boatswain's injuries but there was nothing that could be done and James McLinhie was pronounced dead at the scene. An inquest was later held into the death, one in which Captain Bennett was asked to appear, and a cause of accidental death was pronounced.

The warehouses holding the Loch Vennachar's valuable cargo of wool were almost empty, her hold nearly full, when on the 17th of December Captain Bennett had the ship towed from the Sandridge Pier and floated into Alfred Graving Dock to have the hull cleaned and painted with anti-fouling agents. With final preparations underway, cargo loading began in earnest.

By Christmas Eve the Loch Vennachar had cleared the graving dock and the last of her cargo had loaded. The ship was then floated out into the bay and Captain Bennett was anxious to get underway before the holidays; however, the ship was unable to leave, being shorthanded.

Once Christmas celebrations had been dispensed with and her inebriated crew rounded up and given time to sober up, the clipper was hauled out into Port Phillip Bay in the early hours of Boxing Day by the steamer Williams and cleared The Heads finally on Boxing Day at 7:20 am, headed for London with a hold full of wool.

The Loch Vennachar made her number off the Lizard on March 27th 1885, 91 days from Port Phillip Bay. She was towed into her Gravesend moorings on the evening of the 28th to await a river pilot to con the ship up to London Dock to discharge. The first mate as usual was left to care for the clipper as Captain Bennett took a train to London to visit his agent Thomas Skinner at the Royal Exchange Building in London. From there he headed home to Chatham for a well earned rest.

Whilst Bill Bennett was home, the Loch Vennachar's first mate was in command as she was towed back to Broomielaw to take on another cargo for Melbourne. Loading was completed in double quick time and she was back down to Greenock on April 27th just as Bill Bennett arrived from London having spent the previous evening at another banquet in his honour.

The Flying Huntress was again on hand to haul the Loch Vennachar back out to sea on April 29th, 1885, bound for the North Channel. The weather was thick and foggy, and the tug was kept until they were well clear of Inishtrahull on May 1st. The prevailing north-west winds held true until a light north-east trade was met in latitude 22° 10' north and longitude 24° 29' west.

San Antonio and St. Vincent were sighted on May 23rd, and the ship crossed the equator on June 3rd in longitude 23° 15' west. Southerly winds were encountered in the south-east trades, and much time was lost in having to beat to the eastward; three entire days were taken up in tacking.

After crossing the Prime Meridian in latitude 38° south, the winds became as variable in force as in direction, and, on crossing the Southern Ocean, some exceptionally heavy weather was experienced. In latitude 40° south and longitude 71° east, the wind raged with hurricane vehemence from north-west to west-south-west, and there was a high following sea. The ship ran dead before wind and sea under two lower topsails and foresail until she fairly outran the gale. The worst of it lasted for twelve hours, during which period the glass was at 29.62.

The pouring of oil on the turbulent sea was resorted to, and with effect. Captain Bennett tried this process again outside the Heads, during a south-westerly gale, when the pilot boarded the Loch Vennachar, and the result was again successful. The longitude of Cape Leeuwin was crossed on July 22nd in latitude 40° south, and thence a fine run in was made. Cape Otway was passed at 5:00 a.m. on Tuesday, the 28th of July, 1885, and the Heads were entered at noon, 89 days from Greenock.

The ship was hauled into her berth alongside the new pier at Williamstown to discharge, her 25 passengers glad to again be on dry land. Almost as soon as the clipper's hatches were broached and the stevedores arrived aboard, amongst them were the boarding house runners. These sneaky operators had come to entice the crew members to desert the Loch Vennachar with promises of better pay, free grog and cheap accommodation ashore.

Amongst those who chose to desert was the sailmaker Alexander Brabson. Angered that the man had left the ship taking several key hands with him, Captain Bennett was eager for the absconder to be severely punished when he was arrested by water police. The Williamstown magistrate obliged by sentencing Brabson to six weeks in prison with hard labour.

The Loch Vennachar stayed tied alongside the pier until September 29th when the clipper was shifted into the Alfred Graving Dock for her annual scrape, clean and painting with anti-fouling agents. Once painted the clipper was floated out of the dock and sent back to Williamstown to complete her loading.

Loading was completed on October 9th 1885 and with her 17 passengers aboard the ship was towed out into Hobson's Bay on October 10th, to await her tug to bring the ship down to Port Phillip Heads. There was a wait of several days due to severe west to south west winds and high seas outside of the Heads. Eventually the cold front passed and a new high pressure system moved in from the west allowing the Loch Vennachar and other vessels to safely cross the Rip and set sail for Cape Horn on October 15th.

The Loch Vennachar's run home in October 1885 was without major incident, but her arrival was anything but. She arrived off Deal, behind a tug, on January 5th and was attached to her Tilbury Fort moorings the following morning.

On board was a passenger named Clinton H. Walbridge who was not all that he professed to be. At the height of a howling gale, as the Loch Vennachar was making her way slowly up the Thames on the night of January 6th 1886, a light could be seen approaching the ship. What happened next was a most curious incident, one worth quoting at length as it had never happened before upon a Loch Liner:

Von Biehren was wanted for fraud and deception in New South Wales by Manly Water Police Court, having stolen nearly £800 in gold bullion and cash in order to avoid bankruptcy and his creditors. Using a false identity, that of Clinton H. Walbridge, he defrauded the Commercial Bank of Australia and then, using false identity papers, booked passage on the first fast clipper leaving Melbourne, that being the Loch Vennachar, which departed on the 13th of October.

Following closely upon his heels was Detective George Greaves, who learned from the local harbour pilot that a man matching Von Biehren's photograph had boarded the Loch Vennachar some days before. Leaving for London by a faster route through the Suez Canal was the steamer Ballarat. Taking passage aboard this ship, Detective Greaves endeavoured to get to London ahead of the Loch Vennachar.

The Ballarat arrived at least a week ahead of the clipper, which gave Detective Greaves time to set his trap, the events of which are detailed in the following article.

There was a great deal of media coverage of the incident back in Australia, and it only enhanced Captain Bennett's reputation as an upstanding and honest gentleman. When the trial commenced, Captain Bennett was asked to write a deposition that was to be read to the court in his absence. His sworn testimony, taken by officers from Bow Street, helped put the convicted fraudster Carl Von Biehren behind bars.

Arrest of Carl Von Biehren

"Detective Murphy was very clever and plucky. He reached London before Von Biehren's ship in the Ballarat. The Loch Vennachar was signalled in the Channel, and he at once determined to intercept her before she entered the Thames.

With the assistance of Scotland Yard police, he proceeded to Margate, and having chartered a small pilot boat, lay off Princes Channel, near Margate, for almost a week. At the time, London was in the thick of a great snowstorm which swept the country. On Thursday night, worn out and cold, they were about to give up when a light was observed coming up the channel. They decided to wait to ascertain what ship it belonged to.

They made up to the ship, and Murphy was agreeably surprised to find that it was the vessel he was in search of. He hailed the officer of the watch and told him he wanted to get on board. As a stiffish gale was blowing, he was told it was impossible. But he would take no denial. Eventually, the officer threw out a rope. Murphy had been a sailor in his time, and he determined to make the attempt.

With great courage, he took a leap from the pilot boat in the dark, and succeeded in catching hold of the rope and getting on board. He at once disclosed his identity and in answer to his inquiries found that Von Biehren was fast asleep in his cabin. It was mere chance that he was so, for on the afternoon of that very day a tug was observed near the ship and Von Biehren asked

Carl Von Biehren

*the captain to signal her, saying that he was willing to give £5 to
be put ashore.*

*The tug was hailed and came as near as it possibly could,
but a heavy sea was running at the time and Von Biehren could
not muster up sufficient courage to take a leap from the side of the
ship into the tug. Murphy did not disturb Von Biehren's slumber,
but in the morning took him his coffee instead of the steward.*

*At first, Von Biehren did not recognise him, for Murphy
had shaved off his beard, but when he made himself known, the
distracted grief of the poor German was something pitiful. He
threw his hands up in the air and said, "It's all up with me. It's all
up with me!", and he showed such signs of
agitation that Murphy thought it prudent to take his revolver away
from him. He searched his portmanteau and found about £700.*

*On the Saturday, Von Biehren was brought up at Bow
Street, and formally remanded to take him to Sydney, whither he
sailed home in company with his captor in the Rome yesterday.*
**The Maitland Mercury & Hunter River General Advertiser
Tuesday 23 February 1886.**

The Loch Vennachar and another similarly sized clipper,
the newly launched Falkland Hill, were placed on the berth for
Melbourne, both contracted to load at Broomielaw by Aitken,
Lilburn & Co. Captain Bennett returned home to Chatham on
Thursday, the 14th of January. That night, a dinner was held in
honour of his return after another successful voyage of 81 days
to Portland Bill. He was cordially welcomed home by all his old
friends, who commented that he was looking remarkably well
and hearty. Once the dinner was over, Bill Bennett decided to
walk home, the ground covered in snow, mud and ice.

Just as he reached his residence in the Paddock, he
slipped on a piece of frozen snow and fell heavily to the ground,
striking his head on the stone pavement, where he lay for some
seconds, almost stunned by the blow. He was stunned and left

Astoria 1429 tons. Built at Sunderland. 1885.
SLV Collection.

with a nasty bruise to his head and ego, and over the next few days made a complete recovery.

A month after her arrival in London Dock, the Loch Vennachar was on her way back to Glasgow, passing the Lizard on February 16th 1886. She arrived back at the Queen's Dock berth on the evening of February 19th. Almost immediately, the hatch-boards were lifted and a ballast of pig-iron and iron rails was laid down.

Loading was begun in earnest and lasted until March 18th, when the Loch Vennachar was cleared out from Broomielaw and sent down river to Greenock. Her vacant berth was then occupied by another iron clipper owned in part and managed by Aitken & Lilburn, the 1400-ton Astoria. Bill Bennett was on the train to Port Glasgow as his ship was being towed down the Clyde.

Her time in port was brief, and by March 19th 1886, the clipper had left the Tail o'-the Bank bound for Hobson's Bay behind the Glasgow Shipping Co. tug Hercules. Due to persistent south-westerlies, Captain Bennett took his ship out through the North Channel, passing Inishtrahull on the 20th where the tug was left behind. Out in the western ocean, the Loch Vennachar continued to battle strong south-westerly winds, foggy conditions and rough head-seas.

The storms continued until March 25th, when winds and seas finally moderated. The north-easterly trades were picked up on April 4th as the ship crossed the 30th parallel, and fair winds and seas continued all the way across the trades zone. San Antonio Island was passed on April 9th and the equator crossed on the 25th.

North-westerlies carried the Loch Vennachar south as she began her easting run along the 40th parallel. The prevailing winds swung from north-west to south-west, perfect conditions for which the clipper was designed. The Loch Vennachar flew along before a following wind and sea, covering thousands of nautical miles in just a few short weeks. At times, violent storms would brew up from the south.

One such blow rose up on May 28th. Gale-force winds and high rolling seas pounded the Loch Vennachar as she raced eastwards under a full suite of canvas. One large wave broke over the deck, sending the second officer flying into the scuppers, breaking his arm in the process. The arm was set and the second mate spent the rest of his journey confined to his bunk, or on light duties only.

The line of Cape Leeuwin was passed on June 5th as Captain Bennett turned his vessel north-east. The final approach to Bass Strait was made in heavy weather, keeping most passengers indoors. Cape Otway was passed at 5 am on June 12[th]and the Heads entered through that afternoon.

The voyage had taken 88 days from Greenock and, on the journey, two vessels of note were encountered. The Myrtle Holme, bound for Lyttelton, New Zealand, was spoken to on the 27th parallel. The other encounter was almost her last. The run down to Australia was made in fair weather for most of the trip; it was not until she reached the Roaring Forties that trouble struck.

On her way through the giant waves of a howling gale, the Loch Vennachar almost ran down the steam tug Racer. The little vessel was hove-to, riding out the storm, when out of the darkness the clipper appeared. Sitting athwart her course, the forward lookout cried out that a vessel was right ahead. The helmsman pulled the wheel hard over and the two ships slid past, just 30 feet separating them in the inky darkness. By the time the Loch Vennachar tied up at Williamstown Railway Pier, her cargo was eagerly awaited.

One of the passengers Henry H. Kemp, kept a diary and created a number of sketches that depicted daily life aboard the Loch Vennachar on her voyage from Glasgow to Melbourne in 1886;

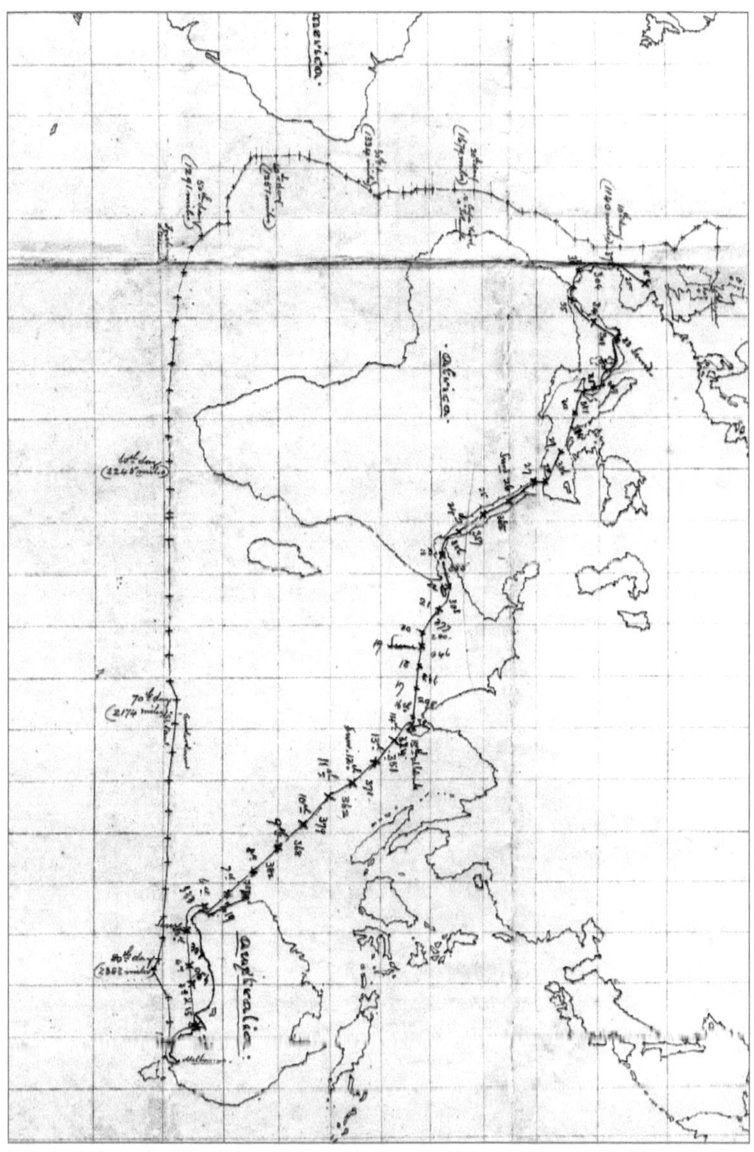

Route taken by the Loch Vennachar and the return route by steamer via the Suez Canal.

Captain Bill Bennett was an avid lover of plants and collected many specimens to take back to Chatham.

The main deck as seen from the break of the poop looking towards the bow.

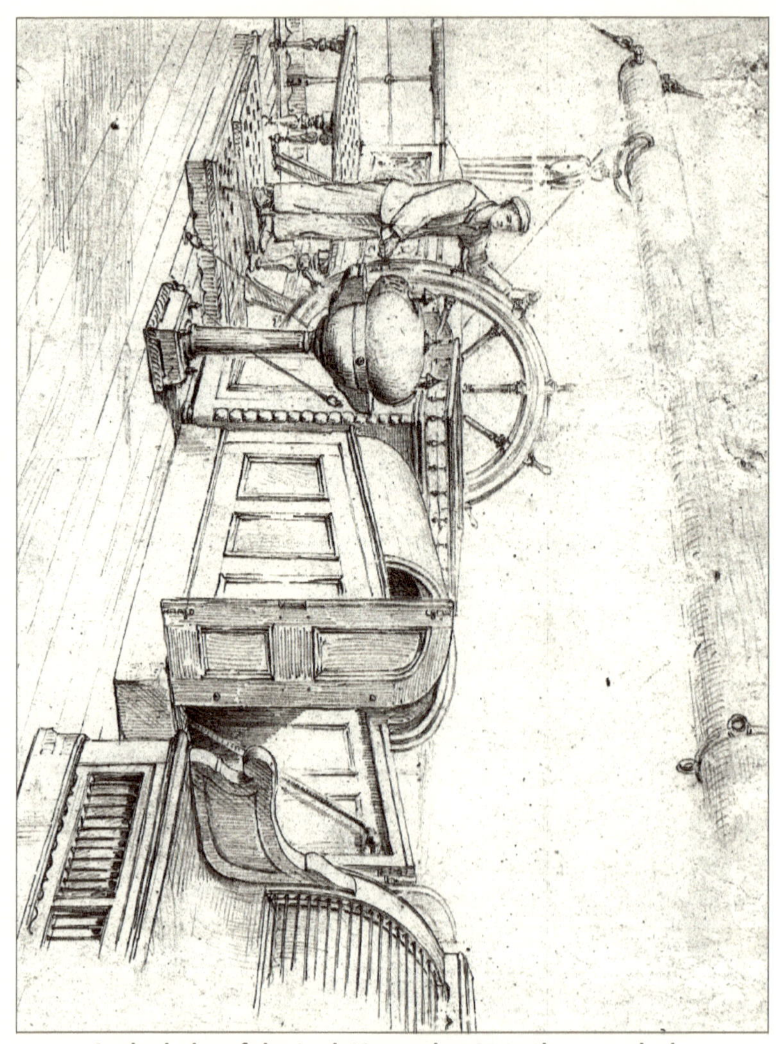

At the helm of the Loch Vennachar atop the poopdeck.

A First Class Cabin.

The Poopdeck as seen from atop the deckhouse.

Captain Bill Bennett waiting for a breeze, on the poopdeck, while stuck in the doldrums.

147

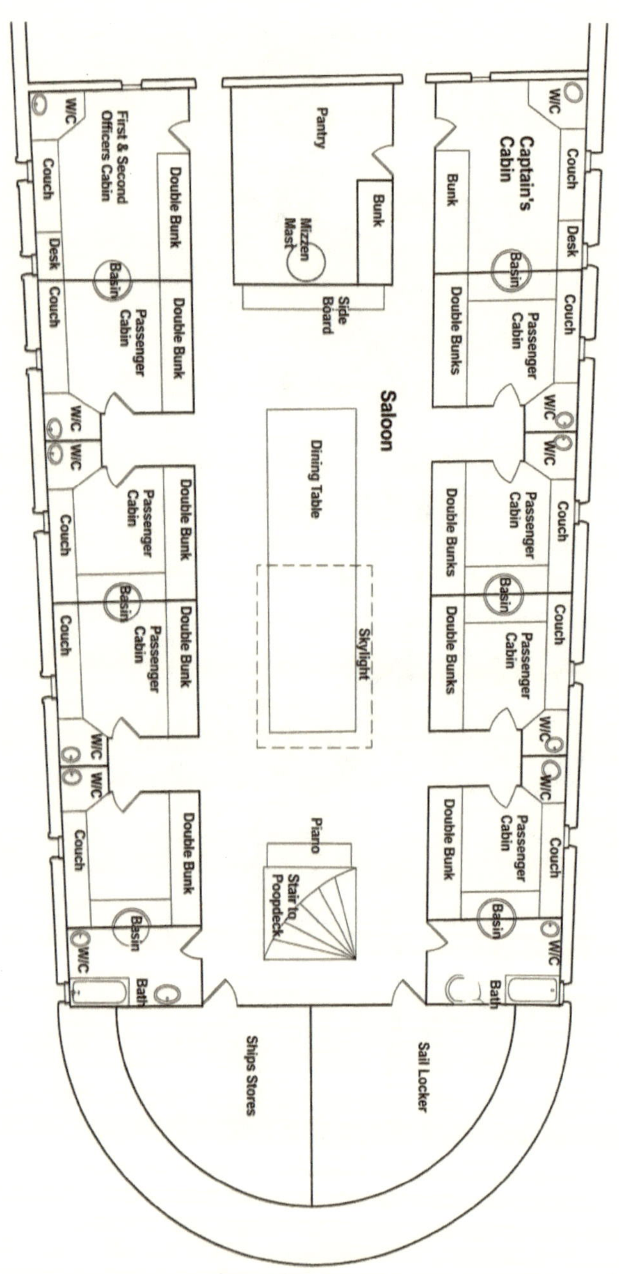

Internal layout of the Loch Vennachar's first class cabins.

The Salamis, wrecked 20th May 1905. Malden Island, South Pacific
State Library of Victoria.

Government Railway Pier, Williamstown.
State Library of Victoria.

The Loch Vennachar spent quite some time tied up at the Williamstown Pier; her cargo was quickly unloaded and snapped up by eager merchants. Amongst the broad collection of items in her hold were 59,000 floorboards, 30,000 clay-fired bricks and 450 tons of pig-iron. The rest of her cargo was a mixture of household items, alcohol, fashion accessories, haberdashery and hardware.

One of the crew was rather taken in drink and assaulted two members of the crew on Sunday, June 27th. J. McAlpine had entered the galley looking for something to eat. The cook was lighting a fire in the ship's stove for the purpose of preparing a meal, and McAlpine brutally and without any cause turned and struck him in the face when the cook told him to wait for dinner to be served. The drunken sailor continued to assault the cook and another sailor who tried to intervene. The water-police were summoned by the mate and McAlpine was arrested. Later in court, he admitted his guilt but showed no remorse; instead of paying a £5 fine, he spent the next month in gaol.

Captain Bennett was away for a time and on September 13th 1886, he answered a summons to appear in the Melbourne Central Criminal Court as a witness at the trial of Carl von Biehren. Bennett took the opportunity to have his ship cleaned and painted in the graving dock before the last of his wool cargo, which was still on its way by the steamer Southern Cross from Tasmania, was loaded aboard.

After an extended delay, having been cleaned and painted and loaded with almost 5,000 bales of wool and general cargo, the Loch Vennachar finally got underway on October 21st 1886, towed to sea by the steamer Hercules. Bill Bennett and the master of the clipper Salamis, William Phillip, had a wager running as to whose vessel would be first to drop anchor at Gravesend, the Loch Vennachar being the first clipper of the season to leave Hobson's Bay.

After a swift journey, the Loch Vennachar passed Beachy Head under tow on January 19th 1887 and entered into London Dock the following morning, catching the January sales with a passage of 91 days. However, she was beaten by just a few days by Salamis and Thermopylae, which made runs of 85 and 87 days, leaving Melbourne and Sydney respectively on October 24th. Still, Captain Bennett's feat earned all concerned a handsome bonus from the ship's owners.

"On Thursday, an unusual and exciting race between no less than three of these clippers, viz., the Loch Vennachar, Thermopylae, and Salamis, took place from the Channel to the Docks; all three vessels taking tugs about the same time. Our readers will be interested and gratified to learn that our esteemed townsman, Captain W. H. Bennett, was successful in placing his vessel, the Loch Vennachar, first in dock, having made the voyage from Melbourne in 87 days.

The Loch Vennachar left Melbourne on 21 October, rounded the Horn 20 November, saw no ice, crossed the Equator 10 December, 28 West; 54 days out. Coming up Channel experienced heavy gales, dense fogs, and sleet, and sighted Lizard 17 January. Capt. Bennett, who looks the picture of health and contentment, is therefore the hero of the 1887 January Wool Sales." **Chatham, Rochester and Brompton Observer, 22 January 1887.**

After discharge of her cargo, the Loch Vennachar cleared out for Glasgow under command of the first mate and crewed by the standing officers, apprentices and a crew of runners engaged for the run home. She passed the Lizard on February 28th before turning north for the run up through St George's Channel.

The tug towed the clipper all the way to the Tail-o'-the-Bank anchorage, and thence to her Broomielaw berth. After her hold was cleaned out, Henderson's of Glasgow began to load a substantial ballast of pig-iron, and then bar and iron machinery and hardware, firebricks, cases of whisky, paints, oils and other chemicals.

Soon her lower hold was full and the clipper was well down on her marks. James Lilburn was on hand to see the hatches battened down and canvas cover secured on the

Glasgow Docks, 1880s.

afternoon of March 16th 1887. He had sent a telegram to Bill Bennett, who was on his way north but was suffering from a bad cold.

By the 28th of March, the Loch Vennachar was ready to head back to Melbourne from Greenock. The weather that evening was abysmal: a howling gale from the south-south-west. Several vessels dragged their anchors, the Loch Vennachar being driven about a mile before the second mudhook managed to find purchase on the river's muddy bottom. The winds began to abate by early afternoon and the tug Hercules began the arduous task of hauling the clipper back to sea. The Hercules stayed with the Loch Vennachar before letting go the tow line off the Calf of Man at 4:00 am on the 29th. The Loch Vennachar reached the western approaches on April 1st and then Captain Bennett set his course to run for Madeira.

The Loch Vennachar arrived in Hobson's Bay on the 25th of June 1887; amongst those aboard were Dr J.T. Harvey and Messrs J. Johnston and Neil Kennedy. Also aboard were 15 second-class and 22 third-class passengers. Her packed hold held its usual assortment of Glasgow goods: 28,000 floorboards, 3,000 cast-iron pipes, hundreds of tons of angle, sheet, plate and pig-iron, furnaces, ovens, general hardware, sewing machines, dye stuffs, tins of herrings, sauces and jams, glassware, paper, cases of scientific instruments, haberdashery, beer, whisky and brandy, and miscellaneous merchandise.

The trip to Australia had been unusually slow by Captain Bennett's usual swift standards, due in large part to the contrary winds encountered for much of the trip. The Loch Vennachar weighed anchor on the 28th and sailed into light north-easterlies down the channel. The tug was parted with off St John's Point and Tuskar was passed on the 31st. Once in open water, east-north-east to north-west winds veered around all the way to the equator. The north-east trade winds failed to appear as San Antonio Island was passed on the 14th of April. Even as she crossed the equator on the 21st of April, the light and inconsistent winds continued to dog the clipper as she ambled south.

Eventually the south-east trades picked up and sailing conditions improved as Captain Bennett piled on the canvas in an attempt to make up lost time. The Cape of Good Hope was passed on the 21st of May along the 39th parallel and the Loch Vennachar ran her easting down along the 40th for much of the run across the Southern Ocean. The Roaring Forties lived up to their name and some excellent runs were made at this time.

The line of Cape Leeuwin was crossed on June 14th at the 42nd parallel, the Loch Vennachar having been pushed well south by strong north-east winds. The ship struggled against strengthening easterlies for more than a week before Captain Bennett tacked north. At this time a westerly change arrived, allowing the Loch Vennachar to make a dash for Port Phillip Bay. After sighting Cape Otway on the 23rd, the weather closed in, forcing Captain Bennett to keep his ship at sea until conditions improved. A pilot finally got aboard outside the Heads on the morning of the 25th of June 1887 and he guided the grateful mariners home to the outer anchorage that same day.

After 88 days, the Loch Vennachar rested at her Hobson's Bay mooring. For most of the trip she had averaged just 200 miles; her best run was a one-day run of 305 miles, and on others the Loch Vennachar covered less than 150 miles in 24 hours. For most of the trip there were no howling gales or hurricanes, just exceptionally fine and mild weather. Those passengers aboard quite enjoyed the trip and were well pleased with Captain Bennett's efforts and the care given them by Dr Harvey, who had signed on as ship's surgeon. During the latter stages of the voyage, Captain Bennett was struck down with the flu and the first officer had to take command of the vessel until the tack northwards was taken. Dr Harvey nursed William Bennett back to health just as the clipper tied up alongside the new Railway Pier at Williamstown.

After three months at Williamstown, Captain Bennett had his vessel cleaned and painted in the Alfred Graving Dock before she loaded the last of her cargo. Being in first-class order, it was hoped she would get away and make a quick passage home. Loaded aboard were 4,500 bales of wool, 900 casks of tallow, 238 bales of scrolls, 100 bales of basils, 24 bales of leather, 29 bales of sheepskins, 2,500 bags of wheat, and a variety of colonial exports all bound for London and Glasgow.

The Loch Vennachar was finally towed away from the pier by the steam-tug Rescue on Saturday the 15th of October and anchored at the outer mooring as final preparations were made for the voyage to London. The pilot came aboard on the Monday morning and the Rescue then towed the clipper out of the bay that same day. The Loch Vennachar cleared the Heads at 7:10 am and, dropping off the pilot, sailed east through Bass Strait.

After just 80 days at sea, they sailed past Dungeness behind a tug on January 5th and made Captain Bennett their number to the signal station ashore. The Tilbury Fort anchorage was reached just after midnight on January 6th. Whilst waiting for two small river tugs to bring the clipper up to London Dock, Captain Bennett boarded the steamer that had delivered a local river pilot and was soon headed for London and then home.

Whilst he was home dealing with some rather serious family business, the first mate had the clipper cleared out through customs on January 31st. Soon a tug was towing the Loch Vennachar home to Glasgow. They passed Prawle Point at 5:30 pm on February 1st, battling fresh to strong easterlies and very rough seas. The pair arrived back at Greenock in the early hours of February 7th, having had to put into several outports once having rounded the Lizard due to strong winds and high seas.

Upon arriving home at his house in Chatham, Bill Bennett was shocked and dismayed to learn that the previous October his son William (Harold William Bennett) and his friend Bertie Dunstan had been badly injured whilst messing around with gunpowder. They were playing in the Recreation Ground and began to let off some gunpowder, a portion of which exploded prematurely. Both boys received very bad flash burns about the face from the explosion, having lost much of their hair; their faces badly charred, the boys' eyes were also burned and it was uncertain if they would be blinded because of the accident. The nine-year-old boys had both recovered from the worst of their injuries by the time Bill Bennett had arrived home, though neither had any freckles nor eyebrows, the skin of their faces and hands being bright pink and fresh.

The first cargo stowed in the hold was 150 tons of pig-iron ballast. This was followed by a general cargo and the personal effects of the passengers. The ship was cleared out on March 17th, yet there was still one thing left to do before departure. Before the Loch Vennachar could set sail, she had to undergo a special Lloyd's insurance survey on March 19th whilst berthed at Broomielaw, in order to maintain her 100 A1 rating.

"All the close ceiling removed from the hold. All the floors, frames, reverses, keelsons, stringers, bulkheads, beams and knees thoroughly cleaned. The cement tested, renewed where necessary. The forepeak above lower deck beams cleaned and all ironwork at this part in the hold above close ceiling repainted and below close ceiling coated with cement wash. Panelling and lining removed from under side lights and other places in poop for examination of plank and frames. The masts, spars and rigging examined. The upper deck boxed. About 700 ft of close ceiling renewed and the remainder replaced." **Lloyd's Survey Report**.

According to the Lloyd's surveyor, John Dawkins, the clipper was in good condition and suitable to set sail for Melbourne with passengers aboard. The clipper was shifted back down to Greenock from her Queen's Dock berth just after midnight on March 19th, stopping briefly at Greenock to receive passengers and allow Captain Bennett to board.

The Loch Vennachar slipped her Tail-o'-the-Bank mooring on the 19th of March 1888. She raced south against the clippers Firth of Solway and Star of Greece. There was little between them at first but however over the vast distances of the Southern Ocean the Loch Vennachar overhauled the Star of Greece so that she arrived in Hobson's Bay on the same day that the Star of Greece dropped anchor at Port Adelaide, June 11th 1888. The Firth of Solway hauled through the Sydney Heads a few days later having threaded Bass Strait.

The Loch Vennachar arrived with 630 tons of pig-iron, sheet iron, pipes, hollow-ware, heavy hardware, bulk beer and spirits, chemicals and general provisions in her hold. Also aboard was a large cargo of gunpowder and general merchandise. The two first class passengers, John Taylor and Neil McKelvie, and the 9 second cabin passengers were glad to get ashore before the gunpowder was lightered off.

The clipper had left on the 19th being towed down the Clyde and into the North Channel. Light easterly winds decided the Loch Vennachar's course as they pushed her quickly eastwards past Inishtrahull at 8pm the following day. Once in the Western Sea a change in the weather brought howling north-westerly gales which continued until the north-east trades were picked up on the 5th of April. The Loch Vennachar whisked on by the Volcano of San Antonio on the Isla De Palma the next day. Rapid progress continued as the ship crossed the equator 8 days later, after just 25 days at sea.

The south-east trades were fallen in with yet easterly winds harried the clipper as she was driven well south against the coast of South America in an attempt to latch onto the westerlies further south. These frustrating conditions continued until May 8th when crossing the 38th parallel the winds turned westerly and excellent sailing conditions prevailed. Moving down to the Roaring Forties the winds turned variable in strength and direction until the line of Cape Leeuwin was passed.

The Loch Vennachar pushed on towards Bass Strait as the weather turned nasty. The winds howled down from the southeast to northeast. Just before entering Bass Strait a powerful gale slammed into the clipper from the northwest. Fierce thunder squalls hammered the ship as great displays of lightning accompanied the clipper as she ventured slipped past the north coast of King Island. This narrow gap had already claimed the Loch Vennachar's sister ships the Loch Ard and Loch Leven so Captain Bennett did not sail this way under a full suite of canvas. The Heads were finally entered on the morning of the 11th of June 1888 but as winds kept pushing from the north it took the clipper all day to reach the anchorage.

The voyage from Greenock to Hobson's Bay had taken just 83 days. The average run for the voyage was 250 miles a day and the best run 320 miles. Despite the at times adverse weather conditions Captain Bennett had made the most of the Loch

Vennachar's fine qualities. Once her gunpowder and passengers had been unloaded the clipper was hauled alongside the railway pier at Williamstown to discharge the remainder of her goods. Despite the passengers' pleasure at such a rapid trip to Australia, one passenger, David Goldie, an architect from Queen Street in Melbourne, died during the voyage and was buried at sea.

Sitting at Williamstown alongside the clippers Loch Ryan, Avenger, Cardigan Castle, Dhawar and Salamis, the Loch Vennachar took onboard her portion of 1888's bumper wheat crop. With so much wheat it was expected that prices would be down, however there had been drought in India and the United States so Australian wheat was much in demand and shipping prices were high, 3s. 7d. per bushel. The freight price per ton rose as high as 27s. 6d., this unusually high rate was being asked and realised by shippers. Aboard the Loch Vennachar were 4500 bags of wheat and flour, and 3600 bales of wool.

On September 12th while the ship was being moved from across the dock to allow the steamer Lady Loch and the ship Avenger to come out, one of the seamen had a narrow escape from being drowned, when he missed his hold and fell overboard. Captain Bennett immediately gave the alarm, and Mr Grimwood, foreman of the labourers at the dock, after several attempts, succeeded in throwing a rope to the drowning man, which he grabbed desperately, but in a panic let go again sank. Fortunately by this time a boat was near the spot, and succeeded in rescuing him; he was taken on board the Loch Vennachar in an exhausted condition, and Captain Bennett plied the near drowned man with whisky with the desired result.

Before the Loch Vennachar was finished loading Captain Bennett had her taken once again to the graving dock to be cleaned and painted. Her hold half filled with wheat negated the need to carry ballast as the hull was scraped and cleaned. The clipper was finally floated out of the dock on Tuesday the 25th of September and was then once again hauled up to the railway pier to finish loading wool ready for the London sales. Loading was

A fogbound Queen's Dock, Glasgow, circa 1890's
Glasgow Life Collection.

The Cutty Sark in Circular Quay, circa 1888.

finished on the 19th of October 1888 and the Loch Vennachar was towed to the outer mooring. The ship was towed to sea by the steam-tug Pharos, during the early morning of the 22nd, and cleared Port Phillip Heads later that afternoon. The Cutty Sark departed Sydney on the 26th and both ships raced to be first to London with their loads of wheat and wool.

The Loch Vennachar made her number off Start Point on January 15th where a pilot was taken aboard and soon after a tug engaged to tow the clipper into Gravesend. The vessels passed Beachy Head at 4:00 pm on the 18th and they arrived at Gravesend on the 19th of January at almost the same time as her sister the Loch Moidart. Yet thanks to some good luck and canny negotiation with the river pilot, the Loch Vennachar beat the Loch Moidart into the East Dock by a few hours and the Cutty Sark by one whole day after 84 days at sea.

As the ship's cargo was being discharged, James Aitken was scheduling the Loch Vennachar to depart on February 23rd 1889. She was slated to berth at Kingston Dock in Glasgow alongside the Loch Ryan under James Ozanne, and the Loch Moidart commanded by Captain Samuel Andrew. The last bales of wool were lifted from the hold on the morning of February 2nd and she was cleared out the same day from London Dock. The following morning the clipper was towed back down to Tilbury and the clipper was towed down the Thames on the 4th.

Having spent the night anchored in the mouth of the Thames, the tug Hercules and her charge sailed past Deal on the 5th, passing Beachy Head the following morning at 10:00 am. Adverse winds and seas meant that the Hercules and her charge were forced to seek shelter off Portland on February 9th sheltering from gales from the west, sou'west. The winds shifted to the west, nor'west and moderated bringing sleet and snow squalls. The weather moderated to fresh to strong northerlies bringing heavy snow and icy rain. The pair made it as far as Penzance before once again becoming windbound alongside several other vessels.

The Loch Vennachar and Hercules were still there on February 12th. The Hercules crew was forced to purchase more coal from Penzance before setting out for the Clyde. Greenock was at last reached on February 14th, the tug being farewelled as Captain Bennett ordered the anchor let go off the Tail-o'-the-Bank. The crew of runners was kept aboard and Bill Bennett left the Loch Vennachar and took a short train ride to Glasgow making for the office of Aitken & Lilburn located at 80, Buchanan Street in the heart of the city. Once there he was greeted warmly by James Lilburn who was thankful that the Loch Vennachar was home intact and ready to be sent away with another valuable cargo.

There was a substantial delay in the loading and departure due to the Loch Vennachar's late arrival. The usual cargo of heavy iron products, firebricks, beer, spirits and assorted sundries much in demand in Victoria. The ship was cleared out on February 27th and departed Queen's Dock just after midnight on the 28th. Stopping briefly at Greenock to take on passengers the tug Conqueror was engaged to tow the clipper out to sea. The westerly winds forced the tug to take the Loch Vennachar down through St George's Channel passing Kildonan on March 1st.

Making excellent time, the Loch Vennachar crossed the Equator on March 28[th]1889, having spoken to the Liverpool-bound steamer Lord Gough.

"The well-known and favourite sailing ship Loch Vennachar arrived yesterday (9th June) from Glasgow, having sailed on the 1st March, which constitutes for her rather a lengthy passage, the time occupied being 98 days. A scrutiny of the log soon explained the cause of delay, there being a great prevalence of easterly winds, which retarded the vessel's progress.

The Tail o' the Bank was cleared on the 1st March, when S.E. and E. winds prevailed until the 7th, in lat. 46 deg. 40 min. N., lon. 19 deg. 37 min. W. Then ensued moderate winds all round the compass to 19th March, in lat. 15 deg. 3 min. N. and lon. 25 deg. 37 min. W., when the winds took very light. N.E. winds prevailed to the 25th, in lat. 2 deg. 6 min. N., when the vessel made only 30 to 50 miles per day.

The Equator was passed on the 28th, in lon. 29 deg. 1 min W., after which very light S.E. and E.S.E. winds occurred to 15th April, in lat. 27 deg. 48 min. S., lon. 25 deg. 15 min. W. Light winds all round the compass followed, with much rain and thick weather. The prime meridian was passed on the 25th, in lat. 35 deg. 38 min. S., and the Cape of Good Hope on the 2nd May, in lat. 39 deg. 9 min. S.

The easting was made in from lat. 39 deg. to 43 deg. S. Then followed a succession of E. winds, the vessel never having the yards off the backstays from the meridian of Greenwich with the exception of three days from lon. 87 deg. E., when 270, 260, and 305 miles each day respectively were run. A continuance of head winds followed.

The Leeuwin was passed on the 23rd May in lat. 39 deg. 59 min. S., when the vessel was blown down with W.F. winds to lat. 45 deg. S. The winds were then S.E. to N.E. to Cape Otway, which was reached on the 6th. After passing Cape Otway the vessel was blown into the straits by a heavy N.W. gale. The Heads were entered on Saturday. During the voyage a passenger, a married man named Peter A. Smith, of Glasgow, died. He was 37 years of age."   **The Argus, 10 Jun 1889.**

Besides her usual Glasgow cargo, the Loch Vennachar carried on her 'tween deck a load of Merino and crossbreed sheep bound for Tasmania. She stayed in London for just two weeks, the time it took to unload, then sailed north for Glasgow. She cleared having finished loading at the Princes Dock on the 28th of February and was joined after by the Loch Moidart on March 23rd.

Fortune began to turn for the worst in 1889 when Captain Bennett brought the Loch Vennachar into Melbourne at the height of another crippling drought. The ship was a long time in getting away, but there was no rush to repeat the same disastrous mistakes that had led to the death of Captain Robertson in Calcutta, so Captain Bennett was happy to wait.

An interesting journal kept by a passenger who travelled on the Loch Vennachar from Greenock to Melbourne in early 1889 is worth examining at length. The journey took 100 days, and the journal was named '*100 Days at Sea*'.

The Lord Gough, an American Line steamship built 1878 at Birkenhead by Laird Bros.
Norway Heritage Collection.

The following extracts give us, the reader, a glimpse of immigrant life aboard the Loch Vennachar from the point of view of a second-class passenger:

29th February. As had been previously arranged, the passengers by the Loch Vennachar met at Greenock today and were taken onboard by a tug, each accompanied by a few friends who had come to wish them God's speed in the voyage they were about to take. After not a few affecting scenes on the part of the passengers and their friends, it was announced that the latter must take their departure, which they did very reluctantly. The tug steamed away from us amidst many kind greetings and a great display of white handkerchiefs which had evidently been washed for the occasion. I did not see any towels used.

2nd March. Splendid weather and got well out to sea. We were wakened this morning by the sailors singing their shanty, which they do when twisting the sails. (This song was a popular halyard shanty, particularly amongst whalers; there are many different versions all following the same tune).

Reuben Ranzo

The air I shall give you when I see you.
Ranzo boys, Ranzo Boys, Ranzo.
He shipped on board a whaler.
Ranzo boys, Ranzo.
The Captain being a good man.
 Ranzo boys, Ranzo.
Took him the cabin.
Ranzo boys, Ranzo.
And gave him rum and brandy.
Ranzo boys, Ranzo.
And taugh him navigation.
Ranzo boys, Ranzo.
And now he's captain, Ranzo.
Ranzo boys, Ranzo.

In the morning a hen died, supposed to have been caused by the passenger who fainted having blown his breath on it. The following are the names of passengers in the second cabin:

Mr and Mrs Wills and baby, Shettleston Miss Cockane, Manchester Mr Clother, Chatham Mr Evelyn, Sydney Mr Smith, Banff Mr Ferguson, Glasgow Mr and Mrs Henderson (mother and son), Dunfermline Mr Low, Edinburgh Mr Smith, Glasgow Mr Davison, Dundee Mr Horne, Glasgow Myself from Johnstone (15 in all)

8th March. Good breeze, and heavy waves lashing over the deck, and some of us who were hardy enough to go out came to grief in rather an undignified way, much to the amusement of others. One of the stowaways sick, got two pills from the doctor which he chewed, and the taste not being quite pleasing to him, he spat them out. Played whist forenoon, afternoon and evening.

13th March. Good day, strong breeze, no sea. The first arranged concert took place tonight on deck and proved a great success. The following was our programme which caused some little amusement: By special permission of Captain Bennett a concert will be held on board the Loch Vennachar on Wednesday evening the 13th of March. The following star artistes have kindly volunteered gratuitously, but will leave themselves to the tender mercies of their appreciative audience for such blessings temporal and spiritual as they see fit to bestow upon them. Patrons are requested to refrain from nasal and bronchial accompaniments and expectorations. Refreshments will be handed round at intervals. Dr Paton will preside.

1st April. There were a few "fools' errands" sent today, but there was no great fun over them. We passed a few old tubs today and signalled two of them. The vessels signal, each flag indicating a letter in the alphabet on getting flag signals. You turn up the book and there you find the information they wish to convey to you. The following is the first one we signalled, viz: LMDK Snow Queen of Halifax; LDWJ from Newport; BNWG to Buenos Aires; WCM 37 days out. The second was the Reyneson from Cardiff to Montevideo, 31 days out. We saw the new moon tonight, which was much clearer than it appears at home. The breeze has freshened today; while it has sent us a bit quicker, it has also kept the atmosphere cooler.

11th April. Today we have had the painful experience of a death and burial at sea. The victim has been Mr P. A. Smith of Glasgow. Ever since he had the fit, he has been gradually sinking, till this morning about 9 o'clock death held its way and he slipped away peacefully. After the doctor had examined him, his remains were sewn up in pack sheet by the sail maker with a bar of pig iron across his legs. This being done, the Union Jack was put over the body and remained on deck till 12 o'clock, the time at which the funeral was to take place.

When 12 o'clock came round the bell tolled and the passengers and sailors all mustered on deck, the body being meanwhile removed to the place at which it was to be put over. After the Captain had read the Church of England funeral service, the remains were consigned to the deep. Mr Smith was 50 years of age and there were no relatives or friends with him.

23rd April. Another lovely day, one would almost imagine we were still in the tropics. The sailors all say that we have had the best weather they have ever experienced.

27th April. The weather has not much improved today, and we have had a good deal of rain. The first arranged concert took place tonight in the saloon, which proved a great success. The following was our "Programme":

Selections violin and piano: Messrs Allison and Williams Song – Tar of the Queens: Mr Clother Song – Father O'Flynn: Mr Cunningham Song – All Love Jack: Mr Brown Recitation: Mr Kennedy Song – Won't You Tell Me: Miss Dewer Song – Finnegan's Wake: Captain Bennett Song – Erin's Isle: Mr Page Reading: Dr Paton Song: Mr O'Brien Song – Sailing: Mr Armour Song: Mrs Paton Song: Mr Currie Song – True Till Death: Mr Maitland Recitation: Mr Duncan Song – Ballyhooly: Captain Bennett Song: Mr Fox Song: Mrs Wills Song – Rule Britannia: Mr Clother Selections violin and piano: Messrs Allison and Williams The concert was brought to an end by singing Auld Lang Syne.

7th May. Glorious day again with fine breeze, but the sea is very heavy, and the deck has been flooded most of the day. We however when we wish to can sit high and dry on top of our cabin and it is a really grand sight to see our little craft battling through the Indian Ocean. We had a run of 230 miles yesterday, which gradually reduces our distance to Melbourne. During the evening the wind fell considerably, and as the moon was shining brightly it was quite a treat to be out on deck.

14th May. Good day again and fine breeze, and we have been going from eleven to twelve knots all day, which is very good business. When we awoke the men were busy scrubbing the woodwork, which is always done before going into port. The sea has been pretty rough and washing over the ship, which did not make walking a great pleasure. But it was delightful to stand in a sheltered spot and breathe in the fresh air which was very bracing. We went 245 miles yesterday.

20th May. An event happened this forenoon which has been the only topic of conversation all day. The Boatswain and one of the men quarreled and prepared to fight it out, but the second mate stopped it in time. However at twelve o'clock when they changed watch, the seaman rushed at the boatswain again, and before you could count two almost all the other men joined in giving the boatswain a hammering.

This lasted for about five minutes, when the Captain came out and flourished a ten chamber revolver about and after a bit stopped the row. But not before the boatswain had been pretty well peppered. There was hardly anyone in the ship sorry for him, although he can hardly be said to have got fair play, as he is a Dutchman to begin with, although he tries to make us believe he belongs to Glasgow. He is very impudent to both officers and men, the Captain being the only man he sneaks under.

9th June. Finale. When we awoke this morning we were safely anchored in the bay of Williamstown, having dropped anchor about 5 o'clock. It was a rather welcome sight to see the land and the fine houses on it. But most of us could hardly help feeling a little sorry at leaving the ship where we had spent so many happy days and nights together. It is a pretty bay and does resemble lying off Greenock a little. We were not long up when the Doctor and Customs Officer came aboard, then some friends of the passengers began to arrive and everyone was busy getting their goods in order for departure.

Extracts taken from: 100 Days at Sea – **Passenger's Journal, Department of Environment and Heritage S.A. Govt**.

The Loch Vennachar was berthed alongside the Williamstown Pier for many months awaiting her cargo of wool; tied alongside was the Loch Ryan. While in port, Captain Bennett had the barnacles and detritus that had accumulated from spending months at anchor removed and her hull repainted with anti-fouling agents before taking her out to the roads.

He had the vessel cleared out on the 18th of October and hoped for a speedy run home. For the last few years, the Loch Vennachar had been the first vessel to clear out for the wool sales. This year, however, the ship Avenger left first, at 11:20 am on Monday the 21st of October 1889, the Loch Vennachar an hour later.

Unfortunately for the skipper of the Avenger, adverse winds kept her inside the Heads for a full day and, as a result, the Loch Vennachar passed out exactly one hour before the Avenger. Once clear, the race was on, as the honour of first across the line carried both bragging rights and a lion's share of the profits for the Loch Vennachar's backers.

Aboard was a loose cargo of animal products, not her usual full cargo of wheat and wool. This was largely because of the drought. Stowed within her hull were bags of mustard hulls, bales of paper shavings, salted hides, 3400 bags of tanning bark, 20 tons of hooves, horns and bones, 3272 bales of wool, 295 bales of skins, 266 bags of refined copper ore, bales of leather, bags of salt, 1535 cases of preserved meats, packets of linseed, 400 bags of copra, machine parts, furniture, and cases of preserved milk.

As more and more passengers and shippers turned to the reliability and speed of steam, profits and margins became tighter. The golden days of sail were waning and the cut-throat tramping days of the 90s were about to begin.

The Loch Vennachar made her number off St Catherine's Point on the 13th of January, at 12:40 pm, three days ahead of the Avenger that sailed down the Thames on the 17th of January 1890. Captain Bennett stayed with his ship as she was taken from

The 3500 ton barque 'Loch Moidart'. Stranded at Callantsoog, The Netherlands, and capsized. On voyage from Pisagua to Hamburg with a nitrate cargo.
State Library of South Australia

London Dock, circa 1890.
London Museum Collection.

Tilbury to London Dock, arriving late in the evening of January 16th, 1890. Her cargo of wool was quickly discharged and a tug was engaged to move the clipper from the East Quay and out to her Tilbury Fort mooring.

It was while they were berthed in London that the crew of the Loch Vennachar learned that the barque Loch Moidart had run aground at Callantsoog off the coast of Holland and capsized with the loss of 30 lives. The loss of the ship and her crew filled all with great sorrow. Captain Andrew of the Loch Moidart had been a good friend of William Bennett and his death shocked all who knew him.

Wreck of the *Loch Moidart*

"The actual loss of life occurred in broad daylight and within the gaze of hundreds of persons assembled on the beach unable to render any assistance... After the ship stuck on a sandbank a boat with five men was dispatched ashore. It survived and... two of the boat's crew swam ashore, Hugh Hossack AB of Inverness and John Frosch AB of Ipswich. The seas washing over the stranded ship caused the crew on board to take to the rigging where they could easily be seen by the crowd. Life saving rockets were procured and fired but failed to carry the lifeline to the unfortunate men. The awful sea running made it worse than useless to attempt to put off in a boat, so the lookers-on watched the breaking up of the ship hoping that when the masts fell with the poor fellows clinging to them some would be carried within reach.

The breaking up commenced amidships and the mainmast and mizzen mast went first. Her crew were nearly all on the other two masts, the fore and jigger masts. Nearly three hours elapsed before the giant force of the waves so crushed in the forward and after parts of the noble ship that the masts went over. It was stated that from that moment on not a soul was seen. An hour later not a vestige of the wreck was visible."

Colonist, Volume XXXIII, Issue 5770, 7 April 1890, Page 3

Bill Bennett was back aboard ship as the clipper was towed from Gravesend on the morning of February 6th, passing the Lizard on the 7th, and dropping anchor off Greenock on March 10th. When the ship was berthed at her usual Queen's

Dock placement, the crew were paid off and Captain Bennett was given extended leave. James Lilburn took charge of the Loch Vennachar as she was due for a complete refit before undergoing a full survey. It was intended that all of the vessel's standing rigging would be replaced by wire rope instead of the traditional hemp ropes. It was going to take at least a month before the re-rigging of the Loch Vennachar could be completed. Her jib-boom also needed replacing, it having been badly sprung during the tow home having been snagged by the tow cable during rough weather.

Repairs were undertaken alongside Queen's Dock during January and early February with the final Lloyd's survey being conducted on March 6th 1890. The Lloyd's surveyor cleared the ship to sail and allowed Aitken & Lilburn to keep the ship at its 100 A1 rating. The Loch Vennachar was hauled out from Queen's Dock and towed to Greenock on the 7th with Captain Bennett aboard. Yet it was here that the ship stayed for another nine days as contrary winds kept multiple vessels moored at the Tail-of-the-Bank, wind-bound, awaiting the last of her crew to appear and for a tug to appear.

The sailors that signed on for the run to Melbourne did so under new articles of agreement. They stated that the crew were to be discharged at the port of Melbourne. This was Bill Bennett's first time signing on a crew under such conditions and he invited them to opt to sign on again for the return run to London. The able seamen were signed on at £3 10 shillings per month plus a sign on bonus.

The tug Defiance belonging to the Greenock Towing Company was eventually engaged to tow the Loch Vennachar out to sea. The pair of vessels set sail from Greenock in the early hours on March 17th 1890, and on the same night they sought shelter in Belfast Bay from a heavy northwest wind. They remained there until the 19th, and then met with west to south-westerlies until the 22nd, the Defiance being left off The Smalls Rocks the same evening. From March 25th until April 4th strong changeable winds from west to west-nor'west were encountered.

The North East trades were then taken and proved light to the equator, which was crossed on April 19th at 25° west. Calms and variables followed to 12° south and 24° west, where the South East trades were fallen in with, but they proved changeable and light and continued until reaching 30° south and 25° west on May 5th. The weather then closed in bringing freshening west to nor'west winds, and they sailed beneath the Cape of Good Hope on May 14th, also in 30° south.

The Loch Vennachar then ran her easting down along 36° south. On the 15th, passing the Cape, a very heavy gale from northwest was met with, and the barque Lady Lonsdale ran foul of her and the helmsman narrowly avoided a collision with the wayward barque. The two following days good running was obtained, with daily runs from 280 to 300 miles being made. Moderate southwest winds followed after passing 33° east to Cape Leeuwin. From thence a heavy sea was lasting 15 hours; light winds were had to Cape Otway, which was passed on June 17th and the Heads passed on the 18th. A dead beat was then made up the Bay to anchorage.

Captain Bennett recorded that it was his most trouble-free voyage ever. He put this down to good weather and a fine crew that did not fight or bicker. This in turn was put down to the practice of 'crimping' being controlled by the government. This problem was solved by the Commissioner of Trade and Customs, Mr Patterson, who set up in Melbourne an office of sailors that ships' masters had to apply to hire crews for their ships. Articles of agreement written to improve a seaman's lot meant that crews were discharged from their ships after arrival in port and were not bound to a ship whilst she was tied up in port for lengthy periods awaiting cargo.

Aboard the Loch Vennachar when she dropped anchor in Hobson's Bay were the ship's surgeon Dr Strangway, John Dickson, Mrs & Mr Fulwood and their three children, Mrs & Mr Parry, and Miss Munro. In second cabin were Eric Sutherland, C.H. Stewart, R. Donaldson, R.H. Logan, W. Cunningham, W. McCallum, and J. Adams. The ship carried her usual cargo of iron – pipes, sheet, angle, plate, plumbers' fittings and pig iron; along

Bargaining with the tug's master to arrange to price of a tow up the English Cannel and into the Thames. No written agreement was concluded, but the terms of the agreement were strictly observed.

with these she carried machinery parts, 2300 bundles of floorboards, 24000 bricks as ballast, paints, paper, bleach, indigo, dyes, starch, lime juice, malt, soap, beer, ale, port wine, whisky, windows, 2 pianos, china, glassware, India rubber, and packets of personal items.

She tied up alongside the Williamstown railway pier to discharge her cargo; despite the industrial action that plagued many other ships she hung on to a fair number of her crew who signed on again for the trip home. Captain Bennett had his ship moved over to a loading berth to take on a load of wool once the Loch Shiel had completed her loading, on the 10th of July 1890. The Loch Shiel set sail on the 11th bound for London, her hold filled to capacity. There was a deal of trouble getting her cargo of tallow and hides loaded as the Stevedores' Labourers Union was out on strike.

Captain Bennett decided to employ his crew and a collection of non-union labour to get his vessel loaded. This caused problems with the Union but gained support from the dockside stevedore company. Even Captain Bennett helped to supervise the loading of her cargo as more bales of wool came in from Tasmania. He even resorted to employing the Loch Vennachar's apprentices to help with the loading of wool into the hold and donned his own dungarees to assist. To avoid possible clashes with striking stevedores, extra police were sent to patrol the docks as a general dockworkers' strike put a stranglehold on the loading and unloading of cargo at Williamstown.

In an effort to end the strike, ship owners made concession after concession to the ever-increasing demands of the unionists who were campaigning for a fair wage and improved working conditions. Captain Bennett avoided trouble by refusing to load wool handled by non-union labour. He also paid them the new rate. This canny and pragmatic business decision allowed him to get union-backed stevedores to load the Loch Vennachar as other ships lay idle. The Loch Vennachar was cleared out on October 24th 1890 and moved into the stream. Bill Bennett managed to get his ship sailed through The Heads on the 27th, passing Wilson's Promontory the following morning, and signalling "All well!" 1890. Aboard were 2600 bags of wheat, 4962 bales of wool, bags of mustard hulls, cases of local wines, 700 casks of tallow, 5200 hides, 1200 cases of preserved meats, bales of leather and packages of general merchandise.

IX

Fighting Bill Bennett

After the lengthy delays due to the dockworkers' strike, Bill Bennett was determined to make the next wool sale. He pushed the Loch Vennachar hard carrying royals and lower stunsails most of the way, doubling Cape Horn on November 19th, 23 days from Port Phillip in company with the clipper Conqueror on her way to Hull from San Francisco. The equator was crossed on Christmas Eve at 37° west before the Loch Vennachar reached Deal on January 21st behind a tug after 86 days at sea, and arrived in London on the 22nd of January 1891.

She stayed in London for less than a month, yet it was more than enough time for Bill Bennett to head home to Chatham. While he was there he was invited to attend the Chatham Volunteer Fire Brigade's annual banquet representing the navy and merchant marine services. Held at the Mitre Hotel, an establishment well known to Bennett being where his Masonic Lodge meetings were often held. Bill also presented to the local botanic garden a collection of plants he had acquired on a short visit to Adelaide, South Australia during his previous stay in the colonies.

Amongst the plants presented to the mayor of Chatham was a rare fern he had collected on a visit to a place called Waterfall Gully, which was gratefully received. His time at home was soon cut short by the need to return to Glasgow. Arriving back at Gravesend on March 1st, Captain Bennett took his ship and crew home on March 2nd 1891, passing Portland Bill on the 6th and rounding the Lizard on the 9th thanks to adverse westerly winds. The Loch Vennachar and her tug did not reach the Tail-of-the-Bank on March 15th, having lost her jib-boom and some of her headgear and the foretopmast having been in a collision with the Swedish barque Superior as they were passing each other under tow. The Superior's master, Captain Anders P. Larson, was furious as he was forced to put back to Greenock to seek repairs.

After a month berthed at Broomielaw, the Loch Vennachar was cleared out on April 9th and she was moved down river to Greenock the following morning to allow Bill Bennett and the passengers to board. There the clipper was given final clearance and a tug began to tow the ship out to sea. A westerly gale prevented the pair from getting past Gareloch for two days, anchoring off Helensburgh until the winds shifted enough to continue the voyage.

Once in port her crew signed off. While in Port Glasgow Captain Bennett had the ship's lifeboats fitted with Mills Patent Engaging and Disengaging Gear. The gear was designed so that when a boat was lowered into the water it would take but a quick release from one man at either end of the boat to set it free from the hooks. The boat would only release once it was in the water.

Finally loaded with her standard Glasgow fare the Loch Vennachar set sail for Australia, leaving Glasgow in the early hours of the 11th of April 1891 and was towed down to Greenock to her usual moorings with a crew of 35 men and boys aboard. By noon sixteen passengers and a ship's doctor were aboard and the last letters home were sent by steamer back to Greenock wharf. The clipper was then taken in tow by a steam tug which hauled the Loch Vennachar out into the head of the North Channel that evening, and out to Inishtrahull where the two vessels parted company at noon the next day.

Winds continued from the west or southwest, light and variable until the northeast trade winds were picked up. The clipper passed the Cape Verde islands on the 2nd of May, and south of here light and squally tropical rainstorms and humid conditions ensued for many days. Eventually the equator was crossed and the southeast trades pushed the Loch Vennachar south around below the Cape of Good Hope and into the Southern Ocean. The clipper journeyed rapidly southeast along the 40th parallel due to rougher than expected weather.

Three days after passing beneath the Cape on June 6th a violent storm slammed into the ship as she ran her easting down. Once through the worst of it the vessel ran ahead of favourable southwest winds, making runs of 300, 310, 290 and 260 miles

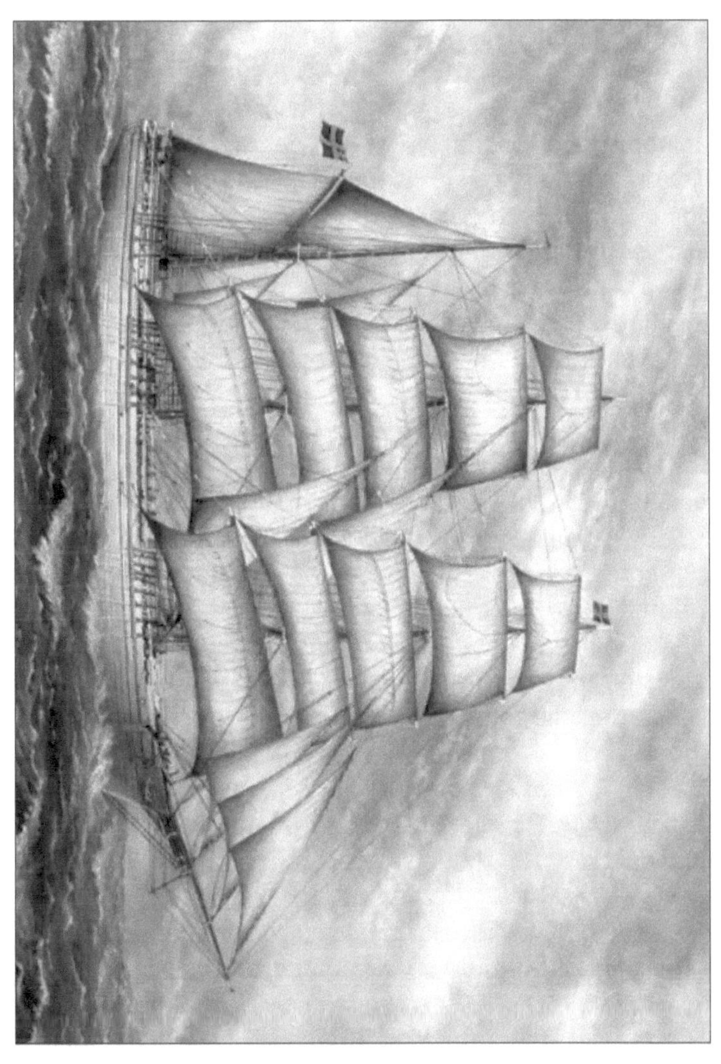

**The Swedish barque 'Superior' Captain Anders P Larson
commanding, circa 1884.**
Artist J. G. Berg.

over a four day period. These rapid runs continued as the Loch Vennachar scudded across the Southern Ocean until the 25th of June.

At the height of a raging storm, at the latitude 38 degrees 58 minutes south and longitude 103 degrees 28 minutes east at 4:30 am, the seas began to rise and a rogue wave struck the stern of the ship parting the hooks of the spanker boom. Fifty-three feet of solid timber yard began swinging in the violent winds, such was the weight when combined with the wind that the swinging boom tore off the port royal top-gallant and the topmast backstays.

Continuing its path of destruction the boom proceeded to tear down the topgallant mast, the topmast head, and mizzen lower topgallant yard. The boom also parted her mounts and swung wildly in the winds nearly decapitating the helmsman who hung on bravely to the helm, keeping the ship steady even as rigging threatened to rain down upon him. The wreckage stayed put aloft and was eventually cut free.

The line of Cape Leeuwin was passed on the 29th of June 1891, when another gale with hurricane like winds and seas again pounded the ship as she began her run northeast pushed along by howling north and nor'westerly winds. Cape Otway was sighted at 7:45pm on the 6th of July and reached the Heads the next day, 87 days from Greenock, but was forced to come to anchor due to northerly winds preventing a safe passage through the rip.

The pilot eventually managed to con the vessel through the treacherous waters but was forced to again bring the Loch Vennachar to anchor at the head of the South Channel, moored alongside was the schooner L'Avenir. The Loch Vennachar eventually limped into port the top half of her mizzen mast completely gone. The passengers and crew were happy to make port, even more so when the large load of gunpowder was lightered off at the outer anchorage.

The bad news continued for Bill Bennett when he learnt that his friend and former first officer John Page, Master of the steam collier Taramung had been killed. His career as captain of

The SS Taramung.
Australian Town and Country Journal 20th June 1891.

Captain John Page, Master of the steam collier Taramung.
Australian Town and Country Journal 20th June 1891

the steamer had been horrifyingly brief. On the night of May 31st 1891 the ss Taramung with a load of 1400 tons of coal aboard sailed from Newcastle. Sailing into a violent storm and beam sea her cargo had shifted and the vessel foundered capsizing off of Wreck Bay 82 miles south of Sydney, going down with all hands.

Things went from bad to worse when a strong southwest gale blowing throughout Saturday June 11th raised a heavy sea in Hobson's Bay. Ships berthed at the Williamstown piers were partly sheltered, but great caution was necessary. The mail steamer Oizaba, scheduled to leave at one o'clock, could not move until two powerful tugs, the Racer and the Rescue, were used to get her into clear water. The Ballarat, being light, got away with less difficulty, though her plunging showed the force of the sea.

As the gale increased during the night, heavy seas swept into the inner piers. The prison hulk Success ground heavily against the breakwater, and the Loch Vennachar, together with the Hollingwood, carried away stern moorings, fresh lines being promptly run out to prevent serious damage. At Port Melbourne boats were sunk, moorings broken, and the river current ran with exceptional force. The storm was the most severe experienced in the Bay for many years.

Upon discharge of her cargo the Loch Vennachar was shifted from new railway pier, Williamstown, to the railway pier to await the first of her outward cargo to be loaded. Then with only part of her wool cargo aboard Captain Bennett put the ship into the Alfred Graving Dock on September 30th to be cleaned, painted and repaired prior to her return journey to London.

However it was not all hard work for the captain and remaining crew of the Loch Vennachar. A market bazaar was held at the Mechanic's Institute to raise money for the Williamstown Sailors' Rest, which was in financial difficulty and in danger of closing. Having opened in 1878, the former Wesleyan Church in Ann Street had been established as a coffee house and place where seamen could take their ease and where the temptations of alcohol and the enticements of boarding house runners were unwelcome.

The market was opened by the Victorian premier Mr Munro. There were many dignitaries in attendance as well as the more mundane folk who had come to join the frivolities and perhaps purchase many of the curios presented for sale. There were six stalls being run by ladies of the Women's Christian Temperance Union who were all dressed in fancy costumes.

With her hold swept and cleaned the Loch Vennachar sits berth
alongside the wharf at Port Melbourne awaiting her cargo of wool,
wheat and skins to he loaded aboard.
Stat Library of Soth Australia.

There was a bachelor's stall and another six stalls, set up by crews of the ships tied up at Williamstown's twin piers. The Salamis, Loch Ryan, Collingwood, Loch Vennachar, Mermerus and Samuel Plimsoll each had tables decorated with bunting and flowers upon which were arranged various curios and handicrafts manufactured by the crews of the vessels so named, also available for sale were goods from England and small artworks created by relatives of the sailors especially for such stalls. The band of the Naval Brigade played a selection of well-known tunes all evening.

Once cleaned and her rigging overhauled the Loch Vennachar was moved back to the London Pier to finish loading her cargo of wool and skins. Tied alongside were the clippers Loch Ryan, Mermerus, Collingwood, Kentmere, and the Salamis. Captain Bennett had his ship cleared out on October 21st, loaded with wool, and sailed through The Heads on the 23rd.

The clipper meandered along south, passing Cape Horn on November 28th, 36 days out. The Equator was crossed on January 2nd in company with the four-masted French ship Cap Horn bound for Dunkirk. Once in the English Channel the tug Guiana was engaged west of Start Point and the pair proceeded to make for the Thames, passing Deal on February 1st, arriving after a long and languorous trip of 101 days.

Upon the discharge of the last of her cargo a ballast of cement was taken aboard and the Loch Vennachar was shifted back down to Tilbury Fort on February 28th 1892. A tug brought the clipper out just after midnight and together they sailed west bound for the Lizard, thence home, arriving off the Tail-of-the-Bank on March 5th 1892.

The Loch Vennachar's fortunes did not exactly improve as she sailed from the Tail-o'-the-Bank on the 6th of April 1892. The ship departed with 34 crew, 12 passengers and a hold filled with general cargo for Melbourne. She had aboard over 200 tons of pig iron and railway track as ballast and was well down on her load lines.

THE BEST BOAT GEAR OBTAINABLE.
"MILLS" PATENT DISENGAGING AND ENGAGING BOAT GEAR.
Approved by Board of Trade, and United States of America Authorities, &c.
SIMPLE METHOD OF ENGAGING.
SIMPLE METHOD OF DISENGAGING.
SIMPLICITY WITH EFFICIENCY-
Thousands of Sets supplied throughout the World, for Liners, Warships, Troopships, Mailboats, Cable Ships, Merchant Vessels, Royal and other Yachts, Pilot Cutters, &c.
Has won the Highest Awards wherever exhibited.
WM. MILLS, LTD., ENGINEERS, SUNDERLAND.
Telegraphic and Cable Address: "ENGINEER, SUNDERLAND."   National Telephone: 552 SUNDERLAND.
American Agents: WELIN DAVIT CO., 305—315, Vernon Avenue, Long Island City, NEW YORK.

The cargo consisted of a diverse mix of industrial materials, consumables, and manufactured goods. A significant portion of the shipment was dedicated to alcohol, including bulk and bottled beer as well as thousands of gallons of spirits in both casks and bottles. Heavy industrial materials made up a large volume of the weight, featuring massive quantities of pig iron, cast iron pipes, steel plates, galvanised tubes, and machinery parts like steel wheels and spokes. The manifest also listed extensive paper and stationery supplies, ranging from printing and writing paper to envelopes and pasteboard. Chemical and painter's supplies were well-represented with items such as linseed oil, white lead, bleaching powder, charcoal, and indigo. Finally, the shipment included a wide variety of textiles and household goods, including thousands of yards of cottons and linens, wool carpeting, hemp twine, cornflour, earthenware, and flint glass globes. The total weight of the cargo was approximately 1,113 tons, not including the ballast, and its value was about £13,010 (equal to £2,146,000 in 2025).

Leaving her tug off Inishtrahull, the Loch Vennachar set out into the North Atlantic, winds swinging from the northeast to southeast. The variable conditions were maintained until May 1st when, upon entering the Horse Latitudes in the vicinity of Cape Verde, a series of calms and baffling airs were encountered all the way to the Equator. The light airs allowed Captain Bennett to set every sail he had in the locker, including stun'sails, watersails, a ringtail and even a jimmy-green on the jib-boom. These extra sails pushed the Loch Vennachar well south as she skirted her way past Cabo Sao Roque. The southeast trades were fallen in with at 3° south and were carried all the way until Bill Bennett altered course to begin the run east down along the 40th parallel on May 29th.

By now the Loch Vennachar had her best suite of sails aloft, the lighter tropical rags and all the extra bunting having long been stowed below in the sail locker. As the clipper began her run below the Cape of Good Hope, the barometer began to fall steadily as an approaching cold front sent fluffy altocumulus clouds ahead of the coming blow. Bill Bennett consulted his first mate Mr MacDougall, and he agreed that they should shorten sail and have the passengers and crew prepare for some rough weather ahead. It was the start of winter and the Southern Ocean hurricanes were notorious.

The winds picked up gradually from the northwest and increased to gale force, bringing fierce lightning and thunder squalls. Scudding along under topgallants, staysails, spanker and headsails, a particularly nasty gust saw the main topgallant blown to shreds and quickly replaced. The nasty weather continued as the Loch Vennachar forged ahead upon increasingly large waves, making over 250 nautical miles that day.

The hurricane winds and mountainous seas intensified on June 2nd as, now sailing under lower topsails, headsails and brailed spanker, the Loch Vennachar's foresail was carried away. By now the passengers were confined to their bunks, with cheese, cold meats and biscuits being the only fare on offer. Lifelines had been rigged fore and aft and rigging nets set about the rails on the poop to catch any who may have been swept overboard. The stormy weather and mountainous seas increased in severity as the day progressed.

June 3rd saw the clipper sailed along at 40° south, 27° east. At 4:00 am the First Mate's whistle sounded, calling *"All hands on deck!"*. They were ordered aloft to shorten sail down to a reefed forecourse and topsails, and a single headsail. At 5:00 am the mizzen lower topsail was blown to ribbons. The ship was labouring very heavily in the horrendous conditions, her lee rail under water all the time; however, the Loch Vennachar had been built to handle such conditions and Captain Bennett was confident that his ship would weather the storm as she had always done. A mountainous sea was running with winds gusting to 90 knots or more. With decks constantly awash and two men always lashed to the helm, it was all the crew of the ship could do to keep her from foundering. The ship was head-reaching under lower topsails and a single fore staysail.

At 6:00 am the ship was overwhelmed by a pair of enormous rogue waves. Standing atop the poop, looking forward, Captain Bennett saw what was coming and, grabbing his speaking trumpet, called the crew aft. He made sure of those men who were aloft on the pitching foreyard trying to furl a sail that had torn loose. The men managed to safely make the poop deck just in time. The Loch Vennachar rode the first wave and sank into the trough at the other side. The sea struck the vessel almost broadside on. While in this position, the second wave came on and broke on deck, filling the topsails with a solid wall of seawater.

With her fo'c'sle buried deep into the green-grey, the entire ship, bar the poop, was covered in swirling, foaming sea and spray. The wall of green water rushed along the deck in a mass of foam and spray, tearing the fore and main masts clean out of the deck, snapping the iron masts like tree trunks. The windward bulwarks were smashed flat and the leeward ones were carried away. The decks were swept clean of everything moveable, and the 60-foot-tall wave picked up three of the ship's boats and over the side they went with everything else.

The forward third of the deckhouse was smashed in, the entire cabin shifted from its mountings. Inside the galley, the two cooks were sheltering from the storm trying to prepare food for the passengers and coffee for the crew. Tons of seawater smashed in both galley doors and blew out the ports. The force of the water smashed the skylight, forcing the second cook, Robert Stephenson, out through the opening; however, William Melvin, the head cook, was washed out of the galley along with everything else and disappeared over the side never to be seen again. His loss was not noticed for several hours after the dismasting, so busy were the crew.

All around was the crashing of falling timber and flashes of sparks and fire from tearing and smashed ironwork; the Loch Vennachar was in trouble. With no masts except a stump mizzen topmast, the ship soon broached and was soon almost onto her beam ends. Without her masts to steady her, the ship rolled dangerously in heavy seas. With the yards flying around wildly, the spanker boom collapsed on top of the wheel, smashing it to flinders; it had been hard up at the time and the helmsmen were left holding the shattered remnants.

As the waters receded from the deck, the Loch Vennachar wallowed violently. For the next nine hours, as the storm raged, those aboard the stricken ship could do nothing except hang on. In an attempt to get the clipper's head to the oncoming seas, Captain Bennett ordered a sea anchor to be set aft and for oil to be poured through the forward scuppers to try and settle the sea around the vessel. The first three sea anchors were carried away by the force of the waves, yet the fourth, of the strongest canvas and secured with chains, held true and the clipper's bow came up into the wind so that the roll was greatly reduced. A jibsail was set upon the mizzen stump as a spanker, which held the ship bow on to the wind, yet the Loch Vennachar had developed an alarming list, her cargo having shifted below.

As the weather began to improve, Captain Bennett had an opportunity to assess the damage; three boats and all moveable gear had been washed overboard, and the fourth boat had been stove in. The poop and forecastle head rails were smashed, bulwarks stove in or washed away, and the cabin outdoors, ports, the bridge rails, and forward end of the deckhouse were smashed and twisted, the house itself having been wrenched very badly from its mounts. The poop deck doors and skylight had been stove in, and the saloon, pantry and cabins were all flooded.

With the spanker gaff having collapsed upon the wheel, smashing it, a jury-rigged wheel had to be set up by the carpenter. Then, as winds settled to a hard, flat blow, the aft cargo hatch was opened and several sailors were sent below to restow some of the cargo whilst others were tasked with throwing much of it over the side. All told, twenty tons of cargo was tossed, allowing Captain Bennett to bring the ship back onto a somewhat even keel.

The crew managed to cut away the wreckage but could do little else until the storm had blown itself out. On June 5th the crew were able to set a mizzen staysail to help steady the clipper's continuous roll. However, Bennett and MacDougall both knew that they needed to set some foresails if they were going to gain some control over the vessel. So, together with the sailmaker and ship's carpenter, they set to constructing, from spare spars, a mizzen topmast and a crossjack to sling from it. Down below, part of the cargo was dozens of railway rails and long, hollow poles. It was these that Bennett and MacDougall decided to use to manufacture a foremast. It took the crew the best part of eleven days to clear away the wreckage, salvage all the usable gear and rigging, shore up the damaged bulwarks and rails with makeshift timber barriers and safety lines, and make essential repairs to the deckhouse and poop.

On June 13th, eleven days after the dismasting, the crew rigged up a makeshift topsail yard and bent on and set a mizzen topsail. The clipper was making some headway but was still adrift on the current, seas still very lumpy. Twenty-four hours later, with the topsail yard holding steady, the men of the Loch Vennachar then sent up a crossjack yard and set a cro'jack sail which provided another half a knot of headway.

With the successful setting of sails on the stump mizzen mast, Bill Bennett decided it was time to add some headgear to the Loch Vennachar. So on June 15th the crew managed to step-in a jury-rigged foremast, an iron rail to which was doubled a long iron tube. They then sent up a salvaged spar to hold a cut-down foresail. The mast was then fitted with fore and back stays and then a fore staysail was set.

During all this time the passengers did what they could to help the crew, many of whom were badly injured; the men helped with clearing away the wreckage and assisted with the repairs, whilst the ladies worked with the limited medical supplies to help Captain Bennett set bones, bandage wounds and tend dressings as and when needed. Everyone aboard was forced to pitch in and help. There were no passengers aboard over the next five weeks.

The weather again worsened on the evening of June 16th and the ship was tossed around at the mercy of the wind and waves. However, the Loch Vennachar was made of stouter stuff and rode out the blow, losing only her crossjack which was blown to ribbons. The weather finally abated on the 21st and another cro'jack was set and a yard was hoisted on the foremast and a small foresail was set. Confident that the foremast would hold, Captain Bennett ordered that a second yard be sent up and a topsail set, thus giving him much better control over the clipper's handling. She was now making a steady 4–6 knots and Bennett had long given up on his attempt to make for his destination. Instead, he set course for Mauritius.

In spite of her jury-rigged masts and sails, the Loch Vennachar covered over 100 miles a day. The southeast trade winds were encountered on July 1stand Mauritius was sighted on the 9th. The weather was squally with thunderstorms over much of the sky. The ship came to anchor outside of Port Louis on the 11th and a tug was engaged to bring the crippled vessel into the harbour the following morning, 96 days from Greenock. It had taken almost five weeks to cover the 1,600 miles since the dismasting and everyone was still alive and in relatively good health.

The Loch Vennachar had been expected to make her usual 80 to 90 day run from Glasgow to Melbourne; however, when she failed to appear after 100 days those connected to her began to get very concerned. People's worries were heightened when word came through that a violent hurricane had all but destroyed Mauritius at about the same time as the clipper was due to make her run across the Indian Ocean. Reports began to filter in that wreckage from an unknown ship had been found after the storm in the vicinity of St Paul Island.

The captain of the steamer Murrumbidgee, upon reaching Melbourne, reported having passed through a debris field, the last remains of a lost ship. The wreckage, including thousands of kerosene tins, timbers and ships' boats, was scorched and burned as if by a fierce fire or explosion. The shattered timbers appeared to have been in the water for just a few hours, and when the steamer passed an entire side of a half-submerged deckhouse there seemed little hope of finding any survivors.

Ships coming into Australia reported that several vessels had disappeared during a hurricane that had raged on the 24th and 25th of June between the Cape of Good Hope and the St Paul

Loch Vennachar arriving at Port Louis after cyclone damage.
State library of Victoria

Port Louis, Mauritius after the cyclone in 1882.
The Graphic, June 11 1892

Islands. The Loch Ryan, that had left three weeks after the Loch Vennachar, arrived safely in Hobson's Bay on the 19th of July; by then the missing clipper was 104 days from Glasgow with no reports of her location coming forth. Checks by Port Melbourne authorities established that the Loch Vennachar had no kerosene in her manifest, so the unfortunate clipper was more likely the missing American vessel Canara, 91 days from New York bound for Melbourne. The ship Canara later arrived much reduced in sail having been heavily damaged by the storm.

Terrible Cyclone Leaves Thousands Dead and Injured on British Isle.

  Port Louis, Mauritius, May 12—"*The colony of Mauritius is only now beginning to recover from the initial shock of horror and despair occasioned by the frightful catastrophe of the 29th of April. Detailed dispatches received from Port Louis confirm that the appalling nature of the visitation was by no means unduly heightened in previous telegrams. An immense and sorrowful toll has been exacted upon our fellow British subjects, with official information now confirming that the number of deaths stands at about 1,200 souls, and the wounded at a grievous 3,000 to 4,000.*

  The calamity descended with a fury seldom, if ever, before witnessed in this prosperous outpost of the Empire. Preceded by a magnetic disturbance lasting three days, the tempest struck with startling swiftness from the north-west, an unusual quarter, reaching a velocity of 113 miles per hour. One correspondent even recorded the wind blowing at an astonishing 125 miles an hour. The violence was so great that the barometer fell to 27.997, the lowest point ever recorded in Mauritius.

  The streets of Port Louis, which was last month one of the happiest colonies, now defy description. They are choked with a confused mass of trees, masonry, brickwork, and timber. At least a third part of the city lies ruined. In the ill-fated Tranquebar section, literally not one house remained standing. Fragile buildings miraculously escaped, whilst massive stone erections were cruelly shattered. Out of 62 churches and chapels in the vicinity, only twelve remain, and these are all damaged. The Royal College and the Cathedral are now little more than heaps of ruins.

The loss of life has been concentrated in the capital, where about 600 were killed. Among the dead are Mr H. Allard of the New Oriental Bank, Mr C. Lamothe, Superintendent of Distilleries, and Mr Delaroche, sergeant of police. The manner of death has, in many cases, been horrible, with bodies dreadfully mangled and bruised by the timbers of falling houses. In the country districts, hundreds of labourers seeking shelter in available buildings were crushed to death in their downfall.

The Acting Governor, the Hon. H. Jerningham, was among the first to act, making a tour of inspection to gauge the extent of the disaster. Orders were instantly issued to distribute food to the needy, and refuges and temporary hospitals were established for the homeless and injured. The troops, detachments of the Royal Artillery and the North Staffordshire Regiment, rendered admirable and devoted service in clearing the streets and assisting the wounded.

The burial of the dead, which went on for six days, has been an urgent, sorrowful task. To facilitate the colony's recovery and alleviate the terrible distress and starvation among the poorer classes, the Imperial Government will be approached for a special relief loan of £600,000, repayable in twenty-five years. It is fervently hoped that the English Press will support the appeal for help for these sufferers." **The Graphic, June 11 1892.**

Upon the Loch Vennachar's arrival in Port Louis, the passengers disembarked to a town in utter ruin, it too having been flattened by the same hurricane that had dismasted their vessel. They were accommodated by the Governor of Mauritius in his own home until passage off the island could be arranged.

Two passengers, David Pembroke and a Mrs Gardener, returned to England on the steamer Pembroke Castle. The other passengers also boarded the departing steamer but disembarked in Colombo, Ceylon, so that they could continue their journey to Australia aboard the steamship Parramatta; Mr H. Moss and a Miss Cummings journeyed to Adelaide, whilst Mr and Mrs T. Grieve and Mr Edmonds carried on to Melbourne.

A sadly odd ending occurred to one passenger, a Mr Wilmot, who had apparently never recovered from his ordeal aboard the Loch Vennachar; he committed suicide two days out

P&O Steamer SS 'Parramatta'
State Library of NSW

from Colombo by jumping overboard in the middle of the Indian Ocean, never to be seen again.

Captain Bennett and his crew were assisted into port by the sailors belonging to HMS Boadicea. The ship's master, Captain George A. Giffard, made sure that the injured vessel was securely moored alongside the naval pier. Later, Captain Giffard came to visit the Loch Vennachar and with him was the commander of the Royal Navy's Indian Ocean station, Vice-Admiral William Kennedy, who once aboard complimented Bill Bennett, his officers and men for their seamanship.

They later handed over cigars and other 'medical comforts', beer, whisky and other treats from the navy store for the crew of the Loch Vennachar. Those crew members still suffering from injury or scurvy were sent ashore to the army-navy hospital that, whilst damaged, was still able to treat the sailors from the Loch Vennachar.

The harbour was filled with smashed vessels and debris from the town and port. Admiral Kennedy offered the services of his carpenters to help make the Loch Vennachar's crew quarters more habitable as both he and Captain Bennett knew that it would be several months before the materials necessary to refit the clipper would be able to be sent from Britain. There was always the chance that the local Lloyd's surveyor may condemn the ship out of hand.

Eventually, telegrams were sent to Lloyd's of London and their agents in Glasgow and Melbourne, notifying them of the Loch Vennachar's safe arrival. The ship was surveyed and the cargo examined and found to be intact, less the 20 tons that had been heaved over the side.

With the cargo secure and the hull watertight, it was decided by Lloyd's to pay out on the necessary repairs required for the Loch Vennachar, so long as it was done by the crew of the Loch Vennachar assisted by the Royal Navy's facilities to help step in new masts.

Back in Glasgow, Aitken & Lilburn authorised Barclay, Curle and Co., the well-known shipbuilders of the Clyde, to

HMS Boudicea leaving Port Louis, Mauritius.
Greenwich Maritime Museum Collection.

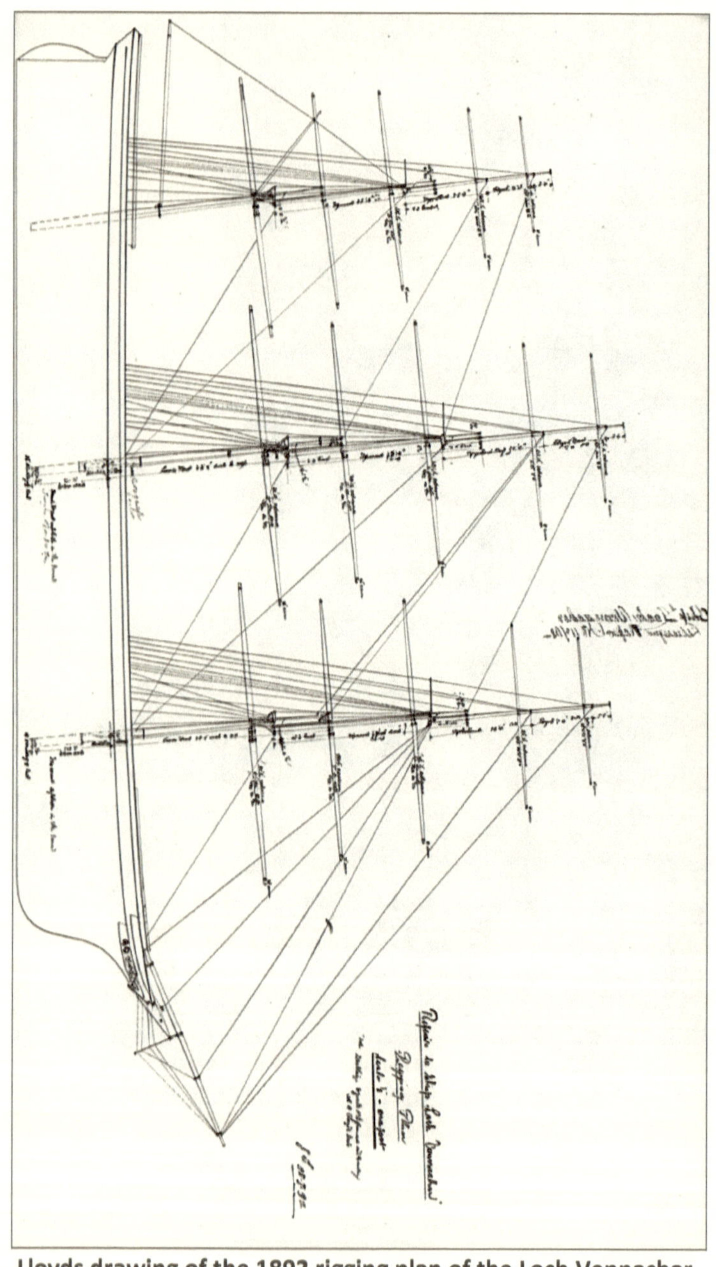

Lloyds drawing of the 1892 rigging plan of the Loch Vennachar.
Lloyds Archives.

Vice-Admiral William Kennedy.
Navy & Army Illustrated.

manufacture new masts, spars, and requisite fixtures and fittings to be able to refit the damaged clipper.

Once manufacturing had been completed, the masts, spars, rigging, fixtures and fittings were loaded aboard the steamer Clan Macdonald and shipped out to Port Louis. She arrived safely at Mauritius on November 1st, having steamed in via Liverpool, Cape Town, Algoa Bay, East London, and thence to Port Louis.

The crew of the Loch Vennachar were ready and waiting for the Clan Macdonald's cargo to be unshipped and sent across to the naval pier where their ship was waiting. All the necessary repairs had been made; bulwarks, rails, cabin doors, ports, and boats had been repaired, patched up, or replaced. The stumps of the old masts had been lifted out and the steps readied for a whole new set to be fitted. The masts and spars were quickly unloaded and sent across where a crane was waiting to lift the lower masts into place.

Once accomplished, the crew of the Loch Vennachar, with help from some eager navy volunteers, sent up the new topmasts, fitted the doublings, and then the topgallant masts. Alow and aloft, the Loch Vennachar was a hive of activity, overseen by the officers of the clipper and riggers sent from the dockyard. Things were going so well that, at first, when the accident occurred, no one seemed to notice. One of the riggers aloft, busily hammering home rivets to secure the topgallant doublings, dropped a heavy iron hammer which struck Able Seaman Hugh Kane on the head, crashing into his skull and killing him instantly.

The man collapsed upon the deck, a pool of blood rapidly spreading from his shattered skull, mouth, nose, and ears. Eventually, someone noticed the fallen sailor and all work was halted just long enough to have the body removed to a local morgue. So shocked were the crew and Captain Bennett that he called a halt to work for the rest of the afternoon to allow the men to recover from the shock. Work continued in earnest the following morning but stopped just after lunch so that all could attend Hugh Kane's funeral.

The refit was completed by November 15th, the bill coming to more than £3000. A number of sailors had already left the island aboard other outbound vessels, so the Loch Vennachar's crew, when she set sail on 18 November, was a mix of old and new hands. The evening before departure, Bill Bennett and his officers, Mr MacDougall, Mr Cromb, and Mr Smith, had attended a dinner at Government House, hosted by the Governor of Mauritius, Sir Hubert Edward Henry Jerningham, and his wife, Lady Anne. There were the usual toasts to Queen Victoria, Great Britain, the Royal Navy, and Lady Anne. After a long and enjoyable evening enhanced by the heat of the languorous Port Louis, Bill Bennett and his officers were driven back to the port to begin final preparations for departure.

The Loch Vennachar, thoroughly renewed, resumed her voyage on November 18th 1892, and met with light winds the whole way to Melbourne, which was reached on the morning of 30 December after a remarkable voyage of 268 days from Glasgow. Almost as soon as the ship had dropped anchor, the crew assembled on deck and gave ringing 'Huzzahs!' for Captain Bennett and his officers, who had brought them through so many dangers to their final destination.

In a letter to The Argus, Captain Bennett described in detail what had happened to the Loch Vennachar on the night she nearly disappeared with all hands:

"We had a terrible smash up on 3 June in lat. 40 deg S., and long. 27 deg (approximately) W. We had been running before fine westerly winds from 26 May, on which day we ran 240 miles, and then 251, 227, 225, 259, 250, 274, and 320 miles consecutively. At noon on 2 June, the wind began to take off and haul to the northward. At 4 pm, we had the main-royal set, with very little wind and the barometer rising steadily to 29.50. It had not been higher than this for two days; I felt very ill at the time. As the weather began to look rainy and dirty, at 6 pm, we took in the main royal and upper topgallant sail. At 8 pm, there was rain with passing light squalls. Barometer 29.50. Shortened sail to upper topsails, as the weather looked dirty, mostly rain with the wind NE. We were braced sharp up, and at 10 pm, the barometer was at 29.20. Shortened sails to lower topsails and made all snug.

At midnight, barometer 29.22, wind ENE and steady, increasing to a gale with heavy rain. At 2 am on 3 June, the barometer had fallen to 29.02 with fine clear weather and not so much wind, and the ship going along splendidly. At 5 am, barometer 28.2, and heavy rains; the main topsail sheet carried away in a squall. At 5.30 am, called all hands as the weather side of the foresail had blown adrift from the gaskets. At 6.15 am, just as daylight was coming in, saw a tremendous sea coming along right down on the port bow. I called out to 'Hold on everyone!', and it rolled right over the ship.

"It was God's mercy that we were not all swept away. The sea swept the decks clean of everything moveable and smashed in the galley door. One cook was washed overboard and another was shot up through the skylight. When we picked ourselves up, it was seen that the masts were gone, except the mizzen mast and upper and lower mizzen topsail yards. The crossjack yard fell across the mizzen rigging and carried that away, all except two shrouds. Well, it was no time to think, and all haste was made to cut away and secure what available wreckage we could. The galley was completely gutted, and we had a bad time of it.

The ship lay in the trough of the sea until 14 June, when the crossjack yard was set up again and sails were bent. Got her out of the trough of the sea and she rolled the cargo in the fore and after 'tween decks adrift. She had a list of about three feet and a half, and so had to throw some pig iron and pipes overboard to get at the other cargo and secure it. She used to roll 45 deg and 46 deg until the chain cables were got up and lashed along the deck. Had a most awful time of it, and it was a hard matter to keep one's feet, the rolling was so heavy. The mizzen rigging lanyards were continually parting owing to the heavy rolling, so got some 4 1/2 lanyard rope, the same that is used for main rigging. Had to make starboard mizzen rigging out of hauling lines (wire), and when the weather got fine, a jury foremast was rigged. It was made out of a spare topgallant and royal mast, and the sprung upper mizzen topsail yard was used for a foreyard.

The cause of the disaster was the seas washing in the port fore-bulwarks from the forecastle to abaft the fore-rigging, and carrying away the chain plates and bulwark stanchions. Of course, when the foremast had no support, over it went, taking the mainmast with it, and also the mizzen topmast just above the cap.

Well, after battering about until 30 June, we gave up trying for Melbourne as I had to keep the ship before the wind when I had a breeze, and she would not steer with the wind before the beam. I knew what a risk I should be running coming on the Australian coast in the winter time, whereas by making for Mauritius we should have finer weather. Well, I had not a chart of the place— only the island marked on the Southern Indian chart, but the sailing directions were in Findlay's directory.

We looked a perfect wreck on arrival. The starboard bulwarks were set out about 2 ft from the perpendicular from the weight of water and wreckage of mast and spars. Thank God we are here safe, but we did have a bad time of it down south. The admiral of the Boadicea (flagship) and his officers visited the ship and complimented us on bringing the ship in, although in such a plight."

The ship's safe arrival in Melbourne was cause for much relief and celebration. The cargo was finally unloaded, and the ship was put into dry dock for a complete inspection of her hull, fittings, and rigging. She was cleaned and any defects repaired before she was released to take on a fresh load of wool for the London sales.

The Loch Vennachar was moved into a berth alongside the Williamstown Railway Pier to discharge; at the same time, her remaining crew were paid off. The only ones to stay by the ship were the officers and apprentices. The rest collected their pay and were off to new adventures.

The cargo was sent ashore by local stevedores, and the clipper was then floated across to Alfred Graving Dock for a clean and paint. Her hull was inspected at the same time and found to be in prime condition. The opportunity was also taken to complete effective and aesthetically pleasing repairs to the Loch Vennachar's poop-cabins and deckhouse, whilst a new wheel and steering gear were fitted.

New boats were also purchased, the ones supplied in Mauritius being swapped out for craft that were fit for purpose. New lifebuoys, safety gear, water casks, and everything that had been lost overboard was purchased new or second-hand from the Port Melbourne ship's chandlery of T.M. Burroughs and Co.

The vessels loading at Melbourne alongside the Loch Vennachar were the Hesperus, Loch Etive, Loch Sloy, Ennerdale, Crown of Denmark, Winifred, and General Roberts. The master of the Loch Etive, Charles Lehmann, and the master of the Loch Sloy, James Horne, were frequent visitors to the Loch Vennachar, and together the three Loch Line captains developed a notorious reputation when on the frolic ashore.

Soon, though, it was time to say farewell to Port Melbourne as the Loch Vennachar's hatches were battened down and the canvas hatch covers were applied. The clipper was cleared out on February 15th, 1893, laden with 3,300 bales of wool, 75 bales of leather, 119 bales of skins, 1,038 bags of tanning bark, and 7,239 bags of wheat. The steam-tug Racer was engaged to tow the Loch Vennachar out through the Heads, which she did at 7:00 am on February 17th.

With as much sail set as he thought prudent, Bill Bennett pushed the Loch Vennachar along the 45th parallel until close to the Horn, when he altered course for the run through Drake Passage. Diego Ramirez was sighted on March 21st, the channel choked with small bergs.

A week later, at midnight of the 27th under a waxing gibbous moon, the lookouts atop the fo'c'sle rang the forward bell for all they were worth. The cry of 'Ice! Right ahead' was screamed out in the darkness, causing the deck officer to blow his whistle three times, calling all hands on deck. The helm was put hard down as crew raced aloft to make sail. Captain Bennett was soon on deck, making careful note of their position: 50° south, 53° west. He estimated that the ice island was about three miles long and up to 200 feet high.

This iceberg was the largest of the 13 that were seen between 52° south and 48° south, and 51° west to 46° west. Once clear of the deadly icefield, the Loch Vennachar continued her run northeast, rounding outside of the Falkland Islands. For much of the voyage home, they kept company with the steel-hulled ship, Carnedd Llewelyn.

Steam Tug Racer was one of a number of tugboats used by the Melbourne Harbour Trust to tow and push larger vessels in and out of Port Melbourne and the Docks.

After 94 days at sea, the Loch Vennachar signalled her arrival to the men of the Lizard light signal station. She was taken in tow off Start Point and arrived off Tilbury Fort on the evening of May 24th, 1893.

Arriving in London, the Loch Vennachar was shifted into London Docks' east quay and berthed alongside the Loch Etive and Loch Long. Once docked, her hatches were broached and her cargo quickly discharged. Once empty, the Loch Vennachar was shifted into Victoria Dock to have her decks repaired, having been damaged during the 1892 storm. The repairs had been considered too expensive to complete in Melbourne and had been deferred until the ship arrived in London. As his ship was being repaired, Bill took the opportunity to head home to Chatham.

William Bennett and his wife Mary (Molly to her friends) were amongst the guests invited to an 'At Home' hosted by Alderman George Winch and his wife Mary, at their home, Holcombe Manor in Chatham. Amongst the entertainments was a Gypsy reading palms, tennis on the lawns, croquet, bowls, and other amusements. Many people took time to wander the expansive grounds, enjoy the carefully manicured gardens, and admire the outdoor sculptures. Most of Chatham's notables were present and spent a pleasant afternoon together raising money for the Chatham Football Club.

The Bennetts' time together was all too brief and soon William was back in London, having received an unusual set of orders from Glasgow. Aitken, Lilburn and Co. had organised a charter for the Loch Vennachar to sail to Sharpness to pick up a consignment of printing paper and other goods. Departing Gravesend on July 3rd, the Loch Vennachar was towed down river and out to sea by the tug Flying Vulture. Together they

Carnedd Llewelyn, 1726 tons. Built by Russell and Co. Greenock.
State Library South Australia.

reached Kingsroad, off Portishead Point, on July 5th 1893. There Captain Bennett had to wait until a local river pilot could be engaged to guide the tug and her clipper up to Sharpness.

Arriving in Sharpness on the 6th, the Loch Vennachar was berthed alongside Sharpness dock near Gloucester; barges began to bring up the ship's cargo from warehouses further down the canal. The local railway network allowed smaller customers to rush their wares from other parts of England to the Loch Vennachar. Stowed aboard were 32,781 bags of Black Horse salt plus 200 cases and 50 casks of vinegar. The ship was finally loaded and ready to be towed down the River Severn on the 17th of July 1893. The clipper was as fit and sprightly as the day of her launch.

By the end of August, the Loch Vennachar had entered the roaring 40s as she began running her easting down, and by the 3rd of September the crew had sighted their first monster iceberg. Conditions were stormy with frequent hail and snow squalls. By the following day, the ship was passing through a field of mammoth bergs, any one of which would have sunk or disabled the ship had she struck one. The weather had abated and conditions were foggy with light winds, and then by the 6th of September the last iceberg was past, or so the crew thought.

For several days Captain Bennett sailed the ship in a north-westerly direction, avoiding several large isolated bergs along the way. Moving north, the Loch Vennachar passed 67 large ice islands. Constant lookout had to be kept to avoid a fatal collision, the kind of catastrophe that had already claimed at least three other Loch Liners in times past.

On one foggy night, the Loch Vennachar passed through a particularly dense field of icebergs, the fog only lifting at 7:00 am the following morning. When the crew could finally see where they were, it was discovered that the ship had seemed to thread her own way through a maze of deadly ice mountains. Five huge, black bergs were threaded by the clipper, and a stiff south-west wind gave the Loch Vennachar enough steerage to make her way clear of the fields at last as she began her final northing run.

An example of the Sterling Siver Llloyds Meritorious Service Medal awarded to Captain W.H. Bennett, whose portrait appeared in the Weekly Times of Melbourne, 21st October 1893.

Captain William Henry Bennett.

Drawings based upon Captain Bennett's descriptions and sketches made later.

Whilst the Loch Vennachar was at sea, Lloyd's of London had decided to award Captain William Henry Bennett with their first ever Medal for Meritorious Service. The Committee of Lloyd's had examined the circumstances of Captain Bennett's conspicuous conduct during the dismasting of the Loch Vennachar in June of 1892. Not only had he saved the ship, her passengers, and most of the cargo and crew, the master of the Loch Vennachar had safely reached Mauritius and, after timely repairs, had completed her voyage, thus limiting losses to insurers to less than £5,000.

The Lloyd's Medal for Meritorious Services, first instituted in 1893, was awarded to those whose endeavours averted damage to, or loss of, vessels and their cargoes. A telegram was sent via Aden to the Ship Masters Association in Melbourne, asking them to inform Captain Bennett of the award once he arrived in port. Cape Otway was sighted and signalled on the 6th of October and the ship finally passed through the Heads at 2 o'clock on the 9th of October and came to anchor above Queenscliff.

The tug Racer steamed down to greet her and was engaged to tow the Loch Vennachar to Corio Bay, where she would then be made fast to Geelong Pier to unload her cargo of salt, which was consigned to Mr Henry Berry. Upon discharging her cargo of salt, the Loch Vennachar was hauled out to Hobson's Bay, where she was tied up to the wharf in Williamstown.

After the Loch Vennachar had made fast to the wharf, the Loch Lomond moved out into the stream and was preparing to drop down to No. 14 shed, when the combined forces of tide and wind caught her stem and drove her on to the Loch Vennachar. The vessels locked together for several minutes, the result of which was that the Loch Vennachar's foretopgallant mast was sprung, the foretopgallant yard snapped in twain, and some of the braces and other gearing carried away. The Loch Lomond also lost several of her braces and a quantity of gearing.

Her cargo was unloaded at the Australian Wharf at Williamstown and her hold filled with a consignment of prime Tasmanian wool destined for the London sales. Upon arrival in Melbourne, Captain Bennett was presented with a medal and certificate for valour by Lloyd's of London for his saving of the crew, ship, and cargo during the hurricane that had dismasted her and destroyed the island city of Port Louis in Mauritius. Captain Bennett was anxious to get underway; he was receiving pressure from his employers to get away quickly and to that end their agents had the ship's cargo ready to load even as she was tying up at the wharf to discharge her cargo.

Having unloaded the last of her cargo at her Yarra River berth, the clipper was towed down to Williamstown to be loaded with wool. Eventually the ship's hold was filled with 6,400 bales of wool. She was delayed from leaving by one day when one of her crew deserted at the last minute. The Loch Vennachar and Loch Ness, commanded by William 'Bully' Martin, were cleared out from Williamstown on December 12th, 1893, and were anchored in Hobson's Bay, each awaiting a tug and pilot.

Leaving Hobson's Bay on the 14th of December, the two ships were towed by the tugs Rescue and Racer from Hobson's Bay at 1 o'clock in the morning. Upon reaching Queenscliff, the Loch Vennachar was taken through the Rip at 7:30 am; the Loch Ness followed 10 minutes later. The twin clippers kept company for much of their trip home, only separating when they approached the Horn. The Loch Ness was bound for Dunkirk, and the Loch Vennachar for London.

The Loch Vennachar signalled her arrival off Prawle Point on March 26th, 1894; a pilot and tug were picked up west of Beachy Head. Captain Bennett's vessel dropped anchor in the Thames in London on the 27th of March 1894; she was beaten by the Loch Ness to Dunkirk by 5 days, which had arrived at Dunkirk on the morning of the 22nd of March.

After a month in port, during which time the Loch Vennachar was again surveyed by Lloyd's, maintaining her 100 A1 rating, she was then towed back to Glasgow in ballast ready for the next voyage out to the Antipodes. Bill Bennett was at home with Mary when a telegram arrived via Glasgow requesting his presence at the offices of Aitken & Lilburn. The Loch Vennachar's owners wanted to add a stopover to her usual run to Melbourne and wanted Bennett's opinion on the matter. The clipper had passed Dublin on May 3rd and arrived back in Broomielaw the following evening.

X
Tough Times Ahead

Upon his arrival at Buchanan Street in Glasgow, William Bennett was handed an invitation to attend upon James Lilburn at his residence in Queens Gardens, an exclusive terraced street set back from Victoria Crescent Road, located in the affluent Dowanhill area of Glasgow's West End. Bennett ordered a shining black Hansom Cab; the driver knew his way out to Dowanhill and soon had his whip driving the horse-drawn cab out to the exclusive neighbourhood.

Upon arrival, he presented his card to the Lilburns' servant, who took it to Isabella Lilburn, who then invited the Captain into the drawing room where her husband James was waiting. She then left the men to their discussion. The meat of James Lilburn's summons was his plan to place the Loch Vennachar on the berth to Adelaide, as the freight rates to Melbourne were falling as steamers began to take over the routes.

The number of people seeking passage out to the colonies aboard sailing vessels had dropped away markedly. Carrying people no longer paid and so the company directors had agreed to add a stopover on most of their clippers' voyages out to Australia. Fares to Adelaide and Melbourne had been dropped to £40 for saloon passengers, down £5. The rates offered on freights to Port Adelaide were equally competitive and catered to shippers whose cargoes were not time-sensitive. It indicated to Captain Bennett that the company of Aitken, Lilburn & Co. was running on razor-thin margins.

She set sail again from Glasgow on June 3rd. The Loch Vennachar was loaded and cleared to sail on June 2nd 1894 and shifted down to Greenock on the evening tide. Bill Bennett was aboard and greeted the few passengers who came aboard just after dawn on the 3rd: two first-class passengers, Messrs Meighan and H. Blair, and three in the mid-deck house. The tug Flying Elf appeared soon after their arrival and proceeded to tow

Clipper 'Loch Ness' under barque rig at Williamstown.
State library of Victoria

the clipper from the Tail-of-the-Bank just after 9:00 am. The captain of the tug later bid farewell to the Loch Vennachar off Rathlin Island on June 4th at 3:00 am.

Winds were light and variable from the southeast, conditions foggy. Three days later they passed the ship Kanawha at 51° north, 14° west and reported 'All well.' She was next reported at 13° north, 25° west by the 1489-ton steamer Stefania on her way to Las Palmas. The light north-easterly winds made for smooth if slow going as the Loch Vennachar began her southing run. The light and variable north and northwest winds continued unabated all the way until the equator, which was crossed on the 1st of July. Moderate nor'westerlies pushed the Loch Vennachar past the Greenwich meridian on the 19th. Captain Bennett pushed south, beginning his easting run along the 43rd parallel, and almost immediately ran into increasingly foul and dirty weather.

The 3rd of August saw the Loch Vennachar pass into a terrible storm with gale-force winds swinging northeast to southeast for several days. The ship ploughed headlong into tremendous seas that continuously broke over the vessel, covering her in green waters. The vessel performed splendidly, passing through the tempest with little damage. Moderating conditions were encountered hereafter and the clipper passed Cape Borda on the 21st, Port Adelaide being reached at 3 o'clock the next morning.

The run to Adelaide had taken 79 days from Rathlin Island. It was whilst in Adelaide that Captain Bennett met the local maritime news reporter for the Adelaide Register, who wrote an article neatly describing the Loch Line's failure to keep up with the times whilst trying to hold onto fading dreams.

"The Loch Vennachar ship is one of the justly celebrated line of Aitken & Lilburn, of Glasgow, who have kept up constant communication with the colonies for many years, having some of the finest sailing ships thus employed. In past years the vessels were the principal passenger carriers, having large staterooms excellently fitted, and in that day altogether superior accommodation. Steam has altered the whole transport service and there was a melancholy tinge about surroundings on

Wednesday on boarding the Loch Vennachar. The cabins and staterooms were in all the original fittings of maple and gilt work, but seemed like a deserted castle falling to decay. No smart stewards running here and there, no brass-bound middies; in fact, the whole concern seemed asleep till the genial old master, who has spent twenty years in the service, came to the gangway."
South Australian Register,23 August 1894.

After unloading 1000 barrels of gunpowder and 700 tons of general cargo, the Loch Vennachar continued her journey on Saturday the 25th at noon. Passing through Backstairs Passage, the ship fell in with a south-westerly gale which continued until after she scudded past Cape Northumberland. From then until the Heads, the winds moderated from south-southeast and then southwest. Cape Otway was passed on August 28th at 6 am, the Heads being passed through at 1:30 pm that afternoon. Captain Bennett ordered the anchor dropped in Hobson's Bay at 5 pm that afternoon, with preparations being made for the vessel to be towed upriver to her Yarra berth early the next day.

Tied up alongside the Loch Vennachar were her sister vessels: Loch Katrine, Loch Tay, Loch Ryan, and Loch Torridon. They were joined on the 18th of September by the Loch Long. After unloading her cargo, the Loch Vennachar was hauled out to Williamstown Pier to begin taking on her outbound cargo of wheat and wool. Lying alongside her was the clipper Avenger. Having almost finished loading, Captain Bennett had the Loch Vennachar floated into the graving dock for regular maintenance. She stayed here for four days before being floated out and hauled back to Williamstown to complete her loading.

Freight rates were falling and the carrying capacity of international steamships was increasing far beyond that which a clipper could safely carry. The asking rate for hold space aboard the Loch Liners was 23 shillings & 9 pence per ton, though most shippers were only willing to pay at most 22 shillings & sixpence per ton. There were many steamship companies that operated with freight rates well below this and who were able to offer cheaper rates due to the much greater carrying capacity and reliability of the large ocean-going steamers.

After having her hull cleaned and some storm damage repaired at the Alfred Graving Docks, the Loch Vennachar was finally loaded and ready to sail. She was towed out into Hobson's Bay by the steam tug Racer and got underway on the 20th of October 1894. It was from here that the clipper almost passed into legend. After 100 days at sea, the Loch Vennachar was reported as overdue by her agents in London. Worries increased when she was listed as missing after 125 days at sea. No other ships reported having seen the Loch Vennachar, and the Lloyds mention in the overdue/missing ships list caused great consternation in both Australia and Britain.

This was made worse by the fact that the ship had a reputation as one of the fastest, safest and most reliable clippers on the colonial run. The clipper had been missing for 140 days and still no word had been heard from or about her. Reports of the sightings of the Loch Vennachar by passing vessels began to appear in the press. She was reported on January 11th 1895 at 5° north, 29° west, then on February 7th at 49° north, 13° west, and finally on February 20th she was sighted by those aboard the steamer Doric, just 50 miles west of the Lizard, and asked to be reported 'All well!'

A pilot and tug were picked up west of St Catherine's Point and then everyone's prayers were at last answered when the Loch Vennachar sailed out of a foggy morning and into the anchorage at Gravesend on the 28th of February 1895. Captain Bennett reported that the ship was delayed by unfavourably light winds between New Zealand and Cape Horn. For 10 days she kept company with the clipper Blackadder as they tried to pass through Drake Passage and make their way around the Horn.

The Loch Vennachar was taken into London Dock to discharge on March 1st and Captain Bennett had a meeting with the masters at Trinity House and then at Lloyds of London to explain why his ship was so overdue. Just 10 days after her arrival, the Loch Vennachar was again being shifted back down to

Loch Vennachar at Williamstown Railway Pier awaiting a load of wheat.
State Library of Victoria.

Former tea clipper Blackadder, 917 tons.
State Library of South Australia.

Tilbury anchorage, Gravesend. She was towed to sea the following morning, just after midnight, and passed Beachy Head behind a tug on March 12th and arrived at Greenock on the 16th with a small amount of general cargo aboard.

The vessel's turnaround time was just two weeks with her departure date set for April 3rd from Broomielaw. She was again on the berth to sail to Melbourne via Greenock and Port Adelaide. She left Queens Dock in the early hours of March 4th, guided down to Greenock by two small river tugs, and departed Greenock on the 7th behind a larger ocean-going steamer.

The voyage was a quick one, crossing the line on May 7th, 30 days out, at 27° west in company with the ship Harland. On June 17th the ship experienced a particularly heavy gale from the southward, which increased to hurricane force, and Captain Bennett was forced to have the vessel heave-to for 12 hours. The ship reached the Semaphore roads on June 28th, 82 days from Greenock.

There was just one passenger aboard, a Mr MacDonald in the saloon, who had taken the voyage for his health. He was sent ashore to stay at a hotel in Port Adelaide and then the Loch Vennachar was shifted out to North Arm so that her 600 barrels of gunpowder could be discharged. After stevedores had unloaded a portion of the cargo, the Loch Vennachar was towed back down the Port River on July 3rd and out to the Semaphore anchorage. She set sail down Spencer Gulf in the early hours of the 4th and took just 76 hours to reach Port Phillip Heads.

The eagerly awaited ship finally arrived back in Hobson's Bay on the 7th of July 1895, passing through the Heads at 8:00 am and sailing up the South Channel to Hobson's Bay. Her cargo of hardware, alcohol and dry goods was discharged at the Williamstown Railway Pier. Yet it would be some months before Captain Bennett could refill her hold with wheat and wool.

Still, he was no idler; being a ship's master was as much about being a good politician as it was about being a master mariner. Society had its demands, and the height of the social season for the deep-sea captains was the Hobson's Bay Yacht Club Cinderella Ball. On the 12th of September, Captain Bennett, the officers of the Loch Vennachar and ship's masters from many other vessels anchored in the bay attended the annual at the Hobson's Bay Yacht Club. Bennett's crew were tasked with providing side lighting from the ship and assisting with the setting up of the ballroom.

Hobson's Bay Yacht Club Ball
By Daisy

"The annual Cinderella Ball of the HBYC was held in the Mechanics' on Thursday evening, 12th September and proved a brilliant success. The hall was decorated nautically, the stage carrying a fleet of model yachts under a full spread of canvas. Immediately in front was a ship's wheel and binnacle, but where was the man at the wheel?

Just for this night they were all masters; each man consulted his chart (programme), pricked out a course, took the tiller, got under way with a good breeze of sweet music and steered clear of all dangers, to the evident enjoyment of the fair freight in his charge. As the breeze died away, the moorings were picked up in splendid style.

There were sixteen of these voyages (dances) to be sailed on that night. At times during the evening some got becalmed, in the doldrums; under these circumstances, it did not seem to be a hardship. The ship Loch Vennachar had lent sidelights; the bright green of the starboard and the rich red of the port lights gave a realistic touch to the scene. A landing stage supported a number of life buoys, whilst oars and many other yacht fixings were artistically arranged at each side. A ship's bell hung from above, and "eight bells" was struck before the first dance commenced.

Numerous flags hung from all parts of the hall, and huge masses of wattle blossom were arranged on each window-sill. A large mirror was conspicuously placed, and how the gentlemen clustered around it (but then gold buttons do look fetching), and on the walls were pictures of yachts and yachting scenes commemorative of cruise time. The supper room was lavishly decorated with lovely flowers. The catering had been done by the ladies in their usual efficient manner." **Williamstown Chronicle, 14 September 1895**

Such social gatherings were commonplace for the well-known sea captains of the Loch and Ben Lines. Often it was here, in these less formal settings, that business deals were discussed and bargains and contracts arranged. It was a poor captain indeed who did not have a few investments and deals underway. Often they would be part owners and underwriters of the ships they sailed on. Many, like William Hawkins, had business interests in other shipping companies as well.

To live a good life in retirement, a ship's captain had to make more money than his commission and sea-going wages provided. The quicker he could load and get underway, often the more valuable his cargo. The captain would take a percentage of the value of the freight rates and fares paid by passengers, but if times were lean, then other income sources had to be explored, and ship's captains were notorious commercial gamblers and speculators. This increased especially when the businesses of crimping and 'slops chests' were curtailed by government regulations.

The clipper was floated into Alfred Graving Dock for her regular scrape, clean and painting with anti-fouling agents and sent back across to the Railway Pier on the 11th. The Loch Vennachar finally upped anchor on the 13th October 1895, loaded with wool and other general cargo. She was hauled out through the Heads by the steam tug Racer at 8:00 am, and put to sea with a favourable breeze running, giving her a fine start for the run home.

Cape Horn was doubled along the 57th parallel on November 8th in company with the ship Cambrian King, and crossed the equator on December 2nd, 50 days out. They spoke to the Danish barque Cimbria at 15° north, 33° west, on December 12th, and entered the approaches to the English Channel on the 29th. A tug was picked up west of St Catherine's Point on December 30th, 78 days from Port Phillip Bay. It was not

Loch Vennachar anchored and drying sails in Hobson's Bay.
State library of Victoria.

Shipping at Port Adelaide, circa 1880s.
State Library of South Australia.

a record, but was one of the fastest passages of the season, especially arriving in the Channel during the middle of a fog-bound winter storm. She passed Deal on New Year's Eve and made her Tilbury Fort mooring just before midnight on the 31st of December 1895. After passing customs and pratique inspections, the Loch Vennachar once again entered London Dock to discharge. She spent a month in port before setting off behind a tug bound for Glasgow on January 28th, and arrived at the Tail-o-the-Bank on February 2nd 1896.

The clipper was slated to take cargo until February 26th; the vessel also needed new sails and cordage. For this James Aitken had contracted the Edinburgh Roperie and Sailcloth Company based in Broomielaw. She had lost a number of sails during the previous runs to and from Australia and, though expensive, the Loch Vennachar was deserving of the best. Bolts of canvas and spools of hemp rope were delivered to the clipper whilst she was berthed alongside Queens Dock.

The company in charge of loading was P. Henderson & Co., who also held shares in the parent company and in the Loch Vennachar as well. It was Henderson's who supplied the pig-iron ballast and many of the steel and iron products much in demand in the colonies. It was a useful partnership with James Aitken that had earned the Henderson and the Aitken families much profit over the years. The company stevedores completed loading the clipper by March 1st and the Loch Vennachar was cleared out for Greenock the same day.

The Loch Vennachar was towed down the Clyde from her Tail o' the Bank anchorage on March 5th 1896 at 1:30 pm. She released her tow that evening and sailed straight into dirty weather as the clipper coasted down St George's Channel as far as Tuskar, which was reached finally on the 8th of March. Stormy weather continued until the northeast trades were picked up on the 28th parallel. The winds were light all the way to the equator which was crossed on April 3rd. The light and variable conditions kept the ship becalmed for two more days when the southeast trades swept in, carrying the Loch Vennachar on light breezes all the way across the tropics. Finally the Greenwich meridian was crossed along the 37th parallel on April 27th when fresh to moderate winds carried the clipper southeast as she passed below the Cape of Good Hope.

Strong gales and heavy seas were encountered. Stormy winds and seas continued all the way to the meridian of Cape Leeuwin when east and northeast winds made for slow progress all the way to Adelaide. She dropped anchor off of the Semaphore at 2 pm on June 4th 1896. After discharging her 900 tons of cargo at Port Adelaide, she set forth again for Melbourne on the 10th, arriving on the 16th having battled strong north-easterly winds all the way to the Heads. Aboard was her usual collection of iron assortments, beers, ales, rum, whisky, port wine, semolina, soda, cornflour, paint, firebricks, paper, red lead, twine, and a variety of loose merchandise.

Whilst in port, Captain Bennett and his friends met to discuss the problems of finding decent English-speaking Able Seamen with enough skills and experience to allow ships in the British Merchant Fleet with English-speaking officers to safely put to sea. It was his opinion that the average merchant crew of the mid-nineties was made up of 15 Norwegians, six Finns, three Greeks, 2 Africans, and an Indian or Malay. He proposed setting up a school under Marine Board Guidance that will teach the new multinational sailors what they need to know to be part of a foc's'le crew. Amongst the proposed subjects were advanced seamanship, advanced English essential for life aboard ship, rope work and knots, and elementary sewing and carpentry.

It was proposed that every element of seamanship be taught by competent experts. The captains felt that if the merchant navy is to survive then such schools were desperately needed. On the 30th of September 1896, Captain Bennett along with 14 other master mariners went to Government House to meet with the Lord of the Admiralty's representative Lord Brassey, to discuss the growing problem of a lack of English-speaking Able Seamen and the growing numbers of non-English-speaking sailors found amongst merchant crews coming out from England. This shortage threatened to have a serious effect on the Royal Navy in the event of Britain going to war:

"Captain Bennett, of the Loch Vennachar, had prepared a paper, and this was the basis of discussion. Captain Bennett stated, and in this all present were agreed, that the abolition of the system of apprenticeship for sailors, and the rating of A.B.'s, had much to do with the difficulty of getting British AB's of the old stamp, though the men were physically as good as ever. Virtually the old school had disappeared with the abolition of apprentices. Many of the foreigners were excellent seamen, but their ignorance of English was a drawback, and in a crisis might be a serious matter. Captain Bennett suggested the adoption of the idea favoured in other countries of limiting the number of foreign sailors on each outgoing ship. The Board of Trade regulations as to manning erred in being under the mark for sailing vessels and the following scales were suggested: 1,000 tons 24 hands all told, 1,500 tons 30 hands, 2,000 tons 35 hands, 2,500 and up to 3,000 tons 40 hands. The best men, it was admitted, now went into the steamboats and special inducements were given them to stay there." **The Argus, 1 October 1896.**

Captain Bennett's words echoed the concerns of many shipowners, captains and those in the armed forces; his words had a terribly prophetic quality about them on so many levels. His foreboding sense of disaster, at least for those who would sail aboard the Loch Vennachar, was something beyond even Bill Bennett's far-sighted ken.

The ship was hauled out from her berth at Williamstown alongside the barque Itata, both of which were scheduled to depart early the next morning. Both ships were bound for London and a friendly wager was placed by the captains. The Loch Vennachar and Itata left Melbourne on the morning of the 17th of October.

The run across the South Pacific was relatively uneventful with distant icebergs being sighted west of Cape Horn. The island of Diego Ramirez was sighted on November 17th, 33 days out. The following day they fell into company with the barque John Lockett, homeward bound from Iquique laden with Chilean nitrate, sailing to Falmouth for orders.

The barque 'Itata' at Bristol.
State Library of Queensland.

The run from the Horn was relatively quiet until they began the run into the Western Approaches on January 8th. The winds were fresh to strong easterlies with frequent squalls and rising seas.

It was during these trying conditions that another vessel, the barque Carla Bauer, out of Rostock, began to take on water. Her master, Captain Otto, directed his crew to do what they could to try and find the leak and plug it. The 962-ton iron barque had been built in 1865 by Denny & Rankin at Dumbarton. The vessel had seen long and hard service as the Duke of Athole before being sold to German interests in 1889. On this voyage she had set sail from Punta Arenas, Chile, heavily laden with a cargo of cedar and mahogany (*Nothofagus Nervosa*).

Her last Lloyd's survey had been in 1889, but since then she had been worked hard as a timber drogher carrying valuable loads of timber from South America to Europe. Ports had been cut in her bow to facilitate the loading of boards and logs. In the trying weather conditions where the Carla Bauer had been bashing her way north through the howling north-easterly gales and huge seas off the Bay of Biscay, one of the timber ports had sprung a serious leak which the crew had trouble stemming.

The Carla Bauer had been in a collision with another vessel back in 1895 and had taken considerable damage on her starboard bow, which had resulted in the barque taking on a lot of water. Towed into Portsmouth and allowed to settle on the mud, the hole in her bow had been temporarily repaired. It was through the starboard timber port and surrounding plates that had been patched after the previous collision that the water had begun to pour in.

Whilst the carpenter and his mates worked to stem the flow of water, other men were set to the pumps. They were old and had not been tended to since 1889. The load of timber had come with chips of wood, bark and other detritus that soon fouled the intakes of the pumps deep in the bilge. Soon both pumps became completely choked and the sea water coming through the leaking timber port could not be stopped.

Captain Wilhelm Otto knew they were in serious trouble as by the morning of January 12th there was almost six feet of water in the lower hold and the Carla Bauer was labouring heavily in the stormy conditions. The crew made preparations to abandon ship; the ensign was inverted and white distress rockets were fired off every hour. A number of vessels sailed within sight but none stopped to help. The lifeboats were swung out on the davits and water, provisions and navigation equipment were loaded aboard. By the morning of the 13th the barque was well down in the water, her decks awash. Yet the crew were not without hope, for sailing into view was another vessel under a full press of canvas heading straight for the foundering vessel.

The Loch Vennachar was up to the Carla Bauer in under two hours, her lookouts having seen the distress rocket. Coming up into the wind, the ship was hove to upwind of the foundering barque and a lifeboat was soon lowered and being rowed across to rescue the thankful crew. Captain Otto was the last to leave the sinking vessel, bringing with him the ship's papers, a sea bag of his most important possessions and the ship's cat.

Once aboard the Loch Vennachar, the exhausted Germans were shown to the saloon where the steward and Captain Bennett took care of the distressed sailors' immediate needs: blankets for warmth, hot coffee and food. The Loch Vennachar stayed hove to for a number of hours, Bill Bennett making sure that no other vessels accidentally collided with the sinking ship. The Carla Bauer finally went down on January 13th at 48° 7' north, 10° 49' west. As she disappeared below the waves, Captain Bennett made a note of the sinking in his log and the Loch Vennachar once again got underway.

The Lizard light was sighted in the early evening of January 19th 1897 and Captain Bennett signalled his vessel's arrival as they passed Lizard light at 7:29 pm. He let it be known that he had survivors from the German ship Carla Bauer aboard. It was cold and dull with low visibility, east to north-east winds and showers. Captain Bennett ordered sail reduced and burned a blue flare at the foremast to attract the attention of a tug.

Heaving to off Start Point light, a pilot was soon welcomed aboard.

He took charge of the Loch Vennachar and allowed for the tug Shamrock to take the clipper under tow on the afternoon of the 20th. The weather was closing in and visibility was down to less than a mile under snow and sleet squalls, made worse by banks of mist. Winds increased from the north-east and strengthened, making for slow going up the Channel. The Shamrock and her charge passed Dungeness on the 22nd but found it almost impossible to progress much further.

The tug captain signalled the pilot aboard the Loch Vennachar that they would have to take shelter from the wind, her coal supply running seriously low. The clipper was towed into Sandgate Bay to wait out the north-east blow. Freezing temperatures and heavy snow had made life aboard for the crews of both vessels all but impossible. Those aboard the clipper simply did not have enough Arctic weather gear to enable them to perform duties asked of them by Captain Bennett and his officers.

Strong to gale force winds and heavy snowfalls followed for the next 48 hours. Yet snugged down in the lee of the hills of the Folkestone Downs, the Shamrock and Loch Vennachar lay safely at anchor until the arrival of a second tug, the Blazer of London, which was soon alongside to guide the clipper as the Shamrock again took up the tow. The harsh conditions continued throughout the 24th, forcing the pilot to have their tugs take the ship into Deal. Safely tucked in behind the Goodwin Sands for the evening, the trio set off again on the afternoon of January 25th, finally arriving off Tilbury Fort on the morning of the 26th.

The crew of the Carla Bauer stayed aboard the Loch Vennachar until she was berthed at 10 East Dock in London Dock. They were then taken to the Seamen's Mission and treated as distressed sailors. Soon the hatches were broached and her valuable wool cargo unloaded and sent to the warehouses of the London Wool Exchange on Coleman Street in time for the first Colonial wool sale of the year on Monday February 10th 1897. The prices realised for the Victorian wool were between 5 to 7

The 962 ton barque Carla Bauer of Rostock (formerly the Duke of Atholl). Built by Denny & Rankin, Dumbarton in 1865.
State Library of Queensland.

pence per pound, 1 penny per pound better than the previous year.

With a crew of runners aboard and the first mate in command, the Loch Vennachar was hauled out from London Dock and shifted down to Gravesend from where she set sail on February 21st. She arrived at Greenock on the 27th and her hatches were immediately lifted and the hold cleaned out ready to take in the next cargo for Melbourne.

After such a turbulent decade of falling trade income, low passenger numbers and increasing difficulties in filling the hold with worthwhile cargoes and finding adequate numbers of skilled sailors, the clipper's return journey to Australia was one Captain Bennett and the Loch Line owners could have done without. On board the vessel were several passengers, all of whom were very grateful to Captain Bennett and his crew for getting them safely to port after a harrowing journey.

The clipper had a full hold of general cargo that was soon transshipped to waiting trains from the Government Railway Pier. Those on board were Messrs W. McReadie, W. Bowie Jnr, James Hume, W.A. Macara, G. Pettigrew, G. McDonald, R. Watson and G.W. Russel. The Loch Vennachar had left Glasgow on the 2nd of April 1897 and stopped at Greenock to take on the last of her passengers and gunpowder.

Captain Bennett decided to take his usual course around the north coast of Ireland. Fresh west to southwest winds carried the clipper south at a fast pace all the way through the trade latitudes. From 40 degrees north, winds became light and variable all the way to the equator, which was crossed on April 29th. The southeast trades were picked up the following day and stayed moderate from there on.

The Loch Vennachar passed beneath the Cape of Good Hope on the 24th of May as she crossed the 39th parallel. From that point on, unsettled weather closed in about the ship as storm clouds gathered upon the horizon. As she began her easting run, violent thunderstorms put on spectacular lightning displays presaging the trouble to come. Stormy squalls were frequent as seas continued to rise.

However, it was not until the 6th of June that the Loch Vennachar's legendary toughness came to the fore. A violent gale swept down from the north as the ship ran her easting down along the 42nd parallel. The winds swung round to the south and increased as the storm cell passed over the area of ocean that the vessel was crossing. Cyclonic winds brought heaving seas as violent winds pushed the clipper scudding along the 43rd parallel.

She passed north of Amsterdam Island as the decks were pounded by huge waves. The ship was constantly awash with foaming green water. One of the boats was smashed in by a large wave which also took with it the break of the poop, the pigs and chickens and anything else loose upon the deck. Captain Bennett shortened sail and at times ran the ship under almost bare poles as the storms pushed the Loch Vennachar rapidly along.

There were very real concerns that the ship may founder and, except for the crew, none aboard were tempted to stroll the decks. One sailor escaped certain death when he was swept from the deck by a huge wave that washed over the ship. The unfortunate sailor was only saved when he was washed into the main braces and pinned there by the force of the wave. When the white water had passed, his incredulous shipmates hauled him back aboard.

Once conditions moderated, all sail was set as rapid progress was made between the 38th and 43rd parallels. Cape Leeuwin was passed on June 16th as she turned northeast. She arrived in Port Adelaide on the 24th of June after just 81 days at sea. After unloading her cargo, she sailed for Melbourne on June 30th, arriving in Hobson's Bay on the 3rd of July. She unloaded her passengers and cargo and was then hauled back down the Yarra to Williamstown Pier for repairs.

Much of the deck furniture had to be repaired or replaced, as did one of the ship's boats and many of her sails. After a refit, Captain Bennett had the clipper floated into the Alfred Graving Dock for her usual clean and paint. Once completed, the Loch Vennachar was again towed off to Williamstown to finish her loading. The Loch Vennachar left Port Melbourne on 24th October bound for London, finally arriving on the 24th January 1898. Thankfully for all aboard and with financial connections to the ship, her return run was met with fair winds and light seas for much of the journey home.

In contrast to previous years, the luck of the Loch Vennachar held good in terms of both income and journeys; 1898 was eventless and profitable. The clipper weighed anchor from Greenock on the 15th of March bound for Melbourne via Adelaide, being towed down river by the tug Hercules. Gale force west to southwest winds and a falling tide forced the tug to bring its charge into Belfast Lough on March 17th until the 19th, when winds shifted to the northwest and moderated enough to allow the Hercules to once more get under way.

The Loch Vennachar bid farewell to the tug once both vessels had cleared the Lough's outer limits as Captain Bennett set his ship's course south by south west, sailing down St George's Channel ahead of a blustery nor'wester. The Cape Verde Islands were passed on the inside channel on March 30th and she signalled a passing steamer and asked to be reported all well on April 2nd.

The northeast trade winds were fallen in with in 28° north, but they proved light, and the equator was crossed on the 14th April. The southeast trades were picked up 3° south of the line, but these likewise were feeble. The prime meridian was passed on the 12th May along the 38th parallel as the Loch Vennachar began to run her easting down under light easterly winds. During the easting run, which was made on the 39th parallel, the wind was almost continuously from the southeast.

Cape Leeuwin was passed on June 11th and, thanks to the light sou'easterlies, it took ten days to reach Cape Borda. Sailing up St Vincent Gulf, the Loch Vennachar dropped anchor off Semaphore signal station on June 21st 1898, after a laborious 94 days at sea. She had two saloon passengers aboard who took the opportunity to step ashore for a few days whilst a portion of the cargo was unloaded.

The ship was hauled out from McLaren Dock on Sunday the 26th and the clipper romped on down the gulf and out through Backstairs Passage, a bone in her teeth as the freshening sou'wester pushed the Loch Vennachar towards Port Phillip Bay, a voyage made in under 72 hours. She passed the Otway light at 2:30pm on the 28th of June, and Port Phillip Heads were cleared early the next morning.

The clipper ship Salamis in Alfred Graving Dock. Circa 1890.
SLV Collection.

She was towed up to her berth in Port Melbourne. Captain Bennett spent time ashore visiting friends, yet he was in no particular hurry to return home. He and his wife had become estranged and Bill spent little time at home in Chatham. Upon discharge of the last of the cargo, the ship was floated into Alfred Graving Dock for her regular maintenance before being shifted down to Williamstown to load wheat and wool for the London markets.

Captain Bennett, a keen shooter, spent his time at Geelong participating in a number of shooting competitions and also at his property down on the Mornington Peninsula. Laden with more than 4000 bags of wheat and as many bales of fine

Merino wool, the Loch Vennachar was cleared out from Williamstown Pier on August 24th and was towed out through the Heads on the 26th. The ship was sailing into promising financial times; a bumper wheat harvest and strong wool prices in London guaranteed that when the ship arrived back in London, she would turn a handsome profit for her backers.

The run home across the Southern Ocean and around Cape Horn was a rough one, the Loch Vennachar encountering heavy weather for much of the run. Icebergs were encountered as they doubled Cape Horn, at 58° south, 69° west. Most of the bergs were small growlers, but they stretched as far as the eye could see, and the ship clawed her way west battling a rare easterly gale which brought sleet and heavy snowfalls. The largest berg encountered was more than 300 feet high and almost a mile in length. Yet despite the dangers, their passage was relatively quick.

The run up through the South Atlantic was without major incident and the equator was crossed on the 12th, 50 days from Melbourne. A pilot was taken aboard on November 16th off the Isle of Wight, and the tug Columbia was engaged off Eastbourne to tow the clipper up to Gravesend the following morning. The voyage came to a successful end two days later when the Loch Vennachar entered London Dock and was tied up alongside the west quay to discharge her cargo.

Captain Bennett stayed with his ship during her stay in London, his wife Mary Ann no longer on speaking terms with him. After 20 years of marriage, Bill was no longer welcome in his own home. In fact, when he had returned home, William had found his former home empty, his wife and children having moved to a very nice three-storey home on The Avenue, West Ealing, London. Two of Bill's sons, Jack and Harry, had become seamen. Harry had served under his father aboard the Loch Vennachar on a number of voyages, whilst Jack was an apprentice aboard a steamer, wanting to become a ship's engineer.

1899 promised to be another bumper year for the Loch Vennachar's backers and her parent company, the Glasgow

Mary Ann Bennett's home in The Avenue, West Ealing, London.

Harry Bennett, aged 21, ship's apprentice.

Shipping Company. The clipper set forth on yet another trip at the height of the Scottish winter on February 25th, outward bound for Adelaide and Melbourne.

She was delayed at Greenock by fierce storms until 4 March, when she finally set sail into a freshening gale that drove her west around Ireland, then south into moderating winds and seas. The edge of the continental shelf was crossed on March 10th, and the further south she sailed, the calmer the winds became, until the equator was crossed on April 9th.

The south-east trades carried the Loch Vennachar onwards as she sailed south to the 20th parallel, where they fell away and conditions became light and rather ordinary. Her easting was run down along the 42nd parallel and, for almost the entire trip, fine weather and light winds prevailed. Captain Bennett and the crew could do nothing to speed along the ship's painfully slow progress across the Southern Ocean.

Cape Borda was passed on June9th and she dropped anchor at the semaphore early the next day, 98 days from the Tail-of-the-Bank. Upon arriving in Adelaide, Captain Bennett and his crew were shocked and dismayed to learn of the demise of the Loch Sloy, which on April 24th had run aground off the south-west corner of Kangaroo Island with the loss of all but three lives.

The story of the wreck of the Loch Sloy was one that could have happened to many a ship's master, especially one unfamiliar with the ship under his command and the currents and geographical conditions of the coast he was approaching. When the ship ran aground, stern first upon the Brothers at the tip of Cape Du Couedic, she was swept clean by the pounding waves; then, upon snapping her keel, she settled diagonally down the sloping face of the reef, her stern visible just six metres below the surface.

The four men washed ashore: passenger David Kilpatrick, Able Seamen William Mitchell and Duncan McMillan, and apprentice William John Simpson, were washed ashore within a few metres of each other. With nothing but a few bottles of whisky and a can of herrings, they scaled the cliffs in search of

The barque Loch Sloy, 1898 Port Melbourne.
State Library of Victoria.

Apprentice William John Simpson.

help. Eventually, the three sailors were rescued by local residents and taken to Cape Borda lighthouse.

David Kilpatrick had been abandoned with the intent of rescuing him later, but he wandered off from his resting place, dying of exposure before he could be found. The lighthouse keepers recovered a number of bodies that were then buried near where they were found.

The survivors were eventually taken to Adelaide by government steamer. The ensuing Marine Board enquiry found Captain Peter Nichol negligent and forced him to shoulder most of the blame. The survivors eventually found their way onto other ships; Willie Simpson was taken aboard the Loch Vennachar whilst she was docked in Adelaide, and he went on to complete his apprenticeship aboard the clipper.

The Loch Sloy's cargo was valued at £30,000,' but when the ship and her cargo were offered up for salvage, only £36 was realised. Salvors managed to retrieve little of the cargo, and the waters were too rough for divers to successfully retrieve any of the galvanised iron sheets that the ship was carrying when she went down. A relief fund was established for the families of those lost, and more than £350 was raised.

Of more importance than the possible salvage of a lost cargo, the loss of which pushed insurance premiums up by 25% for the Australian runs, was the discussion of the placement of a new lighthouse. The two possible locations were Cape du Couedic and South Neptune Island. Captain Bennett's opinion carried a lot of weight in this matter. William Bennett stated that:

'Undoubtedly the Neptunes would be by far the better position. A light on Cape du Couedic would in my opinion only increase the danger. It would no doubt be of service to vessels coming here from Tasmania or New Zealand, but for boats from the United Kingdom or the Continent it would be of no practical use, but rather, as I have remarked, it might do harm. A vessel from those ports would not want to go so far south as to need the guide of a light placed there. My experience in trading here, and it is of many years' standing, is that on the Neptunes the light would be in the right place. A light of a twenty miles radius would put a vessel almost in the middle of Investigator Strait.'

Asked if he would care to express an opinion as to the probable cause of the disaster to the Loch Sloy, Captain Bennett said:

"The Cape Borda light presents a difficulty to the mariner, and in bad weather it is often obscured by the clouds passing over it. It is situated on very high land, whereas if it were lower it could be more clearly and readily seen. I have been close to it before seeing it, and on one occasion I was right underneath it. I prefer to take Althorpe Island light as a guide rather than Borda. In the case of the Loch Sloy it is evident that when the Borda light was expected to show up the vessel was some eighteen miles south of Cape Borda, altogether out of the range of the light. To my mind the chronometers must have been between twenty-five and thirty miles out to have placed the vessel in such a position. At 4 o'clock on that particular morning it appears to me that the extremity of the thirty-mile range of the light should have come into view, but at that time the Loch Sloy was off Cape de Couedic. The position of the vessel was some miles eastward of the line where the light from Cape Borda is cut off." **South Australian Register, 13 June 1899.**

Of the cause of the wreck of the Loch Sloy he was equally forceful in his opinion, an opinion backed by having made more than 40 voyages through the same waters as both an apprentice and as a ship's master:

"There can be no doubt,' said Captain Bennett, 'that Captain Nichol got out of his reckoning. It is so easy to do. Why, I have here the record of the observations of my instruments for the last eight or ten voyages, and they agree in no two instances. I find that, though I have a Sir William Thompson's compass, and carry two of the best chronometers obtainable, I get out in my reckoning. Of course there is no opportunity permitted for this to run the vessel into danger, for a thoroughly systematic record, doubly checked, is made of every movement, so to speak, of the vessel.

That this is so can be seen from a glance at the columns of neatly recorded observations and the results of working them out. Even with all these precautions, with the best instruments, variations will be discovered. The motto which evidently prompts Captain Bennett is, 'It is better to be safe than sorry,' but, as he says, 'Misfortune will overtake the best. It does not matter how excellent a sailor a man may be, he is still liable, from some unthought-of cause, to meet with disaster. Tersely speaking, the accident to the Loch Sloy probably occurred through a slight error in the instruments, or the set of a current causing the vessel to get out of her course." **The Advertiser, 14 June 1899.**

Captain Bennett's words had a prophetic quality, and it would not be too long before he was proved correct about so many in his assumptions, yet so very wrong where it really mattered. Captain Bennett's worry over the fate of the Loch Sloy, or his interviews with newspaper reporters, did not prevent him from maintaining a tight rein over his crew.

On the 15th of June 1899, two sailors, William Heathwood and John Anderson, were tried for the theft of two bottles of whisky from the cargo carried by the Loch Vennachar. Both men had been found drunk on duty by the first officer, John Driscoll, and were charged with the theft of the two bottles, even though they were suspected of pilfering much more. John Anderson was proven innocent, whilst Heathwood, upon being found guilty, was sentenced to a month's hard labour and ordered to pay 36s in legal costs.

After the Marine Board enquiry into the sinking of the Loch Sloy, it was decided that a new light would be built on South Neptune Island. The Board justified the expense by examining their records of inbound passengers and crew that had passed through Investigator Strait in the 5 years prior to the loss of the Loch Line barque:

Year	Number of Persons
1894	80,000
1895	90,000
1896	125,000
1897	133,000
1898	114,000

It was estimated that the number of people passing the Neptunes in the 12 months ending June 30th, 1908, was more than 143,000 people.

With William Simpson safely ensconced in the mid-deck apprentices' quarters, the Loch Vennachar set sail for Melbourne on the 17th of June 1899, arriving after 5 days of contrary winds on the 2nd of July. With so much attention upon Captain Bennett and the Loch Vennachar after the Loch Sloy enquiry, Captain Bennett was interviewed on the 3rd of July about his experiences at sea, and in particular, the first time he saw an iceberg:
Icebergs and Sailing Ships

Terrors of the Sea

"It was the voyage after we had been dismasted in that hurricane off Mauritius and we were in lat. 52 S., and long. 52.20 W., off the Falkland Isles, when I first saw an iceberg, though I have seen many since. The ship was bowling along with all sails set, and though the night was thick and dirty, the moon showed out in occasional glimpses. At midnight the second officer, who was in charge of the watch on the deck, ran down and reported to me that there was a large steamer to the leeward of us.

I asked him how he knew that it was a steamer, and he told me that she must be a big liner, for he could see all her lights burning. I went up on deck, and looked out to leeward, and sure enough, about two miles off, I saw a row of lights that shone with peculiar brilliancy. It looked like a steamer at first, but I was not satisfied, so I put the helm up and ran down to see her at close quarters.

As we neared the lights, I saw that the object was an iceberg about 200 ft high and about 1,200 ft long. What we took to be lights were the reflections of the moon on the points and facets of the polished ice, where the overflowing snow and drift had broken away and exposed the clearer surface beneath. It was a wonderfully beautiful and mysterious sight, and one that I shall never forget.

On the following night, which was March 28, 1883, I was walking the deck with the chief officer at half past 9 o'clock, and I remarked to him that it was cold enough for ice to be about. I had hardly said this when the man on the lookout on the fo'c'sle head sang out, 'A bright light right ahead!' I told the chief officer to go forward and try if he could make it out, because we could not see it from the poop. I remember telling him that it must be a man-o'-war, because merchant steamers bound east always go up on the inside of the Falklands or else through the Straits of Magellan.

It was a clear moonlit night and the mate sang out that he could see a large bright light some distance off and right ahead. Almost at the same moment the lookout man sang out, 'Ice right ahead! Hard up!' The man at the wheel put the helm up instantly and the ship grazed along the edge of a great mass of table-ice which stood 6 ft out of the water and was fully a quarter mile long. We missed it by only a few feet.

We still saw the bright light ahead and soon made out what it was. There was an immense iceberg in front of us about 150 ft high and half a mile in length. The greater part of the surface was of frozen snow that was bluish white in the moonlight, but the upper corner of the edge that was nearest to us had broken off, leaving a large flat surface of transparent ice exposed. The ice was as clear as crystal, and it collected the moonbeams and reflected them with a marvellous brilliancy.

We guessed what we were in for then, and during the remainder of the night it was nothing but port and starboard to get clear of the icebergs that were all around us. I put the thermometer overboard, but it was very little help as a guide, for the sea was not appreciably colder than one would expect in the direct drift of an iceberg. I reported having met icebergs when I got home, and at the request of the Board of Trade authorities, I furnished them with a special memo on the subject, as they said it was the first time they had heard of icebergs at night being mistaken for steamers with their lights burning.

On my next voyage out to Australia in 1894, I had also a very anxious time. We fell in with ice to the southward of Tristan da Cunha, and near that island I saw ten large icebergs. They were quite black on the top, and had evidently capsized from their original position, turning upwards the part which had formerly been embedded in the cliffs of the southern continent. We also passed quantities of floe ice melting.

The huge pieces of floating ice were shaped into all sorts of strange forms, and to port and starboard of us we could see great cathedrals, with the sun shining on their pinnacles, and castles with glistening gates and ramparts. One floe was exactly

Loch Rannoch striking an ice berg, a danger common to south bound clippers that claimed at least two Loch Liners and damaged several others.
State Library of Victoria

like a picture that I once saw of a Pharaoh's chariot and horses, and there it was forging slowly through the water, with the seas breaking on the weather side of it and throwing up fountains of spray that made the most beautiful rainbows in the sunlight.

The night set in very thick and foggy, and I kept all hands on deck, for I knew that we might strike ice at any moment. I had the boats hauled out ready for lowering and the ship was doing four or five knots all night. It was terribly cold and we could see nothing six ships' lengths off. In the morning the fog lifted and I found that the old ship had found her way cleverly through the icebergs.

We had gone straight through a fleet of them in the fog without seeing a single one, and when the weather cleared we saw three big bergs on our port hand and two on our starboard hand. They were covered in glistening frozen snow and were all about 150 ft high, rising out of the water just like enormous cones of white loaf sugar.

Going home the same year, we passed two ice islands on December 2nd in Lat. 58.25 S., and Long. 70 deg. W. They were fully three miles long and were floating side by side, with a space of only 200 yards between them. I saw ice almost every voyage after that, and on November 2, 1897, when we were looking out for the Antipodes Islands, the mate reported land ahead. I knew from the log that we could not have made the islands in that time, and I was a bit puzzled, but I soon found out that it was an ice island.

It was three miles long and 200 ft high, and it was lying about 15 miles southwest of the Antipodes. Luckily we came upon it in broad daylight and had plenty of time to get out of the way. There's more ice met in running in the Australian trade than many people imagine. The Loch Laggan, bound from Liverpool to Melbourne, was posted as missing in 1874 and has never been heard of since. She is supposed to have struck ice.

The Loch Maree is believed to have shared the same fate, and most of all the sailing ships in the trade have had more or less narrow escapes. Why, one of our vessels actually passed over the submerged part of an iceberg and just missed the portion which was above the water. I suppose the biggest iceberg ever seen was the one sighted by a number of vessels in the South Atlantic Ocean in 1855. It was in the form of a hook, the longer shank being 60 miles in length, while the shorter was 40 miles.

This huge hook was a terrible trap for outbound Australian ships and several got caught in it. Most of the ships that got embayed in it succeeded in getting clear, but the emigrant ship Guiding Star struck the ice in the hook and was lost with all hands." **The Argus, Wednesday 5 July 1899.**

The year to date had not been one that filled Captain Bennett with much joy. He had lost a fellow captain, albeit one he little knew; he had spent a lot of time talking to reporters and the Marine Board about ways to prevent further mishaps like the ones that had claimed the Mars, Emily Smith, the Duncow, and now the Loch Sloy; and he had one of his sailors thrown into prison for theft.

So it was with relief that the Loch Vennachar finally left Hobson's Bay on the 15th of August with a hold filled with lesser quality wool and other low-value cargo. The Isles of Scilly were sighted on November 13th, then passed St Catherine's Point behind a tug the following afternoon. Tug and clipper reached Deal on the morning of November 15th before reaching Tilbury Fort anchorage on the 16th of November 1899.

The ship was entered into London Dock on the 18th to discharge, her first mate John Driscoll being left in charge of the ship whilst she was unloaded before being shifted into London Graving Dock for her annual inspection and repairs. Bill Bennett left his officers and the apprentices, including the shipwrecked William Simpson, to look after the vessel. Once back at her London Dock berth, those still aboard the Loch Vennachar were permitted to travel home for Christmas.

XI

That Sinking Feeling

January 5th 1900 saw the survey and repairs completed and the ship moved back to the West India Dock basin. John Driscoll arrived back in London in time to take charge of the clipper as she was taken back to Gravesend on January 14th, from where she was towed back to sea the following morning. The crew of runners who had worked aboard the Loch Vennachar were paid off as she arrived at Greenock on January 23rd, and it was just the standing officers and apprentices who were still aboard when the clipper arrived back at Broomielaw.

**Clyde Shipping Co Tug Flying Buzzard,
built 1895 by Rankin & Blackmore, Greenock.**

The Loch Vennachar again weighed anchor on the 26th of February 1900, being towed to the head of the Firth of Clyde by the tug Flying Buzzard. The tug was farewelled on Tuesday the 27th off the Calf of Man at the height of a north-easterly gale.

256

The dirty weather continued as she sailed down the Irish Channel. Strong winds and rain squalls dogged the clipper as she pushed south until the northeast trades were picked up along the 28th parallel. The clipper sailed past the Cape Verde Islands on the 12th of March amidst very light easterlies that carried her all the way to the equator, which was crossed on March 23rd.

On the following day, the southeast trades were picked up that carried her quickly south. She crossed the Greenwich meridian on April 14th and, upon reaching the Southern Ocean, she raced east, passing below Cape Leeuwin on May 14th. Light easterlies continued as the Loch Vennachar tacked northeast. Cape Borda was passed at 8 am on the 27th of May and she dropped anchor off the Semaphore at midnight the same day, ending a journey of 90 days at sea.

The trip was marked by the fact that fine conditions had followed the ship for the entire passage and not one gale was encountered once out of the Irish Channel. Only one vessel was spoken before the last port was reached: the 803-ton barque Beech Holme, of Napoli, in latitude 38.45 degrees south and longitude 82.16 1/2 degrees, which was bound from Marseilles to Adelaide and was 100 days out.

Whilst in Port Adelaide, Captain Bennett was presented with two watercolours of the Loch Vennachar from the time when she was dismasted in Mauritius. These he quietly hung in his cabin, along with various other pictures from his travels. In the skylight of the main cabin were Bill Bennett's many pot plants. It was the perfect place to put them. With direct access to sunlight, they were protected from the weather and seawater that frequently flooded the poop cabins, wired in place.

After discharging a portion of her cargo, the Loch Vennachar was shifted back out to the Semaphore anchorage on June 2nd and set sail the following morning.

The clipper passed through Port Phillip Heads before dawn on June 8th, and the pilot sailed her up the Western Channel into Port Phillip Bay. A tug then shifted the clipper into Hobson's Bay and she was berthed at the Victoria Dock. The vessel's cargo of coffee, along with several tons of general hardware

Watercolour of the 1892 dismasting of the Loch Vennachar during an Indian Ocean cyclone.

Captain bennet and his apprentices (William Simpson of the Loch Sloy standing directly behind Bill Bennett) aboard the Loch Vennachar, Port Melbourne. 1900.

and pig iron, was unloaded and transshipped to various merchant warehouses along the docks.

Whilst in port, Bill Bennett attended a benefit dinner to raise money for the Victorian soldiers currently fighting overseas in South Africa as part of Britain's war against the Boers, who were fighting for their independence. The gathering was organised by the A.N.A., one of the most powerful and influential organisations in the country at the time, serving a unique dual purpose as both a "friendly society" and a political engine room for Australian nationalism. It was held in the supper room of the Hawthorn Town Hall.

Amongst the guests present were members of parliament, Simon Fraser and J.A. Isaacs; Dr Adams, the Mayor of Hawthorn; Mr Robinson, the clerk of the Legislative Assembly; J. Hamilton, clerk of the Victorian Railways; and Captain Bennett. There were many others gathered to hear the recently returned war correspondent of the Herald and Weekly Times, Major William Thomas Reay. He was a Major in the Victorian Mounted Rifles. The Major talked about the conduct of Australian troops in the roles fighting the Boers in Bloemfontein.

Later, Captain Bennett wrote a lengthy description of the life of an apprentice aboard the Loch Vennachar in reply to an article that appeared in The Herald.

"Captain W. H. Bennett, master of the ship Loch Vennachar, at present in the Victoria Dock, forwards us a lengthy letter on the subject of apprentices, in reply to the article published in Thursday's "Herald" from the pen of Mr John Ebsworth. Captain Bennett writes:—

I was both interested and amused on reading the article in Thursday's "Herald" purporting to give an idea of the life of an apprentice in the mercantile marine. There is more amusement than instruction in the article, which is written with all the assurance of a man who knows, but who, in my opinion, has a deal to learn ere he can hope to pose successfully as the Sir Oracle of the mercantile service. I don't know Mr John Ebsworth, but I have been informed that he is the sailor-lawyer of this city. The amalgamation of these professions is not necessarily conducive to the strictest accuracy, though it may endow a person with a semblance of authority to speak and write on the subject of the sea and those who go down to it in ships. Perhaps I may be permitted, as briefly as possible, to view some of the points raised in Mr Ebsworth's entertaining story, with the object of putting before your readers some facts gleaned in an experience of many years at sea and of many apprentices.

Of course, it is only natural that on arrival at port, after, say, three months at sea, the boys will turn out for their city jaunt in their best "riggery." Brass buttons, smart caps, neat boots, and well-cut clothes; so people think much of apprentices, and particularly of the young fellows dressed in the neat uniforms of the various ships when they turn out. Should any boys ever attend church from a ship if my help could not make a decent appearance? I should take care to bring this to their notice very promptly, because I believe that the ship master and officers are to some extent in the capacity of a parent to them. It is to my interest as well as that of the boys and their employers that they should be properly cared for. I think as a general fact that the appearance of the boys in their best clothes is as good as if an engineer or officer should walk in the clothes which he is accustomed to wear on Sundays and holidays.

Now, as to the duties of an apprentice. These must necessarily be of a varied character, according to the exigencies of the ship and the voyage. A boy sent to learn a trade must start to become an expert, learn at the bench—the very beginning of the trade. The apprentice's work, as a rule, commences in dock, where there are not any seamen on the ship. He has to make himself acquainted with the broom for sweeping the decks, with the proper methods of using a paint brush, and with the object of work he may expect to direct the operations in the future, when in the course of time he hopes to become an officer. It is a most essential part of the control of a vessel that she should be kept thoroughly clean and attractive to the eyes of all on board, and all of the members of a vessel's crew must work.

A lad who learns all this soon finds that when he is introduced to higher work, each task is but a long or a short bit. Mr Ebsworth talks about many uncommon things, such as that boys keep watch on the yards striking bells at half-hour intervals, and paying frequent visits to the binnacle clock, also and indirectly, coming out of the lazarette covered with sugar and molasses. This is truly a beautiful picture of the boy at sea, but it represents a sad lack of imagination on the part of Mr Ebsworth. I should have thought that in trying to impress upon your readers the horrors of this dread occupation, he would have risen to higher flights of fancy.

Seriously, it is ridiculous to say that an apprentice has to rely upon what the A.B.s choose to teach him in the lone hours of the watch. He is taken in hand from the beginning. He is made acquainted with the names and purposes of the running gear, the names of the sails, and the object in view when call is made and shortened; also, he is at times exercised at the wheel with a steersman, and learns the use of the compass and how to steer independent of assistance. All the boys I have had have acquired this art of steering within three months. The boys are certainly told off to grease the mizzen-topmast, top-gallant, and royal mast, and this is neither arduous nor dirty. Besides, it has its purpose, by accustoming them to being aloft, and in giving them the knowledge of the spars only to be gained by practical experience.

Mr Ebsworth says that during the first two years the apprentice has little time or inclination to study navigation or seamanship. I don't know what meaning your contributor puts upon these terms, but I have always understood that the work I have detailed is necessary to the education of a seaman, and part of it is essential to the making of a navigator. But my experience teaches me that the boy does, in the course of two years, acquire a good general knowledge of seamanship, and some of the apprentices I have had, after two years' training, have been very much better than A.B.s. I have at the present time a colonial lad who has been fifteen months at sea, and I am sure he is as good as any able seaman I have on board.

An apprentice's time counts from the day he signs his indentures until the expiry of the same. That means continuous service, and at the end of his term he will—if fit to be at sea at all in any capacity—then be able to pass his examination at once. On the other hand, the ordinary seaman has great difficulty in getting a ship, and during his periods of enforced absence from the sea, must endeavour to support himself in some way or other. The apprentices in the Loch Line, during the time the vessels are at home refitting or in dock, are well cared for in private lodgings at

Glasgow or the Sailors' Home in London, the expenses being borne by the owners.

Apprentices have twelve hours in every twenty-four while at sea, absolutely to themselves. Apportioning eight hours for sleep, it will be seen that they have four hours left at their disposal in which to study navigation. It depends largely upon the lad himself whether he will study diligently. If he is disposed to work, officers are always ready and willing to give what assistance they can. If provided by his friends with instruments and books, a large number of officers of my acquaintance are only too glad to point out and explain the use of the first and the intricacies of the second. No one can do anything with the boy who does not "graft," ashore or afloat, and he is bound to be the loser in the long run. The instructions from masters of the Loch Line are that apprentices are not to be permitted to be ill-used, and to be kept strictly to ship work only.

Mr Ebsworth says that the point in favour of the ordinary seaman is that he is paid from the start. So he is, £1 a month, as a rule, and not too good a time at that. He is generally the drudge of the ship, gets all the kicks and very few of the ha'pence. Now, the apprentice, in our line at any rate, pays £40 as premium, and gets £48 for the term of his four years' apprenticeship, also £2 8s per annum for washing. He is provided with separate and comfortable quarters, medical attendance and medicines when required, and should any accident or sickness befall him during his term, the owners are responsible for all expenses.

As an indication of what actually occurs, a son of Chief Officer Stein, of the Metropolitan Fire Brigade, served his apprenticeship with me, immediately afterwards got his second mate's certificate at the first exam, and is now an officer on an international liner. Mr Stein is so well pleased that he has entrusted another of his sons to the tender mercies of the Loch Line, reckless of the awful warnings so portentously uttered by Mr Ebsworth. He is not afraid that the lad will have to shoulder the spanker boom, do curtain rod drill, get doused with a bucket of sea water, or be subject to any other of the fearful and wondrous things so eloquently written about. Really, I cannot help thinking Mr Ebsworth has confused some stories with which he might have been familiar when he was a boy, and mistakenly brought them into the Herald as the facts." **The Herald 30 Jun 1900.**

Her return cargo was made up of 1400 bags of wheat, 4600 bags of flour, and many large bales of Australian-grown tobacco. This was a first for the Loch Liner and she and the Loch Ness drew much attention from tobacco buyers in London for the quality and quantity of the merchandise they'd brought from the Colonies.

The freight rates for tobacco were cheap enough for local growers to export it to London, and the Loch Line's owners were glad to have the new and hopefully lucrative contract to carry the dried bales of tobacco leaf.

The Loch Vennachar was cleared out from Hobson's Bay on July 14th and was towed down to Queenscliff. However, adverse winds delayed their departure until July 19th 1900 when the Loch Vennachar passed through the Rip. Captain Bennett, with William Simpson aboard for the second year of his apprenticeship, was at the helm.

It was raining with winds light and variable from the west as the Loch Vennachar passed Prawle Point on October 23rd. She was towed to Gravesend on the 25th and entered London Dock at the turn of the tide early the following morning.

Upon her arrival at the London Dock, Captain Bennett was met by a bailiff who handed him a summons from the Chancery Division of the High Court of Justice. The documents were not for him but for William John Simpson, apprentice aboard the Loch Vennachar. The papers demanded that he front up to the court of Justice Cozens-Hardy in a disputed will case. He had to take leave from his ship with accommodation arranged by the agents of Aitken & Lilburn in London.

The case in question was a dispute between Sophia Meyer, the aunt of Blanche Meyer-Edmunds, and Gertrude Leicester, Osmond's stepmother, and involved the disbursement of Blanche's estate, which amounted to more than £12,000. Captain Leicester had convinced a young and naive Blanche Edmonds that he was in love with her. The couple ran away to sea aboard the Loch Sloy to start a new life in Australia, with Blanche taking much of her wealth with her. In her will, Blanche stated that if Osmond outlived her, then all of her substantial wealth would pass to Captain Leicester (or his heirs). The hearing was adjourned several times until all parties involved could be brought together.

William appeared in court before Justice Hardy in mid-November, where he was asked to recount the events of the wreck of the Loch Sloy in all its grisly details. He was questioned at length about Captain Osmond Leicester and Blanche Edmonds's (she also went by the name Mary Meyer) actions during their final moments which amounted to their having climbed the mizzen mast and were still upon it when the mast fell into the sea.

He detailed the last time he had seen either person alive and described the eventual finding of their bodies; Blanche's within the wreckage and Osmond's on the beach a mile to the northwest of the wreck site. In his statement to the court, William Simpson stated:

"I was one of the men that clung to the mizzenmast. I saw Captain Leicester and the lady known as Mrs. Leicester at my elbow. A big wave came and smashed the mizzenmast, and swept it and us into the sea. As I came up first, I saw Mrs. Leicester struggling and screaming in the water, and I saw her face as it sank beneath the waves. The captain had already gone down, I think, for I could not see him anywhere."

Weekly Dispatch (London), 02 December 1900

Lawyers for Gertrude Leicester presented evidence that Blanche Edmonds had made Osmond Leicester her sole beneficiary on December 2nd 1898. They then argued that according to William's evidence, because Osmond had apparently survived Blanche by at least one hour, his body being found well clear of the wreck, then his mother Gertrude was entitled to all of Blanche's remaining estate once any outstanding debts had been settled. Justice Hardy pointed out that it was impossible to prove that Osmond had outlived Blanche and ruled Gertrude Leicester's claims against the Meyer estate groundless. The remainder of the £12000 was awarded to Sophia Meyer in the absence of any other living relatives in England with a viable claim to the estate. William was dismissed once the ruling was made and returned to his ship in company with Captain Bennett,

The old Mucking Bight Lighthouse.

SS Cato, Thompson, E, 1892, Hull Maritime Museum.

who had stood by the boy through the entire ordeal. He had even kept the Loch Vennachar in London two weeks longer than necessary in order that the young man could have a safe place to return to. Aitken, Lilburn & Co. were loath to argue the point as Captain Bennett was their fleet's commodore and his word carried great weight with the Loch Vennachar's owners.

After a successful year, Captain Bennett and the Loch Vennachar's owners were again hopeful that their fortunes had finally turned for the better. The four-masted barques Loch Broom and Loch Carron were turning a solid profit (the Loch Moidart had been lost in 1890, and the Loch Nevis recently sold to the Germans), as were the 1,500-ton ships; there were even promising signs for the ageing 1,200 fleet now that they had all been barque-rigged and their crew numbers trimmed. However, even with these money-saving measures, times were lean and some older ships had to be sold off to foreign interests to cut costs.

The heavily laden Loch Vennachar departed Glasgow on 3rd February 1901 and, after a brief stopover at Greenock, weighed anchor for Adelaide on the 4th, at the dawn of a new age. Australia had become a new nation and there was an air of optimism about the place, even amongst the hard-bitten old-time sailors.

The vessel was towed out into the Firth of Clyde by the steam tug 'Flying Dutchman' and left off St John's Point, Ireland, on 6th February. The Loch Vennachar then sailed through fine weather and freshening winds as she headed southwest into open water. What followed was a series of storms followed by days of unseasonal fogs as the northeast trades proved light and fickle.

Once past the equator, the Loch Vennachar picked up the southeast trades on 6th March. Three weeks of fine sailing ended abruptly on 1st April when gale-force winds and high seas pounded the clipper as she ran her southing down. Stormy conditions from the northwest followed a series of gales that blew on 10th April 1901. Thick and dirty weather punctuated her trip across the Southern Ocean and her best run eastwards was 285 miles in one day.

On May 5th, the Loch Vennachar passed the steamer Oroya at 8:25 am at 35.5° south 125.5° east, as both were headed towards Melbourne. Cape Borda was passed at 12:35 pm on 7th May, and she finally arrived after a longer-than-average trip of 92 days on May 8th at 3 pm; aboard was just one saloon passenger, a Mr Kilgour.

The ship was in port less than 24 hours when the officers and crew of the Loch Vennachar were invited to attend a fundraising concert in the large room at the Prince Alfred Seaman's Home in Port Adelaide, hosted by the Port Adelaide Orpheus Society. A variety of musical numbers were performed, and amongst the performers were apprentices from the Loch Vennachar who provided a choral performance alongside apprentices from several other vessels; amongst these was William Simpson, currently in the 3rd year of his apprenticeship.

After discharging her Adelaide cargo, the Loch Vennachar was cleared out to the Semaphore roads on May 11th and sailed onwards to Melbourne on the 12th, arriving outside Port Phillip Heads on May 15th. However, due to unfavourable winds, Captain Bennett was forced to anchor his vessel off Queenscliff until the winds turned in her favour towards evening. Bill Bennett had the tug take his ship into Hobson's Bay via the South Channel and she dropped anchor late in the evening of the 16th. Tugs were used to bring the clipper up the Yarra to Melbourne Dock so that her cargo could be lifted and sent to the stores.

She lay dockside for quite some time loading more than 8,000 bags of wheat and nearly 4,000 bags of flour for London's millers, 100 tons of tallow, 1,650 bales of wool and skins, 200 tons of copper ore as ballast and sundry other cargo. She set sail on August 12th bound for London, with three passengers aboard: Richard E. Richardson, James F. Styles and William R. Hodges. The run home was a routine event, though Captain Bennett decided to run up along the African coast, crossing the equator on the 1st of November. She passed Dover behind a tug at 11:40 am on November 11th.

The Loch Vennachar arrived in the Thames on the same afternoon. As she reached her anchorage ten miles below Gravesend, opposite the Mucking Light at 11:00 pm, the weather began to close in. By midnight, a howling gale was hammering all the ships on the Thames. Great sweeping storms brought flooding rains to large parts of Britain and Scotland. More than fifty ships were wrecked, and at least two hundred lives were lost.

Just before 4:30 am, during a howling gale, with visibility down to just a few hundred feet, the 1,094-ton iron-screwed steamer SS Cato (owned by T. Wilson & Co of Hull) rammed the Loch Vennachar whilst the clipper was at anchor. The bow of the Cato tore down the starboard side of the clipper aft of the watertight bulkhead, ripping away hull plating and leaving a nineteen-foot-long gash in her hull at the waterline.

With her hold full and taking water over the bow from storm wash, both watches were called up on deck. Captain Bennett and his crew quickly ascertained that the ship was doomed. The Loch Vennachar's hold rapidly filled with water, there being time to launch one of the ship's boats. The Captain and crew, 30 men and boys, and the three passengers had little time to escape, the ship sinking in less than three minutes.

As Captain Bennett raced into his cabin to grab his logs and papers, he passed the pilot. As they were fleeing the rapidly filling cabin, Captain Bennett called out for the pilot to save the ship's mascot, a talkative African Parrot that had been with Bill Bennett and the Loch Vennachar for many years. The pilot just managed to grab the bird before the saloon disappeared below the waves. Of the seven ship's cats kept on board to control the ever-present rats and mice, only one was saved by a member of the crew.

One of the sailors, Alexander J. Jacobson, had received a serious head injury, having been in his bunk sleeping next to the point of impact, and had to be helped into a boat by the bosun, William Logan. The stricken clipper soon heeled over to starboard and sank, a few inches of the bulwarks standing out of the water. The crew were rescued from the water by the crew of the Cato and men from the tug Athlete, and were then landed at Gravesend.

With nothing but the sodden clothes they were standing in, the crew were sent to the Sailors' Home as distressed mariners and offered all help available. Jacobson was ushered off to Gravesend hospital in a serious condition. Apprentice William Simpson, survivor of the Loch Sloy disaster, had been shipwrecked for a second time; he arrived back in Glasgow as a distressed seaman with naught but what the Seaman's Mission had provided for him. This second wreck proved too much for him and for a time he returned to Tobermory, refusing to go back to sea.

The damaged steamer Cato, her stem demolished and her bow stove in, was towed back to Gravesend reach, leaking badly. A salvage expert was dispatched the next day to the site of the accident. He found the ship had sunk on the north side of the mid-channel, half a mile above Thames Haven Pier. She had a list of five degrees to starboard. At the tide's half-ebb, the main deck was ten feet below the water, with 40 feet of water above her deck at high tide. He expected at low tide there to be just one foot of water over the main deck.

The collision was described in detail in a letter one of the crew wrote to his mother, which was later reproduced in a local paper.

NARRATIVE OF A HUNTLY SAILOR.

"We are favoured with the following account written by Mr Gordon Anderson, formerly of Cosmos Lea, Huntly, to his mother:—

You would no doubt be surprised at hearing of our mishap and so near to home. I will try and explain how it all happened. We had sailed up the English Channel as far as Dungeness and there the tug boat took us in tow. This was on Monday. We were towed up until we were about 10 miles below Gravesend and there cast anchor. The officers and apprentices were all asleep in their bunks with the exception of one man on the look-out, on the forecastle, and one officer on the poop.

The accident happened about 4.30 a.m. on Tuesday morning. Mind you we were anchored right out of the way of traffic, in a haven for ships to anchor. The man on watch happened to look over the rail and saw a steamer just about 20 yards off us coming at full speed ahead, making straight for us. The man let out a yell and asked where they were going to? No sooner were the words spoken than she struck us on the starboard bow, ploughing right into the forecastle where the men were all asleep. The men were all thrown out of their bunks and boxes, irons, and everything on top of them. All escaped with the exception of one man named Jacobson, who was completely covered under the debris. One of the men heard him moaning and pulled him out and took him on deck.

The awful bump awoke me, and I was out on deck like a shot (calling to the other boys as I went). I had nothing on me but my sleeping suit. I rushed forward to see what was the matter. I saw poor Jacobsen lying on the deck in an awful state. I got hold of him calling to another man to help me to carry him aft to the cabin. I did not know then that the ship was sinking. The Captain, poor old fellow; I felt quite sorry for him—he was in such an awful state. He said, "For God sake, Gordon, do what you can for that man."

I dressed the man's wounds as well as I could and was just half-way through when the cry went out that the ship was sinking. Everyone made a rush for the boats. I picked the man in my arms and rushed on deck. By this time the only boat was packed full. I cried out to them to take the sick man and I passed him over the ship into the boat to the sailors. I then tried to get back to my room to get a parrot that I had brought from Melbourne for Annie, but the water was rising rapidly so I had to leave the poor little thing to drown.

*I felt very sorry having to leave it after bringing it so far over the sea. Only the first mate, steward, sail-maker and myself were left on the ship. I managed to get on a pair of trousers, and we all rushed up the rigging. We were perched up there for a good while in the cold. The mate got hold of three life-belts and passed me one. The steward said he could not swim, so I gave him mine and we were all going to swim for it. But just then the steamer **Cato** which ran us down sent a boat and picked us up. I can tell you I looked a pretty sight—no boots, no socks, and only a pair of* *trousers and shirt on, and my hands were covered with blood. That is the way I went ashore. We went to the Mariners' Shipwrecked Society, and there got an outfit. All we possessed went to the bottom. We are to be sent home."* **Huntly Express 22 November 1901.**

The Loch Vennachar settled into the Thames mud 40 feet below the surface. Over time, she settled so deeply into the muck that, at high tide, her mainmast spars were completely covered by water.

The Loch Vennachar was left in the Thames mud for 25 days whilst arrangements and preparations were made to raise her. The ship's owners called upon Francis Wagstaff, the former Captain of the Loch Vennachar, to survey the vessel as she lay in the mud. After careful consideration, he recommended she be raised by Thames Conservancy, ship salvage experts.

The stricken ship was lifted from the bottom by Thames Conservancy lighters and hauled further up onto the mudbank on November 27th. It was planned to move the ship further up the bank so that she could later be pumped out and refloated. A week later, the clipper was raised up high enough for the gash to be planked over and the hold pumped out.

Upon being brought off the bottom, Captain Wagstaff inspected her further, finding that apart from water damage to her fittings and a 19-foot-long gash in the starboard bow, the ship was as sound as a bell and well worth refitting. When relatively dry, stevedores were brought in to begin unloading some of the cargo.

December 7th saw Captain Wagstaff direct four tugs to try to haul the Loch Vennachar off the mud. They failed. Two days later, and with the ship considerably lighter and drier, two tugs, the Iona and Guiana, managed to pull the ship off the mud and tow her back to Tilbury Dock for a full survey of the damage.

Many old salts argued that the ship should be scrapped, but the opinions of Wagstaff and Bennett convinced the directors of the Loch Line to invest in the ship's resurrection. When the ship was raised, it was found that the saloon had three feet of Thames mud inside, and every cabin would need a complete refit.

Most of the cargo was a write-off, but salvors managed to save much of the tinned rabbit and other such non-perishables.

When she was finally raised between two barges and floated into Tilbury dry dock for a full Lloyd's survey for much-needed repairs, James Lilburn organised for the ship to be repaired and had the Loch Vennachar shifted across to London Graving Dock for repairs. He spoke to his friend Sir John Denison-Pender, owner of the London Graving Dock Company, to have his engineers repair the Loch Vennachar.

There was an unfortunate incident that took place part-way through the repairs. David Adcock, a forty-year-old ship's rigger, reported for duty at the Orchard House site of the London Graving Dock. He had spent his morning high atop the masts of the Loch Vennachar helping to re-rig the ship. When the midday bell signalled the break for dinner, David began his descent to the quay. As he stepped onto the gangway to head ashore, a steam crane was moving along the very edge of the dock. In a sudden, violent collision, the heavy machinery caught the ladder, sweeping it from its moorings.

David was knocked backward, falling thirty feet into the depths of the dock. Though he was rushed to Poplar Hospital, he was pronounced dead. Repairs were completed at the end of April, the bill coming to £17,000 to completely repair and refit the ship. A great many improvements and additions were made to her passenger accommodation with everything, including the plumbing and lighting, being modernised, making her the grandest 1,500-ton clipper on the water at the time.

The Loch Vennachar finally re-entered service on the 30th of May 1902 after being resurveyed by Lloyd's of London who rated her 100 A1, the highest insurance rating available to a ship of her class at the time. The ship's builders had returned the ship to her glory days but with a thoroughly modern look and feel, unusual for a clipper of her vintage.

The saloon was lined with bird's-eye maple and decorated with gilding and polished mahogany mouldings. A vaulted skylight ran the centre of the saloon, and all cabin

The Loch Vennachar as she is being raised by heavy barge cranes.
'John Ward~McQuaid'

furniture was in keeping with the general design of the ship's cabins. The renovations were carried right throughout with new teak decking, mid-deck house and galley, new rigging, spars, cables, and sails.

The Loch Vennachar left Glasgow on the 30th of May and sailed straight back into trouble. It was found that the starboard freshwater tank was leaking, so the captain put the ship about and anchored in Moville Bay, Lough Foyle, where she waited whilst the tank was repaired. Bad weather forced the crew to wait until the 9th of June 1902 before the ship could again get underway.

Stormy weather and rough seas battered the Loch Vennachar as she sailed down the Irish Channel. Once into open waters, moderating winds were experienced until 6° North, when

the doldrums appeared. The equator was passed when the ship
was 40 days out, and the south-east trades were picked up in 22°
south, 20° west. Then, on the 9th of August, the meridian of
Greenwich was crossed in 40° south as the clipper began her run
east.

The Cape of Good Hope was doubled on the 11th of
August during a series of southerly gales. On the 17th, another
hurricane raged, with the vessel having to be kept running under
three lower topsails. The decks were flooded, and one huge wave
came aboard, smashing the starboard rail of the poop. The best
day's run was 302 nautical miles.

The Neptune Islands were passed at 9:30 p.m. on the 4th
of September, and the Semaphore anchorage was reached at 11
a.m. on the 5th of September 1902, 88 days from Lough Foyle.
Soon after, a tug took hold, and the Loch Vennachar was towed
into port. The Loch Vennachar had finally arrived in Adelaide,
slightly more battered than the pristine condition she had left
Glasgow in.

Aboard her were two characters of note: the urbane
African parrot that had survived the previous sinking, and a
brand-new brass-bound apprentice, Thomas Pearce Jnr. He had
been placed into service by his father, Tom Pearce Snr, one-time
sailor aboard the Loch Ard and Loch Sunart (who survived the
wrecks of both vessels), and now a shore superintendent in
Jamaica for the Royal Mail Steam Packet Company. This was his
first trip with the Loch Line, and the 16-year-old counted himself
most fortunate to have found a berth with Captain 'Fighting Bill'
Bennett aboard the most famous ship in the Loch Line fleet.

The clipper was cleared out on 9 September and set sail
the following morning. She passed through Port Phillip Heads on
the 15th, delayed due to fickle south-easterlies. Upon gaining
pratique, the ship was hauled up the river and berthed alongside
Victoria Dock. The Loch Vennachar was laid up in Hobson's Bay

Captain William Bennett, taken in 1902 aboard the Loch Vennachar as she was docked in Melbourne.

for the rest of the year, as Captain Bennett and the ship's agents struggled to fill her hold. The new 10,000-ton steamers were stealing much of the wheat and wool trade from the larger ports, clippers being relegated more and more to picking up cargoes of grain, wool, and coal from more out-of-the-way locations.

Just before he was ready to depart for London, Bill Bennett was summoned to appear for the defence in the Marine Board enquiry into the stranding of the barque Inverlochy in Hobson's Bay. The vessel's former master, Captain Edwin Kendrick, had been charged by the board with reckless navigation that caused the barque to be wrecked. Captain Bennett was called to defend Captain Kendrick's conduct. He stated quite categorically that:

"He had 27 years' experience of the Port of Melbourne, and it was owing to his representations that a lighthouse was erected at Split Point. He regarded the neighbourhood as dangerous owing to the swell and the current there. There was no doubt whatever as to the current. On one occasion his ship was in danger at this spot, when the wind came off the shore and allowed him to get the ship round." **The Register, 7 January 1903.**

Eventually, the Marine Board enquiry ended without determination and the case was taken to the Melbourne Magistrates' Court, where Captain Kendrick was found to be negligent, had his certificate suspended for twelve months, and was ordered to pay costs of £120. The president of the Marine Board enquiry was critical of Captain Bennett's testimony and abilities as a navigator. Bill Bennett's reply in The Herald was vociferous and pointed. The reply was made public:

CAPTAIN BENNETT. AS MARINE COURT WITNESS. HE REPLIES TO CRITICISMS.

"Captain W. H. Bennett, of the Loch Vennachar, writes this afternoon as follows:— In last night's "Herald", I observed a remark referring to the politeness of the chairman of the Marine Court to me in my examination as to the light at Split Point, and remarking upon his exclamation, "And you call yourself a navigator?"

I shall not follow the bad example set by Mr Panton, as president of the court, by continually ventilating my own opinions and experience, but shall confine myself to referring that gentleman, with reference to his gratuitous expression of his opinion of me as a navigator, to the polished address delivered on 5 July 1891 by Admiral Sir Wm. R. Kennedy, K.C.B., Commander-in-Chief of the Navy, and his description of my capabilities as a navigator as being such as "he would always remember with pleasure as rare or made apparent to every sailor," although from what I saw of the president of the Melbourne Marine Court, it can hardly be expected that he will bow to the judgment even of such a distinguished naval officer.

I have commanded fine ships in the Loch Line since 1878 and have always managed to find my way from Great Britain to Melbourne without any accident as far as navigation is concerned. I was only asked by Mr Traill as to my knowledge of the currents setting towards the shore in the vicinity of Split Point, but when asked as to whether I had seen the white light at Split Point at a greater distance than three miles, I said that I had, according to the distance which I had spaced with my officers.

By continually taking bearings of the light with the wind south-east and easterly, I have found my ship being set inshore and have had to keep altering my course as the vessel approached Split Point, and in this I am corroborated by the evidence of Captain Winsor, master of the ship Celestial Empire, who was in the vicinity about the same time as the Vennachar, and whose ship was carried out of her course five miles in a distance of 17 miles. Captain McMeikan, of the James Patterson, who some years ago spent about a month at the wreck of the Hereford, and who also spent some days at the Inverlochy, also corroborates me as to the current.

This can also be verified by my first and second officers, who are with me at present. I was present in court and heard the remarks the president made to the first mate of the Inverlochy, viz., "That he must either be a fool or impostor." This remark was most unjustifiable and uncalled for; also when the first mate was asked where he had passed for master, he replied, "Aberdeen," when the president interjected, "That it might do for Aberdeen but not for here." Now, sir, surely all the wisdom of the universe has not concentrated itself in Melbourne, though a great many people

*might have thought it had at the time of the land boom. I have
known, and do know at present, some of the smartest and most
able seamen in the Mercantile Marine who are natives of
Aberdeen and have passed their examinations there.*

*Mr Panton, in justice to even himself, cannot really expect
me, a very experienced shipmaster though I am, to possess the
knowledge of my profession as the navigator that he, as a police
magistrate, no doubt considers he has of navigation; and when he
asked me to define refraction, he refused to listen to my
explanation, and when I commenced to inform him of the different
corrections I used in taking meridian altitudes, this scientific
explanation did not seem to fit in with his views, as I was
immediately told to stop.*

*In this morning's "Argus", there is a letter defining
refraction and reflection, and it seems to me that the writer had a
more scientific knowledge of the matter than I. No doubt Captain
Roberts, in his inexperience of handling a large sailing ship in
light winds, thought fit to make the remark, "It is ridiculous for us
to sit here and listen to talk of this sort about the current."*

*I wonder how the Lady Darling went ashore inside
Montague Island in broad daylight! Was it a current? If so, "it
must have been simply ridiculous."* **The Herald 8 January 1903.**

XII
Swallowing the Anchor

The Loch Vennachar was hauled out into Hobson's Bay on January 10th 1903 and cleared the Heads on the 12th, passing the steamer Oonah by Gabo Island on the 14th. The clipper was steering east by south and had on board 5,000 bales of wool, 500 casks of glycerine, 150 small hogsheads of wine, 20 bales of skins, 80 bales of glue pieces, 8 bales of leather, 330 bales of tin offcuts and 4,200 old iron rails as ballast.

After a trouble-free journey, the ship was spoken to by a passing steamer on April 19th, at 49° north, 13° west, and asked to be reported "All well!". The Loch Vennachar arrived at Gravesend on April 27th 1903, and was passed up to London Dock on the 28th of April, in time for the May wool sales.

After discharging her cargo, the clipper was sent north behind a tug. Passing Southend on May 21st, she sailed north for home and Captain Bennett took some time away for a much-needed rest; his age and the unrelenting pace he had kept up for so many years were beginning to take their toll upon his health.

It was not until August 22nd that the Loch Vennachar was towed from her Broomielaw berth and hauled off to Greenock to take on the last of her cargo. On the 23rd of August 1903, the ship was towed down the Clyde on the rising tide to sail again for Adelaide and Melbourne. The tug and clipper entered the Irish Channel and straight into heavy weather from the southwest. St John's Point, at the southern tip of the Lecale peninsula of County Down, was passed on the 25th, and Tuskar was passed on the 27th as the ship sailed into the teeth of a nasty storm. The Loch Vennachar pushed hard for five days before she cleared the Irish Channel and made her way across the Bay of Biscay. The Cape Verde Islands were passed on September 18th 1903, and the German steamer Marienburg was spoken to the following afternoon.

Fresh and stormy conditions marked the trip south to the equator, which was crossed on October 5th. Light and variable winds made for a frustrating run south as the ship sailed into the South Atlantic. Captain Bennett put on as much sail as he could as he brought his vessel down around the bottom of the Cape of Good Hope on October 31st. He began his easting run along the 39th parallel and continued along the 40th in fine and light winds and seas. Light and variable east to northeast winds made headway slow. The meridian of Cape Leeuwin was crossed on the 23rd of November along the 39th parallel, at which time Captain Bennett steered his ship northeast through a series of hard tacking manoeuvres as his ship struggled to make way against the frustrating headwinds.

The Loch Vennachar struggled against gale-force easterlies for four days outside of Cape Borda. Violent rain squalls marked her progress up past the Neptune light and into Investigator Strait. She eventually dropped anchor in the Semaphore roadstead at 2 pm on the 1st of December with just one passenger.

Anchored in the roadstead alongside the Loch Vennachar were the barques Letterewe, Queen, Pehr Ugland and Antares, and the ships Fenice and Pythomene. Once in Port Adelaide, 750 tons of general cargo, whisky and ironware were unloaded before she cleared out for Melbourne. The clipper weighed anchor on the 7th of December and, after battling increasingly strong headwinds, finally tied up at Williamstown on the 12th, just in time for Christmas. On the 13th, she was towed upriver to Port Melbourne's Yarra docks where her cargo was immediately discharged.

Once empty, she was towed back to her Williamstown berth to begin taking on a cargo of wheat and wool. She already had 50 sacks of tanning bark loaded aboard in Adelaide. It was, however, Captain William Bennett's last trip as a ship's master. Whilst staying with friends in Melbourne, he became very ill and was rushed to Bethesda Hospital, where he was to spend many months recovering.

In his place, the well-known and highly respected sailing master, and holder of an Extra-Master's Ticket, William Stephenson Hawkins, current master of the Loch Ness, was given

Port Adelaide, c.1909
State Library of South Australia

command of the Loch Vennachar for her return trip to London. Having developed a well-earned reputation as a "Relief Captain" capable of taking over ships and crews at the last minute, Bill Hawkins was an obvious choice for the Loch Vennachar's owners.

The Loch Vennachar's New Year started with a new captain and a mostly new crew. Besides Captain Hawkins, the ship's new first officer, James Priest, and Bill Hawkins' long-time companion, Dickie Simpson, the sailmaker also joined the ship as she sailed from Australia on the 23rd of January 1904. Aboard her were the apprentices Robert Andrews Jnr, Diarmid Thomson, S.C. Brown, Joe Hadley, Tom W. Pearce, and Sydney M. Stein. The ship arrived without incident after a speedy voyage, dropping anchor at Gravesend on the 4th of May 1904.

The crew were still getting used to Bill Hawkins' hard-driving yet jovial style of captaincy. It was whilst in port that a member of the crew, Syd Stein, received news that every sailor dreaded. On Tuesday the 12th of July, the steamship Nemesis, upon which his brother, William Stein, was serving as second officer, was lost with all hands.

William Stein had begun his career aboard the Loch Vennachar under Captain Bennett, whom he regarded as a friend and mentor. William was 27, married and living in Melbourne; it was he who had gotten Sydney a berth aboard the Loch Vennachar in the first place through his close association with it's old master.

The Nemesis had foundered in heavy seas during the worst storm to hit Sydney's beaches in living memory. Much of the wreckage washed ashore along Cronulla Beach. The wreckage washing up in the pounding surf indicated that the ship's cargo hatches had burst in the heavy sea, the splintered woodwork of the hatches having been recovered.

Also scattered along the northern end of the beach was part of the bridge, much of the mid-deck cabin, and the remains of the saloon skylight. One lifeboat also washed up, appearing to be in good order, but there were no bodies. Sydney, the youngest son of the Chief of the Melbourne Fire Brigade, was stunned and stricken with grief. All sailors knew the risks when they signed on

SS Nemesis 1393-ton cargo vessel built by Thomas Turnbull & Sons at Whitby in 1880.

The boys of the Loch Vennachar in port in 1904: Dairmid Barclay, Tom Pearce, Joe Hadley, and in no particular order S.C. Brown, Robert Andrews, Syd Stein (far right).
Photo supplied by John Boon (Great Grandson of William Hawkins).

to go to sea, but it was not until they were personally affected that such dangers hit home.

The ship had been carrying 1,500 tons of coal and a crew of 31 when she went down. Of the ship and her crew, nothing was ever heard of again, but great piles of wreckage continued to drift ashore for weeks as the hull began to break up on the bottom.

Having recovered from his illness, William Bennett, now officially retired from the sea and having decided to 'swallow the anchor' and reside in Prahran, took charge of the relief efforts to raise funds for the families of those left behind after the wreck of the Nemesis. His efforts raised £128 for the orphans and widows who were being cared for by the Shipwreck Relief Society of Melbourne.

Also, with his keen interest in football, Bennett used his social connections to organise a charity football match between the Caulfield club and the Old Collegians, which was played at the Caulfield Cricket Ground. Bill Bennett also joined the South Melbourne Bowls Club and showed himself to be a dab hand at the old game, once played by Francis Drake. He was approached by the owner of the Herald newspaper and was asked to become a correspondent for the paper, commenting on and reporting on anything to do with the sea.

After a brief stay in London, the Loch Vennachar returned to Glasgow where she discharged her crew. She lay dockside whilst Captain Hawkins visited his family, and James Priest began looking for new crew more suitable to his captain's needs and liking.

The clipper weighed anchor on the 15th of July 1904, arriving in Adelaide on the 18th of October ahead of an approaching tempest. Captain Hawkins dropped both anchors off of The Semaphore and turned his ship into the wind. The crew battened down all hatches and stowed all loose items as the approaching gale whipped up winds of hurricane force across the Gulf St Vincent.

Early the next morning, the tempest brought howling winds and flooding rains; it unroofed buildings and brought down

Captain William Hawkins standing outside of the Orient Steam line after his appointment as replacement skipper of the Brabloch.
Photograph supplied by John Boon.

trees. Towns were flooded and crops were flattened, and one unlucky farmer was killed when struck by flying sheets of roofing iron. However, out in the gulf, Captain Hawkins' preparations and the Loch Vennachar's sturdy and sleek design meant that she rode out the storm, suffering little damage.

On the morning after the storm, Captain Hawkins took his ship into Port Adelaide and unloaded 600 tons of general cargo. He then set sail for Melbourne, arriving in Hobson's Bay on the 28th. After discharging the last of his cargo, spirits and hardware from Glasgow, and filling the clipper's hold with a rich mix of wool, wheat, and skins destined for the London sales, the Loch Vennachar set sail for London on December 15th 1904.

XIII

The Flying Scotsman
William Stevenson Hawkins
b. 1852 – d. 8theptember

William Stevenson Hawkins was born in 1852, in the then busy commercial fishing port of Garlieston, Wigtownshire, Scotland. The village sits on the shores of Garlieston Bay and in its heyday was a commercial centre with a thriving commercial fishery.

Garlieston Boat Builders,
BBC Scotland.

Many of the local boys and men were involved in some way with the trades of the sea. Most young men went to sea but a goodly number were involved in the manufacture of ropes, sailcloth, nets, and other chandlery items. There was a small but important shipbuilding industry that turned out small coastal sloops and schooners, fishing boats and shallow-bottomed traders. It was in this environment that William gained his love for the sea. William was the son of Captain Hawkins, a long-time sailor, and Grace Stevenson, whose father was a well-known and respected trader and ship's master. With his father and grandfather away at sea, the Hawkins household was dominated

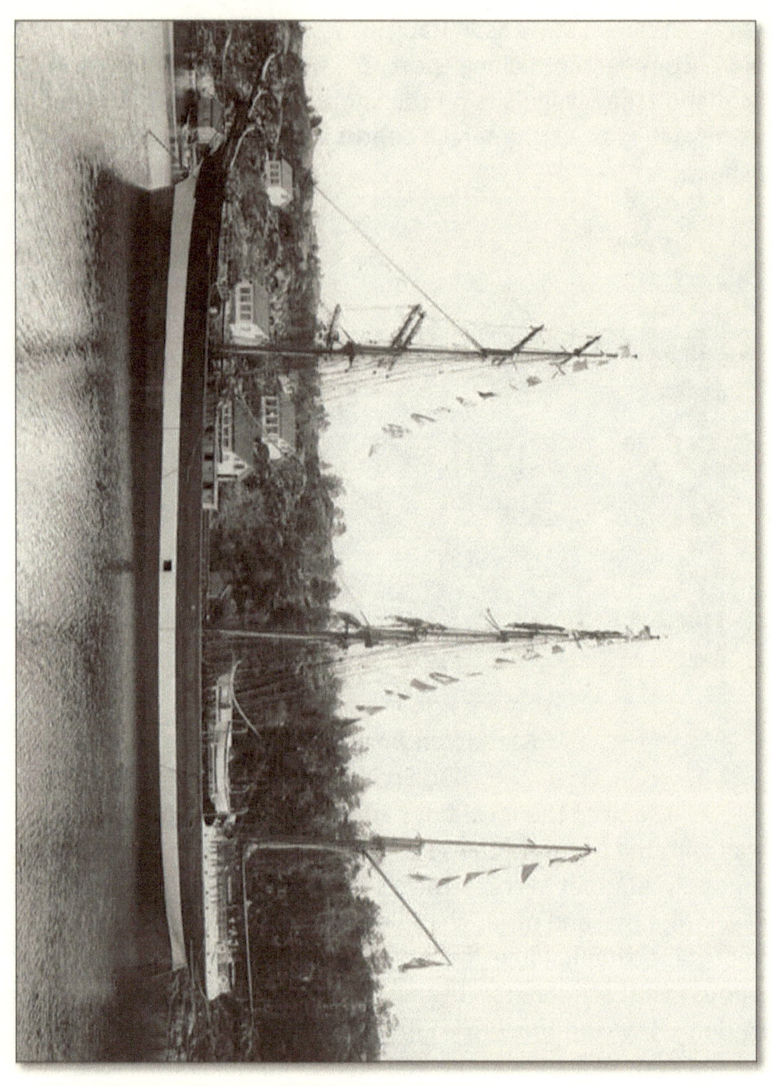

The 1200 ton barque 'Blairhoyle' when she ran under the name 'Pallas' after being sold the Norwegian interests.
www.wrecksite.eu

by his grandmother, the powerful and ever-present Agnes Stevenson.

He had a younger brother, Peter, who was born in 1855. His mother was born in Sorbie, the Stevensons having lived there for generations. William and his brother both grew up in Garlieston, attending the local parish school and being raised in the strict Calvinist traditions.

By age 9 the family had moved to Heads of Garden House in Sorbie; there Agnes and Grace worked as domestic help whilst their husbands were away. Living with them was a young cousin, John McCullock. Despite coming from a small community, William had dreams of larger things. Having grown up listening to the stories of his father and grandfather about life at sea, it was only natural that he would follow them into the family business.

It was his grandfather, Captain Stevenson, who opened up the way for a naive, 14-year-old boy to begin his life at sea, sponsoring his apprenticeship and paying his dues. The newly coated Brass Bounder had so much to learn about being a ship's mate, and his life began in the dockside boarding houses and taverns of Govan, Greenock, and Port Glasgow.

William spent four years constantly at sea before heading back to Glasgow to sit the Board of Trade's exam to gain his Second Mate's ticket. Upon finishing his apprenticeship, William found a berth as Third Mate aboard the clipper "Blairhoyle" under Captain Robert Watson. Captain Watson lived with his wife, Catherine, and their six daughters (Christina, Margaret, Catherine, Marion, Amelia, and Mary) at Avondale Place in Glasgow.

As a fresh-faced third mate, William lived with the Watsons when in port, and it was through this association that he first met his future wife, Catherine, when she was just 13 years old. Over time their friendship blossomed and eventually they married, the couple continuing to live in Avondale Place whilst William and Captain Watson were at sea.

William Hawkins worked for a number of years learning the art of command from his father-in-law, working his way up from Third Mate to First Officer of the Blairhoyle. Spending a number of years working under his father-in-law, William eventually became first mate of the Blairhoyle and soon took the exam for his Extra-Master's ticket.

The time had come for him to take on a command of his own, and an opportunity came again via Robert Watson, who put his name forward to the ship owners Thomas, Dickie & Co., who needed a competent first mate for their newly finished wooden barque, the Craigard. In 1878, at the age of 26, William Hawkins left the Blairhoyle to follow his father-in-law onto the newly launched barque.

William and Katherine Hawkins boarded the barque on Friday 24th May 1878 whilst the vessel was waiting tied to the wharf in Port Glasgow. The vessel set sails soon after and arrived in Sydney on the 7th September 1878, on her first voyage to Australia with passengers and a cargo valued at £43,000. The little clipper had good winds down the Irish Channel, followed by strong westerly winds as she crossed the Bay of Biscay. The north-east trades were soon picked up, which carried the Craigard quickly south.

The equator was crossed 32 days out from port. The south-east trades proved fresh and lively as the barque ran her southing down, passing the line of Greenwich on August 2nd. From then through the rest of the month, strong north-west to south-west winds blowing in violent gales pushed the vessel along, as she ran her easting down along the 49th parallel.

Captain Watson took the Craigard to the edge of her design limits to see what she would put up with, and the little barque did not disappoint as she ran before howling gales filled with hail, sleet, and snow. The clipper rounded the southern tip of Tasmania on the 1st of September and sailed right into the teeth of a violent south-westerly blow. Huge seas battered the barque and one rogue wave broke across the deck, smashing in the front of the poop deck and sweeping the deck clean of everything moveable, including buckets, lifebuoys, and the captain's pigs and chickens.

Once round the east coast the winds abated somewhat and the rest of the trip north was relatively uneventful. The

Craigard passed through Sydney Heads on the 8th of September much the worse for wear. Whilst waiting for the ship's agents to arrange fresh cargo and passengers, Bill Hawkins took the opportunity to leave the cramped confines of the barque and spend some time taking in the sights and sounds of Sydney.

The 860-ton barque waited patiently to be cleared of her cargo of iron pipes, slate flagstones, cordage, muslin, linen, drapery and other articles of haberdashery and hardware. In turn, on September 27th, Captain Watson then had his vessel towed the 60 miles to Newcastle, where it stopped to take on a load of coal.

After waiting for weeks in the crowded roadstead for her turn at the loading wharf, the clipper finally left Australian shores taking her load of 1,180 tons of coal to Hong Kong, a much-needed commodity in the small yet thriving colony where steamers often arrived needing to be refuelled, making the small load a rather valuable yet risky cargo to haul through the pirate-infested South China Sea. She arrived safely on the 24th of November, and the Hawkins' spent their first Christmas away from the Watson home and all its obligatory pleasures.

Having spent Christmas in the tropics, the Craigard then sailed home, firstly via San Francisco and then Valparaiso, to pick up a load of nitrate for the gunpowder and fertiliser trades.

Upon reaching Glasgow, Robert Watson pronounced the vessel fit for trade and passed over command to William, handing him a sextant, chronometers, charts and logbooks, all the necessary tools for a beginning ship's master. William also purchased at this time a revolver and new uniform more in keeping with his new position. With such a promotion came the opportunities to create wealth, something closed to those not in command of a trading vessel.

Apart from the captain's modest wages of less than £50 a month, there were the captain's commission, taken from the profits of a successful voyage. Also, there were the crimper's fees, the fees from the slops chest and the master's share of profits that increased as he invested into other ventures or took out a part share in the ship he was sailing.

William and Katie Hawkins again headed south on another world tramping cruise, leaving on the 4th of October 1879 when the Craigard left Glasgow for Sydney with a hold filled with general cargo, amongst which was 10 tons of gunpowder. The barque dropped anchor in Sydney Harbour on the 5th of January 1880. As well as William and Catherine being on board, the ship's agents, Messrs Brothers & Mason, had returned from a trip to Scotland as well.

The Craigard arrived in the early afternoon off Garden Island, but could not tie up until her 10 tons of gunpowder had been lightered off. The ship had left Greenock and encountered light easterlies as she moved across the North Channel. Once in the north-east trade winds, the clipper made good time, crossing the equator on the 3rd of November.

Despite these favourable winds, Captain Hawkins wanted to make up time, so he pushed his ship and crew, crossing beneath the Cape of Good Hope at the 44th parallel on the 30th of November. The Roaring Forties gave way to the Frightening Fifties as Captain Hawkins rode ahead of a howling storm front that pushed his vessel deep into the icefloes of the Southern Ocean.

It was during this storm that a rogue wave tore across the deck, carrying away a spare spar and tearing ring-bolts out of the decking timbers. The same storm split the upper topsail, which had to be furled by sailors risking life and limb in the cyclonic conditions. Carried for more than a week before the storm, the Craigard was almost dismasted by contrary winds that tore away the mizzen and main topmast staysails. The storm continued until the barque finally turned north around the southern tip of Tasmania on the 23rd of December.

Whilst Christmas aboard the Craigard was a rough and ready affair, the ship's cook broke out stores laid in especially for the occasion and all ate a well-deserved repast, thankful to their Creator that they had survived the harrowing journey.

After a month in port tied to Padbury's Wharf, the Craigard weighed anchor and passed through Sydney Heads on the 26th of January 1880, destined for Port Bassein, Hamburg. The ship stopped in at Newcastle on the way to pick up a load of coal, leaving at the end of December. The vessel made good time, arriving at Port Bassein on the 7th of May 1880.

Upon disembarking in Hamburg, the Craigard's owners, Thomson, Dickie & Co., offered William a job as a shore-based superintendent for ships loading and unloading in Glasgow and in the German ports. The owners saw much potential in the aggressive young captain, and with his father-in-law's support, William settled in Hamburg with his wife, becoming a junior partner in the company run by Captain Thomson, William & Robert Dickie and Alexander Oswald Drysdale, Partners of Thomson, Dickie, & Co., Shipowners and Marine Insurance Brokers, 17 Royal Exchange Square, Glasgow.

The financial windfall allowed William and his wife a certain financial independence; they were still based in the Watson family home in Avondale Place in Glasgow, but they had bigger plans. In 1881, the Hawkins' moved back from Hamburg permanently, choosing to live with Katie's mother, Catherine Watson, and her younger sisters, Maggie and Mary Watson.

After two years ashore, William began to get itchy feet; he was a sailor, and despite Katie being heavily pregnant with their first child, William was determined to once again head to sea. In 1883, he was appointed master of the three-masted iron barque, Blairhoyle, taking over after the vessel's previous skipper, Captain Higgins, had died of fever whilst in port at Calcutta, India. Captain Hawkins was excited to take command of the ship once commanded by his father-in-law. It was a vessel he was intimately familiar with, having served as a mate aboard her for many years.

Refusing to be parted from her husband, Katie moved onboard her father's old ship with its new commander, much to the chagrin of her mother, who wanted Katie to stay at home to give birth. However, the headstrong wife of Captain Hawkins was not to be denied, and it was whilst travelling to Australia from Glasgow that she went into labour just as the Blairhoyle was about to clear the Irish Channel. Pulling into Queenstown,

Ireland, Catherine Hawkins gave birth to Kathleen H. Hawkins, who was named in honour of the woman who helped deliver her.

Mother and child continued south to Australia aboard the Blairhoyle. Upon their eventual return to Glasgow, Kathleen was left in the care of her grandmother, Catherine Watson, as William and Katie Hawkins travelled the world together aboard the Blairhoyle. (In later years, Kathleen H. Hawkins migrated to Canada early in the 20th century.)

The Blairhoyle set sail for Australia in company with the Loch Vennachar, both ships carrying parts of two steam tugs that were to be assembled and used in Port Melbourne. The barque arrived on June 28th. The Blairhoyle, which usually sailed to Sydney, made her best run yet to Melbourne, and it was noted that Captain Hawkins was a skilled and canny navigator and ship's master. William Hawkins was also developing a reputation as a hard-driving, aggressive captain who was willing to put his ship and crew in danger if it meant greater profit for him and his backers.

On almost every trip south, it was noted that he put his vessel into the lower 40s and even into the 50s on occasion, regularly risking dismasting or collisions with unseen icebergs. Nothing seemed to phase Bill Hawkins as he drove for greater efficiency and profits from his ship and crew.

The Blairhoyle was towed from her Tail-o'-the-Bank mooring on the 5th of April 1883, yet it took four more days to pass the Holyhead light due to light winds that at times left the clipper totally becalmed. Moderate variable winds followed until the northeast trades were picked up at 30° north, 21°W west. Freshening winds gave her a boost all the way to the equator, when she once again fell in with light and variable breezes. The equator was crossed 28 days out, and soon after, the southeast trades began to freshen from southeast to southwest.

Fresh and squally westerlies carried the barque to the 19th parallel, when the Blairhoyle was again almost becalmed by light and variable winds swinging south-southeast to north. Slow progress was made until the 30th parallel, when gales and strong winds from the south-west followed to the Prime Meridian. From here, as she began her easting run, strong and favourable westerlies drove the clipper rapidly along as William Hawkins ordered as much sail as possible piled on to make up for lost time.

The meridian of the Cape of Good Hope was crossed along the 45th parallel. Soon after, winds swung back round to the north, becoming gale force as a new weather system moved in. Flying ahead of the approaching front, the foretopgallant yard and sail were carried away and other sails blew out as Captain Hawkins was forced to shorten sail. Continuing along the 45th parallel, the Blairhoyle passed two very large icebergs at 60° east. Captain Hawkins shifted his course north by east to avoid the encroaching icefield and ordered his lookouts to keep a sharp eye out for ice.

From 80° east until Cape Leeuwin, strong gales swinging northwest to southeast hammered the clipper as she battled high cross seas. On Monday the 25th, the barque broached heavily during a sudden wind shift and was struck by a huge wave which poured inwards from the port side, an avalanche of green-white water. The port side saloon skylight was smashed in, and the whole cabin flooded. The ship's gig and cutter were ripped from their mounts and stoved in. The gangways and topgallant bulwarks were washed away, as was everything loose upon the decks.

The damage caused by the rogue wave was extensive but not disabling. The dirty weather continued as Cape Otway was passed on the 27th of June at 3:30 pm in moderating west-southwest winds, and the Heads were passed the next day, 83 days from Greenock. After picking up a tow, the Blairhoyle was hauled to the outer moorings to unload her passengers and gunpowder. Once finished, she was hauled into her berth alongside the Sandridge pier to discharge the rest of her cargo.

Hawkins Family Home c1885.

The Blairhoyle.
State Library of Victoria.

The Loch Vennachar arrived just over a week later, on the 6th of July, when the Loch Vennachar sailed into Hobson's Bay. It was while in port that Captain Hawkins met and spent time with Captain Ozanne of the Loch Vennachar. Whatever passed between the two men will forever remain a mystery, but they had a lot in common, especially as the Blairhoyle had been in Calcutta when the great plague took so many experienced captains, and it was as a result of others' misfortune that both men gained their present commands.

In the end, both men agreed that they had been very lucky. James Ozanne planted within William Hawkins' mind the idea of working for the Loch Lines, and he felt great affection for the Loch Vennachar and her captain. Left with food for thought, William Hawkins had much time to think whilst shipwrights repaired his damaged vessel and altered the interior of the Blairhoyle so it could transport a load of 200 horses to India.

The animals were destined for the British army, and military contracts could prove quite lucrative. The Blairhoyle set sail on the 19th of August, arriving in Calcutta on the 4th of November, having first stopped in at Albany to get fresh fodder and water for the horses. Captain Hawkins was loath to spend too long in the pestilence-ridden waters of Calcutta's filthy harbourside. Quickly leaving India with a load of wheat, cotton, and jute, the barque made her long journey back to Glasgow, finally arriving home in late 1884.

By this time, Bill Hawkins had started to make some serious money. Katie, pregnant at the time, pushed for her husband to find them somewhere more suitable to live: a home in keeping with his growing status as a successful merchant captain on a major trade route.

In 1885, having purchased a home Katie found suitable in a neighbourhood in keeping with the Hawkins' growing social status, the family moved from the Watson home in Govan to a much larger abode in the heart of Renfrew, on Hillington Park Circus, Glasgow. This home was a beautiful two-storey, bay-windowed, sandstone terrace on a hill overlooking Glasgow and the sea. It was set amongst a row of similar dwellings with private back gardens and superb views over the Clyde Valley.

Atop the roof, William had a 'widow's watch' built with large windows facing the sea that held telescopes, allowing the family to keep a watch for ships coming and going down the River Clyde. The main focus was on the Govan docks, at which the Blairhoyle was wont to tie up between voyages. It was not long after the family moved in that the Hawkins' second child, Katherine, was born, much to the delight of her mother; but William wanted a son to carry on the Hawkins name. He loved his wife dearly and was determined to be a better father than his own had been.

Despite his ever-changing domestic situation, the sea and profit ever beckoned the ambitious sailing master. The Blairhoyle and her hard-driving captain arrived in Sydney on the 21st of March 1885, having sailed from Liverpool with a hold filled with migrants and general cargo. As usual, the vessel came in with shredded sails and a rattled crew, but as with past voyages, the ship's owners focused solely upon the profits and the times taken to complete a voyage.

Journey time was dead time to them, and so they encouraged their captains to take their vessels to the edge time and again. Those who sailed with Captain Hawkins knew the risks, but he expected nothing from them that he did not expect of himself. Bill Hawkins lived life to the full. It was during this latest voyage across the Southern Ocean that one of the crew of the Blairhoyle, a man named Garster, fell from the rigging and into the sea. Such was the storm that the ship was running before that the vessel could not put about, and the sailor was drowned.

Tied up at Dalton's Wharf, the barque's cargo was unloaded and stored in the Dalton Brothers' warehouse. After a month of inactivity, the Captain took the Blairhoyle through Sydney Heads headed for Valparaiso, Chile, to take on a load of nitrate destined for the gunpowder mills of England. On the way, he hauled into Newcastle to take on a load of coal. Aboard were a few passengers and a hold filled with barley that could be sold in the isolated port city for a sizeable profit. Valparaiso was

Loch Linnhe, 1400 tons.
State Library of Queensland.

considered the crossroads of the eastern South Pacific, and many a ship called in there before attempting to tackle the Horn.

The barque finally left Chile in July, setting forth once more for Liverpool, her hold full of the vital substance gathered from the remains of countless bird droppings gathered for thousands of years. The Blairhoyle arrived home after a rugged journey through Drake's Passage, and she ran her northing through a storm-tossed South Atlantic at the height of winter.

Taking time away from the ship, William travelled back to Glasgow whilst the Blairhoyle was cleaned and repaired. Unlike the composite clippers with their copper-covered hulls, the iron hull of the barque needed regular scraping to remove the weed and barnacles that gathered on her lower hull. Such growths would wipe knots off a vessel's top speed, and to fix this, the iron-hulled clippers were routinely floated into graving docks to have their hulls scraped and painted with copper- or red-lead-based anti-fouling agents.

In 1886, Katie gave birth to Captain Hawkins' long awaited son, William Hawkins Jnr. Bill Hawkins was not there for his son's birth, again being away at sea. Katie had finally taken her mother's advice and temporarily moved into her mother's home at Blackness, Linlithgowshire. Her eldest daughter Kathleen was still living with her grandmother, and Katherine enjoyed getting to know her elder sibling who up until now had been a stranger in a photograph.

The Blairhoyle had sailed from Hamburg for Sydney on the 22nd of March 1886, arriving there on the 8th of July. With a hold filled with gunpowder, she was anchored off Garden Island before her cargo could be unloaded. Having finished loading her cargo of wheat and flour, Captain Hawkins moved his vessel north to take on a load of coal before sailing once again for San Francisco on the 3rd of August.

Captain Hawkins' reputation as a hard driver of ships and men was cemented in the voyage across the Pacific when the Blairhoyle passed into San Francisco harbour ahead of two other clippers. The clipper Darremman sailed from Newcastle on the 21st of August, followed the next day by the ship Loch Linnhe and the barque Blairhoyle. (The Barremman came to grief just two years later when she ran aground at Land's End and sank with the loss of all hands on the 9th of July 1887).

Both the Barremman and the Loch Linnhe were 1400 ton, full-rigged ships; the 1200 ton, barque-rigged Blairhoyle was not considered a serious threat as the three vessels raced across the Pacific aiming to be the first to reach their destination. Then on the 16th of December 1886, after a long and arduous journey, the Blairhoyle appeared first at the San Francisco anchorage. Over a journey of more than 9000 nautical miles, and averaging 150 nautical miles a day, Captain Hawkins had managed to outsail the bigger and supposedly faster ships. His reputation as a canny and uncompromising navigator was assured.

The crew celebrated their good fortune in the dockside bars and brothels of 'Frisco' as the Blairhoyle awaited a full hold and passengers to take back to Liverpool. Captain Hawkins' officers finally rounded up the crew early in the New Year as the Blairhoyle's hold quickly filled with American-made goods bound for England. The barque weighed anchor at the end of the month making for the port of Hull, on the midlands coast, arriving at the end of April 1887.

Setting sail from Liverpool in early July, Captain Hawkins took his ship back south to San Francisco transporting many immigrants to California, arriving on the 18th of November 1887. One day after dropping anchor, she was towed to the Oakland docks to discharge her passengers and cargo.

On the 14th of December 1887, the ship Montgomeryshire and the Blairhoyle started an ocean race from San Francisco. They were bound for Great Britain and were laden with grain and merchandise. Before starting, their Captains made a wager dependent on the result of their long voyage, and each was confident of beating former trans-oceanic records. Upon his return to England in 1888, William Hawkins received orders to take his ship north to Port Discovery, Washington, in the Pacific North-West; there he was to take on a load of timber for transport to the Port of Iquique in Chile.

Port of Pisagua c.1880.
Pisagua Viejo y Nuevo

The iron ship 'Ardenclutha', 1222 tons, under sail. Wrecked April 12, 1895, Iquique at the end of a voyage from Port Blakeny with lumber. State Library of South Australia.

Valparaiso Harbour, circa 1900,
cumberlandscarrow.co.uk

The barque arrived on the 7th of July and, whilst in port, the Blairhoyle was loaded with refined copper ore and saltpetre. Iquique had become a major trading port after Chile had gained its independence and, as it was on the edge of the Atacama Desert, the Blairhoyle's load of timber was highly valuable. After a long voyage the crew were anxious for home, which Captain Hawkins reached at the end of August 1888.

Christmas was spent at home for the first time in several years; it was a time to celebrate the family's continued good fortune. Even though he had been away for many months, William's love for his Katie and children had only grown stronger. However, love alone would not feed the family or keep them in the lifestyle to which they were becoming accustomed.

So once again William Hawkins went to sea from London, arriving aboard the Blairhoyle in Moreton Bay, Queensland, on the 5th of June 1889. On board were many immigrants seeking a new life away from the squalor and poverty of Britain's polluted cities. On the 6th, the Blairhoyle was towed to its dockside anchorage at Raff's Wharf by the steamer Roko and later in the week began to unload her precious load of passengers and 2240 tons of general cargo vital to the needs of the colony.

Amongst the items on board was a collection of fine oak furniture: bedroom suites, toilets, bookcases, oak and walnut sideboards, overmantels and mirrors, and a vast variety of continental style furniture. The cargo was unloaded in just 72 hours by the ever efficient stevedores of the Brisbane docks.

With no cargo to be loaded aboard, Captain Hawkins sailed from Moreton Bay with 750 tons of sand ballast bound for the Chilean port of Pisagua. The port was a major export point for saltpetre, which was vital for the manufacture of gunpowder. The city was considered a jewel in Chile's economic crown and hosted a large expatriate community of Europeans and was home to banks, hotels, and export companies.

After an extended wait at the crowded anchorage, it was the Blairhoyle's turn dockside to discharge her ballast and fill her hold with bags of the valuable nitrate. The barque finally set sail on the 2nd of December 1889 at the height of the Chilean summer. Bill Hawkins and his crew were more than happy to leave the stifling heat of the Chilean desert port behind. Even though the crew were anxious to get home, it was not to be, as the Blairhoyle sailed for the French port of Dunkirk. She passed the ship Ardenclutha on the 30th of January 1890 and finally dropped anchor off the port of Dunkirk on the 7th of February 1890.

Upon his return to England on the 3rd of March 1890, William Hawkins was offered the opportunity to command the brand new iron-hulled ship, the Edenballymore. After a brief few weeks at home with Katie and the children, William set forth on his new adventure, arriving in Hobson's Bay on the 3rd of July 1890. The owners of the ship, Thomson, Dickie & Company, managers of the 'Maiden City Line', were confident that William Hawkins would be a great success, his reputation on the Pacific runs being well established.

After a brief stay to unload her cargo, the Edenballymore, on the 4th of August 1890, set sail in ballast bound for Valparaiso, Chile, to pick up a load of nitrate. The city served as a major stopover for ships travelling between the Atlantic and Pacific oceans as they passed through Drake's Passage. Always a magnet for European migrants and merchantmen, Valparaiso was known by sailors as *"Little San Francisco"* and *"The Jewel of the Pacific"*.

The booming port city was a vital stopover for ships attempting 'The Horn', especially at the height of the winter storms. Many a battered ship limped into its harbour with passengers and crews telling tales of loss, of mountainous seas, and deadly bergs of black ice. After a long haul northwards, the Edenballymore arrived home on the 1st of November 1890. William spent Christmas at home.

While William was home for the winter, news came from across the Atlantic that Katie's estranged father, Captain Robert Watson, had died on the 8th of January 1891. Captain Robert Watson had been working as commodore of the West India and Pacific Steamship Company, and died and was buried in Manga's Cementerio de Santa Cruz, Cartagena, in the West Indies. His loss hurt the family financially as well as emotionally.

Blackness House.

The iron ship Edenballymore, 1726 tons. Built 1890, Russell and Co. Port Glasgow.
State Library of South Australia.

The Cullmore
State Library of Queensland.

With the death of her husband, Catherine Watson Snr took up a position as head of household at Blackness House; living with her was her eldest granddaughter, Kathleen Hawkins, and her youngest daughter, Mary Watson. There the Watson women ran a house which doubled as a barracks for the regiment of the Cameron Highlanders. To the young soldiers, Catherine was a welcome mother figure and Mary a welcome distraction. Young Kathleen was treated as a younger sister by many of the young troopers staying at the grand home not far from Blackness Castle and port town.

William and Katie Hawkins travelled to sea again, taking the eldest of their children with them, travelling across the channel to Antwerp to pick up passengers and cargo bound for San Francisco. On the voyage to America the next Hawkins child, Grace, was born onboard the Edenballymore.

The ship finally arrived in San Francisco on the 16th of August 1892. On board was a cargo of spirits, wines, and ales from Scotland and Europe; aboard were a large number of immigrants bound for a new life on America's west coast. The Hawkins family continued to make the run from Hull to Antwerp to San Francisco and back home via Valparaiso through 1892 and 1893.

The Wreck of the Culmore

William and Katie's second son, Peter, was born on the return journey to Glasgow and Katie decided then it was time for her to settle in one place. The children were old enough to start school and both she and William wanted more for their offspring than they had had growing up.

William agreed with his headstrong wife and, after negotiation with the Edenballymore's owners and his business partners, Bill Hawkins resigned as master of the clipper and took up a post as a shore-based marine superintendent. He still sailed around the local ports and was based in Hull, the headquarters of Thomson, Dickie & Co. William Hawkins became responsible for the loading and unloading of company ships in Hull, Glasgow,

Liverpool, Antwerp, Dunkirk and Hamburg, often travelling on company ships to the different jobs as required by the company, and for the safe operation of ships and docks and the hiring of ships' masters and crews.

William, it turned out, was a much better ship's master than he ever was a shore-side supervisor of ships and men. With the vessels he was master of, he knew every creak and groan, every rivet, cleat and cable of the vessels under his command; it proved not to be so when dealing with vessels upon which he had not sailed.

This deficit in his knowledge was discovered with painfully fatal consequences in the autumn of 1894. On the 16th of November 1894, the ship the 'Culmore' capsized in heavy seas on her way from Hamburg to Barry in ballast. Of the 26 people on board, only four of the crew were saved, and the ship's master just employed by William Hawkins and the captain's young wife were amongst the casualties. After the accident, a Board of Trade enquiry was held at which Captain William Hawkins was summoned to appear.

"The Culmore discharged a cargo of nitrate at Hamburg in October last. While there she was joined by a new master, P. Halliday, aged 28, who had previously been in command of the Polynesian, which vessel was, as well as the Culmore, under the management of Messrs. Thomson, Dickie & Co. He was described to the Court by Captain Hawkins as being a careful, pushing, and energetic shipmaster.

Four days after the Culmore had commenced to discharge her inward cargo of nitrate, Captain Hawkins arrived at Hamburg to control the vessel's expenses, supervise the work necessary for getting the vessel despatched to sea, and to attend to the other duties of a marine superintendent. On 17th October, Captain Hawkins left Hamburg for Barry. He stated to the Court that before leaving he gave instructions to the master to put up shifting boards in the main hold, and to take in 500 tons of sand in order to ballast the ship for going into the dry dock.

On 25th October, Captain Hawkins returned to Hamburg, and found that the ballast had been taken in and was standing in a cone under the main hatch. He stated to the Court that he was under the impression that shifting boards had been put up in the lower hold, but he was not certain about this. With regard to this matter, the Court is impressed with the fact that, had sufficient shifting boards been put up for some 800 tons of ballast, these shifting boards would have been conspicuously visible after 500 tons of ballast was on board, and that Captain Hawkins should have no doubt as to whether they were there or not, considering that he was especially responsible for the vessel's seaworthiness.

On the 26th October, the discharging of the inward cargo was finished. The vessel was then placed in dry dock, and underwent her No. I. survey. After she came out of dry dock, Captain Hawkins arranged with Mr. Guttery, ballast contractor, to complete ballasting the ship to 850 tons. About 160 tons of this ballast was put down the quarter-hatch, and the remainder down the main-hatch. No shifting boards were put in with this portion of the ballast.

The vessel's draught on leaving Hamburg was 12 ft. 6 in. forward and 13 ft. aft. The water there being brackish, it was estimated the vessel would rise three inches when she got into sea water. About 6.30 a.m. on the 4th November, the vessel left Hamburg and was towed down the river.

On the 12th November, the weather began to turn bad, blowing from west and backing into S.W. with a heavy sea. At midnight on the 12th, the three upper topsails were made fast. The gale steadily increased. By midnight of the 13th, the only sail the vessel had set was her main lower topsail. About 6 a.m. on the 14th, the man on the look-out reported to the second mate that the anchor was coming adrift, and was knocking against the bow. The second mate informed the master, who had been on deck all night, of this.

The master ordered all hands on deck to secure the anchors. While at work securing the anchors, they found the vessel taking a heavy list to starboard, and realised that the ballast was shifting. Hands were at once sent into the hold to trim the ballast to windward. The lower main topsail was cut away and endeavours made to get the ship before the wind, but it was found she was unmanageable. As the vessel was now going over fast, attempts were made to get the topmasts out of the ship. With this object in view, one of the witnesses who appeared in Court went aloft with an axe to break the screws of the topmast rigging. His efforts were unsuccessful. He did not succeed in breaking any of them, and there was not sufficient time to unscrew them. The vessel was now almost on her beam ends. The efforts of the hands in the hold were of no avail with the ballast, as the ship was throwing it to leeward faster than they could shovel it to windward.

About 7 a.m., when the Culmore began to list heavily, the Pelican, of Grimsby, a small screw steamer employed in the fish-carrying trade, came under her stern and lay by her for two hours till she sank. Owing to the strength of the gale, and the condition of the sea, the Pelican was unable to take anyone off the wreck. Just before the Culmore sank, the Swift, a Grimsby steam trawler, also came close to her. The master of this vessel made most energetic measures to rescue the crew of the Culmore from their perilous position. He kept his vessel close to the Culmore's stern, and as soon as she sank he steamed over the top of where she went down and was successful in rescuing four seamen, viz., August Elm, Arthur Norberg, and Konstantine Ivanoff, A.B.s, who appeared as witnesses, and another seaman who, through injuries he received, is at present in the infirmary at Hull. His name did not transpire in Court.

The master and the master's wife were also rescued. They were both alive when got on board the Swift, but died shortly afterwards from injuries they had received in the water. The loss of life was due to the suddenness of the casualty and the extreme violence of the storm at the time, which prevented those on board the Culmore from making use of their own boats, while at the same time it prevented the masters of the steam vessels Swift and Pelican from sending boats to their rescue.

The Court is of opinion that blame attaches to Captain Hawkins for not seeing that the ballast was properly secured before the ship left Hamburg, especially considering the quality of the ballast. The Court is further of opinion that no blame attaches to Mr. Robert Dickie, as he appointed a responsible and experienced superintendent and provided all necessary materials for the equipment of the ship. The Court marks its sense of the gravity of Captain Hawkins' fault by ordering him to pay the sum of £50 towards defraying the expenses of this inquiry, and the Court orders accordingly."

Board of Trade Wreck Report for Culmore, 1894.

The loss of the ship, and more importantly 22 lives, devastated William Hawkins; for a time he headed home to be with his wife and children, taking time to rethink his career options. It was obvious to him and to Katie that he would ever only be truly happy at sea with a rolling deck beneath his feet. William Stevenson Hawkins had salt water flowing through his veins, and in his heart he was a sailor and he was a master at his craft.

However, the Hawkins family needed the money and William had investments to protect, so he continued to work as a marine superintendent, but it was definitely not to his liking as he continued to yearn for a command of his own. During the years 1894–1897, William and Katie's family continued to grow; Christina was born in 1896, and Margaret in 1897.

Despite his best efforts, William had lost the confidence of his employers and business partners, and it became painfully obvious that they would never again employ him as a ship's master. In trying to extricate himself from the company and gain back the money and commissions he was owed, William Hawkins and his employers ended up in court.

On the 5th of March 1898 at Plymouth, after four years working with Thomson, Dickie, & Co., Shipowners and Marine Insurance Brokers, 17 Royal Exchange Square, Glasgow, William Hawkins and his former business partners ended their business relationship in an acrimonious manner in the Glasgow Debts Recovery Court after William was terminated without notice.

Facing ruin, William Hawkins looked to his old friend James Ozanne, and the owners of the Loch Line, William Aitken and James Lilburn. William was received with some caution, and the company did not have an opening upon any of the ships currently in port, so without a berth, he waited, and waited, and waited.

Eventually, the directors of the Glasgow Shipping Company approached Captain Hawkins with a business proposal.

R.M.S. Orotava.
National Library of Australia.

Aitken, Lilburn and Co. had received word that the captain of the Brabloch had fallen ill on the way to Australia and if William was willing, and could get himself there before the Brabloch arrived, he would be given command. Delighted to be given another chance, Bill Hawkins packed his bags and within the week boarded the Orient Line steamship, RMS Orotava, bound for Sydney.

The Orotava arrived in Sydney on the 19th of April 1898. Bill Hawkins disembarked and headed for the offices of the agents who handled the Loch Line's Sydney affairs. Upon arrival at the offices of Briscoe, Drysdale & Co, he learned that the Brabloch had left London on the 14th of January and had passed by the Cape Otway light on the 23rd of April.

Breathing a huge sigh of relief, William made final preparations to take command of the vessel once she had discharged her cargo and anchored in the harbour. The Brabloch dropped anchor off Garden Island on the 28th of April 1898. An anxious Captain Hawkins waited impatiently for the current ship's master to come ashore to receive his new orders and to hand over the ship's certificates, ledgers, logbooks, and charts that came with a change of command.

After her load of gunpowder had been lightered off and her passengers had disembarked, the ship was towed over to the Federal Customs Wharf where the cargo was inspected and all taxes and duties were paid. After clearing customs, the Brabloch was then towed over to Reid's Wharf to discharge her cargo in the first week of May, and on the 26th, Captain Hawkins had the ship towed to her anchorage in Woolloomooloo Bay.

With a new ship's captain came new agents. William, acting upon company orders, looked for and found new agents to act for the ship. The agents William Hawkins employed were A. McArthur & Co, of Macquarie Place, Sydney. They dealt with all of the financial and commercial matters whilst Bill

The steel ship 'Brabloch', 2062 tons, in an unidentified port. She is renamed 'Vinga' in 1917 and broken up in 1924. [steel ship, 2062 tons, ON96072, 278.7 x 41.1 x 24.2. Built 1889 (6) Barclay, Curle and Co. Glasgow. Owners: RK Holms-Kerr, (Aitken, Lilburn & Co. mgrs) reg. Glasgow

State Library of South Australia.

Hawkins reorganised his new ship's officers, then set about signing on new crew.

After three weeks at her moorings, the Brabloch was towed into the stream ready to up anchor for England, which she did on the 16th of June 1898. Aboard the vessel was a load of wool, tallow, skins, mint sweepings, and copra. Captain Hawkins rewarded the faith placed in him by James Lilburn when he brought the clipper into Gravesend on the 30th of September.

Captain Hawkins' position as master of the Brabloch was confirmed and a contract was drawn up utilising his skills as an experienced mariner. He next sailed to Australia, taking the ship on a run to Melbourne via Adelaide. The ship left London in early January 1899 with cargo and passengers bound for Table Bay, South Africa. After unloading cargo and passengers, the Brabloch departed Table Bay on February 22nd in ballast and made quick passage to Adelaide for orders, running her easting down through relatively mild conditions for the Southern Ocean with no ice sighted as the ship scudded across the ocean.

Captain Hawkins and crew dropped anchor off the Semaphore on April 4th before being piloted into Port Adelaide to discharge the last of her cargo. After a week in Port Adelaide, the ship once more got under way headed for Port Melbourne. The ship arrived in ballast in Hobson's Bay on April 19th and soon loaded up again with wool, hides, and wheat. The Brabloch and her erstwhile captain left Port Melbourne on the 14th of June and had to anchor off Queenscliffe waiting for favourable winds, which picked up on the 16th of June.

She arrived in London on the 26th of October 1899 after a laborious run in which the ship encountered contrary winds trying to round the Horn, and was becalmed for many days as she tried to cross the Equator. It was because of the long voyage that William was given no time to travel home for Christmas. He and most of his crew almost immediately set sail again for Adelaide, leaving on the 18th of December 1899. For the Hawkins family it was a miserable Christmas, but food on the table and money in the bank for his children's future was a driving motivator for both William and Katie Hawkins.

The Brabloch sailed forth once again from Gravesend with a disgruntled Captain and crew aboard; however, the owners were insistent that the ship and her cargo get away as soon as possible as there was a charter waiting for them in Australia. Aitken, Lilburn and Co. were looking to increase their profits by trying alternative routes home. Income from wheat and wool freights were falling as steamer companies such as the Cunard, White Star and Adelaide Steamship Companies were offering cheaper rates and faster service.

The firms managing windjammers were being forced to send their vessels to more and more out-of-the-way places that could not accommodate the larger steamers. The Loch Line had already begun to divest itself of the less profitable 1200 ton vessels, concentrating on the super clippers, the giant four-masted barques, the 1500 tonners Loch Vennachar and Loch Garry, and the new steel clipper, the Brabloch, which was lighter, stronger, larger than and as fast as the 1500 tonners. The Brabloch was a state-of-the-art steel-hulled clipper, the peak of her design, but a design that had increasingly limited application and appeal to the everyday importers and exporters who looked to steamships for their business.

The Brabloch left Gravesend on December 18th and sailed down the English Channel with strong east to southeast winds. Winds swung round to the southwest to northwest as she made rapid progress, passing Madeira 13 days out. She had had two calm days in the Bay of Biscay before picking up the northeast trades which carried the ship briskly into the tropics where once again she was becalmed. After losing the trades she suffered through nine days of light and variable winds.

On the 5th of January a member of the crew, John McEwin AB, died and was buried at sea. He had been laid up with illness since just after the ship had left port and only appeared briefly on deck on December 24th. The Equator was crossed on the 12th in hot and sultry conditions with little wind punctuated by occasional rain squalls. The southeast trades were finally picked up and Captain Hawkins piled on the sail as the Brabloch pushed south, passing the line of Greenwich along the 42nd parallel as she began to run her easting down.

She made her easterly run along the 43rd parallel passing beneath the Cape of Good Hope on the 5th of February. Moderate winds, fine weather and calm seas were experienced for much of the trip across the Southern Ocean to the meridian of Cape Leeuwin when the usual westerly gales picked up as the ship drove northeast. Freshening northwest to southwest winds and rising seas followed the Brabloch all the way to Cape Borda; once into Investigator Strait strong west winds prevailed as she headed into the gulf.

The Brabloch arrived in Adelaide on the 5th of March at the end of an eventful voyage, and after discharging her cargo of general hardware she was taken on charter to the Port of Thio, New Caledonia. There she was to pick up a load of copra and sago for export back to Glasgow. Aboard were several plantation owners and their families returning to Scotland. Despite this venture into literally unknown waters, the trip back to Scotland, which began on the 25th of April and ended at Greenock on the 30th of July 1900, proved to be unprofitable once all the ship's expenses and crew's wages were paid out.

There was some dissatisfaction amongst officers and crews of various vessels within the fleet and thus several sailing masters were offered new commands. Amongst those marked for change was William 'Bully' Martin, a straight-shooting, no-nonsense captain with a poor reputation amongst the crews, was facing problems on the Loch Ness, so was given command of the four-masted barque, Loch Broom. With a reputation as a reliable 'relief' captain, Bill Hawkins was appointed as the interim commander of the Loch Ness.

The crew were greatly relieved to be serving under a master with the reputation of Captain Hawkins. To most, he was known as a hard-driving yet careful navigator, a man who drove his ships and crews hard but never lost his hearty and jovial nature. One particularly relieved was the ship's sailmaker, Richard 'Dickie' Simpson, who had served under Hawkins before and knew what to expect from the man while at sea.

The Loch Ness.
State Library of Victoria.

Thus began another chapter in Bill Hawkins' career. With a new ship and a new crew, he had a great deal of work to do and not much time to bring the vessel and her crew up to his expectations. Bully Martin had run a very tight ship, but he was a cautious captain who took few risks. This proved popular with the ship's owners, but he was considered somewhat of a tyrant by those who sailed under him.

The time between commands gave William a chance to head home to Glasgow to spend time with Katie and his ever-growing family. The Hawkins home was a hive of feminine family activity, for besides Catherine, now aged 43, ruling a house of eight children, she did so with the help of her aged mother Catherine Watson,75, her spinster sister Margaret Watson, and her nanny and housekeeper Bridget Moan from Ireland. Katie also ran the family business interests whilst her husband was at sea, and with so many people underfoot, William, who for so much of his life was a master to be obeyed, became just another member of the Hawkins 'crew' whenever he made it home.

Hence, it was with a mix of melancholy relief that William once again headed off to sea at the helm of the Loch Ness on the 23rd February 1901, sailing from Glasgow to Melbourne.

The Loch Ness, barque, left Greenock on the night of February 23, at 8.30, with light westerly winds. She anchored at Belfast Lough next day, and sailed thence on 27th, with a heavy westerly gale. She was eight days in the channel. The wind blew hard from the west until Madeira was reached on March 16. The trades were picked up in 23 N. and 26.48 W., and the equator was crossed on April 2 in 26.48 W. The south-east trades, which were only moderate, were lost in 22 S., 29.8 W. On April 18, in 28.18 S., 19.8 W., two starboard foretopmast backstays were carried away by a heavy south-west gale, and they had to be secured with tackles for the time being. The Cape was passed on April 27, in 44.41 deg. Then heavy gales were encountered, waves coming aboard and washing away all loose deck gear. The gales lasted till the Leeuwin was reached, and then the wind fell, and calms were experienced for five days. On May 25 the heaviest gale of the voyage blew, and the ship ran under lower topsails until it moderated. The Borda was passed at 3 a.m. on Sunday, and the anchorage was reached on Monday night. **The Register 28 May 1901.**

The barque arrived in Adelaide on the 27th May 1901 and, after discharging part of her cargo, sailed directly for Melbourne without incident. As was his way, Captain Hawkins had driven the Loch Ness hard through some quite violent weather, but such was his mastery of a vessel in such conditions that neither he nor the crew were in any great fear of their lives.

She dropped anchor in Hobson's Bay on the 3rd of June 1901, her hold filled with general merchandise. Such runs were commonplace for Bill Hawkins, and he knew the waters well. He spent what time he did have in port visiting friends and conducting company business. After a four-month stint in Hobson's Bay, Captain Hawkins and the crew were anxious to get underway once again. Having had her hull cleaned and painted, and her hold filled with wool, wheat, and other items of produce from the colonies, the Loch Ness set sail for London on the 3rd of October at 1:30 pm. Fair winds allowed the vessel to clear the heads before nightfall and she was once again on her way south-east heading for Cape Horn and home, arriving on the 17th of January 1902.

Word came back to the wool buyers in London that southern Australia was once more slipping into drought and the amount of fine wool available would be quite limited. Thus it was that the first ships to port stood the greatest chance of filling their holds, and getting away early enough would see a massive increase in profits for the trip.

Captain Hawkins, who had been hoping to spend some time in Glasgow with Katie, had to cable her with the unwelcome news that he would again be at sea before the year was out. Such was the price to be paid for being a successful ship's master. The Loch Ness put to sea on the 21st of March headed once again for Adelaide and Melbourne. William pushed his ship hard, for he could smell a profit and he was racing against some of the finest clippers on the colonial run.

Despite the crew's best efforts, the weather did not co-operate with the Loch Ness and her impatient captain. Fighting a

Hobson's Bay Railway Co's Pier. Sandridge.
State Library of Victoria.

north-westerly gale, the barque finally dropped anchor in Port Adelaide on the 9th of June 1902. On board for her call in Adelaide was a selection of earthenware and hardware, linens, chemicals, explosives, beer, and fine spirits. She had more such cargo bound for Melbourne's warehouses.

Upon arrival in Hobson's Bay on the 29th of June, the Loch Ness was towed to her Williamstown moorings and began to discharge her cargo. The trip had taken 96 days, and there were times when he and the crew thought they'd be lucky to get to Melbourne at all.

Captain Hawkins commented that during the trip several fierce storms were encountered. Seas were so rough that oil bags were used to slow the ship and keep her from broaching in the heavy seas. Horrendous hail-filled gales lashed the ship, at times reducing visibility to almost nothing. Vivid lightning bolts accompanied the storms, adding to the nightmarish quality of the storms. The Loch Ness came through with little damage, though, and even as she entered the Straits to Adelaide, she had little trouble finding her way in the stormy conditions.

After an eventful trip, Captain Hawkins was more than a little anxious to get underway again, the ship having been surveyed for damage by a Lloyds inspector and given the all-clear. However, the weather gods continued to conspire against Bill Hawkins' plans for a quick dash home.

Having been scheduled to leave port in October, the driest year ever was recorded and sheep numbers fell by more than half. With little wool on the market and freight costs rising, the Loch Ness and her crew were forced to look for other cargoes to fill the hold. After months of rescheduling and delays waiting to fill the ship's hold, the Loch Ness finally set sail for London on the 22nd of December, arriving home on the 24th of March 1903.

"The year 1902 cannot be placed among the bright years of Australian history. It has been badly marked by natural calamity... The ravages of the drought are one of the great facts of the period which closes today. When the year was entered upon, it was hoped that the worst of the prolonged drought in the northern states had been experienced. Tremendous losses of stock

The Hinemoa, a four-masted steel barque built in 1890 by Russell & Co., Greenock.
State Library of Queensland.

had been sustained... The copious rains did not fall, however, until November and December, and meanwhile the enfeebled flocks succumbed by the millions."

The Argus, Wednesday 31 December 1902.

The times that William and Katie spent together throughout their long marriage were precious and few. They loved each other greatly, but it was impossible for them to spend great lengths of time together. This was no different when Captain Hawkins walked out of his front door at Hillington Park and walked the few blocks down to the wharf. After checking in with the harbourmaster and the weather and tides, he took the ship's gig out to her moorings and there waited for passengers and the last of the crew to come aboard.

The Loch Ness slipped her moorings and was towed from her Greenock anchorage on the 15th of May 1903. After a swift journey, the Loch Ness was forced to anchor in the outer moorings of the Semaphore Anchorage as, when she arrived, Port Adelaide was already full dockside with another dozen vessels waiting to discharge their cargoes. Eventually, the Loch Ness unloaded her 400 tons of whisky and sailed on to Hobson's Bay.

Upon arrival, Captain Hawkins received word that he was to await other Loch Line vessels. By the middle of October, the Loch Katrine, Loch Rannoch, Loch Ness, Loch Garry and the Loch Etive had arrived. A late arrival was the Loch Tay with a sick Captain Bennett aboard. All awaited their share of a meagre wool clip.

By Christmas Day, the Loch Ness had begun loading more than 10,000 bags of wheat at the Williamstown Wharf. The Loch Ness, along with six other clippers, was contracted by the British Government to combine with five other ships to take the excess wheat harvest to Europe in one large fleet. The other ships loading alongside the Loch Ness at the Williamstown Pier were the Enrichetta, the Pharos, Cambrian Monarch, Belfast, Apollo, and the Hinemoa.

This was one trip long overdue and William Hawkins was anxious to head home as by now he knew Katie would have given

Captain John W Peden.
Townsville Daily Bulletin, Monday 25 August 1930.

birth; but as to her health and that of the child, he had to wait. Katie Hawkins gave birth safely to Patrick Hawkins at the family home earlier in the year.

Events were to overtake Bill Hawkins when the master of the Loch Vennachar fell gravely ill and was rushed to Bethesda Hospital. Word was sent to James Lilburn for advice and, not long after, Captain William Hawkins was asked to bring the Loch Vennachar back to Glasgow.

The Loch Ness's first officer was given command of for the return journey, but first he had to replace his sailmaker as Dick Simpson followed his friend to Hawkins's new command. On the 15th of January 1904, the Loch Ness left Melbourne with a new captain, John W. Peden. After a delay to transfer command of the vessel and settle Captain Bennett's affairs, the Loch Vennachar left Melbourne on the 23rd with William Hawkins as its new master. Both ships were headed for Hull with over 2,000 bales of wool and 10,000 bags of wheat for the London markets.

Born in Kilmarnock, Scotland, Captain Peden would go on to have a long and distinguished career as a ship's master and later as a harbour pilot in Rockhampton and Brisbane. The Loch Vennachar arrived safely on the 3rd of May 1904, anchoring at Gravesend with her load of wheat and wool. The early arrival allowed Bill Bennett to spend time at home. He was overjoyed to meet his new son, Patrick, for the first time. The Hawkins family celebrated this time together, those precious few weeks when they were a complete family again.

It was just before the Loch Vennachar was due to leave Glasgow that one of her apprentices, Syd Stein, received word that his elder brother William had been killed when the steamer he was first officer on, the Nemesis, was lost with all hands off Cronulla on the 13th of July 1904. Despite Syd's grief, the Loch Vennachar weighed anchor on time, on the 15th of July, her hold filled with general cargo bound for Adelaide and Melbourne.

After a rugged 97-day trip plagued by storms and heavy seas, the Loch Vennachar arrived at anchor off the Semaphore, Adelaide, ahead of a violent storm on the cloudy morning of Tuesday the 18th of October. The storm blew in all morning, covering the gulf and most of Adelaide in a huge dust storm that brought with it cyclonic winds, hail, belting rain, and dozens of injuries as a result of flying debris and fallen trees. Captain Hawkins, a veteran of such storms, safely secured his ship, which along with the barque Isabel Browne rode out the gale without problems.

When the winds finally abated in the early morning, Captain Hawkins signalled the Semaphore that he would need the pilot so he could unload his 600 tons of spirits and cargo destined for the Port Adelaide docks. Whilst the Loch Vennachar was tied up in port, one of the passengers who had been travelling on the sailing ship for his health passed away suddenly from the effects of tuberculosis:

"On Thursday morning Thomas Erskine, a passenger from Glasgow to Melbourne by the ship Loch Vennachar, which is at Port Adelaide, died in his cabin of consumption. Erskine, who was a groom in the employ of Messrs J. & P. Coats, the well-known thread and cotton manufacturers of Paisley, Scotland, was a single man, aged 28 years. He suffered from consumption and, prior to coming to Australia, was 18 months in a sanatorium. Messrs Coats & Co. paid his passage to Australia, and on arrival in Melbourne he was to meet one of their agents, who was to arrange for him to go on a farm to regain his health. Erskine was not actually ill on the passage out, but was very weak. He was dressed and on deck as usual on Thursday morning, and requested the steward shortly before 8 o'clock to remove his sleeping apparel from the upper to the lower bunk. As soon as this was done he went down in his cabin, and three minutes later was dead. Erskine, who was a native of Scotland, had, it is believed, only one sister living, the rest of the family having also died from consumption."

The Advertiser, Friday 21 October 1904

Happy to be away from the events of Adelaide, the Loch Vennachar passed through Port Phillip Heads at 9:10 am on the 28th of October 1904. Before she had left, however, Captain Hawkins had all of the bedding from the cabins occupied by Tom Erskine burned and had the ship's steward replace it with brand new linen and mattresses.

What followed was six weeks of waiting for her cargo of wheat and wool to be loaded. The weather was fine and cool, more like a Cornish summer. The crew also thought so and several members gave Captain Hawkins quite a few headaches. One of his apprentices, Sydney Stein had completed his time as an apprentice. As his home was in Melbourne the master of the Loch Vennachar permitted the young man to leave the ship in Melbourne, endorsing his completed indenture papers.

Four days after their docking in Port Melbourne, the ship's cook, James McDonald, stepped ashore after lunch and was supposed to be back aboard by 6 pm. He did not return and Captain Hawkins fined him 14 days pay. Three days later, once her inward cargo had been discharged, sveral of the crew signed off, having fulfilled the terms of their sign-on articles. David Johnston, Assistant Steward, and Able Seamen Angus McDougall, A. McSporran, John McDonald, Neil McKechnie, Harry Gillespie, T. Chalmers, R. Tucker, J. Archer, and John Best. They were joined by other members of the crew for a run ashore visiting the pubs and other establishments. Except for those discharged sailors, everyone returned to the ship that evening except sailmaker, Dickie Simpson. A seasoned drinker, the fractious Scot had gone on the ran-tan and was somewhere ashore three sheets to the wind.

The ships cook, James McDonald still had not returned after a week and Dick Simpson finally surfaced on November 3rd having been fined a months pay. Ten days later Simpson again disappeared on a three day bender but was found by James Priest and others and returned to the ship much the worse for wear. Then after three weeks Bill Hawkins decided to replace his cook. He was officially listed as having deserted the ship, taking his effects with him. He was already at sea aboard an outbound vessel.

Ten days later a new cook was signed on, William McLean joined the Loch Vennachar on December 10th along with R.H. Rolton as 3rd Mate. William Baird, Richard Tucker, R Pusch, G. W. Johnson, George McCoppin, Alex Stewart, B. Hansen who all

Steam-Tug Guiana. Built 1886 by Uskside Shipbuilding Co. Ltd.

signed on at 4 pm just before the ship cleared out on December 12th.

With the last of her crew safely aboard the Loch Vennachar passed through the Rip on the 14th of December 1904, loaded with wool and wheat for the London sales.

After a voyage of 91 days the Loch Vennachar made her number off Prawle Point on March 13th. 1905, being towed up channel by a steam tug, reaching her Tilbury moorings that evening. Two days later a pair of river tugs hauled the clipper up to London Dock, the ship being entered inward on the 15th, the Loch Vennachar coming to rest alongside warehouse 1. Most of the crew were paid off in London though several including First Mate James Priest and sailmaker Dickie Simpson stayed aboard for the tow home to Glasgow.

The Loch Vennachar departed the Thames on April 11th behind the steam-tug Guiana bound for the River Clyde. The pair arrived at the Tail-'o-the-Bank on the 16th. She was then shifted up river to Queen's Dock, Broomielaw the following morning.

XIV

Crew of the Final Voyage

James Priest, 35, North Shields, Tynemouth – First Officer

First Officer James Priest.

Engraving of the Red Cross Line tea clipper Royal Edward.

James Priest was born on December 11, 1869, at North Shields, Tynemouth. He was the son of Captain Samuel Priest and Margaret J. Priest (née Errington). James was the second eldest of nine children: Jane, Samuel, Ann, Isabella, Margaret, George, Lily, and Florence. When James was a baby, the family lived in a stone terrace on Linskill Street, North Shields. However, with more children on the way, the Priests moved to Gardner Street, North Shields. James's father, Samuel, was a mariner who married the daughter of a mariner and whose own father was a mariner too.

He first went to sea with his father's blessing, signing on as an apprentice aboard the 1,500-ton tea clipper Royal Edward, operated by H. Fernie & Sons. On April 4, 1886, aged just 16, James joined the crew. Captain Robert McCleave sailed the Royal Edward from Sharpness on April 20, 1886, with a full cargo of bagged salt for Melbourne.

The ship was first damaged by heavy gales in the South Atlantic at 29°S 18°E, which destroyed two boats, swept away all loose deck fittings, and severely strained the vessel, causing leaks and water ingress from the deck. Periodic pumping was required to continue the journey. Around June 30, at 40°S 27°E, she encountered a hurricane-force gale that severely damaged her and washed away the cabin. The ship took on more water as the leaks increased.

After three days of pumping, the crew was exhausted. Fortuitously, the Norwegian barque Bellona arrived and, at great risk, rescued the crew on July 3. They were delivered safely to Sydney on August 12. When the Royal Edward was abandoned, she was in a sinking state.

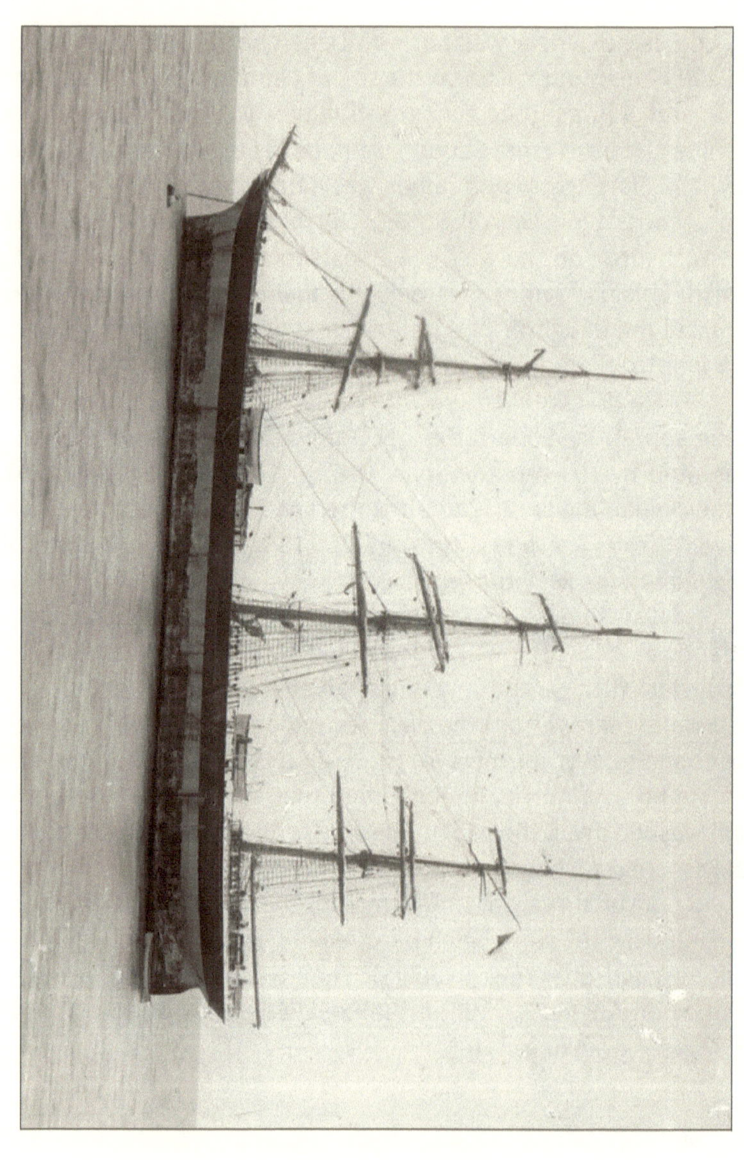

The iron ship 'Aristomene', 1795 tons, at anchor.
State Library of South Australia.

Still under indentures upon his return to Britain, Fernie & Sons placed James aboard the 1,188-ton barque Royal Alice late in 1886. He finished his apprenticeship aboard the iron clipper ship Aristomene in April 1891, before staying aboard as an Able Seaman for another 15 months. He eventually left the ship in Vancouver, Canada, where he sat for and gained his Second Mate's certificate in February 1892. The Aristomene then sailed back to Liverpool laden with wheat.

James Priest briefly returned home to North Shields to visit his family. The only ones at home were his parents, Samuel and Margaret; his brother Sam, who was an apprentice butcher; his sister Isabella, a tailoress; and the youngest, Edith, who was still at school. His brother George had also gone to sea as an ordinary sailor aboard another Fernie clipper.

Priest's first berth as a Second Mate was aboard the brand-new 1,500-ton steel barque Annie Speer, a coal and saltpetre boat running between Shields and Iquique. He boarded her in August 1892 and returned to Liverpool a year later. Once there, James returned home to Shields to sit for his First Mate's certificate. His application papers described Priest as being 5 feet 5 inches tall with a fair complexion, light brown hair, and blue eyes. He had tattoos of a ballerina and a British ensign on his right arm. James was successful, despite having to sit the exams twice after failing the navigation exam using a chronometer on his first attempt. Priest was granted his ticket on October 7, 1893.

Soon after gaining his Mate's certificate, James began working for the Dundee Shipowners' Co., securing a berth as First Officer of the Glenfyne. Under the management of W.O. Taylor & Co., the Glenfyne operated as a classic deep-water "tramp," traversing treacherous routes between the UK, Australia, and South America. In 1894, she was a frequent sight in the coal ports of New South Wales, often hauling fuel to South Australia before venturing across the Pacific.

After leaving the Glenfyne in May 1897, James Priest returned to North Shields to study for his Master's certificate, which he successfully obtained on January 27, 1898. In April 1898, he signed on as First Mate of the Glenogil, a four-masted

The 913 ton, barque 'Glenfyne', under a coaling staithe at Newcastle
H. Built, 1882, in Aberdeen by Alex Stevens.
State Library of Victoria.

steel barque of 2,271 tons. Continuing his employment with the Dundee Shipowners Company, he sailed from London to New York and then on to Melbourne. He remained with the Glenogil until July 1900, at which point he rejoined the Glenfyne.

The 1901 Census confirms that James Priest was serving as First Mate aboard the Glenfyne while the vessel was docked at Millwall Dock, London. At 31 years old, he was building a significant reputation within the company, having served reliably aboard their premier vessels.

Working for the Dundee Shipowners' Co. as First Mate aboard the barque Glenfyne, under Captain William Hossack, a Scottish master of many years' experience, James had made the London-to-Sydney run quite regularly. His transfer to the Loch Vennachar was not that much of a change for this toughened ship's officer. Following his service for the Dundee Shipowners' Co., James transitioned to the prestigious "Loch Line" (the Glasgow Shipping Company), known for its fleet of fast iron and steel clippers.

He joined the crew of the Loch Vennachar when the previous First Mate, Gordon Anderson, left to join another of the Loch Liners in 1903. James Priest was being groomed to become the next master of the clipper when Bill Hawkins moved on. He was on only his third trip to Adelaide, yet was no stranger to the route or hazards to be found along the way.

As Chief Officer, James Priest had many duties. He was responsible for all aspects of the ship in Captain Hawkins' absence. In matters of crew discipline, he was wont to use his fists, and it was not unheard of for sailors and stowaways to be beaten, flogged, or worse. James Priest kept a fairly tight grip on the crew and was a fair if hard man. When on watch (usually 4 to 8 am, 4 to 8 pm, or the dog watch), James would stand on the poop deck beside the helmsman, an Able Seaman, and would coordinate with the lookouts, navigate the ship, and respond to dangers as they arose.

In port, when Bill Hawkins was away, James Priest held responsibility for the discharge of the vessel's cargo. Captain Hawkins had learned the hard way to personally supervise the loading of his ships and the placement of a vessel's ballast. James had to manage the upkeep of the vessel and supervise the maintenance work carried out by the crew. Even when the ship was taken into dry dock, James had to superintend major repairs. Working alongside the steward, William Molseed, and the carpenter, James Reid, James Priest had to ensure that required equipment and materials were purchased and stowed for use.

Working with Fred Lake, James ensured that all safety equipment, lifebuoys, belts, safety lines, buckets, boats, and rocket gear were kept in good working order. James would often stand watch with Fred Ward, teaching him the roles and responsibilities of a ship's officer and overseeing his progress in undertaking command of the ship and its crew.

Charles Radcliffe, 21, Michigan, USA - Second Officer

Charles Radcliffe was born in 1884, in Michigan, in the United States of America whilst his family were travelling on business from Britain. The family was originally from Blackburn in Lancashire, a market town in the Burnley borough of Lancashire. During the Industrial Revolution it grew into one of Lancashire's most prominent mill towns. At its peak, it was the world's largest producers of cotton cloth, and a major centre of engineering.

Charles was the son of Samuel George Radcliffe, a wealthy land owner, cotton merchant and business man (he ran his father-in-laws' Cotton Mills and sold the products), and Isabella M Radcliffe (the daughter of wealthy merchant, alderman and cotton spinner, Samuel Smith of Lancashire). The whole family was tied closely to the firm Samuel Smith and Sons, Plumbe St, Burnley. The company and Isabella's father dominated their lives and provided the Radcliffe's with a comfortable standard of living. The family lived in a stately two story home in Whitegate Lane, Burnley. Charles was the oldest of three children; his sister Frances, and his younger brother Richard.

The 148 ton topsail schooner Sunbeam coming into Runcorn.
Unknown Artist.

The iron barque 'Ednyfed', 1115 tons, Built 1882, Doxford and Sons, Sunderland.

Being from a family with money and having travelled frequently with his father overseas Charles developed a love for the sea. Rejecting a life amongst the cotton mills, this fascination led him to away to sea. His choice of vessel was a schooner rigged barge named Sunbeam sailing out of Liverpool for Runcorn. Her master Captain R.M. Ham was happy to have the extra hand aboard though he was only a ships boy paid just a 10 shillings a month. Charlies time aboard the Sunbeam was short lived.

The Sunbeam, heavily laden with pipe clay lay at anchor off Erith Pier in Anchor Bay when she was run down by a large steamer and sunk at her moorings. Charlie and the crew were saved but were left with just what they were wearing. After such a disastrous start to his maritime career, Charlie's father decided that if his son insisted on becoming a mariner then he would do so as an apprentice.

To this end Samuel wrote to his friend ship owner Robert Thomas if he would find a berth aboard one of his vessels with a master who would provide Charles with a solid education in the laws and lore of the sea. The vessel chosen for Charlie was the 1115 ton iron barque Ednyfed, under the command of Captain David Jones. He signed indenture papers with Robert Thompson, and agreed to serve aboard the Ednyfed for not less than 48 months. He signed the articles March 3rd 1900. The barque was scheduled to sail from Liverpool on March 15th 1900 bound for Fremantle, Western Australia, yet did not depart until April 17th.

The Ednyfed arrived off Fremantle on July 7th 1900, 81 days from Liverpool;

"The barque encountered moderate weather, with a couple of heavy gales, which prevailed to the Line, which was crossed 25 days out. Thence to Tristan d'Acunha fine weather prevailed. The Cape was rounded 55 days out and thence up to arrival at the port bad weather was encountered. Some very heavy north to south-west gales prevailed, with heavy seas and fierce rain squalls. The ship came through the rough weather without any material damage. Rottnest Island was sighted at 7 a.m. on Saturday, the

pilot boarded at 2 p.m., and the vessel anchored in Gage Roads at 4 p.m." **The Daily News (9 Jul 1900.**

Whilst in port Captain Jones gave a revealing interview to a reporter for the Daily News;

"The Ednyfed is under the command of Captain David Jones, a fine specimen of the genuine Welshman. He is a very practical skipper of the old school, a real old "sea dog," very plain spoken, and hospitable. A representative of The Daily News dropped in on Captain Jones during the week and found him in his very comfortable cabin on his vessel. In answer to the reporter's questions, Captain Jones stated that he had been at sea since his thirteenth year, a term of 44 years. Of that time, he has been for 20 years master.

Captain Jones hails, as his name will at once imply, from Wales. His birthplace is the small seaport town of Nevin, in North Wales.During his long experience of sea life, Captain Jones has only been wrecked once, and that was many years ago, when sailing in a vessel under the command of the father of a sea-captain now at the Port. No lives were lost. During his time as master, he has been very lucky, not suffering shipwreck, nor ever having any serious damage done to the vessels in his charge. He has, however, at times seen vessels wrecked, and he has several times passed abandoned vessels at sea.

Asked his opinion as to sea life, Captain Jones said that, from a captain's point of view, the life is very hard. It is a very responsible life, and one in which a shipmaster has to put up with many annoyances and troubles; from a sailor's point of view, the life is far harder. Plenty of work, and many privations make it a very unsatisfactory life. For a young man it is very pleasant, but after one reaches the age of 30 or 40 years, he is no longer fit for the sea.

As regards sailors, the captain says that the average seaman is a fool. He is easily led and will believe anything that is told him. He will work for about a year, and then, when reaching port, he gets his money, sometimes £40 or £50, and perhaps in a few days he will have spent every penny. Taking them all round, sailors are all right, very hard workers, etc., but the real fault with them is that they have no will of their own. One bad man in a forecastle can turn all the sailors bad.

As regards the employment of so many foreigners in British ships, Captain Jones said that, in his opinion, the reason was that foreigners had not enough ships of their own, so they were forced to serve in British vessels. British sailors now prefer steamers and will not, unless hard pressed, serve in a sailing vessel. Again, as a general rule, foreigners are quieter and more careful than the British sailor.

From a shipmaster's point of view, Captain Jones expressed the opinion that England as a shipping nation was on the decline. She was yearly losing trade, which was picked up by the Germans. The cause of this loss Captain Jones put down to the strikes that are so frequent in England, and as an example quoted those recently in South Wales. He spoke in very deprecatory terms of the several agitators in England and Wales, who were gaining money by stirring up strife. Referring to the maritime laws of England, the skipper thought that, though they were as strict as foreign mercantile laws, they were not so strictly enforced.

As to the shipping ports, Captain Jones said he thought that Cardiff was the greatest shipping port in the world regarding the number of vessels leaving there every year. London and Liverpool were about equal. Of the shipping ports of Australia, he thought that Sydney was the principal." **The Daily News 14 July 1900.**

Upon discharging the last of her cargo the Ednyfed set sail in ballast on August 10th for Newcastle NSW to load coal for Iquique. She arrived safely on September 1st. Upon his arrival at the Seaman's Mission located in North Stockton, Charlie found a telegram waiting for him. It simply read *"Father died, home, 22/8/1900 – Mother".* Charlie was devastated. In spite of his grief Captain Jones expected him to pull his weight and show up for work as usual. Charlie and the other apprentices stayed at the Seaman's Mission when not at work aboard the Ednyfed. Jones did not want them getting into any trouble whilst in port.

The ship set sail on November 8th heavily laden with 1650 tons of coal. She reached her destination on South America's West Coast on January 7th 1901, after a laborious 60 days at sea.

Iquique Harbour, circa 1908.
Chile-Iquique Archives.

Iquique was a vital hub in the global nitrate trade, with significant maritime activity connecting it to Europe. The Ednyfed departed Taltal on March 6th bound to Falmouth for orders, arriving on June 28th 1901, after a short layover a tug was engaged to tow the barque across the channel to Ghent to discharge 1600 tons of nitrate.

After leaving Ghent-Flushing Captain Jones sailed the Ednyfed back to Port Talbot to collect a new crew. Once there he received orders to sail to Taltal once more with coal. She set sail once again on August 29th with Charlie Radcliffe still aboard now in the second year of his apprenticeship. Arriving at the end of November the barques precious cargo of coal was discharged and then began a long wait until stevedores could be organised to load the bags of nitrate into the hold of the Ednyfed. She finally departed the port on February 2nd 1902 bound to Falmouth for orders and made her number off the signal station on May 11th, 98 days from Taltal. From Falmouth the barque was towed to Bristol to unload.

The barque was docked at Bristol for a month, allowing Charlie to head home to Hornsea to visit his mother, sister Frances, and brother Richard. The family lived in a three story terrace home on East Bourne Road. This was the first time Charlie had been home in two years, and it was strange because his father was absent. Samuel had left his wife Isabella a sum of money that would with careful thrift allow her to and the children to live comfortably, plus there was the ongoing income from investments her husband had made that were meant to be for their future retirement.

East Bourne Road, Hornsea, Yorkshire. Circa 1905.

The Ednyfed was towed from Bristol across to Penarth, Wales, on June 12th to take on a load of coal for East London, on South Africa's west coast. They set sail on July 23rd 1902 with Captain Jones still in command. The barque arrives safely off the mouth of the Buffalo River on October 20th after 89 days at sea. Upon Discharge of her much needed cargo of coal, Captain Jones received orders to sail to Newcastle, NSW in ballast to take on another load of black-diamonds for Chile.

Charlie was looking forward to meeting old friends and going on a spree ashore as the Ednyfed was towed into Stockton harbour on January 16th 1903. Captain Jones was less sanguine, the Ednyfed had not secure charter and so was stuck in the Hunter River until her agents could arrange one. However this time it was not Chile, but the Peruvian port town of Salaverry to which the barque was to carry 1600 tons of coal. After a month in Port they set sail on February 16th beginning one of the slowest most painstaking voyages of the year across the Pacific.

It took the Ednyfed 106 days on a voyage that usually took less than half that time. The barque finally dropped anchor on June 2nd 1903, her crew hungry worn out and suffering the effects of tropical sores and scurvy. The barque had been badly damaged during a series of storms whilst running her easting down along the 44-46th parallel. She had lost sails, the foretopmast, boats, bulwarks and the like whilst her windlass had been destroyed. Captain Jones had been badly injured during the voyage and was immediately sent to hospital upon the vessels arrival. The barque could not set sail from Salaverry until repairs had been made.

There was no outward cargo to be had from Peru and so Captain Jones decided to sail to Barbados for orders. The set sail from Peru on August 25th 1903, however Captain David Jones was in no fit state to command the barque and the first mate, Richard Evans, had assumed command. As a final year apprentice, Charlie Radcliffe had been promoted to acting third mate.

After safely reaching Barbados the Ednyfed was docked for much needed repairs. Captain Evan received orders to sail for

Liverpool when the barque was ready. She set sail on December 13th 1903, and after a month at sea passed the Old Head of Kinsail on January 17th 1904, arriving back in Liverpool on the 20th.   Upon docking Charlie applied for his discharge but was informed by Captain Evans that he still had almost three months left on his indentures.

However Richard Evans was not a harsh man and knew that Charlies mother needed his support. To that end when the Ednyfed was towed to sea on March 19th, the son of Isabella Redcliffe was on his way back to Hornsea to study for his Second Mate exams. The family home, Eastbourne Villa, in Eastbourne Road, Hornsea, was quiet when he arrived at the end of the month.   His mother Isabella had hired a domestic to help with the housework and his siblings were ar school when he arrived. He was warmly welcomed, and once safely settled into his own room Charlie took the books Captain Evans had given him and began to study in earnest for his upcoming exams.

After completing their 4-year apprenticeship, candidates had to submit their indenture papers and discharges to the Superintendent at the local Marine Board (Board of Trade) in Hull to qualify to sit the exam. The Board of Trade examinations for Masters and Mates were conducted at the local Mercantile Marine Office in the vicinity of Whitefriargate-Custom House Road. Charlie travelled to Hull during the first week of May to submit his indenture papers and discharges to the Superintendent at the local Marine Board to prove he was qualified to sit the exams.

For an apprentice to qualify for a 2nd Mate's certificate (Foreign Trade) he had to pass strict Board of Trade examinations focusing on navigation and seamanship. Requirements included competency in arithmetic, using a sextant and chronometer, and proving sobriety and proof of good character. He was quietly confident, that he knew his Navigation and Mathematics, he knew to use a sextant to find latitude and a chronometer, was an expert seaman after more than four years at sea, and was physically fit.

Eastbourne Villa (Left) and the more famous Sunbeam House (Right).

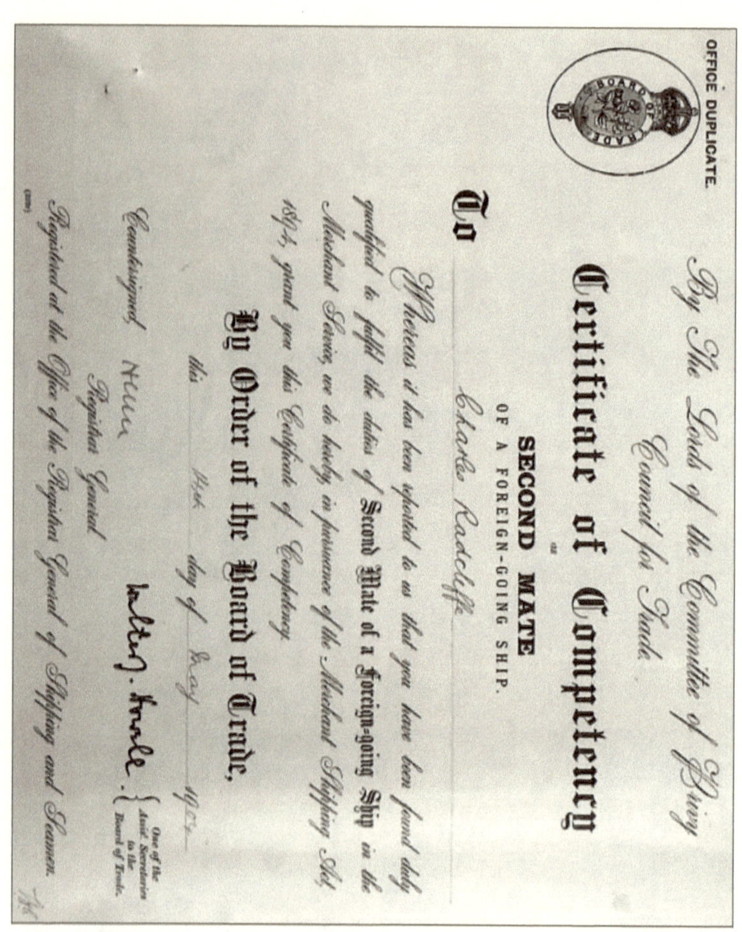

His initial application describe Charlie as being 5 feet, 9 inches tall, with a fair complexion, brown hair and blue eyes. This paperwork was submitted on May 12th and he successfully sat his exams that afternoon. His Second Mate's ticket was issued four days later and a proud Charles Radcliffe made his way home to share the news with his family. Now all he needed was a berth aboard a reputable outbound square rigger, unfortunately for Charlie there the many more qualified mates than there were jobs available in Hull. Instead he knew he would have to send out applications to a variety of merchant shipping companies. At first he looked through classified advertisements in daily newspapers and shipping gazettes.

It was many months before Charlie received a positive reply from one of his many letters. In February of 1905 a registered letter arrived in Hornsea addressed to one Mr. Charles Radcliffe RNR. A clerk from the Scottish firm of Aitken, Lilburn and Company invited him to travel to Glasgow for an interview with James Lilburn.

Thus with a new sea-chest packed with his belongings, books, a new sextant, well worm knife, needle and palm, his old ditty bag and several changes of clothes. Charle boarded the train at Hornsea Town station, travelling to Hull. Alighting in Hull he caught the next train to Newcastle via York, before transferring to an express train that took him to Edinburgh. Staying overnight at a local inn, he freshened up and donned his best attire before catching the early morning train to Glasgow for his 10:00 am appointment at 80 Buchanan Street.

The interview went well and James Lilburn was obviously impressed with Charlie. He was familiar with Captain Jones and knew his as a sober and intelligent sea captain with an excellent reputation for producing apprentices of quality. He was happy to offer Charlie a position aboard one of the vessels his firm owned and managed, as soon as a suitable opening became available. But for the nonce Charlie would just have to trave back to Hornsea and wait. A telegram arrived at the beginning of April summoning Charles Radcliffe to attend upon James Lilburn esq as soon as possible for his position aboard the ship Loch Vennachar sailing to Australia in June.

After a long and sad farewell dinner with his family Charlie again boarded the train to Hull bound for Glasgow and new life as an officer working for the Glasgow Shipping Company.

Fred Lake was born 1883 in Hamilton, Victoria. He was the son of Joshua Lake and Elizabeth Rebecca Lawes Wilkinson (daughter of Julia Owen and Frederick Wilkinson a leading Melbourne barrister). The Wilkinson's and the Lakes were both prominent families from Sussex and Essex in England. Fred was named after his grandfather Frederick Wilkinson the former Master of Equity for Victoria. He was the second of five children. He had an older brother William, and a younger sister and brother, Mary and Geoffrey. He did have another brother named Edward who died as an infant.

None of his siblings followed him into a life at sea. Fred spent his early years in Hamilton where his father was headmaster at Hamilton College Hamilton College, at Clinton, N.Y.; coeducational; founded 1793 by Samuel Kirkland as Hamilton-Oneida Academy, chartered 1812 as Hamilton College. It was named for Alexander Hamilton. Originally a men's college, the school began admitting women in 1979. in western Victoria from 1882 to 1885.

From there the Lake family moved back to Melbourne when Fred's father was appointed as General Superintendant of Fine Arts for Melbourne's great Centennial International Exhibition in 1888-89, and an adviser to the National Gallery of Victoria.

Fred's father was a prominent community figure and philanthropic member of the Old Melburnian Society. Frederick Ward grew up in Malvern, one of Melbourne's leafier suburbs and attended Melbourne Grammar School (1897-8), where his father was a former master from 1872 - 85. Fred lived with his parents until leaving home to become an apprentice with the Loch Line. He started his career as an apprentice aboard the Loch Garry.

Captain James Horne took the wool clipper Loch Garry from the Tail O' the Bank anchorage on June 3rd 1899. The ship was outward bound for Adelaide and Melbourne. The island of Inishtrahull was pass the following evening as the ship and her tug, Flying Fox, headed through the North Channel and into the Atlantic Ocean. The vessels parted company that same evening 10 miles northwest of Inishtrahull. The clipper rolled along, a bone in her teeth sailing across the face of a freshening west to southwest wind, deep into the North Atlantic.

The Loch Garry arrived off Port Adelaide, dropping anchor opposite the Semaphore signal station on September 12th, 100 days from Torr Head, Ireland.

"The Loch Garry, ship, which arrived on Tuesday afternoon, having explosives aboard, went to the North Arm to discharge. She had a most tedious and vexatious passage for a great part of the way from Glasgow, owing to light and adverse

winds. The only good running was through the trade winds and from the Cape of Good Hope to Cape Leeuwin. The best day's run was 306 knots, which showed what the ship could do if she only had suitable winds.

Glasgow was left on June 2, and Greenock on the 3rd, and passing through the North Channel a departure was taken from Tory Island on the 5th. Very light winds prevailed while west of Ireland till reaching the parallel of 30 deg. N. latitude, when better breezes were met with. The north-east trade was met with in 28 deg. latitude, and was moderate in force. St. Antonio was passed in sight on the 26th. Over a week was spent in the doldrums, and the equator was crossed on July 8. Till the end of July the winds were provokingly light, and at times ahead, so that the prime meridian was not reached till August 5, in latitude 42 deg. S. The meridian of Cape Leeuwin was passed on August 31.

The running was fairly good, averaging 215 knots daily. After passing the meridian of Cape Leeuwin much detention was caused by light winds and calms, so that Cape Borda was not sighted till the 9th, and, to keep up the character of the passage, the ship was detained for two days in Investigator Strait. Three gales were encountered while running the easting down. The first was a stiff north-east gale, bringing up a high sea on the day after passing Tristan d'Acunha.

The next was on August 12, in latitude 40 deg. S. and longitude 27 deg. E., from the north-west, during which the ship was hove-to for 20 hours. The oilbags were used with good effect. The last one was a severe and long-continued gale, commencing on August 25, in latitude 38 deg. S. and longitude 84 deg. E., lasting for four days till reaching longitude 104 deg. E. and latitude 39 deg. S. This gale raised a very high sea, compelling the ship to be kept well before it. The ship came through them all with very trifling damage. The Loch Garry was towed up, and touched the ground near No. 9 beacon, but got off after a short detention."
The Advertiser 13 September 1899.

Upon discharge of a portion of her cargo Captain Horne had the ship moved back out into the stream ready for the short run to Port Melbourne.

The Loch Garry left Port Adelaide on September 19th and sailed into a series of heavy gales for three day, passing through

Port Phillip heads on September 24th. After discharge of the last of her gunpowder the ship was towed upriver to Port Melbourne so the rest of her cargo could be hoisted ashore. Several of the crew were signed off and Captain Horne was left to find at least a dozen sailors for the run home. He also signed on a new apprentice, one Frederick Ward-Lake, the son of well know artist and Free Mason, Joshua Lake.

He was a friend of Captain Horne, who often stayed at the Lakes palatial two story home of Aldersbrook in Toorak. The Lake family were well known in Melbourne Society and regular patrons of the arts. Captain Horne was glad to have his friend's son aboard, even though it was unusual for Aitken and Lilburn to take on Australian apprentices.

Captain James Horne   **Joshua Lake.**

With a fresh crew and new apprentice aboard, the Loch Garry set sail from Melbourne on Monday November 27th heavily laden with wool and wheat bound for the Melbourne sales. She passed through the Heads at 10:00 am. Settling course to sail south by south east Captain Horne sailed below New Zealand and cross the South Pacific deep into the Roaring Forties. Cape Horne was passed on Christmas Day, 28 Days from Melbourne, and finally picked her tug up off of Prawle Point, on February 19th, after a voyage of 84 days. She had a record run sailing through the tropics, crossing the Tropic of Capricorn on January 14th and 14 days and two hours later she crossed the tropic of Cancer, a trip of almost 3000 nautical miles, a speed record that was not bettered by a commercial square rigger. On February 4th and 5th, while positioned between latitudes 40° North and 38° North and longitudes 42° West and 34° West, the vessel encountered a very heavy gale blowing from the West-Northwest. This weather system produced a dangerously high sea.

The following week, on February 11th and 12th, at latitude 45° North and longitude 27° West, the ship was struck by another heavy gale, this time coming from the East-Northeast and Northeast. The conditions were severe enough that the ship was forced to heave to for 24 hours to ride out the storm.

Finally, on February 16th, 17th, and 18th, between latitudes 48° North and 49° North and stretching from longitude 19° West to 9° West, the vessel faced a strong westerly gale. During this period, the ship experienced a high following sea as it continued its approach. It was another cracking run by James Horne and the first of many voyages for Fred Ward who by now was aloft with the best of the old sailors and taking his regular tricks at the wheel.

The ship was soon taken from her Gravesend anchorage by a pair of river tugs and moved up to her London Dock berth. The Loch Garry's cargo was amongst the first of the season and fetched a good price at the March wool sales. After taking on a crew of runners the Loch Garry left London on March 20th 1900, and was towed all the way back to Glasgow and placed back on the berth for Adelaide and Melbourne.

Once in Glasgow Fred lake as introduced by Captain Horne to the owners of the Loch Vennachar. They were happy to have him aboard and looked forward to him repaying their faith

Broomielaw Bridge, Glasgow, circa 1900.

with long service with the company. Fred was quartered at a residence Aitken & Lilburn had set up for their apprentices just a stone's throw from Queens Dock, Broomielaw. Named after the Brumelaw Croft, a stretch of land along the Clyde, the Broomielaw extended from Victoria Bridge to Anderston Quay in Glasgow.

After taking on a new cargo of heavy irons wears from Henderson's, barrels of whiskey and assorted homewares for the colonies the Loch Garry was shifted down to Greenock and her Tail O' the Bank anchorage. Before her passengers joined the ship, James Horne had the clipper towed across to the powder hoys to take on her cargo of explosives. Moored at the mouth of Gare Loch the ship was soon joined by a pair of red painted barges from which kegs of gunpowder were hoisted abord the Loch Garry and sent into the main hold before the main hatch was sealed.

The Loch Garry was towed from Greenock on June 2nd and left off Inishtrahull the following evening. After a voyage of 97 days the Loch Garry dropped anchor in the Semaphore roadstead on September 8th 1900. After discharging a portion of her cargo the clipper with her four passengers still aboard cleared out from Port Adelaide on September 13th bound for Melbourne.

"The Loch Garry left Greenock on June 2nd, passing Tory Island on the 4th. A long continuance of adverse south-westerly winds hindered progress, and the island of Madeira was not passed until June 24. The N.E. trades proved light and disappointing, so that the equator was only crossed on July 14. In the southern trade region the breezes were, however, of a more wholesome character. Tristan D'Acunha was sighted on July 30th.

The meridian of the Cape of Good Hope was crossed on August 7th. During the run across the Southern Ocean the ship chiefly experienced winds south of west, and a long south-westerly swell. Between the meridians of 38 and 52 degs. east, in about 41 degs. south, severe gales were encountered. The gale of the 14th August was a very "wicked" one, raging with such fury that the vessel was "hove to," and the expedient of using oil bags to quell the turbulent seas was adopted with marked benefit. The Loch

The 1565-ton Loch Garry under tow headed down the Clyde.
Built by J&G Thomson, Glasgow.

Garry, although sorely pressed, emerged from these trying engagements without suffering damage, a fact which speaks well for her "storm fighting" capacities.

The meridian of Cape Leeuwin was crossed on the 30th. On August 25th, in lon. 96deg. east, another gale of exceptional force presented itself. A noteworthy feature of this storm was a terrific squall of large hailstones, which sounded like the rattle of musketry as they struck the decks. For three days the ship was put upon her best behaviour, and she acquitted herself satisfactorily. On September 4th and 5th a moderate gale was met.

Adelaide was reached on September 9th, where 900 tons of cargo were landed, and whence the voyage to Melbourne was resumed on the 14th inst. When off Cape Northumberland, on the 19th inst., she passed through another severe atmospheric disturbance with flying colours, but then her troubles ended. A spell of adverse winds succeeded, till the 23rd inst., when a fair start occurring the ship bowled along merrily to her destination."
The Argus 26 September 1900.

After a brief stay in Melbourne, just long enough to repair the storm damage and take on 4500 bales of wool, 5100 bars of lead ballast, 4800 bags of wheat, and other miscellaneous cargo. The ship was cleared out on October 26th, and was towed down to Port Phillip heads on the 29th by the tug Racer. Such was the rough weather and horrendous sea conditions going through the Rip, that the pilot, Captain Strickland was forced to stay aboard after the tow hawser snapped. Captain Horne shaped his course to pass below Wilson's Promontory with plans the heave to and transfer the pilot aboard an inward bound vessel.

When he finally returned to Port Melbourne Strickland had quite a story to tell;

"Pilot Strickland states that the Loch Garry left her anchorage in Hobson's Bay at half-past 1 o'clock on Monday morning, in tow of the tug Racer, the wind blowing light from the nor'-west. As the vessel proceeded down the harbour the breeze freshened, and when she was off the Quarantine Station at half-past 7 o'clock Pilot Strickland consulted with Captain Horne as to

whether they should proceed to sea or anchor until a more favourable opportunity arose. As far as could be seen there was not much of a sea running in the Rip, and it was therefore determined to make the passage immediately. All went well until the tug and the ship were abreast of Point Lonsdale, when the wind, which was blowing fresh from the westward, suddenly chopped round to the sou'-west, and gathered additional strength, whilst a remarkably high sea got up, causing the ship to strain greatly on the tow-line.

Then an incident occurred which filled those on the Loch Garry with dismay. The tow-line, which was relied upon to hold the vessel securely until she was sufficiently far out to sea to become independent of the assistance of the tug, suddenly parted, and lurching round into the trough of the sea the ship was confronted with the danger of stranding on a lee shore. Immense waves were rolling in, and the vessel laboured fearfully. At times she almost completely buried herself, and, as the crew were washed about the deck, the task of getting sufficient sail on the vessel to keep her off the shore was made extremely difficult. Fortunately, although the waves ran so high, the wind was only of moderate strength, and at last enough sail to get headway on the vessel was set.

Meanwhile the anchors had got adrift, and the formidable task of again securing them whilst the ship was plunging had to be undertaken. With such sail as had been put on her the vessel managed to stand out to sea, but the wind then freshened considerably, and the ship laboured so terribly that it was found hopeless to get any more canvas spread. For some hours afterwards she was buffeted about with frightful force. Great volumes of water broke over her, deluging the decks fore and aft, and doing considerable damage to fittings. One immense sea thundered on deck, knocking down several of the crew in its course, and swept into the forecastle, reducing the compartment to a scene of chaos.

Then the boom of the ship, yielding to the heavy pressure put upon it by the seas as the vessel repeatedly buried herself, went by the board, and in their efforts to get it in again the crew passed a sensational time. A number of them were so badly knocked about that they were incapacitated from further duty. The second mate, overcome by excitement, fell to the deck in a fit, and had to be carried for safety to the cabin, where the united efforts of three men were required to hold the unfortunate officer until his sudden seizure was over.

Whilst this episode was taking place the chief mate and some of the apprentices—the rest of the crew were disabled—worked manfully to secure the boom, which was dashing against the hull of the ship so violently that it was feared a hole would be knocked in her. Their endeavours, fortunately, were ultimately rewarded, and thus a pressing danger was removed, though only at the cost of great hardship to those employed in the perilous work. The afternoon was well advanced when the boom was recovered, and all on board were worn out by their trying experiences, but success had crowned their efforts, and the good ship was then well off the land and comparatively safe. Towards 8 o'clock in the evening the wind veered round to the west-sou'-west—a fair breeze—and before it the vessel ran away towards Wilson's Promontory." **The Argus 5 November 1900.**

One of the apprentices who distinguished himself during the emergency was Fred Lake who was later commended for his bravery by Captain Horne and Captain Strickland.

The voyage was relatively slow. They passed the four-masted barque Claverdon, on Christmas Eve, at 34° south, 30° west, and the barque, Mexico, on January 11th, as they crossed the Equator at 29° west.

The Loch Garry encountered rough weather for much of her voyage but particularly in the north Atlantic. After sailing past 30° north 41° west, on January 27, the Loch Garry encountered a continuous succession of easterly and south-easterly winds for three weeks, afterwards amounting to strong gales, raising high seas. Captain Horne was compelled to heave the ship to several times. On one occasion, from February 7 to 9, they were hove-to at 50° north, 30° west, for 48 hours. Horne ordered the use of oil bags to smooth the waters around the ship to great effect. Despite the trying conditions the Loch Garry reached Gravesend on February 28th, after 122 days at sea with a many of her crew still badly injured and laid up in their bunks.

The ship was soon at her London Dock berth on the South Quay to discharge her cargo. There she stayed until March 26th when under tow the clipper was towed back down the Thames and onwards to Greenock. They arrived back in Glasgow on April 3rd 1901. The Loch Garry needed an overhaul yet her owners were running their ships on razor thin margins and so the clipper was immediately place back on the berth for Australia.

The fully laden vessel was towed back to sea behind the tug Flying Phantom on May 11th 1901, the tow hawser being dropped off of Inishtrahull at 4pm on the 12th. The following afternoon the Loch Garry was sighted by the inward bound steamer Sicilian at 55° north, 30° west. What followed was a voyage dominated by light flukey winds. Only on sixteen occasions did the ship travel more than 200 miles in a day. Her poor luck continued when she was struck by an easterly gale as the clipper tried to round the Cape of Good Hope. This 'dead-muzzler' held the Loch Garry up for a week. The ship made her number off Cape Borda lighthouse at 3pm on August 26th, after a tedious 106 days at sea. They arrived off of Semaphore the following afternoon and dropped anchor whist the customs and health inspectors motored out to the waiting ship and her crew.

After four days moored at Port Adelaide Captain Horne had his ship moved back out to the Semaphore roads. The voyage to Port Phillip Bay took just 54 hours, anchorage to anchorage, a significant enough time to be mentioned in the local press.

Their stay in port was the usual three months before the Loch Garry was towed to sea behind a tug on December 20th 1901. It was whilst they were sailing home that apprentice Fred Lake completed his time and studies to become a mid-shipman in the Royal Navy Reserve. James Horne, himself and officer in the RNR was happy to confer this rank upon Fred on February 27th 1902. It was a proud moment for the brave young man he having been inspired by Captain Hornes own exemplary naval service during the Crimean War.

The Loch Garry sailed up through the English Channel, making her number off Prawle Point on April 3rd and arriving in London the following evening. The ship was hauled up to her usual London dock berth where her cargo of whet and wool and quickly discharged. Captain Horne made sure that Fred Lake's naval seniority was properly registered. They stayed in London for the month as the clipper needed her rigging repaired after damage incurred rounding Cape Horn.

She was again back at sea by April 29th, making her number off Dungeness as she passed, arriving back at her Victoria Dock mooring in the Clyde a week later. Captain Horne was due for leave but decided to continue stay aboard the Loch Garry for another run to Melbourne. By this time Fred Ward was at times promoted to acting Third Officer to give him experience as commander of a watch whilst the clipper was at sea.

The Loch Garry began her next voyage behind the tug Flying Coot on Sunday July 6th 1902 when she parted with the tug off of the island of Inishtrahull. Captain Horne put the Loch Garry on the port tack and ordered all plain sails set as the clipper rolled on out into the North Atlantic, winds moderate from the west. She experienced light airs and fine weather down to the region of the south-east trades, which were picked up three degrees north of the equator, which was crossed on the 12th of August. The prime meridian was passed on the 29th, and the Cape of Good Hope was doubled on the 5th of September. Their easting run across the Indian ocean was marked by moderate breezes, with an occasional gale.

The ship made her number off Cape Borda on October 3rd, at 10:35 am, headed up Investigator Strait, and was berthed at McLaren Dock, Port Adelaide on the evening of the 5th 1902. Her stay in Adelaide was a little under three days and soon the ship was back at sea headed for Por Phillp Bay. She passed through the Rip on October 10th and came to anchor in Hobson's Bay the following morning.

The ship was brought up to Port Melbourne's South Wharf to discharge the remainder of her cargo, and after making sure that all was in order, Captain Horne allowed Fred to head home to visit his family. He was a permitted to sleep ashore on weekends much to the delight of his mother and sister May. It was during this time in dock that another of the apprentices, 16-

year-old John Caughey fell from aloft and landed upon a belaying pin which pierced his thigh. The young sailor was taken to hospital to have his wound dressed before being sent back aboard to recuperate.

After almost three months in port a fully laden Loch Garry set sail on January 30th 1903 bound for Hull to discharge her load of grain. She passed the steamer Tokomaru on March 2nd whilst doubling Cape Horn at 56°south. Captain Horne at last made his ships number off Prawle Point on April 27th, after 87 days at sea. A tug and pilot were engaged soon after to guide the clipper onwards to Hull. The tug and her charge arrived off Hull on the 30th and soon after the Loch Garry was tied up alongside Albert Dock.

The Loch Garry was back at Greenock on May 16th 1903 and set sail from there again on July 9th once again bound for Adelaide and Melbourne. She was towed to sea by the tug Flying Scotsman, being left off St John's Point, of Donegal Bay, on the 10th. Once into the zone of the northern trade winds they passed the steamer Tarragona, on her way to the island of St Vincent. Moderate winds and fine weather were experienced to the equator, which was crossed on August 7th at 21° west.

The ship made excellent progress through the south-east trades, the prime meridian being passed on August 25th , at 38.5° south as Captain Horne began his run eastwards. The Cape of Good Hope was doubled on August 29th 42° south, 49 days out. The islands of Madeira, St. Antonio, and Tristan D'Acunha were sighted as the clipper ran her easting down. From 12° east to 30° east a continuous succession of strong south-west and south gales were encountered, frequently rising to hurricane force, bringing dangerously high seas with them, driving the Loch Garry far off her usual course.

This prolonged the passage between the Cape and Australia, but the ship came through all the bad weather without damage. The meridian of Cape Leeuwin was crossed on September 25th. After a voyage of 84 days the crew of the Loch Garry let the anchor go off Semaphore Pier on October 2nd 1903. She carried 1000 tons of general cargo for South Australians, mostly iron and steel products and ingots of pig-iron, that took the best part of a week to discharge.

The ship was towed from the Port River and put back to sea on October 9th, bound for Melbourne. The run to Melbourne was punctuated by frequent thunder storms, high seas, and periods of dense fog. They arrived off Port Phillip Heads on October 13th and was hove-to awaiting the arrival of a pilot. Once through the Rip the Loch Garry was met by a tug that towed the clipper up to Hobson's Bay. She was then sent up Yarra to Victoria Dock to discharge the reminder of her cargo.

Also docked at Melbourne were the Loch Rannoch, Loch Katrine, Loch Ness and Loch Etive. Their captains and crews, all employees of Aitken & Lilburn, were frequent visitors to each other's vessels and several crew members swapped vessels for the run home to Britain. The Loch Garry was cleared out on December 9th with several crew members having transferred across from other Loch liners. The ship passed through The heads on the morning of December 11th following the vessels Alcinous and Perthshire, all bound for London.

Captain Horne sailed his ship out through Bass Strait and set his course to run south of New Zealand. The Loch Garry encountered a southwesterly gale and huge seas on her way southeast. She was sighted by the crew of the SS Moeraki at 45° south, 161° east, on the 15th at 4:00 pm, and asked to be reported 'All well!". The clipper arrived in the channel on February 27th , after a cracking run of 78 days, and after picking up a pilot and tug was towed up to Gravesend, arriving on March 1st. She was soon hauled into London Dock and berthed alongside the Loch Etive at Warehouse Number One.

Upon arrival, Frederick Lake had officially completed his indentured time as an apprentice. He had spent the last year serving as Third Mate of the Loch Garry and now having completed his time aboard he reported to HMS President a Doterel-class sloop-of-war that was being used as the drill ship and training establishment, for the London Division of the Royal Navy Reserve. It was here he was to receive training designed to turn civilian volunteers into proficient naval officers. Midshipmen

Council for Trade.

Certificate of Competency

as

SECOND MATE

OF A FOREIGN-GOING SHIP.

To   Fred Ward Lake

Whereas it has been reported to us that you have been found duly qualified to fulfil the duties of **Second Mate of a Foreign-going Ship** in the Merchant Service, we do hereby, in pursuance of the Merchant Shipping Act, 1894, grant you this Certificate of Competency.

By Order of the Board of Trade,

this   1st day of July 1904

Walter Howle.

One of the Assist. Secretaries to the Board of Trade.

Countersigned,

Registrar General.

attended regular drill nights on the President moored in the Thames. raining included instruction in basic seamanship, naval gun drills and field gun drills. They were taught naval discipline, semaphore, signaling, and knotting/splicing. They had to train until they were deemed "efficient" by Admiralty standards.

Fred spent five weeks in London attending regular training days aboard HMS President. He attended his first five-day training session starting on April 12 1904, and finished his last week of training on May 16th. Upon completing this first block of training Fred Lake stayed in London with family friends to study for his Board of Trade exams. He managed to successfully pass the tests and gained his Second Mate's ticket, in early June but then had to depart London for Glasgow without staying long enough to collect his certificate. (The ticket was eventually issued on July 1st 1904 while Fred was at sea). He was almost immediately posted to the position of Third Mate of the four masted barque Loch Torridon, serving under Captain Robert Pattman.

Having travelled back to Glasgow expecting to rejoin the Loch Garry as she was berth alongside Victoria dock, Fred was informed that the position of second mate had already ben filled. However Bob Pattman, master of the Loch Torridon, moored alongside, had an opening and was expecting Frederick Lake RNR, to report to him as soon as possible. After a meeting with Pattman during which he was thoroughly grilled by his new captain about his knowledge, conduct and previous service. James Horne had already filled Captain Pattman in on the qualities of his new third officer and so this meeting was more of a way for Bob to assesses the young man's character under pressure.

The Loch Torridon left Queen's Dock, Glasgow, at noon on June 14th, with a general cargo, including four locomotives, and the Tail of the Bank, where the ship was detained, wind-bound, on the 18th. Tuskar Rock light was passed on June 20th. The equator was crossed on July 15th, 27 days from Greenock. The south-east trades proved to be strong throughout, and took the ship into 28° south and 31° west longitude on July 23.

Captain Robert Pattman.

From this point onwards the Loch Torridon encountered strong north and north-west winds and gales to the meridian of Cape of Good Hope, which was crossed on August 3rd along latitude 44° south, 19 days from the equator and 44 days from Tuskar. On August 4th an easterly gale was encountered. It commenced in south-east, and finished on August 8th. From this date she had north and north-westerly gales to the south of Tasmania, with a day or two westerly and south-westerly winds intervening. Much foggy and rainy weather was also met in the Southern Ocean. The meridian of Cape Leeuwin was crossed on

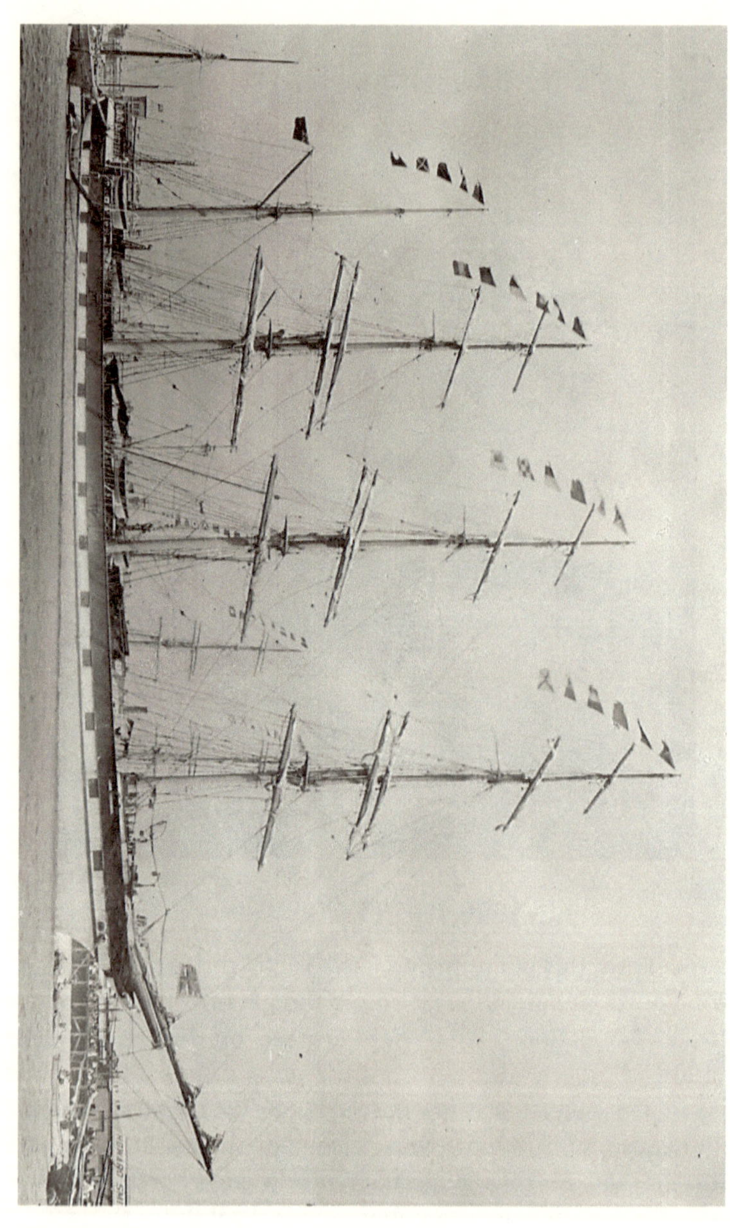

The barque Loch Torridon, 2081 tons, built by Barclay, Curle & Co, Glasgow.

August 24th, 21 days from the Cape of Good Hope, 40 days from the equator, and 65 days from Tuskar.

The Loch Torridon proceeded south of Tasmania, and on August 18th fell in with another easterly gale, lasting 24 hours. She rounded Tasmania on August 31st, and then had a fine run to port, with south and south-west gales. The barque anchored off Mosman's Bay on arrival. The ship completed the run from Greenock in 77 days, and from Tuskar, the last point of departure, in 75 days.

The barque was berthed at Walker's Wharf, Miller's Point to discharge, which was completed by September 16th and after which the Loch Torridon was towed across to the Darling Island anchorage. During her time berthed alongside Robert Pattman was feted by the local press and a number of lengthy articles about his life and the career of the Loch Torridon, spanning sone twenty four years. He was entertained aboard his own ship by friends and admirers and the officers, and apprentices of the ship, including Fred Lake, were invited to be part of the celebrations.

When loading was completed the Loch Torridon's hold was filled with almost 7919 bales of fine Merino wool, 1291 casks of tallow, 3195 pieces timber laid down as flooring in the lower hold, 200 cases of meat, 25 hogsheads of whiskey, and 10585 bags or chromium ore as ballast. This was said to be the largest wool cargo ever taken by the four-masted clipper.

The vessel was cleared to sail on November 26th 1904, and she was towed out through Sydney Heads on the 28th at 11:00 am, by the tug Advance. Cape Horn was sighted on Boxing Day, 28 days out. Yet the return voyage did not live up to her reputation as a very fast ship. The Loch Torridon made her number off Southend on the morning of March 6th 1905, after a laborious 98 days at sea. She made Gravesend behind a tug that afternoon, and passed into London Dock just before midnight.

Once her cargo was discharged and the Loch Torridon was ready to depart for Glasgow, Fred Lake took his leave from the ship and returned to HMS President for another eight weeks of training. He spent weekdays aboard the training ship and stayed with family friends on weekends.

Fred finished this lengthy stint on May 21st, 1905, after receiving word of his next posting from Aitken & Lilburn in Glasgow. Taking the next train north, Fred made his way to the sailors' home used by the officers and crews of the company's vessels. Once settled in, he returned to Buchanan Street and reported to the Loch Line office for his newest assignment: Third Officer of the line's flagship, Loch Vennachar, which was currently on the berth for Adelaide and Melbourne.

Fred was considered by many to be a handsome young man who was likable and popular with passengers and crew. On board the Loch Vennachar he was fourth in command and responsible for the '8-12' watch from 8 am 'til noon, and from 8pm until midnight. He was also responsible for maintaining the ships safety equipment and for making sure that the officers and crew followed correct procedures whilst on board. Fred often stood watch with James Priest whose job it was to teach him the finer arts of commanding a ship and, it's at times, volatile crew.

Amongst his many duties as Third Mate Fred had special responsibilities to keep the ship, the people on board and the environment safe. After the wreck one of the ships life boats was found washed up in the surf at Vivonne Bay on Kangaroo Island. The boat had 100' of rope wrapped around it and its bottom torn out. The boat had obviously been launched but foundered in the heavy seas drowning all who had taken to her before the survivors could reach safety. It was poignant to note that amongst the wreckage washed ashore was a bunk railing with the words Fred Ward hastily carved into the wood but unfinished perhaps indicating that Fred was off watch and asleep in his bunk when the ship struck the cliffs.

tember.

The tablet had been crowned by his brother-officers of the R.N.R., with a massive wreath of white lilies and roses, twined on the ribbons of the R.N.R. and the ship, and resting on a draped Union Jack. Below it, hung a life-buoy, inscribed by his father, with the names of the ships on which he had sreved—the "Loch Garry," "Loch Torri'don," and "Loch Vennachar," and H.M.S. "President," with the flag of the line and the ensign of the service, resting on the Jack. On the left wall hung a wreath, sent by "The Old Melburnians," with the Oxford ribbon and silver mitre of the Melbourne Grammar School. A white-satin and chrysanthemum wreath. "from his Mother." adorned the opposite flank, and the ledge beneath the tablet was draped with a white linen altar-frontal carrying ferns and lilies and chrysanthemums; a large sheet anchor of blue-gray sea-lichen and immortelles hung pendant to the ground as an offering of hope from his English Uncle and family.

At the anthem-interval of a beautiful

Memorial Tablet to Frederick Ward-Lake, Mid-Shipman, R.N.R.

381

James Reid, 29, Dumbarton, Scotland – Ships Carpenter

James Reid was born in Dumbarton in 1876. His parents were John Reid, himself an ironturner and shipwright, and Mary (b. 1845). She was an Irish woman whose parents had migrated to Glasgow at the height of the Great Potato Famine. Her father, a carpenter, had found work in the Clydeside shipyards. It was while living in Dumbarton as a young woman that she met the young apprentice shipwright, John Reid.

John worked at the shipyard of William Denny & Brothers. The Denny yard was situated near the junction of the River Clyde and the River Leven. The company built all types of ships but was particularly well known as a producer of fine cross-channel steamships and ferries.

James was the second of four children: John Jnr (b. 1874), Robert (b. 1878), and Mary (b. 1880). Together they lived with their parents in a small tenement at 60 High Street, Dumbarton. All three boys joined their father in the shipbuilding trade. However, as wooden ships gave way to iron and steel, there was less call for carpenters.

So, by the age of 21, having completed his journeyman years, James Reid found himself working as an ironmonger for D. and W. Henderson and Company. The company was famed as both shipbuilders and marine engineers, were part owners of various Loch and Ben Line vessels, and suppliers of the iron and metal fittings to the shipbuilder responsible for maintaining their vessels.

Like his father before him, James's job involved fabricating custom metal objects such as specialised bolts, fasteners, and tools, bridging the gap between raw iron and finished ship parts. He was also involved in procurement and inventory management, supplying the massive volume of iron, steel, pipe, and hardware needed for maintenance and construction.

Postcard of Dumbarton, circa 1882.

383

By 1901, James was married to Agnes, and they were sharing a room at a boarding house in Rhu, Dumbartonshire, owned and operated by blacksmith and ironmonger Archie Donald and his wife Nelly. However, James was looking for something different and decided to sign on as a ship's carpenter for Aitken, Lilburn & Company. Thus, after several voyages aboard the company's vessels, he found himself assigned to the *Loch Vennachar* for another run to Australia.

William Molseed,31, Greenock – Steward

William Molseed was born on March 17th, 1874 in Greenock, Renfrewshire. Both originally from Ireland, his parents were James Molseed, a journeyman painter, and Jane Given, an immigrant from Derry.

James had an older sister Jane and several younger brothers and sisters, George, John, Annie, Andrew and Agnes Molseed, and all grew up in West Blackhall Street, Greenock. Living nearby were his uncle Andrew and his wife Helen Molseed, also painters. Also living with the family were boarders Samuel McInnes, John Walker and Robert Shields, painters and gilders working alongside William's father, James, as painters and decorators.

By 1891, the family had moved to more spacious accommodation at 22 West Stewart Street in Greenock. William had left school and, along with his brother George, had started work as apprentice painters and gilders, working in the family business alongside his father and uncle, but this soon paled. This life, however, was not for William; he had dreams of bigger things away from the painting business.

In 1901, at the age of 27, whilst still living at home, William had left the family business and, despite being a disappointment to his father, had started working as a spirit dealer's assistant.

William was afflicted with a restless spirit and a longing to see a world outside of the crowded streets of Greenock. It was whilst working for the spirit dealer that he met men who worked

West Blackhall Street, Greenock, circa 1890.

upon ships as stewards and ship captains who were carrying cargoes of spirits across the seas. It was after listening to their stories, and upon their suggestions, that William found his way upon the Loch Vennachar. Not qualified or experienced enough to be a proper sailor, William's work with spirits and beverages, and a good head for inventory and accounts, saw him perfectly suited to life as a ship's steward. Coming from such a large family, and living in a busy seaport, it was only logical that William would seek a life away from the crowded streets of Greenock.

As the chief steward, it was William's job to oversee those members of the crew not directly involved in its sailing operations. William oversaw the preparing and serving of meals; cleaning and maintaining officers' quarters; and passengers' wants and needs, including medical matters. He was involved in the receiving, issuing and inventorying of stores. William, as steward, also planned menus, compiled supply lists and controlled the ship's records. Working alongside Bill McLean and James Priest, William was in charge of requisitioning and purchasing stores and equipment. When many passengers were present, William, along with young William Turnbull, would assist the ship's cook in the baking of bread, etc.

William McLean, 49, Glasgow – Ships Cook

William McLean was born in 1855 in Glasgow, the son of foreman baker John McLean and Margaret McLean. Billy was the fourth of eight children: Janet (Jessie), John (Jack), Ann (Nan), Margaret (Maggie), Susan (Susie) and Christina (Christy).

Janet worked as an umbrella maker, Agnes in the cotton mills, and Billy and Jack in the family business as apprentice bakers. The family lived in a spacious two-storey home in Lanark Street, St Andrews, Glasgow.

Billy completed his apprenticeship by 1873 and worked for a time in his father's bakery. He did not stay long, though, and as soon as he was able, William McLean shipped out to sea as a ship's assistant steward and baker aboard the transatlantic

Postcard of Lanark, pre-Word War One.

RMS Gallia built in 1879, taken while approaching New York.
United States Library of Congress.

Late 19th century, Buchanan Street, Balfron, Stirlingshire.

steamers sailing from Glasgow and Liverpool. He later became a ship's cook, working aboard a variety of smaller steamers and sailing ships.

By 1881, former baker Jack McLean had sold his share in the bakery and had become a wine merchant. The family home and shop were on Stirling Road, City of Glasgow, Blackfriars, located at the east end of Cathedral Street, opposite the Royal Infirmary. Billy was seldom home, though his family was rather well-to-do by now.

In the mid-1880s, Jack and Maggie McLean retired from life in the big city and purchased the Coach House Inn in the village of Balfron, Stirlingshire. The McLeans operated the bar and a spirits shop on McLeans Land in Buchanan Street and lived in a home attached to the bar and shop. Whilst at sea, Bill was working as a waiter aboard the Cunard liner, the RMS Gallia, that sailed between Liverpool, Queenstown and New York.

In 1905, Bill McLean, a qualified Able Seaman, was serving as the cook aboard the *Loch Vennachar*, a position much envied during rough weather and cold nights. A favourite dish of the crew was plum duff, and Bill's cooking had to be good enough to grace the table of Captain Hawkins and the now infrequent saloon passengers who travelled upon the clipper.

Richard 'Dickie' Simpson, 57, Greenock – Sailmaker

Richard Simpson was born on the 20th of July 1847 in Greenock, Renfrewshire, to Douglas and Elizabeth Simpson. Douglas, a gardener, and his family lived in a tenement in Union Court in Greenock. Known as 'Dickie' to his parents, he was the youngest of 6 surviving children, and the only boy. His sisters were Maggie (Margaret b.1831), Bella (Isabella b.1837), Betsy (Elizabeth b.1839), Jessie (Janet b.1843) and Nan (Ann b.1845). In 1851, the elder girls worked in the cotton mills, whilst the younger children were at home or attending the local primary school.

By 1861, the family had moved to East Shaw Street, Greenock. Douglas still worked as a gardener and Elizabeth in a

Post Card of Union Street, Greenock, late 19th century.
Scotland Photographic Memories.

shop. The only children left at home were Nan, now working as a machine closer in the local cotton mill, and Dickie, who had a job as a sailmaker's apprentice in the sail loft of Thomas Black & Sons. His workplace was located at Dock Breast and Brymner Street, just to the east of the Customs House. A former sailor, Thomas Black crafted sails, cutting and stitching large pieces of fabric to make hardy sails that would withstand continued use in the toughest sea conditions. This expertise, working with fabric that would be exposed to the worst weather, gave workers at Black's of Greenock the skills required to make durable canvas sails.

Life had taken an interesting turn for Richard and his mother by 1871. His father Douglas had passed away and Elizabeth and Dickie had moved into his sister Betsy's home. The eldest daughter had married William Forbes, a marine engineer, and now had four children of her own. They all lived together in a fine two-storey home in John Street, East Greenock. Richard, now 23, was a sailmaker still working for Thomas Black, though he was starting to get itchy feet and wanted to see the world outside of Glasgow and the River Clyde.

Yet before this, he met and married Agnes Campbell on the 13th of November 1874. Richard and Agnes had three daughters, Sarah (1876), Elizabeth (1878), Catherine (1880) and one son, Richard Jnr (1888). Dickie, Agnes and the family lived in a two-storey terrace house in Armadale Place off Bank Street, Greenock for many years. It was where the girls and Richard Jnr were born and where they grew into adulthood. For Dick, it was home; with him away, the Simpson home was a hive of family life, ruled over by Agnes.

In 1897, the family was still living in Armadale Place. Whilst Dick was probably at sea, Catherine married Alexander Taylor, a joiner from Gourock. The wedding took place at Crawford's Hall in Greenock West on 4th January 1897. In the intervening years, Richard was away for much of the time. He only made it home for a few weeks or months every year whenever his ship was in port for a refit or to take on cargo.

Inverclyde, Greenock at the turn of the 19th and 20th centuries.
Discover Inverclyde Archives.

In 1901, Agnes was looking after her son Richard, and she was determined that he would stay at school. Also living in the family home was Sarah Simpson, who worked as a grocer shopkeeper's assistant, Sarah Hamilton (aged 57), who was Agnes' sister-in-law, and Sarah Hamilton Jnr, Agnes's niece.

Sometime between 1901 and 1905, the growing family moved to a more spacious home at Regent Street, Greenock, Scotland. Regent Street in Greenock had a long history, serving as a key residential and commercial thoroughfare near the town's bustling docks. In the 19th and early 20th centuries, this area was home to many families connected to the local maritime and shipbuilding industries.

On receiving news of the loss of the *Loch Vennachar*, there was much sadness in the Simpson household, for it was hoped that Dick would be home in time to give away his daughter Elizabeth when she married John Farley, a blacksmith, on the 29th December 1905 at the Simpson home in Greenock. The day was bittersweet as Sarah Simpson was getting married to Alexander K Campbell, a plater, at the same time in a double wedding.

With the last of her daughters married, Agnes found herself alone with their youngest son, Richard, aged 17. Sarah and her new husband, Alexander Campbell, continued to live at the Regent Street home for some time.

Richard 'Dick' Simpson, aged 57, after more than 30 years at sea, was the oldest member of the crew and a veteran sailor, who had previously served on the Loch Ness. As a sailmaker he came over to the Loch Vennachar with his old captain and friend William 'Bill' Hawkins, under whom he had served aboard the Loch Ness. The captain often, as not, usually kept to himself and occasionally spoke to the sailmaker for company.

Dick Simpson was responsible for maintaining the ship's sails and all canvas work, from mending and repairing sails to the manufacture and repair of pennants and jacks, deck buckets etc. Sailmaker's mates were also known as idlers, as they did not stand watch. Dick Simpson answered only to Bill Hawkins and to the carpenter, James Reid.

SIMPSON.—Lost on the Australian coast, by the wreck of the Glasgow ship, Loch Vennachar, Richard Simpson, sailmaker, beloved husband of Agnes Simpson, 11 Regent Street.

Greenock Telegraph and Clyde Shipping Gazette 12 December 1905.

Eugen Broberg, 28, Stockholm, Sweden – Sailmakers Mate & Able Seaman

Eugen Östen Bernadotte Broberg was born in Stockholm, a major trade and port city built on fourteen islands along Sweden's south-central east coast at the mouth of Lake Mälaren. He was the son of Fredrik Broberg and Augusta Charlotta Kastman. Eugen was the eldest of twelve children: Signe Annette, Frederick Olof, Lilly Charlotta, Georg Helmer, Karl August, Oscar Walfrid, Carl Helge, Gustav Vernon, Hildan, George, and Richard Broberg.

The Broberg family later moved to the port city of Norrköping in Östergötland. By the early 1890s, Fredrik was determined to give his family a fresh start. On 26 April 1895, the family boarded the steamer Georgia, which departed from Gothenburg bound for New York. Upon arrival at Ellis Island, the family was processed and eventually settled in Worcester, Massachusetts.

At the time, Worcester was one of New England's largest manufacturing centers. The city's major industries specialized in machinery, wire production, and power looms, and Worcester was once considered the wire capital of the world, supplying products for telegraph systems and fencing. Fredrik found work in a factory as a wire cable maker.

Unwilling to follow his father into factory work, Eugen instead boarded a train to Boston, where he secured a berth as an ordinary seaman aboard an outbound sailing vessel bound for Britain. During his time aboard square-rigged ships, he learned the craft of sailmaking and became a well-respected able seaman. Eugen was one of hundreds of thousands of Nordic sailors who plied their trade aboard British ships.

Much sought after, such sailors were a mixed blessing. They were highly skilled and easily found work aboard the thousands of windjammers that cruised the world's sealanes. The downside was their lack of English, which at times was cause for great concern, particularly amongst the older master mariners. Men like Bill Bennett rued the day when laws changed, making it difficult to gain apprentices, and most British sailors turned to steamships for their greater creature comforts and better rates of pay.

Donald Mathieson, 26, 1879, Portree, Isle of Skye, Invernessshire, AB

Crofters Houses near Portree, Isle of Skye, circa 1900.

Donald Mathieson was born in 1879 in Portree, the largest town on the Isle of Skye. He was the son of Kenneth and Christine Mathieson and the fourth of six children. The eldest child was also named Donald, followed by Neil, Alexander, Donald (the younger), Flora, and Kenina.

Kenneth Mathieson was a crofter who supplemented the family income by operating a fishing cutter during the herring season. The vessel was crewed by his brother, Archibald Mathieson, and his sons. Donald's father died before he was ten years old, leaving the boys to run the croft and keep the fishing smack operating in order to help support their long-suffering mother.

Eventually the family left the farm and moved into North End House in Portree town. There Donald snr became toe major bread winner, working as a wall-paper stainer. After his mother's death Donld snr migrated to Canada with several other members of his extended family.

Donald the younger left home to seek his fortune at sea in about 1895. His career took him around the world, but it was brought to a sudden end in 1905.

Anders Andersen, 24, Kragerø, Norway - Able Seaman

Anders Andersen, age 24, was an Able Seaman from Kragerø, Norway. He was born on 11 February 1882 in Kragerø, a town and municipality in Telemark. Anders stood 5 feet 10 inches tall, with fair hair and light blue eyes.

Kragerø was one of Norway's largest port cities at the time. By the end of the nineteenth century, its fleet numbered around 170 ships, and the town served as the focal point for nearly 500 surrounding islands. Trade and industry were largely controlled by a small group of wealthy merchants who owned mines, ironworks, shipyards, sawmills, mills, and waterways.

Anders was the son of Anders Andersen, a Swede, and Hansine Olsen, a Dane from Vemmelev. A devastating fire struck Kragerø on 15 June 1886, destroying three neighbourhoods, burning down 192 houses, and leaving approximately 1,500 people homeless.

Shipping in Kragerø Harbour during winter. Circa 1909.
Norsk Folk Museum Collection.

The following year, Anders's father died. His mother later remarried Emanuel Amundsen, a renovator, and together they had another son, Victor.

At the age of 16, Anders went to sea. His younger brother later followed him, being apprenticed to a Norwegian tall ship. The last time Anders spent an extended period at home was in

1900, when he was recorded in the census. Shortly thereafter, he shipped out aboard the steamer Jane Radcliffe.

After learning of Anders's death, Victor emigrated to Mobile, Alabama, in the United States. He eventually settled in Pensacola, Florida, where he worked as a sailor and fisherman.

Edward (Ned) McEwan , 36, Greenock- Able Seaman

Edward "Ned" McEwan was born in 1869 on the shores of Lochgilphead. His father, John McEwan, was a labourer from Ireland, and his mother, Margaret Dunbar McEwan, was from Greenock. Ned was the youngest child in the family. His siblings were Mary Ann, Patrick (who died at birth), Margaret, and his younger sisters, Elizabeth and Catherine.

After many years at sea, Ned met and later married Bridget Hogan in 1891. Their first son, John, was born on 8 May of that same year. The family lived in a brownstone terrace at 9 Crawford Street, East Greenock. Ned's wages as an able seaman were not sufficient to support the household, so Bridget was forced to take in boarders: Dick Clark, a miner; his wife Jane; and their son, Dick junior.

Ned was often away at sea for years at a time, and as a result his son grew up barely knowing his father. After Ned was killed, Bridget remarried, emigrated to the United States, and went on to have more children.

Lochgilphead, circa 1880.

Hugh Humphrys, 55, Porthmadog, Wales, Able Seaman.

Hugh Humphreys was born around 1850, though he himself was unsure of his exact date of birth. His birth was registered at Caernarfon in 1851, but the precise year remained uncertain. He grew up near Port Madoc (now Porthmadog), an environment dominated by shipping, slate, and coastal trade.

On 21 February 1867, Hugh was indentured as an apprentice aboard the brigantine Zenobia. His age was entered in the registry as 13, although malnutrition had left him small for his years; in reality, he was likely closer to 16. He was placed under the care of Captain Thomas Richards. The Zenobia was a timber drogher, frequently carrying cargoes of wood to continental ports such as Hamburg.

Hugh spent the next four years aboard the Zenobia. His apprenticeship ended abruptly in 1870 when the vessel was wrecked.

In 1871 Hugh joined the barque Glenara as an able seaman, having just completed a voyage aboard a schooner. He remained with the Glenara until mid-1872, when he signed on to the schooner Lizzie, sailing out of Aberystwyth. He served aboard her for more than a year and eventually became acting mate, though he was never formally recognised by the Board of Trade.

Despite not officially completing his apprenticeship, Hugh remained in the employ of timber merchant and shipowner Peter Jones, owner of the Zenobia. In 1875 Jones gave him command of the brigantine Adria, trading between Port Madoc and Hamburg. Hugh held this command for two years before being replaced in 1877 by Captain Hugh Lloyd.

This promotion allowed Hugh to leave the boarding house and move into more comfortable lodgings in Snowdon Street, Porthmadog, a well-built bluestone cottage just back from the inner harbour.

After losing his command, Hugh returned to sea as an able seaman aboard the schooner Mela of Aberystwyth for one voyage. Early in 1878, while ashore in Liverpool, he signed on to the Southern Cross for a deep-water voyage around the world.

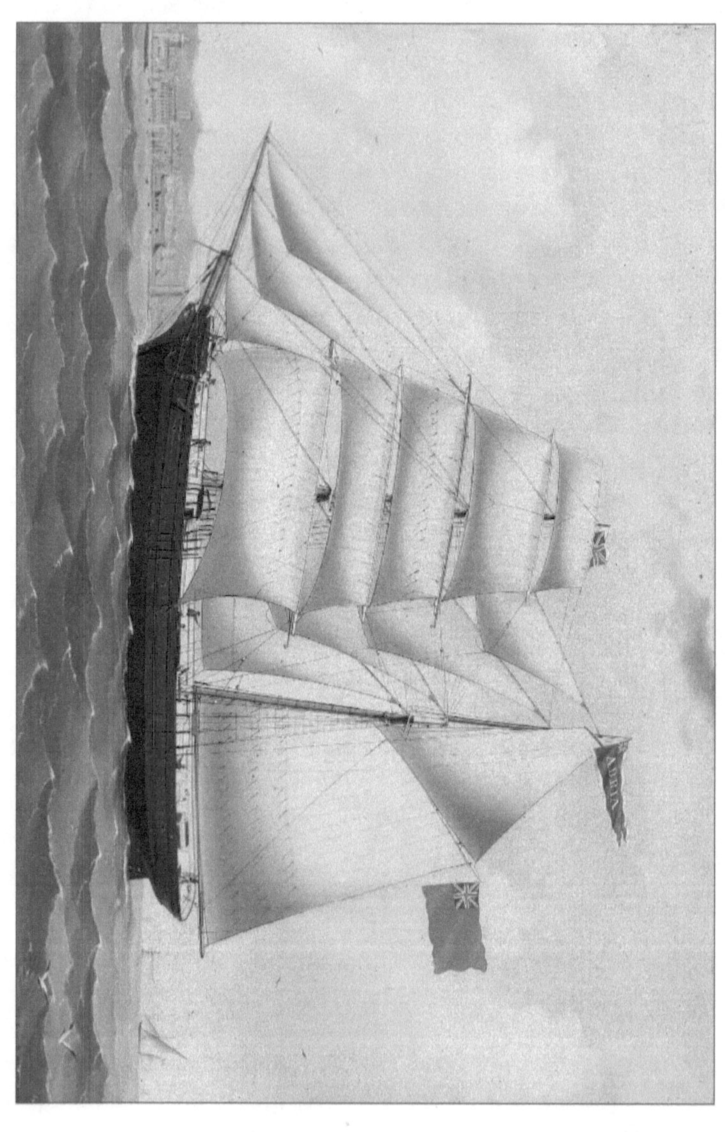

Brigantine Adria of Port Madoc by L. Renault Leghorn 1878.

Surname	Given name	Station	Age	Of what Nation
ROBERTS	HUGH	MASTER		
HUMPHREYS	H J	MATE	37	PORTMADOC
SCHONERN	C	CARPT & SEAMAN	26	FLEMBURG
MEYER	P	COOK & STEWARD	30	HAMBURG
ISAKSEN	Y	A. B.	37	NORWAY
REUTER	H	A. B.	20	LUBECK
PETERS	A	A. B.	28	DANTZIC
RASSMUSSEN	K	A. B.	19	DENMARK
SOARRER	J	A. B.	22	DENMARK
ALLENTSEN	L	A. B.	19	DENMARK
JONSSON	C	A. B.	22	SWEDEN
HOLTZ	N	A. B.	29	WINTRON
BOYE	H	A. B.	17	DENMARK
MENTZ	R	A. B.	19	BRESLAU
BOYERS	L	A. B.	18	SWEDEN
ELLIS	J R	BOY	14	PROHILIA
GRIFFITHS	GRIFFITH	BOATSWAIN	28	NEVIN

Crew list of the Braidwood, sailing from Hamburg to Sydney 1885-6.

On his return to Wales he made his way back to Aberystwyth.

Between 1880 and 1881 Hugh worked ashore in Liverpool as a longshoreman. Restless once again, he returned to sea in early 1882 aboard the John Ewing, sailing from Liverpool to Canada and back.

By early 1883 Hugh had accumulated sufficient experience to be appointed mate of the Aberystwyth brig Prince of Wales, having just come off the Liverpool vessel Cygnet. The voyage lasted less than a month: on 20 April 1883 the Prince of Wales was wrecked off Milford-on-Sea, opposite the Isle of Wight. Hugh sustained injuries in the wreck that left him ashore for several months.

Hugh's next recorded berth was as first mate of the Quebec-registered barque Braidwood in 1884. She sailed from Liverpool to Valparaíso with coal, then to Iquique to load guano, copper ore, and phosphates for Falmouth for orders.

Rounding Cape Horn, the Braidwood encountered appalling Antarctic weather, snowstorms, freezing temperatures, and violent seas. The vessel was badly damaged, and several crew members suffered chilblains and frostbite. One seaman developed gangrene in his frostbitten hands and later died while being treated in hospital at Valparaíso.

After returning to Europe, the Braidwood discharged her cargo in Hamburg and almost immediately sailed again on 14 September 1885 for Sydney, New South Wales, laden with general cargo. She arrived on 20 January 1886 after a meandering passage of 128 days.

Captain Hugh Roberts relied heavily on Hugh Humphreys to manage a small crew, many of whom spoke little English. On 21 February 1886 the Braidwood again sailed for Valparaíso with coal, thence to Iquique to load nitrates and copper ore for Hamburg and Liverpool.

Hugh next appears in the crew lists in 1890 as an able seaman aboard the steamship SS Inventor, sailing from Liverpool to Calcutta via the Suez Canal. After being paid off, he joined the steamer Vesta for another voyage to India in 1891. He spent much of that year at sea before returning home to Aberystwyth, where he again worked ashore as a stevedore and longshoreman.

In 1893 Hugh returned to sail, joining the fast dandy-rigged schooner Maid of Meirion as bosun. She carried a variety of cargoes but was frequently employed in the Porthmadog slate trade, transporting roofing slates to ports such as London and Ramsgate.

On December 20th 1893, the Maid of Meirion was caught in a severe gale in the English Channel near the North Foreland. Her sails were shredded, she was leaking badly, and the exhausted crew were forced to man the pumps continuously as the vessel drifted dangerously close to the Goodwin Sands. The Ramsgate lifeboat Bradford and the steam tug Aid were dispatched and, despite terrific seas, succeeded in boarding the schooner and towing her safely into Ramsgate Harbour. Both vessel and cargo were saved, and their survival was credited to Captain Jones's decisions and the swift response of the Kentish rescuers.

The iron barque 'Primera', 597 tons, in New Dock, Port Adelaide [iron barque, 619 tons, ON74484, 173.7 x 28.6 x 17.5. Built 1875 A Stephen and Sons, Glasgow. Owners: William Sherwen and Co., registered Liverpool.

Hugh remained with the Maid of Meirion and other slate-carrying schooners owned by the Lewis family of Borth for several more years.

In 1900 Hugh signed on as an able seaman aboard the iron barque Primera, laden with coal and bound from London for Walfisch Bay, Africa. The voyage ended in catastrophe when fire broke out in mid-Atlantic. After explosions tore through the hatches and the ship became unmanageable, the crew and passengers abandoned her in two boats.

Hugh was among those who endured 25 days adrift at sea with minimal food and water, suffering extreme thirst, starvation, and exposure. After sighting Ascension Island, the survivors were finally taken in tow by naval authorities and brought ashore more dead than alive. Following recovery, Hugh returned to England aboard the Union-Castle liner Galeka.

After surviving yet another shipwreck, Hugh joined the schooner Telegram at Runcorn on 1 August 1901. She traded between Runcorn, Plymouth, Newhaven, and Preston before being laid up for winter refit on 28 November 1901.

Hugh then returned to Liverpool and signed on to several steamers owned by Robert Napier & Sons of Glasgow and Aberdeen. He voyaged to Cape Town aboard a Napier steamer, where he disembarked, and in December 1904 joined the steamer Moravian for the return voyage to England. He left the vessel at Plymouth and travelled back to Port Madoc to visit family and friends.

While staying at the Blue Anchor Inn, a public house in the heart of Porthmadog's harbour district, Hugh received word from his friend Anders Andersen inviting him to join a voyage to Australia aboard a Loch Line ship, the Loch Vennachar.

Blue Anchor Inn, Porthmadog.

Alexander Dunlop, 16, Rothesay – Able Seaman

Ballianlay Schoolhouse, Ballianlay, Isle of Bute, Buteshire. Circa 1900.

A heavily pregnant Annie Dunlop stood at the door of their cottage behind the Ballianlay Schoolhouse and farewelled her husband, Alex. While Alex was away, Annie supported herself by working as a shop assistant and as a cleaner in the schoolhouse for her brother-in-law, Jamie Duncan, the Head Teacher of Ballianlay. She waved goodbye as the trap carrying James and Alex disappeared down the narrow country lane on its way to the harbour at Rothesay.

Later, with sea bag in hand, Alex boarded the ferry to Wemyss Bay and from there travelled by train to Glasgow Central. From Glasgow, he took an overnight train bound for London. On arrival, Alex caught a cab to his lodgings at 210 East India Road, Poplar. Situated opposite the East India Docks, it was a convenient address for a seaman awaiting a ship.

Although he held an Ordinary Master's ticket, Dunlop was serving as First Mate aboard the City of Cadiz, a 1600-ton barque on which he had once served as an apprentice. Her master, Captain Robert Davidson, lived aboard with his wife and three children, giving the ship a distinctly homely atmosphere. The Cadiz lay berthed in the East India Docks awaiting the final members of her crew. She carried a general cargo valued at £30,400 and was bound for Sydney, New South Wales.

The barque was hauled from the dock on June 5th and moved downriver to Gravesend, where she lay for two days awaiting a tug. She was then towed to the Downs but, owing to light and contrary westerly winds, was forced to wait with dozens of other vessels sheltering behind the Goodwin Sands. Captain Davidson eventually ordered anchors weighed and the tug took them out to sea. The City of Cadiz cast off the tow off Start Point on June 11th.

As the English coast faded astern, the crew settled into their routine, though the weather remained unsettled. The ship drifted through variable conditions until she finally picked up the northeast trade winds, which blew lightly but steadily toward the equator. Alex and the men watched the stars shift overhead until they crossed "the Line" on July 7th, thirty days into the voyage, at longitude 24° West. Once in the Southern Hemisphere, the ship truly found her stride. The southeast trades were strong and consistent, allowing the Cadiz to make excellent time as she surged southward toward latitude 28° south.

The easy sailing soon vanished. The warmth of the tropics gave way to the bitter cold and thunderous seas of the Southern Ocean. Strong westerlies and frequent gales battered the barque. By July 27th, she fought her way across the meridian of the Cape of Good Hope at latitude 43°30′ south. For days afterward, she ran her easting between the 43rd and 44th parallels, trapped in a world of screaming northwest-to-southwest gales and towering slate-grey seas.

Conditions worsened. Massive seas crashed over the bulwarks, flooding the decks with walls of white water. One particularly violent wave smashed into the deckhouse, splintering a door and stoving in one of the ship's boats. Several crewmen were injured, thrown about by the force of the water. Despite the damage, the Cadiz proved herself a thoroughbred of the "Bay" line. She flew before the wind, often covering 300 miles in a single day. During one remarkable seventy-two-hour stretch, she logged 960 miles, with a best day's run of 350 miles—numbers that must have filled Captain Davidson with pride.

The ordeal eased at last as the ship rounded Tasmania on August 16th. The roaring gales faded, replaced by gentle, welcoming winds that guided the weary crew northward. At 6 a.m. on August 20th, 1888, the City of Cadiz passed through the Heads and dropped anchor in the quiet waters of Neutral Bay, her long voyage from London finally complete.

While Alex was at sea, Annie gave birth to a healthy son, whom she named Alexander after his father. Her sister Jessie Duncan, a doctor from Rothesay, attended the birth along with the local midwife. Annie was confident she would soon see her husband again; the day after the Cadiz arrived in Sydney, she received a telegram from Alex announcing their safe arrival. Jamie Duncan replied in turn, informing Alex that his wife and newborn son were well.

The City of Cadiz quickly discharged her cargo and was shifted to Circular Quay's coaling staiths to load 2,200 tons of coal bound for San Francisco. The barque had a reputation for being "crank" and tender when heavily laden, and Captain Davidson was both anxious and angry that his agents had contracted for such a heavy coal cargo. Coal was dangerous and unstable, prone to shifting in heavy weather or spontaneous combustion. Yet few other paying cargoes were available for the American run, where the owners had a wheat cargo awaiting shipment back to Britain.

The City of Cadiz cleared Sydney Heads at 2:50 p.m. on October 20th, 1888. She carried a full complement of twenty-seven men and boys, as well as Mrs. Davidson and the couple's three children. Captain Davidson planned to round the southern tip of New Zealand, then follow the Great Circle route along the 45th parallel before swinging northeast across the Pacific. Contemporary meteorological reports from New South Wales noted unsettled spring conditions, with persistent southerly and southeasterly winds in the Tasman Sea.

To reach the prevailing westerlies needed for the crossing, Davidson would normally have stood well south. Instead, continual southerly winds and heavy seas forced him to remain closer to the coast than intended. For the first three days, strong southerly blows generated short, steep seas, particularly dangerous for a deeply laden and tender vessel like the City of Cadiz.

Her crank nature soon became apparent. Captain Davidson and his First Mate, Alex Dunlop, grew increasingly alarmed as conditions deteriorated. The heavy coal cargo and prior storm damage placed immense strain on the ship's structure. Seams between her steel hull plates began to leak, initially manageable by pumping, until coal dust clogged the pumps.

As the ship wallowed in the heavy seas, her stability worsened. Rolls grew deeper and recovery slower. Some fifty miles offshore, sailing south-southeast in appalling conditions, the City of Cadiz was in grave danger. Water flooded the hold, the pumps were useless, and the coal cargo had shifted violently. One heavy squall and a succession of large rollers were enough to force the barque onto her beam ends.

The end came suddenly in the early hours of October 24th. With no watertight bulkheads below, the ship rolled completely over and sank in less than three minutes. She vanished somewhere between Montague Island and Green Cape, forty to fifty miles from shore.

No further word was ever heard. One hundred and nine days later, Lloyd's of London officially listed the City of Cadiz as overdue. In April 1889 she was declared missing, and in June a fragment of a boat's transom bearing her name washed ashore at Bermagui, New South Wales—the only trace of the vessel ever found. A Board of Enquiry quickly absolved all parties of responsibility for sending an unsuitable ship to sea.

Annie Dunlop, grief-stricken, was left to raise her infant son alone. She continued working as a shopwoman and cleaner at Ballianlay, living with her sister Jessie and helping raise the Duncan children. When young Alexander was old enough, he was enrolled at Ballianlay School and remained living with his aunt and uncle.

Eventually, Annie moved to Glasgow to live with her sister Sarah and brother-in-law James Niel at their handsome three-storey terrace on Leyden Street, Maryhill. She worked as a live-in housekeeper and, after the birth of their first child in 1899, as a nanny.

As a young man, Alexander Dunlop often heard stories of his father's many adventures from local seamen. When old enough, his uncle Jamie enrolled him in the Naval Lads' Brigade run by the Royal Naval Reserve detachment at Rothesay. The primary naval presence on the Isle of Bute was the Royal Naval Reserve Battery at Battery Place, manned by professional merchant seamen and local fishermen. These part-time professionals trained for immediate Royal Navy service, and local boys were organised into brigades that emphasised discipline, seamanship, knot-tying, and signalling.

Rothesay Harbour was the centre of the cadets' world. Amid constant traffic of steamships and fishing boats, boys learned by observation as much as instruction. Eventually, Alex accumulated sufficient sea time aboard the Clyde training ship

1,800-ton steel sailing vessel Queen Elizabeth. Owned and operated by Black, Moore & Co. of London.
Historic Ships Collection.

Empress, moored in Gareloch Bay. In 1902, at just fourteen years of age, he graduated and was rated an Ordinary Seaman.

Much to his mother's grief and horror, Alex joined the 1800-ton steel sailing vessel Queen Elizabeth. Owned and operated by Black, Moore & Co. of London, she carried him on a successful voyage from Taltal, Chile, to Baltimore with a cargo of nitrates and copper ore. When he signed off in February 1904, he did so holding the rank of Able Seaman.

After a spree ashore, he headed north to New York to try his luck. Once in the Big Apple, Alex Dunlop began searching for a passage back to Britain. After tramping the docks for several days, he eventually found a berth aboard the Liverpool-bound Cunard steamer Campania. He signed articles on April 22nd, 1904, and went aboard at 6:00 a.m. the following morning, sea bag and dunnage slung over his shoulder.

The Campania was towed from her New York berth at 10:00 a.m. that same day, with Alex aboard as she steamed down the Hudson River and out into New York Bay. With a top speed of 22 knots, the great liner made a fast crossing, arriving back in Liverpool on April 30th. Alex signed off there, having earned £1 10 shillings for the voyage.

It was enough money to carry him home to Bute, where he visited his aunt Jessie and uncle Jamie at Ballianlay. After a warm welcome, he learned that his mother was still working in Glasgow as a housekeeper and nanny for his aunt Sarah and her husband, James, in Leyden Street, Maryhill.

After several weeks' rest at home, Alex boarded the ferry to Wemyss Bay and caught the train for Glasgow.

Launched in September 1892, the Cunard liner RMS Campania, made the astonishingly fast trip on her maiden voyage of 5 days, 7 hours and 12 minutes giving her the Blue Riband for that year.

Cunard Postcard Cassier's Magazine 1893.

His arrival in Leyden Street was an emotional one. Annie had never wanted her son to become a sailor, let alone a blue-water mariner serving aboard square-rigged ships. Now that he had returned home safely, she was determined never to let him leave again. It was a forlorn hope, but Alex's mother resolved that if her son were to go to sea once more, it would be with a company of solid reputation.

As it happened, this soon proved to be the case. After a period ashore spent studying for his mate's certificate, Alex discovered that he still lacked sufficient sea time aboard blue-water, square-rigged vessels. As a result, in 1905 he signed articles at the offices of Aitken, Lilburn & Company at 80 Buchanan Street, Glasgow. All that remained was to secure a berth aboard one of their outbound ships.

Magnus Jenson, 26, Aarhus, Denmark, Able Seaman.

Them Parish Church, Skanderborg County where Magnus and his
siblings were baptised.

Magnus Jensen was born on September 17th, 1877, to Ole Jensen and Ane Marie Christensen. He was the second of seven children: brothers Peder and Kristian, and sisters Gjertrude Marie (a foster sister), Helene, Gjertrude, and the youngest, Thomasine. Living with the family was Ole's mother, Gjertrude Marie.

Magnus was born on the family farm of Viserbjerg in the rural district of Skanderborg County. The nearest village with a church was Them Sogn. At the time, the population consisted of approximately 1800 residents, the majority of whom lived on scattered farms or in small clusters of thatched housing. The economy was strictly agrarian, focused on rye cultivation and cattle grazing, though much of the land remained uncultivated heath and moorland. The local church served as the primary administrative and social center; the village still lacked the industrial infrastructure and cooperative dairies that would later define its development. Infrastructure was limited to primitive sand roads connecting the parish to the market town of Silkeborg.

Ole Jensen was a smallholder (husmand), and as the second son, Magnus knew he was unlikely to inherit the farm due to the Danish tradition of primogeniture. His options were limited: he could remain a hired farmhand (tyende) for his own brother or strike out to build a different life.

Like many younger sons of that era, he looked to the sea for his future. Located just 45 miles from the port city of Aarhus, Magnus headed for the coast as soon as he was old enough. Aarhus was undergoing a massive transformation during this period; by the late 1800s, it had surpassed other regional towns to become Denmark's second-largest city, largely due to its expanding harbor. For a young man with grit, the maritime world offered a level of upward mobility, from ordinary seaman to mate or even captain, that was nearly impossible within the rigid social structure of rural farming.

Aahus Havn, circa 1900.
Aarhus Havn Museum Collection.

So, with few options open to him, Magnus signed on aboard one of the many outward-bound vessels, and from that time onwards, he was rarely ever at home. His family eventually lost track of his whereabouts, and his death in 1905 went unrecorded back home in Viserbjerg.

David Hansen, 30, Bergen, Norway, Able Seaman.

David Hansen was born in 1875 in the bustling port city of Bergen, Norway, into a family that embodied the great 19th-century migration from the rural fjords to the urban coast. He was the youngest of six children born to Anders and Thora Hansen. While his parents had roots in the rural parishes of Jølster and Gloppen in the Nordfjord and Sunnfjord regions, they moved to Bergen shortly after their marriage. By the time David was born, the family had fully traded the agrarian life of the countryside for the dense, commercial atmosphere of Norway's premier trading hub.

Life for the Hansen family was centered around the merchant yards of Strandgaten, the primary commercial artery of Bergen. David's father, Anders, found employment as a Gaardsdreng (yard hand and laborer) for Jacob Michelsen, a prominent merchant and stockbroker. This position defined the family's social and physical world. As a Husleier, or tenant, Anders lived with his wife and six children (Anne, Berntine, Thore, Hans, Caia, and David) in the modest tenement sections of the Michelsen property. While the merchant family enjoyed the grander front-facing portions of the estate, the Hansens lived in the shadow of the warehouses and stables where Anders worked.

As a yard hand, David's father was responsible for the heavy lifting of the merchant trade: maintaining the grounds, handling shipments of goods, and caring for the horses that moved cargo through the city's narrow streets. Notably, the household where David spent his infancy was the same one that produced Christian Michelsen, the merchant's son who would eventually lead Norway to its independence in 1905.

Strandgaten, Bergen, circa 1910.
Bergen Archives Collection.

Bergen, Norway c.1890.
Library of Congress.

Bergen's bustling port, with its exotic sights, sounds, and smells, was much more alluring for a young man who had no intention of working as a merchant's laborer like his father. Thus, at about the age of 15, David Hansen left Bergen and signed on to one of the many vessels that lined the harbor. This began a career that saw him in 1905 sign on to the 1500-ton clipper, Loch Vennachar.

Edward Holden, 38, Newark, New Jersey, USA – Able Seaman

Edward Holden was born in 1867 in the town of Newark, New Jersey. His parents were George and Caroline Holden. He had four younger sisters: Emma, Aran, Nellie, and Mabel. When not at sea, Edward lived at the family home at 13 Sussex Avenue, Newark.

His father, George Holden, was a clerk and bookkeeper who had served as a soldier during the American Civil War, enlisting as a private in the 8th New Jersey Volunteers in 1861. Like his father, Edward had hazel eyes and dark brown hair.

Unwilling to join either the army or the navy, Edward instead left home to go to sea. He worked on the Great Lakes aboard both sailing vessels and steamers before heading to Canada, where he signed on to various Atlantic packet ships sailing between Nova Scotia and Britain. In 1892, he sailed from London to Liverpool aboard the Nova Scotian barque Recovery. The captain was a hard-case "Bluenose" master, and Edward deserted the barque rather than endure poor treatment.

Edward's mother, Caroline, died in 1891. After her death, his father remained at the family home with his new wife, Carrie Holden, and Mabel, the youngest daughter, who helped care for her aging father. Caroline's death devastated George, whose drinking worsened, and he soon afterward moved to the Disabled Soldiers' Home in Leavenworth, Kansas.

John Bickle, 20, Edinburgh – Able Seaman

John Bickle Jr. was born in 1884/1885 in Edinburgh to John Bickle, a telegraph clerk, like his father, Josiah Bickle, before him, and Margaret McKenzie Bremner. John's father was originally from Hayle, Cornwall, and met his future wife while living on Kempock Street in Gourock, Greenock.

John was the fourth of five children. He had two older sisters, Christina and Elizabeth; an older brother, David; and a younger sister, Margaret. John's maternal grandfather, David Bremner Sr., was a sea captain of some distinction/note. Margaret's brother, David Bremner Jr. (born 20 January 1879, Westray, Orkney), followed in his father's footsteps and pursued a life at sea. Serving as a mate (and from 1912, Master) aboard the coastal trading steamship Ploussa (Reg 119711), David Bremner Jr., who later received a CBE during WW1 (London Gazette of 7 June 1918), introduced the young John to the life of a mariner.

Before going to sea at the age of fifteen, the Bickle family moved frequently between company houses as John Sr. advanced from one posting to another, with the quality of accommodation improving with each promotion. Their residences included Kempock Street in Gourock, where John's parents first met; East Claremont Street in Edinburgh, where they married; followed by Rintoul Place, Bellevue Crescent, and finally Eyre Crescent, all in Edinburgh. At Eyre Crescent, a beautiful four-story brownstone in one of the more well-to-do areas of Edinburgh, a cousin, Jessie Polson, boarded with the family.

John's father died at Burntisland, on the northern shore of the Firth of Forth, in 1903, aged 51. He died intestate and estranged from his wife, leaving just £165 17s and tuppence to Margaret. John Jr.'s wages contributed significantly to supporting his widowed mother and his younger sister, Margaret, who was only fourteen years old when John was killed aboard the Loch Vennachar.

Eyre Crescent, all in Edinburgh, circa 1905.

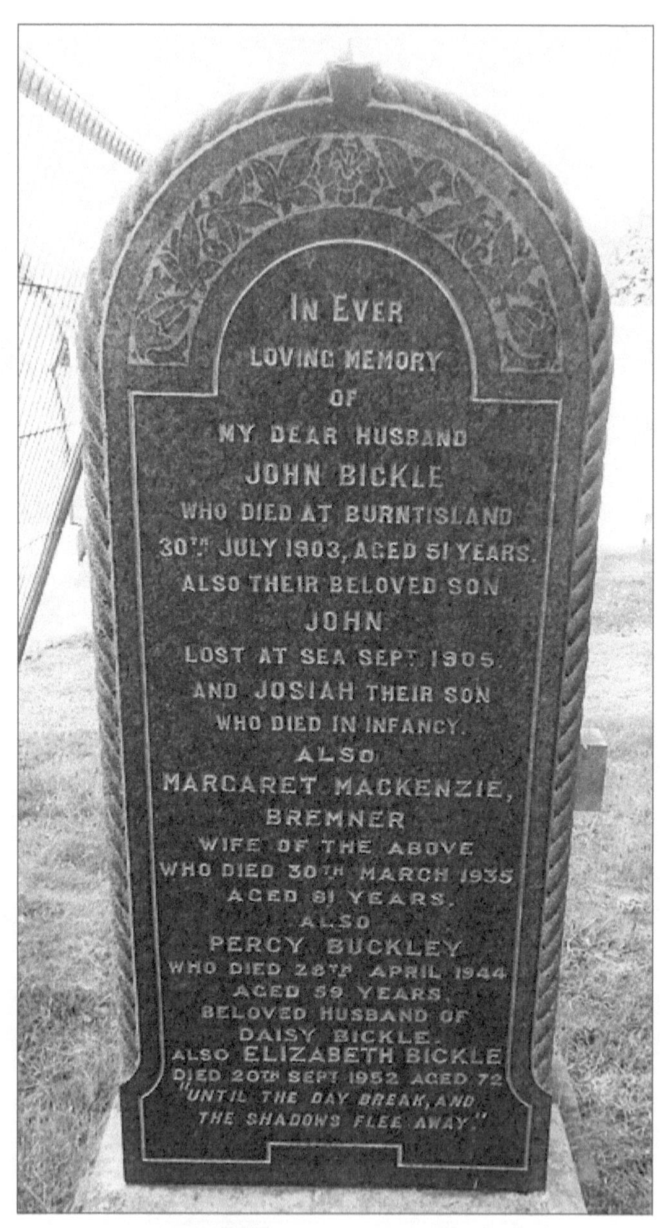

The Bickle/Bremner family plot, Edinburgh.

Tomas Andersen, 26, Arendal, Norway, Able Seaman.

Tomas Andersen was born on the 19ᵗʰ of March 1879 at Barbu, Aust-Agder, on the edge of the city of Arendal in Norway. At the time, Barbu was a thriving independent municipality that overshadowed its neighbor, Arendal, in both population and size. While Arendal was the prestigious seat of wealthy shipowners, Barbu served as the region's industrial heart, housing approximately 6700 residents within its urbanized coastal borders.

Tomas was the youngest of six children born to the Swedish master carpenter Anders Andersen and his wife, Anna Christine. His older siblings were Andreas, Mathilde, Margrethe, Sophie, Ingrida, and Carl. The family's resilience was tested early when Anna Christine died while Tomas was just a young child, leaving Anders alone to raise his large family.

The environment they lived in was defined by the shipbuilding trade, the very lifeblood of Barbu. The town was well known for its many shipyards, or verfts, which lined the shorelines of the Tromøysund. Skilled craftsmen like shipwrights, smiths, and caulkers lived in tight-knit clusters near the water, their lives dictated by the rhythm of the hammers and the launching of vessels from prominent works like the Pusnes Støberi & Mekaniske Værksted. By the turn of the century, Barbu was a hub for the construction and repair of the wooden sailing fleet that had made the region famous, even as it felt the pressure of the global transition to steam and steel.

It was into this industrial landscape that Anders Andersen had been drawn. Eventually, the family shared two flats at Kittelsbugt 189 in Arendal. Given their surroundings, it was no surprise that the three sons, Andreas, Fredrik, and Tomas, all became sailors. Each boy started working in the shipyards as a child before eventually going off to sea, beginning with Andreas, then Fred, and finally Tom. This seafaring life came with a heavy silence; when Tomas died in 1905, his passing went unremarked for many months before the family was finally notified late in 1906.

Barbu Township, Arendal, Norway, circa 1910.

430

William Clifford Barry, 20, Port Adelaide - Able Seaman

William Barry AB

William Clifford Barry was born on the 20th of June 1885, at Semaphore, South Australia. He was the son of Johanna Croll and Captain John Charles Barry. William was the second of eight children; Edgar, Horace, Robert, Doris, Mary, Arthur and Leo. Originally from Dover and Folkestone, England, using his middle name Charles Barry migrated to Port Adelaide in 1878. It was whilst he was working as a wheat broker in the Clare district that he met Johanna, the only daughter of bootmaker, James Croll. The couple were married in Clare on February 3rd 1883 soon after they moved down to Southwark, Adelaide where almost a year to the day later, Edgar was born.

Soon after the family moved to Semaphore when Charles decided to resume his career as a mariner. He Charles went to sea as a boy in ships trading to China. Later he came to Australia in sailing ships of' the Orient Line ar a 'one-shilling- a-month man.' He arrived at Port Adelaide in 1873 in the sailing ship Hesperus under Captain Legoe. Before settling in South Australia, Captain Barry traded to New Zealand and Tasmania, and was once wrecked in the Tasman Sea. He served as mate on the steamer Wakefield, was chief officer of the steamer Warooka, and later took command of the steamers James Comrie, Warooka, Kooringa, Warrawee, and Karatta.

Three of his sons Edgar and Robert, and William followed their father to sea, Edgar eventually becoming a master mariner. William went to sea later in life than the average sailor. In the years before heading to sea, he was a delivery runner and copy boy within the Register newspaper offices at Port Adelaide. He began his apprenticeship as an Ordinary Seaman under the tutelage of Captain Robert Pattman aboard the Loch Torridon, incidentally working alongside Fred Ward when he was an apprentice. In early 1904, after completing his time aboard the Loch Torridon he left the four-masted barque when she berthed in Sydney.

From there, he travelled back home to his parents' house at Turton Street, Semaphore, in South Australia. Once done visiting family, William then boarded the steamer SS Yongala for Perth before boarding the steamer Caledonia. This then sailed back to London, after visiting family he caught an overnight train to Glasgow. He carried with him a recommendation from Bob Pattman.

It was unusual for Aitkin Lilburn & Co to hire Australian officers and seamen. However with Pattman's endorsement ensured he could take up a position as an Able Seaman with the Loch Line. With the Loch Vennachar's return to Broomielaw, William was welcomed aboard by First Mate James Priest. He was soon in his dungarees and helping to prepare the ship for her upcoming voyage.

SS James Comrie in the Port River, SA. 1904 .
Post Card.

Postcard sent by William Barry to a friend, written whilst aboard the SS Caledonia.

"New York 30/05/05 Dear old Pal, Am present in above (SS Caledonia). Trust you are in capital health spiritual & otherwise. Leaving Glasgow in "Loch Vennachar" for Adelaide approximately June 10th. Always Yours Wm Barry."

Loch Vennachar's Apprentices

Horace Eastwood, 15, Knottingley, Apprentice.

Horace Eastwood was born on the 23rd of May 1890 in the town of Knottingley, in West Yorkshire, on the River Aire, a centre for boat building; its shipyards built and maintained both inland and seagoing vessels. His parents, Captain Charles Eastwood and Annie Eliza Taylor, had married in the summer of 1889, and Horace was baptised on July 13th 1890 at St Botolph's Church, where his father was officially recorded as a mariner. Horace was the son of Captain Charles and Annie Eliza Eastwood, Master of the ship Mary and Ann, and the elder brother of John William Eastwood, a Second Lieutenant in the 10th Battalion, Sherwood Foresters, who was killed during the Great War at Pas de Calais on January 28th 1918, aged 21, having lived at Rose Villa, Knottingley.

Horace came from a long line of seafarers on both sides of his family. His paternal grandfather, Thomas Eastwood, had been master of the 56-ton schooner Mary and Ann until his retirement to the family home in Aire Street, Knottingley. The vessel was a "Billyboy" schooner built in 1858 by John Harker, a fixture of the local shipyards. Horace's maternal grandfather, William Taylor, was also a Master Mariner, ensuring the boy was immersed in maritime tradition from birth.

Horace's father Charles, who had worked as first mate under his father, took over command of the family vessel. Charles operated the Mary and Ann with his younger brothers Nathan and Thomas Jnr, and the ship became a family home for a time as Annie Eliza accompanied Charles on many of his trading trips.

Charles's older brother John Eastwood also followed their father to sea, eventually becoming Master of the schooner Rosa Alba, operating out of Portland, Dorset. Charles and Annie Eastwood moved from the family home in Aire Street once Horace was born, settling into a comfortable life at Rose Villa on Cow Lane, on the outskirts of the town.

Forge Hill Lane
SOUVENIR OF KNOTTINGLEY
KTGY.15
SOUVENIR
Ropewalk
Weeland Road
Canal View

Aire Street, Knottingley.

Charles continued to operate the Mary and Ann alongside John Matheison, his first mate, and his brother Nathaniel Eastwood, whilst Annie stayed home with young Horace. Nathaniel lived with his wife Ruth, who looked after old Thomas Eastwood. On March 21st 1891, in the year after Horace was born, the family suffered a double blow. Nathaniel Eastwood died early in the year, aged only 24, and shortly after, Charles's older brother Thomas was killed.

During the recent gale, the steamer Neptune of Newcastle, bound from Guernsey to Dover with a cargo of stone, encountered the full force of a blizzard in mid-channel. The hatches became loosened, and the captain and mate while endeavouring to fasten them were washed overboard and never seen again. The sea afterwards swept the decks clear, totally dismantling the vessel, and finally extinguishing the fires. The crew, who numbered seven, then manned the lifeboat and abandoned her, landing safely at Weymouth on Wednesday. The drowned officers were both Knottingley men. The master Tom Eastwood was about 40 years of age, and resided in Aire Street, where he leaves a widow and three children. The mate Ephraim Green, was 45 years old, and leaves a widow and four children.

Thomas's death, came not long after Nathaniel had died, leaving his wife Ruth alone. Left with little choice, Ruth had to bring in boarders to the Aire Street home to provide an income for the family. Charles and Annie helped out when they could, but Tom's death placed even more of a strain upon the family's already stretched resources. Grandfather Thomas Eastwood eventually passed away on October 20th 1894, aged 72. Charles's brother Tom and his wife Rachel had three sons: Tom, Joseph, and John. The family lived in Aire Street but after Tom's death moved to Victoria Place, Low Green, Knottingley, with Rachel's mother, Mary Watson. Mary's father, Joseph, was a well-known ship owner from Doncaster.

Charles's other brother, John, spent much time at sea whilst his wife Eliza Eastwood lived in Moon's Yard, Knottingley, waiting for her husband to come home. They had two daughters, Florence and Annie Eastwood. Mary Watson died around 1890 and the girls moved to Rose Villa to live with Annie and Charles. Not long after Mary's death, John gave up his life at sea and moved back to Knottingley, eventually finding his way to London to work as a paint agent. In London he met and married Mary, and the couple moved to Upland Road, Camberwell, and had three daughters: Ivy, Eva, and Daisy Eastwood.

In 1897, Horace's brother John William was born. By now a seven year old Horace was beginning to take an interest in the sea like his father and uncles. In 1901, the census recorded the eleven year old Horace as a scholar, and he likely attended the Knottingley National School while his father continued his coastal voyages. Despite the family tragedies that had already taken his uncles Tom and Nate, Horace was determined to go to sea.

In 1904, whilst visiting his Uncle John in London, Horace was introduced to John's friend William Hawkins, a veteran of the Loch Line, who offered him a position as an apprentice aboard the Loch Vennachar. John Eastwood agreed to pay his nephew's indenture and training fees, and Captain Hawkins took young Horace on as an apprentice mate. Leaving Gravesend in early 1905, the Loch Vennachar with Horace Eastwood aboard sailed for Greenock, Glasgow, to take on general cargo bound for Adelaide and Melbourne, Australia.

Joseph William Hadley (1884–1905) was born in Wivenhoe, Essex, a small but historically significant fishing and shipbuilding port on the River Colne, which served as the principal port for Colchester. His birth was registered in the Lexden district in the fourth quarter of 1884, though some accounts give his birth year as 1885.

He was born into a large maritime family and was the eldest of thirteen children. Most sources identify his parents as Joseph Hadley and Mary Ann Hadley (née Kent), while some

Wivenhoe, Essex, circa 1900.

census-based records suggest William Hadley and Elizabeth Hadley (née Bond). This discrepancy likely reflects either a recording inconsistency or the presence of closely related Hadley families in Wivenhoe, all part of the same seafaring community. By 1911, five of his siblings had died, a common reality for large families of the period, and his surviving brothers and sisters included Albert (b. 1887), Rawdon (b. 1890), Harry (b. 1892), Lewis (b. 1893), Thomas (b. 1895), Alice (b. 1896), Gladys (b. 1899), and Lily May (b. 1905).

Joseph grew up at the heart of Wivenhoe's maritime world, living first on High Street and later at The Quay, locations that placed him in daily contact with shipbuilding and seafaring activity. The Hadley family had deep roots in the local maritime trades, including fishing, boat building, and command of trading vessels. His grandfather, also named Joseph Hadley, was a Master Mariner who received his certificate in Colchester in 1864, while his father followed a similar path, going to sea at a young age and eventually becoming the owner and captain of the 36-ton schooner Neaira. Some records also describe his father as a yachtsman, reflecting Wivenhoe's role as a wintering port for elite racing yachts of the Edwardian era.

Joseph began his own maritime career early. By the 1891 census, he was recorded as a schoolboy aged six, and by 1901, at sixteen, he was listed as an Ordinary Seaman, evidence that he had already begun formal seafaring work and basic training. After gaining experience as a deckhand, likely aboard his father's vessel Neaira, he sought to advance his career in the merchant service. In 1902, he began a four-year apprenticeship aboard the iron-hulled clipper Loch Vennachar under Captain William Bennett. During this time, he formed a close friendship with fellow apprentice Robert Andrews.

By 1905, Joseph was nearing the completion of his apprenticeship and was due to finish his training in May 1906, at which point he intended to sit for his Ship's Master Certificate, an important step towards command.

Thomas William Pearce, 19, Southampton – Apprentice

Thomas William Pearce was born in 1886 in the major port city of Southampton, Hampshire. Situated at the northernmost point of Southampton Water, at the confluence of the River Test and the River Itchen, the town experienced significant expansion during the 19th century, with its first dock opening in 1842.

Tom, known as Tom Jnr, was the son of Captain Thomas Richard Pearce (formerly Millet), the hero of the Loch Ard, and Edith Pearce. When Tom was three years old, his younger brother Robert was born. The family lived in a handsome brown-brick, slate-roofed, two-storey terraced house at 6 Fitzhugh Place, Southampton.

In 1901, Thomas joined the Loch Vennachar as an apprentice, shortly after the vessel had been raised from the bottom of the Thames. He was sponsored by his father, himself a ship's captain associated with the Royal Mail Steam Packet Company, and followed in the footsteps of both his father and grandfather. The Pearce family had a long and distinguished maritime tradition, and it was expected that both Tom and Robert would, in time, become shipmasters.

Their grandfather, Captain James Pearce, had been master of the steamer Gothenburg and lost his life in its wreck on February 24th 1875. Because of this tragic family history, some superstitious sailors labelled young Tom a "Jonah" and refused to serve aboard the Loch Vennachar while he was part of the crew. Captain Hawkins, however, dismissed such superstition outright.

Thomas came from a well-to-do family with a proud seafaring heritage. After returning to England from his last voyage aboard the Loch Vennachar in 1904, he secured a position as a midshipman in the Royal Naval Reserve. During this period, he served for a month aboard a warship in Southampton.

When the Loch Vennachar later sailed from Greenock, Tom was on what would be his final voyage as an apprentice mate. He was due to complete his apprenticeship the following May and intended to present himself for his Second Mate's Certificate.

Tom looked forward to arriving in Melbourne, where he would finally reunite with his younger brother Robert—then an apprentice aboard the Loch Garry—whom he had not seen for two years.

Captain James Pearce (top)
Thomas Richard Pearce (bottom)

Dairmid Stewart Barclay Thomson, 18, Melbourne – Apprentice

Dairmid Stewart Barclay Thomson was born in 1886 in Melbourne, Victoria, the eldest son of Dr Matthew Barclay Thomson and Emily Kate Thomson (née Dowling). He grew up in a well-established colonial family with strong medical, pastoral, and political connections.

Tragedy marked the very beginning of his life. In October 1889, before Dairmid had reached his first birthday, his mother Emily died at just twenty-four years of age in South Yarra. Her

Dr Matthew Barclay Thomson.

death followed a severe and painful heart attack after taking chloroform, administered by her husband for persistent chest pains. She left behind two infant sons, Dairmid and his younger brother Noel Barclay Thomson (born 1888), in the care of their grieving father.

Emily came from a prominent Victorian family. She was born at Jellalabad Station near Darlington in 1864, the daughter of Thomas Dowling (1820–1914), a pastoralist, magistrate, and long-serving member of the Victorian Legislative Council. Dowling was a significant figure in colonial Victoria, associated with the development of the pastoral industry and local government in the Mortlake and Camperdown districts.

Dairmid's father, Dr Matthew Barclay Thomson (1857–1943), was himself the son of Scottish migrants William Thomson and Emma Hutchinson. A trained medical practitioner, he

447

became known as a pioneering doctor in the treatment of typhoid, later serving as government Health Officer for Dandenong. He was also active in civic and social life, including membership of the Old Melburnian Society, and was a keen golfer, serving as a judge at the Victorian Amateur Golf Championships in 1923. Following Emily's death, he remarried in 1892 to Jane Ariadne (Ardnie) McLaurin.

Dairmid was educated at Geelong Grammar School before continuing his studies at Malvern College in England. After completing his education, he chose a maritime career, pursuing his ambition to go to sea. In January 1903, at just sixteen years of age, he began a four-year apprenticeship as a Master Mariner with the Loch Line, joining the sailing ship Loch Vennachar. He was the last Australian apprentice accepted into the company.

This decision may have been influenced by Captain William Bennett, a former master of the Loch Vennachar and a family friend, who later retired to Dandenong and became a prominent member of the local community. Still only eighteen, Dairmid was on just his third voyage when the Loch Vennachar was wrecked.

XVII
The Last Voyage of the Loch Vennachar

The Loch Vennachar being towed to sea.

On the 15th of March 1905, the Loch Vennachar arrived safely at the Gravesend anchorage. Eager to get word to the wool brokers that the ship had dropped anchor at her usual mooring opposite the Mucking Light, Captain Hawkins sent word ashore via signals alerting the port authorities of her safe arrival. Word is passed onto the wool stores, allowing Captain Hawkins to sell his valuable cargo for a premium price at the March sales in London.

By the 18th, the Loch Vennachar had been towed into the Thames and tied up at the London Docks so stevedores could begin discharging her load of wool, wheat, and general cargo. Fresh supplies of food and water for the week were taken on board and some crew, those not immediately necessary, were allowed a little shore leave to enjoy the delights of the London dockside. After a week discharging cargo and rounding up the crew, the Loch Vennachar sailed once again for home, arriving off Greenock at the end of March.

Arriving in port aboard the ship were: Captain William Hawkins, Chief Officer James Priest, Second Officer John Cameron, Carpenter William Davis, Sailmaker Dick Simpson, Steward Edward Minto, Assistant Steward David Johnston, Cook James McDonald, Able Seamen A. McDougall, James A. G. Brass, C. M. Sporran, John McDonald, W. T. Mansom, M. McRekine, H. Gillespie, T. Chalmers, R. Tucker, F. W. Archer, John Best, Ordinary Seamen Charlie Muir, William Hawkshaw, Apprentices Robert Andrews Jnr, Dairmid Thomson, Samuel C. Brown, Joe Hadley, Tom W. Pearce, and Sydney M. Stein.

Syd Stein, an apprentice on the trip out, had refused to take the return trip, leaving the Loch Vennachar one hand short. Syd Stein's parents refused to allow him to stay on the Loch Vennachar as his mother had had a premonition of disaster, just like she did when her other son, William Stein, failed to heed her warnings. He was drowned when the ship Nemesis sank with all hands off Botany Bay in July 1904. Robert Andrews left the Loch Vennachar to continue his career under Bob Pattman on the Loch Torridon, and Sam Brown transferred to the Loch Vennachar's sister ship, Loch Garry, under James Horne.

Upon arrival, the ship was towed to the docks where the crew and miscellaneous cargoes were discharged. Upon emptying her hold, Captain Hawkins has the vessel towed to her loading berth alongside the Glasgow Docks. He planned to have the ship cleaned and scraped once he arrived back in Melbourne. Instead, he had the ship's torn sails and rigging replaced, and those parts of her hull showing wear or rust were chipped and painted with red or grey lead. Captain Hawkins superintended the ship's long-needed overhaul whilst placing notices in the Seamen's Mission and the local pubs and boarding houses, beginning advertising for new crew.

Several old hands stayed on, including Dick Simpson and Charlie Muir, who would qualify as an Able Seaman upon completion of the next round trip to Melbourne. Dick took the time to head home, where he discovered that two of his daughters were to be married later in the year. Much of Dick's accumulated wages went straight into the family's coffers, in part to pay for the upcoming nuptials that Dick did not really want to miss. Whilst the ship was in dock, the steamer SS Caledonia arrived in London and an eager young sailor, William Barry, travelled north from London to join his new ship.

May saw the ship returned to her regular anchorage after a period of refit and maintenance. After a period of time away with their respective families, Bill Hawkins and James Priest met again at 80 Buchanan Street in Glasgow to go over the ship's inventory and to sign on the new apprentices they needed to replace the ones who had left the ship after her last trip. Joe Hadley, Tom Pearce, and the third-year apprentice, Dairmid Thomson, were once again listed on the crew manifest, and a new lad, Horace Eastwood, was introduced to his new skipper and taken down to the Loch Vennachar before proceeding to Mrs Brown's boarding house across the Clyde.

When space became available, the ship was towed to the Queen's Dock and began taking on a general cargo destined for Adelaide and Melbourne. With an absence of paying passengers, many of the regular luxuries and supplies available to saloon and second-class passengers are not loaded, making room for extra cargo in the 'tween deck storage spaces.

The search for experienced sailors with a British background was proving difficult, so James Priest was forced to accept applications from several experienced Scandinavians who were willing to sign on at rates below what they might have gotten elsewhere. Captain Hawkins only wanted experienced foreigners upon his ship, and one unlucky applicant was a young Australian who wanted to head home to Adelaide to see his father. Geralt 'Garnet' Kemp of Port Germaine was an Ordinary Seaman of little experience who tried to find his way home by working to pay for his fare and lodging. After much searching, Garnet Kemp found a fo'c'sle berth aboard the Loch Broom, which was currently under command of Bully Martin.

Before the Loch Broom left, he wrote a letter to his father in Port Germaine telling of his failure to gain a berth aboard the Loch Vennachar and of its nice captain and crew. In an ironic twist, Garnet Kemp, who was serving as an Ordinary Seaman aboard the Loch Broom, was struck by a falling tackle block whilst standing watch in the port main lower rigging. Knocked out cold, he fell overboard into a roiling sea and was drowned. He lost his life on the 20th of November 1905 just west of the Canary Islands.

Signing onto the crew as second officer came Charlie Radcliffe, of the Burnley Radcliffes. He was an unknown quantity, and Bill Hawkins took him on strength as his family were well-known and well-connected clients of the Loch Line. Fred Lake transferred over from the Loch Torridon as third mate. James Reid, a very experienced sailor and shipwright, came aboard as ship's carpenter; he and Dick Simpson had sailed together before and Captain Hawkins counted himself fortunate to have signed him up. After losing both ship's stewards, Captain Hawkins reluctantly took on Bill Molseed, a spirit merchant's assistant, as his steward.

Princess Dock, Glasgow.

This was his first trip aboard a large clipper and was the true beginning of his career as a blue-water sailor. Despite the Captain's initial misgivings, he impressed Bill Hawkins with his head for figures and his grasp of bookkeeping, ordering, and inventory management. Bill Molseed also had many connections within the Scotch whisky industry and knew how to sweeten a deal. Signing on as ship's cook, after a long stretch in prison, was Bill McLean. He was a hardened man, eager to escape his past and the dark poverty of the Glasgow dockside.

James Priest was hard-pressed to find experienced Able Seamen. To fill the ship's crew register, he signed Don Matheison, an old shellback from Skye. Donald began his career aboard the old barque Fusilier and from there worked his way around the world many times. Joining him was another old salt, Anders Anderson, a man with a short temper and one not to be crossed. With them was Ned McEwan, an experienced mariner from the grimy backstreets of Greenock.

Signing on for a different life was the Welshman, Hugh Humphries, another world traveller. Hugh began his career sailing the Americas hauling phosphate and fish; he was after something more and the large clippers offered this. Joining these senior sailors were men from all over: Alexander Dunlop, a cousin of the Laird of Bute in Rothesay; Max Jenson, a Dane from the busy port of Aarhus; David Ranson, a mariner hailing from Bergen in Norway who worked on the British ships because the pay was better. Next on the list was Edward Holden, from Newark in the United States, a man who usually did the London to New York run. Edward Holden was of the old school and brooked little foolishness. Then came a swag of young sailors, experienced Able Seamen, but with few sea leagues beneath their belts when compared to the old salts of the crew.

Counting himself fortunate to have found a berth aboard the Loch Vennachar was John Bickle, whose father ran the telegraph office in Edinburgh. Another was Tom Anderson, a likeable young man with many friends amongst those from the Loch Torridon and Loch Garry, upon which he had served. Will Barry was a South Australian who had sailed all the way from

Adelaide so he could take up his post aboard the Loch Vennachar; he showed up at Mrs Brown's eager to head to sea.

Joining this band of young adventurers was a group of boys on just their first or second voyages across the ocean. There was sixteen year old Eddie McPhee, from Morven, who had escaped a life working his father's forge. Willie Turnbull, fifteen, who was small for his age, had gained a job as a deckboy, the ship's 'Peggy', for his first trip to sea. Joining them in escaping a life of poverty was William Martin, whose parents had been driven from their lands by the Highland Clearances. All these men and boys joined Charlie Muir and Dick Simpson, who had already signed back on to join Captain Hawkins for another trip to the far side of the world.

Two apprentices, Robert Andrews and Sam C. Brown, left the ship, transferring to other Loch Liners. Staying on board were Joe Hadley and Tom Pearce, both senior apprentices who were undertaking their last voyage before presenting themselves for their second mate's exams. Also staying on was Dairmid Barclay, a friend of Fred Lake's who had been introduced to Captain Hawkins by Fred's father, Joshua Lake, whilst Bill Hawkins was in Melbourne. Rounding out the crew was young Horace Eastwood, a lad of fifteen and a newly frocked brassbounder.

On the 22nd of May, bad news reached Captain Hawkins at home when a telegram arrived informing him that his good friend, Captain J. H. Paterson of the barque Isle of Arran, had died of a heart attack midway to Queenstown, Ireland. Captain Hawkins and his wife travelled to Ireland to help Mrs Paterson. Katie Hawkins invited her to stay with them in Glasgow until she had sorted out her husband's affairs.

To relieve Mrs Paterson of some of the burden, Bill Hawkins agreed to transport Captain Paterson's belongings back to Adelaide aboard the Loch Vennachar, where he promised to personally see them delivered to the Paterson home in North Adelaide. Mrs Paterson planned to travel back to Adelaide aboard a steamer and hoped to be in Adelaide in time to receive both Captain Hawkins and her dead husband's things. She was greatly distressed to hear of the loss of the Loch Vennachar and

The White Star liner 'Suevic'.
State library of New South Wales.

the death of her great friend William Hawkins. It seemed to her that the sea was destined to take from just about everyone she cared for.

Mrs Paterson was delayed in leaving Scotland and travelled later to Adelaide aboard the White Star liner Suevic, arriving home on the 3rd of November 1905. The Suevic herself would later be wrecked on the 17th of March 1907 when she ran aground off Lizard Rocks, Cornwall.

The Loch Vennachar spent most of early June tied up alongside the Queens Dock, with its railway lines, derricks and warehouses as local stevedores began loading cargoes for Australia.

The cargo destined for Adelaide was: seventy cases herrings, 1 tank pipes, 10 cases fish, 5 doz clay pipes, 15 doz. castor oil, 6 doz dry colours, 1 doz glass, 143 do. paint, 3 do. wire netting, 11 do. printing paper, 2 do. capsules, 3 do. labels, 10 do. ale, 75 do. bloater paste, 45 do. beer, 985 do. cornflour, 10 do. oatmeal, 1 bale, 8 cases, 1 truss merchandise, 79 pkgs. stoves, 24 casks glassware, 275 bdls. steel, 10 bales nets, 471 casks, 386 kegs white lead, 20 do. rails, 50 do. rivets, 20 do. boracic acid, 65 drums oil, 4 casks castings, 1,045 sash weights, 1,685 single tubes, 6,731 bdls. do., 58 casks fittings, 9 casks spirits, 544 steel plates, 5,851 steel bars, 150 tons pig iron, 3 casks potash, 15 do. rum, 15 bales twine, 10 casks aerated waters, 150 cases, 20 octaves, 15 casks, 57 qtr casks whisky, 2 bales corks, 19 pkgs. bottles, 4 cases baths, 1 case, 15 bales cordage, 5 cases sundries, 100 cast iron pipes, 71 cases, 56 bales paper, 90 kegs Epsom salts.

The cargo for Melbourne consisted of: 150 pkgs. ale, 5 pkgs. paper (R.R.W. & Co.), 38 bdls. twine, 6 and 4 pkgs. do., 10 pkgs. stoves, 6 cases castings, 1 case stoves, 1 pkg. rollers, 2 pkgs. handles, 15 tons pig iron, 40 pkgs. gypsum, 50 cases whisky, 6 bales jute cordage, 14 bales newspaper (A.H.M.), 25 cases whisky, 35 cases merchandise, 425 pkgs. cocoa essence, 100 cases cornflour, 150 pkgs. ale, 330 pkgs. whisky, 27 cases material, 1 case artists' material, 88 cases painters' material, 331 pkgs. whisky, 10 hogsheads ale, 1 bale corks, 50 cases cornflour, 25 cases fish, 3 bales canvas, 135 bales cordage, 6 pkgs. paper, 6

Lamlash Bay, Isle of Arran.

Lamlash Bay was used as a shelter bay by hundreds of ships every year in the face of heavy weather. It was a place of relative safety well known and used by ship passing to and from the Clyde. A permanent coastguard station was maintained there as well as a telegraph which made a fortune passing messages from ships anchoring in its sheltered harbour.

www.johnstonsmarinestores.co.uk/about-lamlash/

pkgs. dye, 20 pkgs. oil, 360 kegs white lead, 24 pkgs. stoves, 438 pkgs. steel plates, 5 pkgs. granite, 370 cases fish (G. M. Davidson, mark D in diamond), 20 cases ale, 25 cases stout, 96 bales paper (Detmold), 21 pkgs. charcoal, 9 pkgs. alum cake, 96 pkgs. red lead, 92 bales sheets, 16 pkgs. traps, 150 pkgs. pipes, 20,000 bricks, 1 case shovels, 20 kegs ochre, 10 pkgs. siliceous, 25 cases essence, 257 pkgs. firebricks, 35 cases paper (Spicer & Son, mark J.S. and Co.), 33 pkgs. stoves, 20 pkgs. castings, 15 cases, etc. whisky, 50 tons pig iron, 279 pkgs. fireclay.

Loch Vennachar sailing 'Full and by'.

William Hawkins wrote to his friend, Herbert Veal, a Customs & Shipping Agent in Melbourne. In the letter he expressed his views of his upcoming voyage with hopes that he would make a smart passage and be able to renew his acquaintance with old Melbourne friends. He proudly boasted that the Loch Vennachar had had a fine trip home from Australia, arriving on the 89th day.

The voyage home was completely free of storms, and the ship made such an excellent run to the Horn that he was hopeful of completing the round trip in unusually quick time, even though at that time the ship had not been in dry dock for two years.

By Monday the 12th of June, the last of the crew had embarked aboard the Loch Vennachar. The ship was towed by a steam tug from the Glasgow docks and out to the Tail o' the Bank and anchored for the night, the anchorage in the upper Firth of Clyde immediately north of Greenock and Gourock. This area of the firth had gained its name from the sandbar immediately to its east which marked the entrance to the estuary of the River Clyde.

Then on Tuesday the 13th at 8:00 am, Captain Hawkins gave the order to slip the mooring lines that kept the ever anxious ship tethered and the Loch Vennachar began to move away from the Tail o' the Bank, towed downstream and into the Firth of Clyde by an ocean going tug. Captain Hawkins took his ship out through the Irish Channel. The clipper sailed straight into the teeth of an approaching storm with gale force winds coming from the southwest, before swinging to the northwest.

The following day, lashed by hurricane force winds and snow, the Loch Vennachar sought shelter in Lamlash Bay to wait out the storm. For three days she lay at anchor alongside a dozen other vessels before at last weighing anchor and heading south into the Irish Sea. The tug towed the clipper as far as the Isle of Mann, the tow rope being let go off Chicken Rock lighthouse. As the ship passed Tuskar the following morning, the crew took a last long lingering look as they left Ireland in their wake.

The ship crossed the Bay of Biscay and headed into the North Atlantic, encountering freshening westerlies and rising seas. The clipper was shaken by the rough seas but made good headway in the trying conditions. Winds moderated and the fresh and fine conditions continued all the way to the Azores, when a further line of storms and squalls were encountered.

Captain Hawkins had the ship under full sail as she ran south-southwest. The ship soon picked up the northeast trade winds, and with moderating seas she made good progress, averaging 12 knots as she beat her way southwest around the rump of Africa. Moving further south, she picked up the hot winds of the Sahel blowing its dust-filled tendrils out across the sea. The superheated air made conditions difficult as the sirocco blasted the West African coastlands.

Continuing her fast progress, the Loch Vennachar slipped past the Cape Verde Islands on Sunday July 2nd. The forward lookout cried out, "Land ahead!" James Priest, the officer on watch, shouted "Where away?" as they sighted the volcanic island of Santo Antão on the port quarter, its sulphurous peak 7,400 feet above sea level.

Captain Hawkins took the time to calibrate his instruments and mark the ship's position in the ship's logs. The volcano was the highest point in the island group and made a useful navigation point. The four-masted steel barque Vimeira, under Captain Mason, from New York was spoken to on July 7th, at 12° north, 27° west. From there, light winds and fair seas were encountered all the way to the equator.

The 11th of July saw the Loch Vennachar cross the equator just east of Saint Peter and Paul Rocks; in company with the Danish barque Olga, (formerly the 1042 ton ship Caroline). Several violent tropical storms dogged her progress before she spent several days lolling about in the doldrums before picking up a freshening trade wind once again heading south. The lads who had never 'Crossed the Line' were baptised with all due ceremony by Dick Simpson acting the part of King Neptune and his helpers. Edward McPhie, William Turnbull, William Martin and the new Brass Bounder Horace Eastwood were all inducted into the brotherhood of mariners by Neptune and his helpers as the Loch Vennachar crossed the equator.

The four-masted. 2233 ton, steel barque Vimeira.
Built 1891 by Charles Connell and Co. Glasgow.
State Library of South Australia.

Accompanying the Lord of the Sea was Amphitrite, his queen, the judge carrying a list of those to be initiated, a priest, barber and coal-faced guards. To Neptune's chant the young men were given a rough treatment, being covered in coal tar and soap then ritually shaved all over with a mock razor. The initiates were then dunked into a tub of sea water and scrubbed clean by the guards. After a few hours of light-heartedness by those crew members not on watch, the youngest members of the crew were given a few hours off to enjoy the experience in the hot and humid conditions. Afterwards the young men were presented with certificates that proclaimed they had been transformed from Greenhands to genuine Shellbacks.

The Loch Vennachar passed into the Roaring Forties on August 12th. She had already passed close to Ilha da Trindade, before curving south-east past Tristan da Cunha. Once into the forties, she entered the ice zone, the area of the Southern Ocean where the chance of encountering icebergs increased with every degree southwards the ship headed. Captain Hawkins was no stranger to these seas, never feeling more alive than when he commanded a ship racing through the southern squalls. Common sense would have dictated running east along the 40th parallel; yet it was the great circle route from the Cape of Good Hope to Australia, curving down to 60 degrees south, that was 1000 miles shorter and offered the strongest winds.

Running down past the Cape of Good Hope was done along the 43rd parallel. It was in these latitudes that Bill Hawkins had made his reputation, regularly taking vessels under his command deep into the forties and even into the Frightening Fifties to save time on the trip east. Captain Hawkins took the Loch Vennachar south deep to the edge of the ice fields, his only fear being the black bergs, those ice islands that turned turtle in the night and were invisible to lookouts. Weighing the risk of ice against a fast passage, Bill Hawkins pushed his ship and its crew to a line between the 43rd and 45th parallels as the Loch Vennachar began running her easting down.

As she scudded easting, the Loch Vennachar ran before early spring gales. High seas and roaring winds of 50 knots plus made for a swift yet perilous voyage. The main topgallant and royal, along with one of the headsails, were shredded and several large waves threatened to sweep away members of the crew as they washed across the deck. The ship, however, suffered little real damage in the clipper's swift passage across the Southern Ocean. Captain Hawkins maintained a sure line between the 43rd and 45th parallels across the southern seas. Several large icebergs were passed on the morning of the 21st of August, but their blue-white majesty posed no genuine threat.

At this point in the trip, Loch Vennachar averaged between 240 and 300 miles a day, and the journey promised to be well under 90 days. At times even the experienced hands had a hard time of it as Captain Hawkins drove his ship for Adelaide through the trying conditions. The voyage to South Australia from latitude 44 degrees south, longitude 80 degrees east, was marked by a series of severe gales with winds from north nor'west south sou'east, accompanied by high cross seas. The ship threatened to broach several times as huge waves lashed the decks. Captain Hawkins ordered the crew to loosen the chains to give the ship more flexibility as she climbed up mountainous waves and plunged bow-first into the cavernous troughs on the other side.

Yet no matter how much punishment she took, the Loch Vennachar held together, just as her designer, Captain William Martin, knew she would. By Friday the 1st of September 1905, the Loch Vennachar was running under topsails and headsails as she headed north-east in a heaving beam sea, the winds coming from the north-west before swinging west-south-west. Captain Hawkins and his crew worked to keep the ship from being rolled or pooped. Heavy rain and sleeting hail lashed the vessel as she continued on her journey. The approaching front threatened to make the next day or two uncomfortable indeed.

The storm front passed rapidly over the Loch Vennachar on Saturday the 2nd, bringing with it howling 70-mile-an-hour winds, thunder and lightning and more than an inch of pounding hail and rain. The barometric pressure dropped to below 28.5 as the eye of the Southern Ocean cyclone passed over the ship. The clipper experienced exceptionally high waves, with very large patches of foam, driven before the wind, covering much of the surface of the boiling, spume-covered seas.

The storm moved rapidly eastwards, leaving heavy conditions in its wake. The crew breathed a sigh of relief as they sailed north-east, confident of reaching port in well under 90 days. The winds swung west-south-west, announcing the approaching high with its fine weather. The cook again began preparing hot meals and the last pig was prepared for slaughter, ready for a fine meal of roast pork that the ship's crew would share once they sighted land.

Showery weather continued, but conditions abated as the ship sailed east. By Sunday the weather was fine and the sea moderate to rough, with winds from the south-east tending north-east later in the day. Captain Hawkins began final preparations for the Loch Vennachar's stop in Adelaide. He had James Priest, along with Dick Simpson and the ship's carpenter, make a survey of any damage the ship had taken and asked the cook and steward to prepare an inventory of supplies, including water in the tanks. Sailors began writing letters home and made plans for what they intended to do once they had safely reached port in Adelaide or Melbourne. Even as she raced north, the ominous grey clouds of another storm appeared upon the horizon and the ocean's colour turned dark green once again.

By the morning of the 4th of September, conditions had moderated even further. The sun was out and shone through a sky filled with scattered showers and long fine breaks. A cold, freshening breeze blew up from the south and south-west. Progress was swift, and Cape Leeuwin could only have been a day or two away according to Captain Hawkins' calculations. The weather continued to be unsettled, but it was nothing compared to the conditions that the Loch Vennachar had encountered on her trip across the Southern Ocean.

Captain Hawkins was looking forward to his stay in Melbourne, and William Barry planned on spending a few days visiting his parents after spending months at sea travelling to and from Britain. The rest of the crew had plans for their time in

Melbourne; Joe Hadley and Tom Pearce would celebrate their final voyage home as Brass Bounders by lifting an ale or three. Upon arrival back in Glasgow, they would sit the exam for their Second Mate tickets and then their real careers would begin. They may have only been able to gain berths as third mates posted in charge of the fo'c'sle, but they would at least gain a taste of command. Tom also hoped to catch up with his younger brother Robert. The brothers had not clapped eyes on each other for two years and, after the recent death of their father, Tom senior, they were all each other had in the way of family. Dairmid Thomson's father was anxious to see his son again and show him off at the Old Scholars' upcoming dinners.

The fine if cold conditions continued as a complex weather system moved into the ocean to the south of Cape Leeuwin, which was crossed on Tuesday, the 5th. Winds swung around to the east-north-east, forcing Captain Hawkins to a port tack earlier than he would have liked as the ship veered close to land. Cloudy conditions continued, making the reading of the ship's exact position difficult. This was nothing new for the 40-year veteran, and he pushed on, confident that his sea logs and chronometers would more than make up for any minor navigational variations.

James Priest did his best to instruct Fred Ward and the lads new to the sea on the finer points of being a sailor. He was a hard man, but at least he was fair. But heaven help the poor hapless sailor who disputed anything the mates ordered them to do. Of the three ship's officers, only Fred Lake, with his laconic good humour, saw an easy rapport build between him, the apprentices, and the older shellbacks of the crew.

The approaching low-pressure systems winds blew in from the north-east as it moved towards the south coast, with gale force winds and squally, rough, and showery weather increasing in ferocity as it progressed eastwards. Windy squalls were common, and the cold, overcast conditions became worse as winds slowly shifted to the west and south-west. The Loch Vennachar, as she entered the Bight south of Cape Leeuwin, benefited from warmer and gentler north-easterlies as she started upon her starboard tack. The night was windy, the sky hidden by low cloud; a quarter moon struggled to shed its sickly light through scudding clouds as the Loch Vennachar raced under full sail across the Bight.

"In addition to the Loch Garry, which arrived at Melbourne last week, three representatives of the Loch line fleet, the Loch Etive, the Loch Lomond, and the Loch Ness, are now in Melbourne, having arrived some time ago. Three others—still the Loch Rannoch, Loch Torridon, and Loch Vennachar—are on their way to Melbourne, whilst, according to latest advice, the Loch Carron and the Loch Katrine were also loading for that port. The efforts made to popularise the 'Loch' liners as passenger as well as cargo carriers were attended with very satisfactory results, and, according to a Melbourne exchange, even now, when steamers secure the great bulk of patronage, the 'Loch' liners continue to receive a fair share of it. The present voyage of the Loch Garry from Glasgow to Adelaide stands as one of the best that she has yet made. She arrived at Adelaide on the 74th day out. For 30 days she averaged 240 knots, her best daily run being 313 knots. This feat for consistently good sailing is remarkable. Captain James Horne is still in command of the Loch Garry."

Examiner, Wednesday 9 August 1905.

By the 5th of September, the Loch Rannoch and the Loch Torridon were just a few days behind, their crews expecting the Loch Vennachar to have safely arrived in Port Adelaide ahead of them, and the Loch Carron and Loch Katrine were well on their way, being just a week or so behind. The sun set with the winds coming from the port quarter; with topsails and headsails set, the clipper barrelled along, her captain and crew confident of an early arrival off the Semaphore within the next two to three days. During the night, the winds shifted to the north-north-east and freshened with the dawn.

Wednesday, September 6th dawned to overcast and unsettled conditions, the clouds in the east taking on a reddish hue. Billowing clouds of precious topsoil drifted down from the east with the approaching dust storms. The winds had freshened as the sun rose at 6:29 am.

Loch Vennachar last seen by S.S. Yongala.
State Library of Victoria.

Conditions were perfect for sailing as, with the sunrise, Captain Hawkins called the port and starboard watches to the yards with orders to lengthen sails, adding upper-gallants, staysails and royals. He moved the Loch Vennachar from the port to the starboard tack, ready to make her run below the Neptune Light and into Investigator Strait.

As the sun rose higher in the sky, First Officer James Priest attempted to take readings to establish the ship's current position. From the ship's chronometer, he knew that they should have been at a longitude of 133 degrees east; however, because of the ever-present low cloud, establishing the ship's latitude was proving to be troublesome.

As the morning progressed, the forenoon watch came on deck and James went below for breakfast, handing over the con to Fred Lake, who was able to take readings as the cloud blew away to the south. His readings were confirmed by Captain Hawkins when he appeared after breakfast in a light and jovial mood.

Midway through the forenoon watch, as the Loch Vennachar sailed east-south-east across the Great Australian Bight, the forward lookout shouted out that he saw smoke ahead. As the two vessels closed on each other, Captain Hawkins realised it was the Adelaide Steamship Company steamer, Yongala, on her regular run from Fremantle to Adelaide, 160 nautical miles west of South Neptune Island.

Captain Hawkins checked his watch; it was 10:00 am in the morning. The weather was fine and clear, the seas slight and the winds gentle from the south-east. As the Yongala approached, Captain Hawkins ordered signal flags be raised asking the Yongala for the current longitude. The Yongala replied with signals of her own indicating their current position: latitude 33.21 degrees south, longitude 133 degrees east.

As the two ships passed astern of each other, Captain Hawkins ordered a further signal be sent saying, "*Loch Vennachar – Please report we are all well.*" Being unable to make out the signal, Captain Rees of the Yongala ordered his ship about

SS Yongala
State Library of Victoria.

Last sighting of the Loch Vennachar seen standing into the land at dusk.
State Library of Victoria.

and to close upon the stern of the Loch Vennachar so he could read the flags.

The Yongala came close enough to the Loch Vennachar that her captain and crew could see the steamer's name clearly upon the bow. Captain Hawkins stood upon the poop next to the helmsman talking to James Priest and Charlie Radcliffe. As the two ships passed abeam, Captain Hawkins raised his arm waved farewell to the passengers and crew of the steamer, the Yongala's captain returning the gesture. According the Captain Hawkins, their position put them some 160 miles west of Neptune Island. The wind was light from the south-east, and the vessel was steering east-north-east. The clipper was sailing close-hauled on the starboard tack, laying on a course almost directly for Adelaide

The Loch Vennachar continued on her way under full sail, making a crisp 11 to 14 knots as she headed towards Adelaide in an east-north-easterly direction. The pale quarter moon rose high above the clouds at 11:13 am, but no one saw it as the gathering clouds began to fill the sky.

Next day, 7th September, conditions remained the same, Captain Bennett recorded in his log for the all four watches; 'Cloudy, dull and light haze, sea smooth'. The Loch Vennachar stayed her course for the rest of the day. Just before dusk, a schooner was sighted by lookouts in the distance. She was too far off to be signalled and the pair of vessels went their separate ways.

The following morning of September 8th, the wind veered to the north-east but remained light, logged at Beaufort Force 1. The sea remained smooth and the haze persisted. Bill Hawkins now faced a wind which was 'dead muzzler' for Port Adelaide. He now faced the prospect of having to beat up through Investigator Strait. To remain close-hauled to starboard meant sailing west, by nor'west towards Neptune and Gambier island groups off the Eyre Peninsula. He chose instead to wear-ship and once through the wind the Loch Vennachar stood on east, sou'east, close-hauled on the port tack and closing in towards the northwest corner of Kangaroo Island. James Priest made sure that the lookouts on watch atop the fo'c'sle-head kept a sharp lookout for land and the welcoming light of Cape Borda.

At 8 bells, marking the end of the Morning Watch conditions winds were fresh, sky cloudy, a low haze concealed the horizon, with a moderate sea running. By noon the northeast wind had freshened, the gloomy, hazy atmosphere continued, as seas roughened. With the change of watch Second Officer Charles Radcliffe assumed his place beside the helmsman, he ordered the emerging watch to reef the mizzen and mainstays. Captain Hawkins ordered the main course to be reefed as the wind began blowing harder from the north-east, carrying with it the smell of dust-filled rain that began to fall.

Checking the instruments on the binnacle in front of him, Bill Hawkins noted that the barometric pressure had begun to drop sharply to 29 millibars and continued to fall steadily, indicating an approaching change. He did not need instruments to know that another blow was on its way, but before going below for lunch, he made sure that Charlie Radcliffe would keep an eye on conditions and shorten sail if the winds began to strengthen.

All through the afternoon watch, weather conditions continued to worsen. Clouds were building in the west, the wind had continued to freshen, swinging north-east to north-west, and seas began to rise, becoming choppy as the northerly winds knocked the tops of the rollers. Barometric pressure continued to fall throughout the day.

By 4:00 pm, at the start of the first dog watch, light passing rain-showers, gloomy light, and a hazy atmosphere greeted Captain Hawkins as he came on deck had come back on deck and ordered hands to shorten sail even further as the blustery northerly winds continued to strengthen. With no sun to take readings from, Captain Hawkins relied upon his experience, speed recordings, and the ship's twin chronometers to try to maintain an accurate fix on the ship's position; however, dead reckoning was the best that he could do.

As James Priest came on watch, he ordered lookouts forward and topmen to clew up sheets that had come adrift in the strengthening winds. The off-watch joined the idlers in the deckhouse for dinner, as the ship's steward served Captain Hawkins and the apprentices in the saloon the leftover pork from the previous day's roast. The officers and brass-bounders enjoyed a rare moment of civility as the crew tucked into their meal of sea-biscuits, salt laden bully beef, and twice-baked bread and apricot jam, washed down with copious amounts of lukewarm tea.

The sun set at 6:00 pm, the start of the second dog watch. It was already quite dark out, and the feeble lights from the ship's lanterns barely pierced the growing darkness. By this time, skies were very overcast, squally rain was pelting down and thick haze, seas rough to very rough By the end of the second dog-watch the winds had freshened to near-gale conditions from the north-west, and those on watch followed orders from James Priest to prepare two of the ship's boats and to attach lifelines to the ship's rails. Forward lookouts were warned to keep a sharp eye out for the Cape Borda light, though the mate had difficulty relaying these orders to his Scandinavian crew members. The night was becoming dirty and safety-lines were rigged fore and aft. The helmsman, dressed head-to-toe in wet weather gear, was joined by a lee helmsman, both were ordered to don lashings to keep them attached to the wheel as waves began to smash against the rudder.

By the start of the First Watch at 8:00 pm, when Fred Lake appeared on deck, rugged up in oilskins and several layers of wool, the weather conditions had worsened considerably. Skies were overcast and squally with showers of driving rain, and hail in places, with rough to very rough seas. Winds had become strong to gale force from the nor'nor'-west and threatened to strengthen further. Still the Loch Vennachar stood to the east-south-east, as close to the wind as possible. Standing, braced on the windward side of the poop Hawkins stared into the gloom hoping to catch a glimpse of the elusive flash of the Cape Borda light.

Towering waves as high as 6 metres caused the ship to roll violently and threatened to put the Loch Vennachar over onto her beam ends as they washed over her pitching deck. Visibility for the lookouts was down to just a few hundred metres, the moon offering no light to speak of as low cloud and driving rains made navigation by instruments, logs, and charts an absolute necessity. Captain Hawkins set a conservative course, convinced the ship was on track to pick up the Borda light, even as the ship ran before the wind.

Fred Lake took over from James Priest, who went below for his evening meal. Fred was no stranger to these waters, having spent his time as an apprentice making the run from Britain to Melbourne via Adelaide a number of times. As the night progressed, the ship sailed onwards, driven at speed even under shortened sail. Even under shortened sail a crisp 12 to 14 knots was logged as they sailed across the face of the wind close hauled on the port tack. With no stars to steer by and an elusive, waxing, quarter moon providing little illumination, the mates did well to keep the ship headed in the right direction. Despite the thick haze Bill Bennett was sure they were on course to clear cape Borda however he had not allowed enough sea room for the lee way the ship was making and the strong easterly set of the current.

When Charlie Radcliffe came on watch at midnight, the deck was awash, topsails and headsails were set, and the ship was running before a rising sea, propelled along by gale-force winds. Towards midnight, Captain Hawkins came on deck just before the change of watch, checking the ship's speed and relative position against his logs and charts. He ordered a further shortening of sail as he ordered the helm put down sending the Loch Vennachar in an east-north-east direction. Lookouts had not yet sighted either the Neptune or Cape Borda lights, and Charlie Radcliffe was under strict orders to keep sails set as they were and true to course. Lookouts were placed aloft upon the foremast, and lifelines, safety gear, and lifebelts were made ready.

Despite the captain and crew's best efforts, none of them could accurately tell just how far south the ship had been driven. What was not obvious was the strong eastward current that was prevalent at this time of year, further complicating a navigator's

Cape Borda Light with vessels signalling in the distance.
State Library of South Australia.

ability to accurately judge the ship's position. To further complicate matters the moon had disappeared and the thick haze grown worse. Unknown to all on board, Bill Hawkins included, there was an invisible line inshore of which the Cape Borda light was obscured by the adjacent hills to the south of it.

A sleepy and irritable mate came up onto the poop deck, having roused the change of the watch from their bunks in the fo'c'sle. He was already soaked through to the skin, having been drenched by the waves that continued to break over the bow of the ship as she ploughed relentlessly through the walls of white water. It was just after midnight and Charlie was greeted with stormy, overcast, and squally conditions, with showers, sleet, and hail in places, and rough to very rough seas. Strong to gale-force west to south-west winds, a rising barometric pressure, and 6-metre high waves were making navigation difficult.

Visibility for the lookouts was down to a few hundred metres, and those on watch could never hear what was being yelled at them from the poop. Not that it made much difference, as no one on the poop deck had any chance of hearing a call from the forward lookouts above the roaring wind and waves. In total darkness, the Loch Vennachar barrelled forward, with an anxious watch officer eager to get back to his bunk and the warmth of the saloon's relatively warm and dry luxury.

The Loch Vennachar put to sea six foremast hands short, and had had to make do with young, inexperienced ordinary seamen and Nordic crew members with poor English skills, taken on board as crew because there was a shortage of experienced British sailors. The night promised to be long and trying. Thus was the life of a ship's officer on the graveyard watch. Unable to chat blithely with the twin sailors manning the helm, there was little more lonely a position aboard the ship, with only his own mind for company.

By 3:00 am weather conditions had begun to moderate somewhat and the watch promised to pass without further incident. James Priest had wandered onto the deck to check the ship's progress. The Cape Borda light had not been sighted and James Priest was nervous. He noted that lookouts had been

The relative positions of the two lights the crew of the Loch Vennachar were searching for.

placed, one on the foretopgallant yard, another on the forecastle head; a man was sent aloft and forward every 15 minutes to keep an eye out for the Borda light that the Captain was certain would be seen somewhere to the southeast. The log was hurled but no bottom was reached the current being too strong.

Visibility was almost zero due to the squally, overcast conditions, punctuated by sheeting curtains of rain. The Cape Borda light was hidden by low cloud and high cliffs that shielded

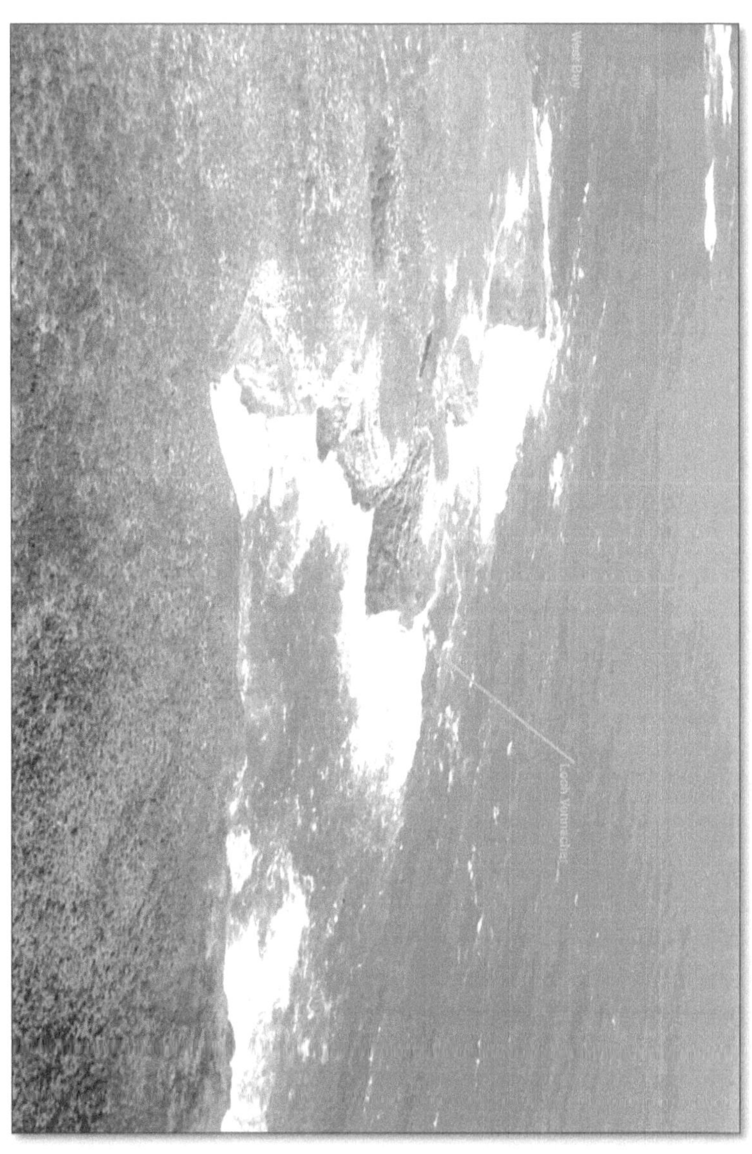

Vennachar Point, the place where the Loch Vennacharan aground on the morning of the 7th of September 1905.
Photograph by Terry Drew, original member of SUHR that surveyed the wreck site in 1977.

the light in the atrocious conditions. She was not the first ship to lose sight of the Borda light. This was despite the lamp having an effective range of 21 nautical miles on a clear and calm night. The light's signal sequence, of a group flash 4 every 20 seconds (Latitude 35° 45' 3" S, Longitude 136° 35' 7" E), was not that different from the other light the lookouts were searching for.

Sometime before 4:00 am just as the morning watch were appearing on deck, a cry was heard from the forward lookout that he had sighted breakers ahead. Madly ringing the ship's bell the lookout, a young apprentice, then ran aft struggling to stay afoot on the pitching deck. At first, those abaft could neither properly hear nor understand what the frantic man was screaming about. Another man ran forward, sighting the same grey-white line of surf directly ahead. Running back to alert the watch officer of the approaching danger, the lookout struggled to make himself heard above the wind and waves.

The James priest grabbed his whistle sounding out three shrill blasts. *"All Hands on deck!"* he ordered all hands to the braces and the helm put hard down as he attempted to bring the ship around. Captain Hawkins was summoned to the deck. The normally jovial Scotsman awoke cursing and angry, livid to find his ship upon a lee shore with breakers right ahead. The Loch Vennachar was less than a mile from the cliffs as Captain Hawkins called out to 'bout ship!

All hands rushed up on deck, calm and professional in their reactions. The mate ordered the crew to set headsails as others manned the winches to bring round the yards on the mainmast. There was no time to release the anchors or cable, and even as the ship began to come around as the helm was ported, Captain Hawkins realised it was too late. She'd missed stays. Thick, heavy rain squalls and low cloud almost down to sea level obscured everything.

As she struck the rock shelf at the base of the cliffs, 100 feet high, under full sail, her masts bowed forward, the back braces straining then tearing away the chainplates. The ship's headgear folded upwards as the fore and main topmasts collapsed and shot forward. The topgallant masts stuck fast high upon the cliff, dislodging rocks and showering the crew with spars and rigging. The masts of the ship were interdependent; as soon as one went, the others quickly followed. The jib-boom and bow sprit were snapped like matchwood the figurehead being sheared off at the base.

The debris fell upon the deck and hung over the side, a tangle of spars and cables. The wreckage slammed against the hull, maiming those trapped beneath. The rigging, sails, and spars from the fallen mizzen covered the ship's boats atop the skids. Two of the ship's boats had their hulls stove in, and the lookouts and those atop the fo'c'sle peak were pitched into the sea. The Loch Vennachar was hung up upon the cliffs by her fallen masts, and no boats could be launched until the crew managed to cut the sails and metal cabling away.

With her hull stove in to beyond the collision bulkhead, water poured in to the lower hold. Held firm in a jagged cleft of the cliffs the ships decks were awash and many a sailor was swept to his doom.

As the ship passed over the rock shelf, the hull plating aft of the bow split and wave action drove her deeper onto the cliffs. The ship began to settle bow-first upon the rock shelf, her rigging being torn away and covering the deck. Only the lower mizzen mast remained. As waves swept across the deck, many of the surviving crew gathered upon the poop and deckhouse roof. Others climbed to stump of the mizzen mast attempting to stay clear of the crashing waves and swash.

The crew managed to cut away some of the rigging with axes, leaving deep marks upon the bulwarks and gunwales. Waves swept over the deck as the ship settled lower into the water and an attempt was made to launch the gig and cutter. The shattered remains of the Loch Vennachar were drawn back off the rock shelf by the weight of water and wave action, and as she settled, anything atop was washed away. The few survivors climbed into the remaining rigging, crowding onto the shrouds and clinging to the crossjack and the crosstree.

The ship quickly sank down atop a reef 20 feet below the surface, the weight of the water already in her hold and the pounding of the waves breaking her keel and splitting her open at about the mounting of the foremast. This area had been weakened when she struck the cliff and the mast was torn from its mountings, compromising hull integrity in the process.

As the ship split in two, the larger aft section began to spill cargo as waves smashed over the poop and quarter decks. The mid-deck house was lifted off the deck and smashed into several large pieces as the saloon and 'tween decks flooded. The mizzen stump finally gave way, throwing the last few hardy souls to their deaths in a sea filled with churning foam and wreckage.

One of the ship's two surviving boats managed to get clear with several survivors; however, anyone who had been in the forecastle was dead, as the bow settled more or less intact in a wide trench between the rock shelf and the shallow reef just out from the cliff base.

The larger stern section was now picked up by monstrous waves, turned sideways, and pushed into the cliffs, the rudder pointing south. The stern swung wildly in the heaving seas, the pounding surf pushing the port railing hard against the cliffs, shattering the hull. The waves that swept the aft section onto the rocks just as quickly tore her off again. Anyone still aboard at this stage had little hope of survival.

The heavy masts and cable-bound spars were dragged into the surf. Lighter parts of the ship, including the gutted remains of the mid-deck house, were washed away, and the hull began to break up as it was pounded against the cliffs. The aft section of the Loch Vennachar slid off the rock shelf, her hold completely flooded, and slid into deeper waters on the seaward side of the reef that had snapped her keel.

The donkey engine, pig iron, and bricks tumbled to the depths, covering the bottom about the wreck. Teak decking and timber fixed with brass fittings washed into the gorges and ravines surrounding the point into which she'd run. Great rolls of newsprint were washed out of the shattered aft cargo hold and swept out to sea.

The surviving boat was quickly overwhelmed and smashed against the cliffs, the occupants drowning. Others were swept off of the deck and fallen rigging into sea caves at the base of the cliff just north of the wreck site, their bodies torn apart as they were driven deep into the cave by pounding waves with tons of debris from the shattered ship.

Those not killed by fallen rigging or drowned in the foundering lifeboat, were swallowed by the huge seas, or were smashed to death by wreckage, or torn to pieces against the jagged rocks at the base of the cliffs. There were no survivors.

XIX
One of Our Clippers is Missing

An early Admiralty chart of the waters around Kangaroo Island.

The Adsteam ship SS Yongala arrived in Port Adelaide less than 48 hours after she had crossed paths with the Loch Vennachar. After tying up at the dock and discharging his passengers, Captain Rees reported to the harbour masters that he had spoken to Captain Hawkins aboard the clipper and that he had instructed Captain Rees to report the clipper and her crew as all well.

Maritime authorities expected the ship to appear at the Semaphore anchorage within a day or two at most. Stormy weather continued in the gulf and waters around Kangaroo Island, but little fear was held for Captain Hawkins and his crew.

Concerns increased, however, as with each passing day the Loch Vennachar failed to appear. After a week, the Marine Board sent a telegram to the keepers at Cape Borda to keep a sharp lookout for the clipper and to report any sighting of her as soon as possible. The ship was officially listed as missing on the 13th, and there was growing speculation amongst the local newspapers as to her fate. The common theory was that the Loch Vennachar had been blown off course by the northerly gales and would make her way around the bottom of Kangaroo Island, coming into Adelaide via Backstairs Passage. To this end, the keepers at Cape Willoughby were alerted to the clipper's possible appearance and were asked to notify maritime authorities if she was sighted.

Loch Vennachar Overdue Adelaide, Thursday

"Some anxiety is felt at Port Adelaide concerning the ship Loch Vennachar, which is 93 days out from Glasgow. On September 6 she was spoken by the steamer Yongala 33.21 S, 133 E, or about 160 miles west of Neptune Island. She then desired to be reported "All well". Eight days have elapsed and no further word has been received. The vessel, under ordinary circumstances, should have entered the gulf two days after being sighted in the position indicated, but the possibilities are that she has been blown down to the south and has not been able to recover her position in the heavy gales which have raged during the week." **The Argus Friday 15 September 1905.**

SS Coolgardie.
State Library of Western Australia.

West Bay Shelter Hut 1906.
State Library of South Australia

After being 94 days out from Glasgow, authorities in Adelaide and Melbourne were more than a little concerned that the ever-reliable Loch Vennachar had yet to make an appearance. Another ship was also reported overdue at the same time. The steamer Coolgardie had run through storms from Fremantle to Adelaide, and was late arriving at port. Her master, Captain Nightingale, reported that the weather his ship had encountered was the most severe he ever faced.

A ship that arrived safely in Port Adelaide was the steamer Grantala; her captain reported that she had encountered strong north-westerly gales and mountainous seas as she crossed the Bight. With the safe arrival of the Coolgardie and none of her passengers or crew having spotted the missing clipper, speculation increased that the Loch Vennachar had met with misfortune.

By the 17th of September, the Marine Board had made the decision that if no word of the Loch Vennachar had been received by the following day, then Captain C.J. Clare, Superintendent of the Life Saving Department, would dispatch Captain Patrick Weir in the government steamer Governor Musgrave to search the south and west coasts of Kangaroo Island as well as any other locations the Board deemed appropriate. When no word was received by the morning of the 18th, the Cape Borda telegraph had sent no message and no one else had reported the Loch Vennachar either, the Governor Musgrave left Port Adelaide that afternoon. As she left, Captain Clare was confident that the Loch Vennachar would be found safe as Captain Hawkins was an old and experienced navigator, well able to handle any problems his ship and crew may have had to face.

Leaving at 5 pm and heading south at best possible speed in rising seas, the Governor Musgrave set course for Cape Willoughby, Pelorus Island, South-West Rocks, Young Rocks, North Rocks, and Vivonne Bay. It was planned that Captain Weir would follow the coast to Cape de Couedic, West Bay, and Cape Borda. Upon arrival at Cape Borda, he was ordered to telegraph the Marine Board to report his progress before heading north-west for Neptune Island.

Captain Weir completed his initial sweep of the specified locations with a cursory search of Kangaroo Island's rugged coastline and the surrounding islets and reefs. Upon arriving at Cape Borda on the evening of the 20th of September, the Governor Musgrave anchored off Harvey's Return, near Cape Borda lighthouse. After transmitting a progress report, Captain Weir received instructions to head north to Rocky and Greenly islands and thence to Coffin Bay and other points along the west coast. Eventually, after anchoring at Cable Bay and sending a message back to Adelaide, Captain Weir received word that the Loch Vennachar had not arrived and he was to return to port, there being nothing more he could do. Thus, the Governor Musgrave arrived back in Adelaide after an unsuccessful five-day search for the missing clipper. Those aboard the steamer had apparently completely missed the Loch Vennachar's final resting place.

Conditions throughout the trip had been fine, though seas continued to be heavy and the sky overcast. Aboard the ship was C.P.O. Staples of the Life Saving Department, in charge of the Rocket Rescue Gear; A. Darby, representing G&R Wills, the agents of the Loch Line; and various reporters and photographers. Captain Weir and the crew of the Governor Musgrave had been instructed to search a great many locations in a short amount of time. This gave them time for only cursory glances at each location as they steamed past. Much of the time, because of the poor conditions, the steamer was 500 yards or more away from the islands and coasts they were surveying.

There was a certain air of the frivolous and macabre with the press along, and Captain Weir was ever conscious of what may be reported back to the wider world. The steamer cruised rapidly along the south coast as far as Remarkable Rocks and Cape de Couedic, the ship being rocked by giant swells that slammed into the cliffs that lined much of the island's south coast. Captain Weir took time to inspect the waters around the Casuarina Islets. These large granite outcrops were awash, standing 50 feet high and constantly covered by rollers powering in from the Southern Ocean.

Winds were coming from the south-west to south-east and light patchy rain and showers were frequent in the area. Conditions continued to moderate throughout the day but stayed overcast with deep ocean swells. Turning north-west, the Governor Musgrave steamed into Maupertuis Bay where lookouts sighted the shattered remains of the Loch Vennachar's sister ship, the Loch Sloy, and another wreck, the Mars, at Cape Bedout. The afternoon wore on cold and grey, with 12 to 18 foot rollers pounding the cliffs.

On the way north, lookouts were instructed to keep a watch at certain points for Life Saving Department shelter huts and fingerboards for signs of use or deterioration.The hut erected at Cape du Couedic appeared to be untouched, and the fingerboards at Remarkable Rocks, Cape du Couedic, at the site of the wreck of the Loch Sloy in Maupertuis Bay, and at Cape Bedout were all intact. The shelter huts and fingerboards had been erected by the Life Saving Department after the wreck of the Loch Sloy, in which one of the survivors died for lack of food and shelter.

The fingerboards were white wooden posts with painted signs located on prominent landforms, giving the distances and directions to the nearest places where help could be found. The steamer passed close to the mouth of West Bay at just after 4:00 pm on the 19th of September. Lookouts spied out the shelter hut and saw the beach clear of wreckage and the shelter hut door still closed. Assuming that there were no shipwrecked sailors in the vicinity, Captain Weir steamed rapidly north, bypassing the Loch Vennachar's final resting place in the early evening light.

Lookouts failed to take note of the wreck. At this stage, the hull was still mostly intact, with the rigging keeping most of the spars tied to the ship as she rested in 40 feet of water. The heavy seas and gloomy, overcast conditions made spotting a sunken wreck all but impossible, especially when the lookouts were in no way expecting to find one in the vicinity.

The wind and currents had already pushed the loose wreckage either deep into the cove and caves on either side of the wreck site, or further out to sea than 500 yards. The Governor

Musgrave finally anchored briefly off Cape Borda, arriving at 5:45 pm, in time to see the sun setting a brilliant orange as it dipped below the oppressive grey clouds.

On the 25th of September, there was some consternation amongst those hoping for the Loch Vennachar's safe arrival when it was falsely reported in some papers that the vessel had arrived safely in Adelaide. The hopes these reports raised were dashed a few days later on the 27th, when reports came in that fresh wreckage had washed ashore on the south and east coasts of Kangaroo Island.

The Marine Board sent the Kingscote Postmaster south to investigate the reports of wreckage east of Cape du Couedic and along the beaches of Cape Gantheaume. Just over three weeks after the wreck, people's worst fears were realised when Captain F. Peters of the ketch Fanny Watt picked up a roll of blue printing paper in St Vincent's Gulf, just 20 miles from the Goannas, 18 miles north-east of Port Adelaide opposite Port Gawler.

When brought to Adelaide, the paper's external markings matched the paper bound for Adelaide's newspapers: the Register, The Observer, and the Evening Journal. Despite this, many people still refused to believe that the paper could have come from the Loch Vennachar, being so far from where she was last seen.

Reports continued to come in from Kangaroo Island that fresh wreckage had washed ashore along the island's south-east coast. At Cape St Albans, the lower half of one side of the ship's figurehead washed ashore, still covered in white paint and gold gilt. These reports prompted the Marine Board to order a fresh search of Kangaroo Island and its surrounds.

So, on the 28th of September, Captain Weir took the Governor Musgrave out once again to search, this time for the possible wreck site of the Loch Vennachar. In Melbourne and in

Glasgow, employees and owners of the Loch Line were all equally confident that the Loch Vennachar had simply been blown off course and would, any day, turn up either in Adelaide or, at worst, in Melbourne very soon.

The search by the Governor Musgrave had a great many people's hopes and fears riding upon it. The steamer arrived at Cape Willoughby on the 29th, and after two days searching along the coast to Cape Hart, enough wreckage was recovered to convince Captain Weir that it was from the Loch Vennachar.

Reported Discovery of Wreckage

Captain Clare received a telegram from the postmaster, James Rumble, Kingscote, Kangaroo Island, to the effect that wreckage had been found on the south coast of Kangaroo Island, and that there was a rumour that some bales of paper had lately been washed ashore in the vicinity of Cape Willoughby.

A man named William Burgess told the postmaster that he had met a woman who said she had found a spar with a lot of piping around it 16 miles east of Cape du Couedic. Captain Clare authorised the postmaster to organise a search party and, with Bill Burgess, thoroughly scour the coast.

A search party will travel across Kangaroo Island to the locality where the wreckage was reported to have come ashore 16 miles east of Cape du Couedic, and then search the coast westward to Rocky River. They have been instructed to report to Captain Clare as soon as possible. The Marine Board received a report from Cape Willoughby that a spar about 30 feet long, with a sheave inlet in it and two iron bands, had been seen a mile out to sea.

Final confirmation of the ship's fate was received in Adelaide on the 30th of September, when a report was received that a ship's boat bearing the name "Loch Vennachar" on its stern had washed ashore at Vivonne Bay on the south coast of Kangaroo Island. The boat was clinker-built, 26' long with an 8' beam; her bottom was completely stoved in. Wrapped around the boat was over 100' of rope, indicating an attempt by crew members to get clear of the doomed ship.

Some of the wreckage recovered on the second search including a piece of the skirting from the ships figurehead.
State Library of South Australia.

Searchers scouring the coast discovered an abundance of fresh wreckage strewn along the coast from Cape Gantheaume to Cape St Albans. Amongst the wreckage recovered was a 9' length of the jib boom, pieces of whisky cases, a 20' length of teak decking and a large corner of the teak deck-house. None of the crew was found amongst the scattered debris, and few clues as to the wreck's whereabouts could be ascertained.

With mounting concern for the safety of the 28 missing sailors, authorities started speculating as to the exact location of the shattered ship. Chief amongst the locations were Young and Pelorus Rocks, chosen because of the distribution of the flotsam along Kangaroo Island's south coast. By early October, wreckage was beginning to wash up on the southern tip of the Fleurieu Peninsula and all along the coast to Victor Harbor.

With the discovery of the wreckage confirming the loss of the Loch Vennachar, speculation was rife as to her location and many were the opinions espoused by experts all and sundry. Captain Robert Pattman, master of the Loch Torridon and friend of William Hawkins, and Captain William Bennett, former master of the Loch Vennachar, were interviewed in early October by a reporter:

"If I had any doubt about the vessel being lost," he said, "the finding of that cargo in the gulf has convinced me. Captain Bennett was more optimistic than I was. He gave her till Saturday (tomorrow), but the finding of the reel of paper has convinced him, too, that his old ship is gone. Of course, vessels are delayed in a remarkable fashion sometimes. I remember once I was coming in my ship from Adelaide bound here, when I struck head winds and bad weather, and was not heard of for 21 days. You can easily see the absence of any news about the Loch Vennachar would not satisfy us, but the news today is too conclusive.

I think she struck the Young Rocks. She had 1,330 tons of cargo aboard, and Capt. Bennett, who knows her well, reckons she would be within 18 inches of her Plimsoll mark, so she would be in tip-top sailing trim. I don't see how, with south-westerly and westerly winds, she could get ashore on Kangaroo Island. You see she would have 12 points to come out on if she did get behind Cape

Hart, and Captain Hawkins would know as soon as he had got too far in, for Cape Hart shuts out the Willoughby Light.

Of course, if his ship were disabled or partially disabled, he might get in under Cape Hart and not be able to come out again; if that is the case, the coast along there will be piled high with pieces of the ship and all she had in her. Wreckage could easily travel from Young Rocks to the head of the gulf; it is only a journey of 130 miles. It would take about a fortnight for the reel to travel that far, I should say, and the barnacles point to the same time. She must have been wrecked very soon after the Yongala sighted her."

The Register & Argus, Saturday 30th September 1905.

Captain Clare, Superintendent of the Life Saving Department, ordered Captain Weir and the *Governor Musgrave* south, this time to look for survivors and pick up any wreckage. The steamer left promptly on the 9th of October and returned on the 12th after a fruitless search of the southern coast of Kangaroo Island and the waters around Young Rocks and Pelorus Island.

Like his more famous counterparts, Patrick Weir was also of the opinion that the Loch Vennachar had foundered off Young Rocks. He put little or no effort into searching the western end of Kangaroo Island and the Marine Board, perhaps swayed by the opinions of Captains Bennett and Pattman, did not push Captain Weir to pay close attention to this stretch of coastline.

This was especially so when so much wreckage was washing up on the coast from Vivonne Bay to Cape Hart. The waters around Young Rocks were deep and it was thought that if the clipper had struck the reef in a heavy gale, she would have gone down in minutes with a total loss of life. Still, James Lilburn and his partners back in Glasgow were confident that Captain Hawkins would bring the ship home. They had not yet received the latest reports coming from the Island and Adelaide.

Searching for wreckage and bodies on the south coast of Kangaroo Island.
State Library of South Australia.

Pelorus Island.
State Library of South Australia.

Aboard the Governor Musgrave searching for the Loch Vennachar.
State Library of South Australia.

The government steamer Governor Musgrave.
State Library of South Australia.

The loss of another ship off the south coast of Kangaroo Island fuelled the debate on the need for another lighthouse on the south-west corner of the island. Earlier debate swayed by Captain William Bennett had seen the building of the light on South Neptune Island. Critics blamed the government for another failure and tried to make political mileage on the backs of the deaths of 28 mariners. The issue went all the way to Federal Parliament when the Prime Minister, Alfred Deakin, was asked by an opposition member when a lighthouse would be built on the south coast of Kangaroo Island. In typical political style, the issue was referred to a committee for further deliberation.

Meanwhile, the search for the Loch Vennachar and her crew continued. A mounted Trooper, R.C. Thorpe, had been sent south to coordinate the land search parties that were scouring the island's south coast. Trooper Thorpe had discovered a piece of the ship's railing with fresh axe marks in it on the beach near Pennington Bay.

This find and others encouraged the authorities to continue the search with the mounted trooper leading the investigation. With a lack of further finds of fresh wreckage, and the Young and Pelorus sites thoroughly explored, local fishermen convinced Captain Clare to send the Governor Musgrave to the Pages Islands, a small rocky group of granite outcrops to the east of Cape Hart. These islands were searched as part of the third search by Captain Weir and proved as fruitless as all the other explorations by land and sea.

By early October, further wreckage had washed ashore at Victor Harbor and William Burgess and his search party, also containing Mr Rumble, the Post Master, had discovered parts of the ship at Stunsail Boom River, west of Vivonne Bay. Bill Burgess had searched from Rocky River to Vivonne Bay and had also claimed to have checked on the shelter huts at Cape Du Couedic and West Bay. But if he had, he would have noticed the wreckage beginning to come ashore as the wreck broke up out by the point.

By this time, a great amount had been washed far inland up West Bay Creek and timbers had started to come ashore with the wind and tides. It seemed at this stage that the needs of the locals and those of the authorities were beginning to diverge. That, or the search party had not searched as far west as they had claimed. Either way, the exact location of the Loch Vennachar's final resting place continued to elude government authorities.

The debate about erecting a light at Cape Du Couedic continued unabated even as the search for the Loch Vennachar began to be wound down. Most harbour pilots and local ship's captains were of the same opinion as Bill Bennett: that the light on South Neptune was in the right place, the Loch Vennachar had gone aground at Young Rocks, and a light on the south-west corner of Kangaroo Island was a waste of time and money. In fact, some even espoused the opinion that a light placed on Cape Du Couedic would be a death trap, luring ships in to their doom on the reefs around the cape.

None of this conjecture did anything to shed light on the fate of the Loch Vennachar or her ill-fated crew. Another wild theory was put about when a Southern Right Whale was found in Backstairs Passage, having been sliced in twain by a passing ship. The theory was that the whale had been killed by the Loch Vennachar, which had then been dismasted and foundered in heavy seas. It was a convenient theory, but one with little substance, considering the timing of the find and the location of the whale's corpse. It was posited that a large steamship had accounted for the whale and this was all the more likely considering the time of the last sighting of the Loch Vennachar, the amount of wreckage already found, and the state of decomposition of the whale.

There was still considerable interest in the Australian newspapers as to the fate of the missing clipper and her crew.

Grave of the Unknown Sailor from the Loch Vennachar made from a capstan-bar and decking timber.
State Library of South Australia

There was little doubt as to their collective fate, but no one knew quite where. The clues were tantalising, but nothing definitive indicating her whereabouts had been found. By the 11th of October, £1 10s 6d had been donated for the benefit of the crew's dependants. There was a concerted campaign by locals in Adelaide and Melbourne to raise considerably more, but without any survivors there was no public face to invoke the sympathies of the people of South Australia like there had been when the Loch Sloy had come to grief six years earlier.

With the interest in the wreck ongoing, the editors of the Argus in Melbourne began a campaign pushing for a light to be built at Cape Du Couedic. State and Federal authorities continued to drag their feet on the issue as public pressure continued to mount for something to be done to ensure that future accidents were averted. The political pressure began to bear fruit through the Premier of South Australia in response to a question by Mr McGillivray. Having all but abandoned the sea search for the Loch Vennachar, the Premier of South Australia directed the Marine Board to send Captain Weir and the Governor Musgrave to Kangaroo Island to look for and survey possible sites for a new lighthouse on the south coast.

By the 15th of November, media interest had all but disappeared even as Trooper R.C. Thorpe continued his investigations into the missing ship's final resting place. Resigned to the loss of another of their ships, Aitken, Lilburn and Co. officially notified Lloyd's of London that one of their clippers was missing.

A limited search was being maintained by Trooper R.C. Thorpe, who was being assisted by Charles May, a settler from Rocky River Homestead. Together the two men were again checking the more likely spots along the south-west corner of Kangaroo Island. It was whilst they were inspecting the Shelter Hut at West Bay that they came upon a most distressing sight.

"Trooper Robert .C. Thorpe,

Doubtless you have seen in the papers the result of my visit of inspection to the Shipwreck Shelter Hut at this bay, and the sad discovery we made – I had a man named May with me for company, as it is both a rough, scrubby and dangerous place to come to alone. He is a farmer living 15 miles from here. We first visited the Cape De Condie (Du Couedic) shelter shed two days previous to coming to this one and found all the stores, etc. intact.

On Sunday, the 26th November, we rode to this bay and tied our horses up at this creek where I have pitched my camp. We walked to the beach through dense scrub for a mile. My mate was walking some distance from the creek whereas I was keeping close to the bank, and after going nearly half a mile I called out, "Hullo! There's some casks from the Loch Vennachar!"

He came to me, and as we walked towards the mouth of the creek where it empties into the sea, we saw casks all over the beach, some full, some three-quarters full, some half and quarter full of whisky. A lot of it was "Vanguard" whisky in 18 gallon casks; also a hogshead full of probably English draught ale branded 'Fosler Prestonpans, also some casks of "Taymouth" whisky, also some casks 'McPhersons' whisky, 36 gallons, also some casks of "Bon Accord" whisky, also some "Dewars" whisky, also one cask of oil. All were consigned to Melbourne, and also a number of casks of whisky consigned to Adelaide firms. Also a host of bales of paper, same as this piece I have written this letter on.

There are a lot of reels of greenish blue paper consigned to the "Observer" Office Adelaide; it is the coloured paper they generally use for the cover of their weekly paper "The Observer". Loose tins of "Davidson's" tinned fish is also strewn all over the place. We found two casks intact; they are consigned to a

"There are piles of wreckage from almost every part of the ship - cabin doors, legs of tables, settees, pillows, mattresses" – Constable Robert Thorpe.

Melbourne firm. Such articles as hair brushes, clothes brushes, brooms, etc., are also to be found, and pipes that have been smoked out of, pieces of flannel, under shirts, and under pants, white linen shirts, pieces of serge, and tweed trousers with pieces of braces attached, also pieces of ladies underclothing marked "B. Patterson" and a man's sock marked "J. H. Patterson".

The last named two articles were part of Captain Patterson's (deceased) effects which Captain Hawkins was bringing out for Mrs. Patterson. She came to Melbourne in one of the mail liners, her husband had died aboard his sailing ship en route to England – and as Captain Hawkins of the Loch Vennachar was a great personal friend of Capt. and Mrs. Patterson, he promised to bring the late Captain's effects out and probably she put some of her own underclothing in the same boxes, which accounts for them washing up.

"There are also two 60-foot spars and a number of smaller ones, all chewed about by the rocks, which are very sharp on either side of the bay. There are piles of wreckage from almost every part of the ship - cabin doors, legs of tables, settees, pillows, mattresses - some of the wreckage is to be found in crevices and on ledges of rocks over 20 feet from the level of the sea, showing clearly what a dreadful sea there must have been the night or day the poor old gallant "Vennachar" met her fate. I can quite understand why it is none of the poor fellows reached shore alive. The rocks would chop them to pieces, so sharp and hard are they, besides this coast is teeming with sharks, and the sea that must have been running then, why nothing could live in it.

We have some dreadful seas off our southern and south-west coast. The island is one continuous formation of high rugged cliffs over 350 feet in many places and a straight drop into the seething waters. There are heavy pieces of the ship's bulwarks over 30 feet long, with the top rail and sides and great heavy iron stays attached. The spars have long pieces of wire rope and heavy iron hooks, etc. attached. I gather from these that the ship must have struck a sunken rock not far out from the mouth of West Bay because such terrible heavy wreckage could not possibly float far. The ship has probably been dismasted during the terrible weather she met and drifted inshore. It is only twelve miles to the south of Cape Borda lighthouse.

We then turned our eyes to the north end of the beach, and seeing something dark lying on the sand just near the shelter hut, I said to my mate, "I believe that's a body." We could not tell for certain owing to the distance. We however drew nearer and there we found the decomposed body of a poor young fellow, probably not more than 17 or 18. It smelled awfully bad. It was lying on its back, the skin was dry, all the features were completely gone and the flesh was leaving the skull, the left leg was thrown clean across the body and was almost detached at the hip joint. The right leg and arms were somewhat naturally shaped, they did not appear to be as shrunken as the left leg. It was a rather prettily shaped body, being slight yet compact, about 5 ft 7 or 8, remarkably tiny hands and feet (more like a female), the teeth were evidently perfect, no hair or clothing. It was much too decomposed to get a good description.

My mate and I carried the body up to a flat and buried it in its lonely grave, without a friendly tear, except our own. It is a dreadfully lonely place, high towering sand hummocks, and cliffs, and dense scrub, which made our sad task ever so much harder. The place, save for the roaring waves, is as still as death. I got a brass tipped capstan bar and nailed a cross piece on to form a cross, and with the aid of a stick and tin of black paint recovered from the wreck, I marked on the cross, "Body from the Loch Vennachar 26-11-05."

Since then the Government has appointed me Receiver of Wrecks for Kangaroo Island, and as I have recovered 44 casks of whisky etc.(majority full), I must remain in this terribly lonely camp for God knows how long - anyway until a vessel can get in the bay to take it away. It will be a risky job whoever takes it on. I shall be glad to get home to my family again – 30 miles away.

We have to live on wallaby and damper and black tea from brackish water. I left home on Wednesday 22nd November and am in camp still. I have had a terribly rough job of late riding and walking over the terribly rugged cliffs and through dense

Trooper Robert C. Thorpe and Mr Charles May standing outside their tent on West Bay Creek, November 1905.
State Library of South Australia.

*scrub; I have at times been fairly dead beat. I have secured you
some nice pieces of wood and will forward them to you as soon as
I get home.*
Yours Faithfully,

Robert C.Thorpe,

Mounted Constable."

The finding of the wreckage and the body removed all
doubt as to the fate and probable whereabouts of the Loch
Vennachar. But the mystery was not yet solved. It had just moved
to a new phase. Now authorities knew roughly what had
happened to the ship and approximately where, the only things
left to ponder were: where exactly was the wreck, how she'd
foundered, and why.

In answer to these riddles, there were some things that
the Loch Vennachar's crew had taken to their collective watery
grave. Trooper Thorpe reported via Cape Borda that upon
sighting the beach they discovered it was strewn with wreckage:
ships' spars, ships' fire buckets with the name 'Loch Vennachar'
stamped upon them, the stern of a ship's boat, a wooden ladder,
cases of tinned fish, reels of newsprint paper, a sailor's work coat,
and more than 30 hogsheads of whisky, most too large to haul
off of the beach.

The rocks were strewn with heavy wreckage and some
casks were found half a mile up the West Bay Creek, its tidal flows
having carried the lighter flotsam well inland. Trooper Thorpe
was instructed to stay camped beside the wreck until
arrangements could be made to salvage the remains of the cargo.
He was there for several weeks before the Governor Musgrave
arrived with a salvage crew. Whilst he waited for salvagers to
arrive, the Marine Board was canvassing opinions as to the
possible location of another light on Kangaroo Island. Cape Du
Couedic was the popular choice, but there was much bickering
about the cost, who would foot the final bill, and provide the
labour and materials for the project.

The announcement of the discovery of the whisky, which was only one small part of the cargo carried by the missing ship, provoked interest from locals on Kangaroo Island who were seeking to salvage the spirits and sell them at a higher price. The only thing standing in their way was Trooper Thorpe and the customs that was to be paid on the recovered whisky. Much of the whisky was never recovered, and it was likely that savvy locals were unwilling to surrender all that they had salvaged.

Industrious Islanders also salvaged most of the valuable timber washed ashore at West Bay and much of it became furniture and parts of houses, for worked timber was a rare and valuable resource on the wild western end of Kangaroo Island. Early December saw more wreckage come ashore; included amongst the flotsam were articles of the Pattersons' clothing, indicating that the aft section of the ship, including the saloon, had begun to break up.

The number of whisky casks rose to 44, and barrels of ale and other spirits also made their way into the bay as the stern finally split asunder under the constant pressure of the pounding waves. Amongst the unusual pieces that came ashore were the ship's binnacle and the gig's sail, complete and untorn.

The Governor Musgrave left Port Adelaide on the night of December 8th to survey Cape Du Couedic and other possible sites for the new lighthouse being planned. Once this had been achieved, she was to anchor at West Bay to allow a shore party to examine the wreckage found there and to take on board all that could be salvaged and sold by the ship's underwriters after customs duties had been paid.

On board the steamer were the Marine Board president, Arthur Searcy; Wardens Gibbon, Vasey, and Berry; the Chief Marine Engineer, A.B. Moncrieff; P.H. Upton, manager and agent for the South British Fire and Marine Insurance Company of New Zealand; and P.D. Haggart, secretary of the Adelaide Steamship Company. The survey of sites settled the question as to where the light would be placed. There was still a question of who would provide the money and when the project would eventually get underway. The extreme isolation of the site and a means of providing supplies to the light and its keepers presented its own set of problems for the chief engineer and his wardens to solve.

The Governor Musgrave then moved onto Adelaide with seas running high. Despite this, a boat was put ashore so that the chief engineer and wardens could inspect the wreckage. To their minds, and those of other members of the Marine Board present, there was no doubt that the Loch Vennachar had foundered near the entrance to West Bay and, in the absence of any survivors or bodies other than the one already buried, there were no survivors. With the survey and inspections over, Captain Weir headed back to Adelaide, taking with him samples of the wreckage for the board's investigation and final report.

Having finished the survey work, the Governor Musgrave sailed back to West Bay almost immediately to begin salvage operations. Even though conditions were rough and treacherous, the wardens managed to get a boat and line ashore and establish communications between Trooper Thorpe and the steamer. Over the course of the next two days, the cargo and wreckage of value were taken aboard the steamer.

Wreckage of the Loch Vennachar

"On Saturday morning, the steamer Governor Musgrave returned to Port Adelaide from West Bay, Kangaroo Island, with some of the wreckage of the Loch Vennachar. She sailed for West Bay on Wednesday night, called en route at Harvey's Return, and there landed a few packages for Cape Borda light station, and reached West Bay on Thursday at 8 a.m.

"There was a big roll on," remarked Captain P. Weir, when interviewed on Saturday morning. "We could get no nearer than 500 yards to the beach. Otherwise the weather was favourable for our object. I did not discover the exact locality of the wreck. As a matter of fact, I was too busy to spare the time to search for it. There cannot be any doubt that she is lying close by West Bay. There is an immense amount of wreckage lying behind the sand hills and rocks there, but strange to state it cannot be seen from the sea. It is marvelous how the wreckage could have got there. The large topgallant mast we have brought back in the Musgrave was at the back of a sand hill 100 yards from the beach, and some of the casks of whisky were nearly half a mile from the

beach, evidently having been blown up the West Bay creek. I meant to have searched for the wreck, but as I have said, I was kept too busy."

The Governor Musgrave brought to Port Adelaide 43 casks of whisky, a few of them ullage (part filled with air), one cask of beer, three rolls of printing paper, a ship's binnacle, and a spare topgallant mast. The rolls of paper are comparatively useless for printing purposes, but the topgallant mast is uninjured. So also is the whisky.

When the Musgrave had steamed in as close as Captain Weir considered it prudent to go, she was securely anchored with two anchors, one of which was to prevent her going further inshore, and the other to prevent her drifting out to sea. A line having been passed ashore by means of a boat, and made fast to the rocks, a block was hauled ashore.

By means of an endless whip, the casks and other wreckage were hauled on board. Four casks at a time were hauled through the water. At times, especially when the huge rollers broke against the casks, the strain on the whip was very severe. The rope parted twice. All except seven casks, two on the rocks on the north side and five on the south side, were got on board by means of the endless whip. The seven were taken off to the steamer by boat.

Only the wreckage considered worth saving was conveyed to Port Adelaide. Mr. T. Bickers went with the steamer from Port Adelaide to represent the Customs. The whisky has been placed in bond at Port Adelaide.

C.P.O. Staples, of the life-saving service, also was a passenger by the Governor Musgrave. He went as far as Breakneck River and erected a fingerpost directing any possible wanderers who might come across it to the West Bay shelter hut, which during the Musgrave's stay he painted. The body of the youth found by Mounted Constable Thorpe has been buried in the sand hills between the shelter hut and the beach."

The Advertiser, Monday 18 December 1905, page 7

AUCTION SALE.

MARINE BOARD AND NAVIGATION ACT, 1881,
PART IV., SECTION 256,

The undermentioned Cargo, recovered from West Bay, Kangaroo Island, and supposed to have been washed ashore from the wreck of the barque Loch Vennachar, will be offered for sale by public auction, pursuant to the above Act, under instructions from the Receiver of Wrecks, at the Bonded Warehouse of Messrs. George Ferguson & Co., Port Adelaide, on Thursday, the 15th day of March, 1906, at 11 o'clock a.m.

    3 qr. casks and 3 octaves Taymouth Whisky.
    1 qr. cask Sandy Lawson Whisky.
    6 octaves McLaren's Whisky.
    6 octaves Red Star Rum.
    2 octaves Bon Accord Whisky.
    1 hogshead English Ale
    12 qr. casks Dutton's Glenlivet Whisky (special), Rolis Paper (pale blue).
    1 Topgallant Spar.
    1 octave Oil Cream Special Reserve Whisky.
    1 qr. cask King's Liquedr Whisky.
    2 qr. casks and 1 octave Dewar's Whisky.
    2 qr. casks White Horse Whisky.
    1 qr. cask Mate's Scotch Whisky.
    9 octaves Vanguard Whisky.
    1 qr. cask Wee McGregor Whisky.
    1 Bundle Paper (cut).

For particulars of Marks, Numbers, and Contents see "Government Gazette" of March 8, Sale slips, with full particulars, may be obtained from Marine Board Office, Port Adelaide, or the Government Auctioneer, Taxation Office, Adelaide.

B. SOLOMON,
Government Auctioneer.

Captain Weir made several pertinent observations about the distribution of the wreckage and its placement out of sight of those viewing the wreckage from the sea. It seemed at first glance that the wreckage was storm-tossed and could easily have been accounted for by tidal storm surge. But this would have left a great deal of wreckage scattered across the beach hard up against the base of the fore dunes and perhaps into the swales behind.

However, for the wreckage to be invisible from the shore when so much other wreckage had been so obvious on other parts of the coast hinted at a more human reason for a lack of high-grade flotsam on the beach. Of the over 400 casks of spirits, ale, aerated water, baking soda and the like, only a few dozen hogsheads of whisky were retrieved, the rest being described as being too smashed up.

The spar retrieved from the back of the sand hills had to be carried and rolled over 100 yards back to the beach. The tantalising possibility that the wreck site had been kept secret for some weeks before Trooper Thorpe laid claim to the salvage began to look more and more like the truth.

Authorities in Adelaide were well used to "wreckers" plying their trade along the state's rugged coast and knew that poverty-stricken island folk were not beyond helping themselves to bounty thrown up by the sea. This was why Constable Thorpe had been instructed to stay with the wreck for as long as he was able to. There was a long history of smugglers using the island to hide goods to avoid paying government tariffs, and a free load of whisky and beer, along with many other easily reuseable items, would have been a temptation for all but the most God-fearing islanders.

Although the evidence was largely circumstantial, it did mount up, thus prompting the Marine Board to act quickly when the wreck site was finally located. Chief amongst those suspected of withholding information from the Marine Board and police were those men from the island deputised to help with the search; William 'Bill' Burgess and Mr William Rumble from Queenscliff both came in for close attention.

If the wreckage had been pushed behind the dunes as discovered by Trooper Thorpe and Captain Weir, then Bill Burgess and his party, when they 'inspected' the West Bay Hut, would have discovered it quite quickly. Instead, they gave the site the all clear. The more valuable wreckage itself, including several heavy hogsheads of whisky and a valuable topgallant mast, were discovered far inland out of sight of the sea.

Bill Rumble made some quiet and detailed enquiries as to the salvage and sale of the whisky discovered at West Bay. He seemed quite keen for the whisky to be salvaged by him so it could then be sold after customs duties had been paid. Much of the whisky was never recovered. William .E. Rumble later became a mounted constable himself.

A salacious article appeared in The Advertiser on Saturday, November 6th 1937, which stated that the lighthouse keepers from Cape Borda had discovered 17 bodies in a steep, wave-swept gorge near West Bay. If the report of keepers discovering the wreck site and not reporting the find to authorities had any substance at all, then the other evidence of smugglers and wreckers began to carry a much more genuine flavour. For the rumours to be true, the evidence appeared to implicate a number of notable locals.

Thoughts of such possibilities passed most people by as the Marine Board focussed on avoiding another such catastrophe as had befallen the Loch Sloy and Loch Vennachar. It had been learned that in the weather systems that had swept away the Loch Vennachar, another six vessels had been listed as missing since the clipper had smashed into Kangaroo Island. Amongst those missing were the French barques St Donatien and Lafayette.

The Marine Board had decided to build a first-class light at Cape Du Couedic and engaged the Surveyor General to begin the planning process. The board finally acknowledged that the Borda light was not perfect and its effective range should be improved as soon as possible.

Wreckage continued to wash ashore well into January, and close exploration of the coastline around West Bay revealed more whisky that the Governor Musgrave was sent to pick up. The latest find was discovered beneath a large pile of wreckage by Charles May. Echoes of the tragedy continued to play out in the media when it was claimed that a message found in a bottle

Wreck of the French barque Montebello.
State Library of South Australia.

was from Captain Hawkins claiming that he and the crew were ashore on Althorpe Island, dated 29th of October.

The media ran the story, but investigations by Trooper Thorpe proved the note to be a fabrication, a cruel hoax. Still, people were fascinated by the mystery of the ship's final resting place. Once in Adelaide, the final cask of whisky taken from West Bay was placed with the others in Ferguson's Bond Store, where they were being held until a government auction to be held on the 15th of March at Port Adelaide.

The auction went ahead at 11 am and achieved solid prices for the salvaged goods, totalling £125 for the lot. With the disposal of the salvaged goods and the yet incomplete investigation into the loss of the Loch Vennachar, the Marine Board members were more than happy to move on from the whole sorry affair.

Attention moved onto the building of the new light at Cape Du Couedic. The Marine Board met on Wednesday the 11th of April to discuss the appropriation of funds for the construction of the new lighthouse. It was recommended that the Board request funds from the State Government and that £5000 to £6000 would be more than adequate to complete the task. Some members were against the scheme, but the board's president, Arthur Searcy, was of the firm opinion that if the light had been built in the 1890s, then 60 lives from the Lochs Sloy and Vennachar would have been saved.

By June 1906, the Marine Board had still not delivered its findings into the loss of the Loch Vennachar. The secretary of the Board was directed to draft a finding, but Arthur Searcy stated that the board's marine investigator, Captain J. Sheridan, had still not located the hull even though he was of the opinion that it lay just outside the mouth of West Bay. Each time he had journeyed to the location, the weather had been too rough to locate the wreck of the lost clipper.

At this point, no further action was taken by the board and an open finding was recorded: that for reasons unknown, the Loch Vennachar, on or about the 7th of September, found herself 15 miles south of where she should have been. Then, for reasons unknown, she foundered against the cliffs in the vicinity of West Bay, Kangaroo Island.

There were no survivors found, and neither did searchers locate the hull of the Loch Vennachar. Yet, there was enough wreckage located to conclude beyond doubt that the ship had gone down against cliffs and then been smashed to pieces by the actions of the waves. Only one body had been found, and another 27 whose bodies were not located had died of drowning or impact with debris or rocks.

While the politicians quibbled about the price of a new lighthouse, serendipity forced their hand when, in the early hours of Sunday the 18th of November 1906, the French barque Montebello ran aground below the cliffs near where the Loch Sloy and Loch Vennachar had been lost.

The 2300-ton vessel, in ballast and bound for Port Pirie to take on a load of grain, was lost, though all hands were saved. The Marine Board immediately set about establishing an enquiry into the wreck, whilst the loss of the Montebello reignited calls for the building of a light upon Cape Du Couedic as soon as possible to avoid any further losses of property or life, the Marine Board pushed the government for the immediate funding needed for the establishment of a manned light at Cape Du Couedic. To prevent the loss of any more lives or property, especially when two clippers had foundered either side of the cape within the previous 14 months, £5000 seemed a trifle. A footnote to the use of government funds came when the costs incurred when searching for the Loch Vennachar, £230 1s 2d, was paid out to the Marine Board from the proceeds of the wreck.

By January 1907, the moves to build the Cape Du Couedic light were in full swing. The Governor Musgrave arrived off of the cape on Thursday, the 10th of January. On board was the Assistant Engineer of Harbours, Mr Labatt, who selected a site for the lighthouse and a jetty that would need to be built first.

The only place to build it was in the little cove on the eastern side of the cape, an anchorage that was named Weir Cove in honour of Captain Patrick Weir of the Governor

The survey of Cape du Couedic, 1906.
State Library of South Australia.

Construction of the Weir Cove Jetty, Governor Musgrave at anchor.
State Library of South Australia.

Cape du Couedic Lighthouse, c 1908.
State Library of South Australia.

Musgrave. The jetty would be built at the bottom of a 300-foot cliff with a storehouse at the top to hold the keepers' supplies. The light itself would sit about 200 feet above sea level, looking out over the Casuarina Islets, Remarkable Rocks, and Maupertuis Bay. The surveyors discovered the secret sealers' camp, a sea cave known as Admirals Arch. It was the heart-rending beauty of the cape that made its fell reputation all the more poignant and heartbreaking. The light would be built, but the impossibly rugged and isolated nature of the location meant that everything and everyone needed to complete the task would have to be brought in by sea.

In February, the *Governor Musgrave* returned with surveyors from the Surveyor-General's Department so that the final survey could be done before the jetty builders arrived to construct the Weir Cove pier. The chief surveyor, Mr Furner, and three assistants used as their references the charts and measurements of the coastal features created by the early French explorer Nicolas Baudin's chart-maker, François Péron, as he sailed aboard the ships Le Géographe and Le Naturaliste, mapping the southern coast of the island in 1801.

The charts and sketches were so accurate that the surveyors could not fault them, and they played an important role in the final site selections for the jetty, lighthouse, and the keepers' cottages.

In 1908, the construction of the lighthouse was well underway at Cape du Couedic, whilst further up the coast, the northern point at the entrance of West Bay was named Vennachar Point in honour of the lost clipper, even though her final resting place had never been established.

The light itself had arrived from England and the jetty had been completed, even though the trip up a 300-foot cliff was a hazardous affair, especially when the wind was from the south-east. The engineers had set up a flying fox to haul supplies up the cliff from Weirs Cove. When heavy loads or rough weather prevented the hauling of supplies up the cliff, the flying fox was used to carry both cargo and passengers up the cliff to the waiting stonemasons and engineers above.

The flying fox could haul up to a ton of cargo 270 feet up a narrow cutting, and the winch was powered by an oil-powered donkey engine. The storehouse was made of local limestone blocks and divided into five sections: three to hold the stores for the three keepers' families, one for stores for the light, and one to hold rescue and safety gear to replace that currently held by the Shelter Hut, which still sat at the base of the point. Included in this set was a full Rocket Apparatus and wooden ladders and ropes designed to help with the rescue of stranded mariners.

The three keepers' cottages, the engine and storehouses, and the light tower itself were all made from locally sourced dressed limestone blocks. The tower stood 55 feet above the cape and the light itself 70 feet; all were connected by carefully laid paths and a road from the storehouse to the cottages. A telephone line was constructed to connect Cape du Couedic with Cape Borda in 1908 and served as the only means of communication. It joined the line at Cape Borda and thence to Kingscote.

The light and surrounding buildings were finished in 1909. On the day it was due to commence operations, the weather was so rough that the party aboard the Governor Musgrave, including the President and Wardens of the Marine Board, were unable to land. Signals were sent to the keepers to turn on the light.

With the activation of the lantern, not another ship was lost from 1909 until the light ceased to have major commercial importance when it was automated in 1957. The men and boys of the Loch Vennachar perhaps had not died in vain, but their deaths could so easily have been prevented if the lessons learned in 1899 after the loss of the Loch Sloy had been applied sooner. It took, however, the loss of three expensive clippers, tens of thousands of pounds of lost cargo, and the loss of more than 30 lives for the message to get past the penny-pinchers and naysayers and for the light at Cape du Couedic to finally be built.

XX
Mishap Turns to Mystery

West Bay and Vennachar Point.
Google Earth

With the sale of the salvaged items from the wreck, the Marine Board enquiry was delayed to the point where the President seriously considered abandoning it altogether. However, in the absence of witnesses or a wreck, the enquiry recorded an open finding.

The board's report surmised that the ship, whilst way off course, had run aground and become wrecked somewhere close to West Bay, probably to the north side as indicated by tides and the distribution of wreckage. Of the crew, there were no survivors and most, if not all, had drowned or been dashed to pieces by wreckage or rocks.

Searchers never found the hull of the Loch Vennachar, so exactly what happened could never be determined. Thus, with this finding, the Marine Board's investigation was left open pending the production of further evidence, and the story of the missing ship passed rapidly into legend.

Stories of the vessel having a Jonah onboard, of it being an unlucky or even cursed ship, filled people's superstitious minds with a myriad of theories as people sought to explain how and why the Loch Vennachar came to grief with the loss of 28 lives.

The loss of the Loch Vennachar was not a unique occurrence; already at least three other major vessels had been lost in the area under similar circumstances. In 1877 the 129 ton, wooden brigantine, Emily Smith ran into the cliffs near West Bay. For four days before she came to grief the Emily Smith had been running before a storm, her captain unable to take regular navigational observations because of the overcast conditions.

It was just after 4:00 am when the ship ran upon a reef at the base of the cliffs near Cape Bedout, seven miles north of Cape Du Couedic. The Cape Borda light was impossible to see being covered in low cloud and the northerly winds followed by a south-westerly gale had blown the brigantine off course. From this wreck there were just three survivors. The area's deadly reputation continued to build with the destruction of the Mars.

In 1885 the 487-ton barque was making for Port Pirie from Melbourne when unable to pass through Backstairs Passage because of contrary winds. The captain decided to make a detour around the bottom of Kangaroo Island. The vessel passed Cape Du Couedic in the early hours of the 19th of June steering a course north by east ahead of a south-west wind. At 5:00 am breakers were seen on the leeward quarter and the captain put the ship onto the starboard tack attempting to come about.

Instead the barque ran aground and slewed around onto her beam ends, the captain and two others being immediately swept away and drowned. The ship had gone ashore against the cliffs just off of West Bay much like the Loch Vennachar would do twenty years later. If there had been a light at Cape Du Couedic then Captain Pringle would have steered away from the coast and eventually would have seen the Cape Borda light which had been hidden by the cliffs to the northward. Three more men had died for the want of a light on the south-west corner of the island.

The losses of the Emily Smith and the Mars were tragic accidents that should have prompted the Marine Board to act, but it was not until 1899 when the 1200-ton clipper, Loch Sloy came to grief in Maupertuis Bay that serious consideration was given to erecting a light at Cape Du Couedic. At 5:00 am of the 24th of April 1899 the lookout of the Loch Sloy alerted the helmsman that there was land ahead. The crew were expecting to see the Cape Borda light but had miscalculated their position.

The ship was immediately put to port to bring the clipper about, but the manoeuvre was too slow. Within moments the Loch Sloy was amongst the breakers upon a reef about 200 yards from shore. The vessel was swamped in short order and settled down by the bow. Of the 35 souls aboard, 31 were drowned and of the four who came ashore alive, only three made it to safety. The Board of Trade's report into the disaster stated:

"Taking into consideration the facts mentioned in the foregoing account, it appears to the Board that the loss may be attributed:

(1.) To an error in the ship's position, she being fully 25 miles too far to the eastward.

(2.) To the vessel proceeding all night, and right up to the time of imminent danger, at a high rate of speed, viz., 10 or 11 knots per hour. As she was running on to a somewhat dangerous

coast, no land had been seen for upwards of 100 days, and Cape Borda was expected to be made before daylight, it would have only been prudent to have shortened sail and reduced the speed to 6 or 7 knots so as to make the land after sunrise, especially as she was approaching Cape Borda on a course which would render her dependent on the accuracy of her chronometers.

(3.) To insufficient look-out, particularly in regard to no one (as far as is known) having been sent aloft at intervals, especially after midnight.

(4.) To the chain cables not being on deck, or the anchors ready for use. If they had been available and let go there was a chance that they might have held the ship as was the case with the "Duncow" under precisely similar circumstances.

(5.) To the spanker not having been set when tacking ship. The flying jib, foretopmast stay-sail, and maintop mast stay-sail were set, and there was little time to spare, but the spanker was most important.

(6.) If the vessel had been first put on the port tack instead of the starboard tack, she would probably have gone clear."

John Darby, Secretary Marine Board. Marine Board Offices, Port Adelaide, 2nd June, 1899.

The aforementioned clipper, 'Duncow', was a near miss but highlighted the need for a light at Cape du Couedic. In 1897, the 1700-ton, fully rigged ship was sailing from Puget Sound to Port Pirie with a load of timber. In attempting to round Cape Borda, the ship was coming up from the south travelling north by east, with the wind from the south-west.

"About 8 a.m. on 25th May, the wind being strong and the sea heavy, sail was shortened. At noon the weather was clear, with a strong breeze and high sea, the ship making 10 knots. At 10 p.m. the night was overcast and cloudy, with rain squalls and no stars visible; one hand on the foretopgallant yard, another on the forecastle head on the look-out, the master and the first mate on the poop. At 11.50 p.m. the look-out aloft called out, 'Put your helm hard down, there is land right ahead.' The master at once felt that the vessel was in the vicinity of Cape Couedic, and immediately brought her to the wind on the port tack, and made more sail. One point of land was weathered, and the Casuarina Islets were seen (one ahead and another on the port bow), but not

the passage between, a thick heavy rain squall obscuring everything. Both anchors were therefore let go, each with 75 fathoms of cable, in 14 fathoms, and the vessel brought up about 3/4 of a cable length off the cliffs, which for many miles along the coast are nearly perpendicular, and from 300 to 400 ft. high. Clewed up and made everything fast, and stood by until the morning."

By morning, the crew found themselves in the lee of 300 ft cliffs with more foul weather approaching. The captain decided to abandon ship and the crew rowed and walked for help, taking six and a half days to reach safety in Kingscote. The tug dispatched to check upon the ship discovered her just as she had been left, anchored within the little cove at the base of Cape du Couedic. The Duncow was then made safe and towed to Port Pirie undamaged.

The resultant Marine Board investigation found that the captain had committed several errors which contributed to the near tragedy. He had failed to account for the strong easterly current that ran around the south of the island and:

"secondly, in running on to a dangerous coast in weather that would not permit the land, which is high, to be seen until close to, especially as no land or lights had been seen since leaving Cape Wickham; farther, even if his reckoning, according to the evidence, had been correct, the course was a dangerous one, inasmuch as the ship would probably have fetched the land at the western end of Kangaroo Island, somewhere near Cape Bedout or West Bay, where there are dangerous rollers (marked on the chart), and where the Cape Borda light is obscured."

John Darby, Secretary, Marine Board. (Issued in London by the Board of Trade on the 2nd day of September 1897.)

The Duncow below Cape Du Couedic, 1897.
State Library of South Australia.

The Captain of the Duncow had been lucky, but he had made the same errors in judgement that dozens of other captains had made before him in approaching Kangaroo Island from the south-west at night during bad weather. The difference was that he had almost paid for his mistakes with his life and the lives of his crew.

The masters of the Emily Smith, Mars, Loch Sloy and Loch Vennachar had made similar mistakes but had not been anywhere near as fortunate as Captain Graves and his 25 crew. None of these mishaps would have occurred if the much-warranted lighthouse had been built. But it was not, and whilst politicians and bureaucrats argued and quibbled about the price, many sailing vessels came to grief and innocent people died.

The final commercial sailing ship to come to grief on this stretch of coast was the French barque Montebello. In 1906, whilst travelling to Port Pirie in ballast, the Montebello was attempting to round the western end of Kangaroo Island. The ship was travelling north by east with a south-westerly wind. The weather had been stormy and overcast for several days and, though the captain thought they were 60 miles south-west of the Neptune light, this was calculated by last known position and dead reckoning based upon logs and the ship's chronometers.

The ship had been travelling under shortened sail all night on the starboard tack when, at 2:00 am on the morning of the 18th of November, the lookout called "Breakers ahead". The ship was put about but struck rocks 150 yards from shore just west of Stunsail Boom River within sight of Cape du Couedic. The crew all made it to safety, but the ship's master had made the same mistake as the others and had run his ship too close inshore on a dangerous, unlit coast.

These five wrecks and one near disaster occurred in the space of just 29 years along a well-travelled but highly treacherous trade route, and these were just the accidents people knew about. There were persistent rumours that at least one sealing supply vessel, or more likely an American whaler, had come to grief in the years before settlement. There was a great deal of mysterious wreckage, already aged by the sea and sun, scattered along the coast when settlers first began to officially settle upon the southern side of Kangaroo Island.

The cause for the loss of the Loch Vennachar seemed obvious in hindsight, but without a wreck to examine, the theories about her demise flew thick and fast at both the time of her initial disappearance and in the aftermath of the location of the body and wreckage at West Bay. The armchair experts and professional mariners alike had their own ideas about how the ship came to grief and the location of the wreck:

In the weeks immediately after the disappearance of the Loch Vennachar, the carcass of a Southern Right Whale was found floating in Backstairs Passage. The whale was almost cut in two and at first glance it appeared that the whale had been hit by a steamship, such was the damage to the corpse. It was later posited by certain maritime 'experts' that the whale may have been struck by the Loch Vennachar, which was then either dismasted or holed.

One well-respected clipper captain put forth the idea that the Loch Vennachar was dismasted during a sudden wind shift. The ship was backed up whilst under full sail and turned around. His theory stated that probably the topmasts were torn off and the spanker boom and rigging crashed down upon the wheel, smashing the steering gear and binnacle. This rendered the ship unable to manoeuvre and she then came to grief upon a reef or cliffs.

A third option put forth by pundits in the weeks after the Loch Vennachar's disappearance was that the ship was blown off course by the strong northerly winds. She was then dismasted in the storm and then struck one of a number of reefs to be found south of Kangaroo Island.

A variation to the above theory put forth by many local captains, including the retired Captain Bill Bennett, led many to believe that the ship was driven south by the northerly winds and, whilst the Loch Vennachar was attempting to round the bottom of Kangaroo Island and come into Adelaide via the Backstairs Passage, she ran aground on either Pelorus Island, Young Rocks, or upon a previously uncharted reef. All of which were to be found within 30 miles south of Kangaroo Island. The ship then foundered and broke up, spilling wreckage all along the southern and eastern coast of the island.

A ships chronometer. 1870 - 1880.
Power House Museum Sydney NSW.

A less obvious theory was that the Loch Vennachar was lost due to poor navigational knowledge. This simple navigational error was based upon the fact that whoever was watch-keeper on the night of the 7th of September 1905 failed to recognise their position because they confused the 3 flashes in 20 seconds of the Neptune light with the 4 flashes in 20 seconds of the Borda light. This confusion was made worse by the stormy conditions, low visibility and a lack of moon or stars to navigate by. Twelve miles south of the Neptune light would have put the Loch Vennachar in the middle of Investigator Strait, whilst 12 miles south of the Borda light put the ship smack into the cliffs by West Bay.

Once the wreckage was discovered at West Bay, the theory that became the most popular with the experienced captains of the various Loch Liners was that the Loch Vennachar had been driven south by northerly winds and, coming up from the south-west at night, failed to see the Borda light because it was hidden by the cliffs and headlands. Upon sighting breakers ahead, the ship, already heading north by east, turned on the starboard tack attempting to avoid the cliffs and instead drove into the cliffs near West Bay. Journalists interviewed Captain Robert Pattman of the Loch Torridon and Captain William Bennett, ex-skipper of the Loch Vennachar, and both men agreed it was easy to be driven 10 to 20 miles north or south of a ship's predicted course during stormy conditions.

A less popular theory, but one that most professional mariners agreed with, was the role that a faulty chronometer may have played in leading to navigational errors that put the ship too far south and east. Right up until the adoption of radio checking and beacons, there was always the possibility for a ship's chronometer to be slightly out. This would lead to inaccurate reckoning of a ship's longitude, combined with the inability to take accurate celestial measurements of a ship's latitude due to poor weather conditions. The combination of factors would lead a navigator to use dead reckoning based upon a ship's speed, course and last known position. Inaccuracies in a ship's chronometer would only have to be small to cause a ship to be off course by even just a few miles. Whilst this would not generally be a problem in open waters, in the confines of a narrow strait or channel filled with treacherous islands, reefs and shoals, a small course error could have disastrous consequences.

Captain Telfer, master of the Loch Rannoch in 1899, made quite a few relevant observations about the loss of the Loch Sloy that were equally applicable to the loss of her sister vessel, the Loch Vennachar. During the night, the winds were from the north-east, which would compel her to tack. The ship, forced by the adverse winds, would have made a longboard to the south-east, which would have taken it south of Kangaroo Island.

The ship then met the south-west wind, which caused her to retrace her course, forcing the ship to head north by east, her crew expecting to eventually pick up the Cape Borda light. Captain Telfer said of the light that it was a splendid one and, in fair weather, visible for 25 miles, but it was shut out to the southward by the land, so vessels coming from that direction would have no idea of their position in foul weather.

When the captain made his longboard to the south-east ahead of the cold front and then returned on a change of the wind, then the crew could not have seen the Cape Borda light until the ship had passed the south-western extremity of the island. It would have been shut in by the land.

Captain Telfer went on to explain that, regardless of whether or not the ship had been miles out of her course from some cause other than the weather, a quarter of a point or so in the compass would easily make that difference on a long course. He also commented that a chronometer is only a chronometer, a fancy clock. He put it pointedly when he stated that it all depended on when the ship's captain last sighted the sun and whether a ship's chronometers were out even by a small amount.

He was adamant that even the best chronometers were often a little out, and that a chronometer out by two minutes meant a 30-mile course deviation. For a ship that was not in sight of land, such a trifle could make a great difference in navigation. He went on to state that, unlike a steamer that could hold its course even in poor weather, a clipper very much depended on the wind for her course. He stated that even though the ship would have to travel in a north-easterly direction to make the Cape Borda light, a sailing ship cannot travel in a straight line; it all depends on the wind and the weather.

Lastly, he made note of the currents about Cape Borda. The admiralty charts indicated that the waters about the western end of the island were marked as variable, and there was a general drift to the east along the south coast of the island. All of these factors were to be brought into account when trying to account for the loss of the Loch Sloy, factors which very much played out in much the same manner with the losses of the Emily

Smith, the Mars, the Loch Vennachar, the Montebello, and almost the Duncow and dozens of other vessels whose near misses or foundering went unrecorded.

It did not matter at all who came up with what theories; without a wreck or witnesses, there was no way to accurately gauge just what had killed the Loch Vennachar and her 28 crew. The Marine Board investigators eventually gave up on their inquiries; unable to reach a satisfactory conclusion, the board recorded an open finding and society moved on.

Not everyone, though, was willing to let the matter rest. From time to time, a newspaper would run an article on the mystery of the missing ship and her lost crew. The names of the lost were forgotten, and the only physical reminders of the lost clipper were a lonely grave and an isolated headland on an island at the far end of the world.

As time passed, the story of the Loch Vennachar passed into legend. People still occasionally scoured the cliffs for any sign of the wreck, but with no success. The locals on Kangaroo Island did not let sentiment stand in the way of their need for dressed timbers and metal fittings. Many a building and quite a few pieces of furniture contained recycled wood from not just the Loch Vennachar, but from many other vessels that had dashed themselves to pieces upon Kangaroo Island's rugged, lonely shores.

The mystery of the Loch Vennachar remained unsolved for more than 70 years, and when she finally surfaced again into the light of history, she did so in a most unusual way.

XXI

More Questions Than Answers

**Seated upon the restored bower anchor of the Loch Vennachar
is the Mr John Boon, great grandson of Captain William
Hawkins.**
Photo courtesy of John Boon, 2005.

Latitude 35° 53' South, longitude 136° 31' 57" East. These
are the coordinates of the shattered wreck of a noble clipper that
came to grief in the early morning of September 7th 1905.

As the ship approached Kangaroo Island travelling north
by west with a south-westerly wind behind, she was battered by
howling gales. These were punctuated by murderous
thunderstorms, blinding white squalls of pelting rain, hail and
sleet. The winds gusted up to 70 miles an hour and the rollers
topped 50 feet in places. Low cloud made taking any navigational
readings all but impossible as the ship moved north-east, her
lookouts attempting to sight the Cape Borda light. However, the
light was closed in by the high cliffs and dense low cloud as the
ship raced up from the south. Visibility for the lookouts was

The end of the Loch Vennachar. 8-9 September 1905.

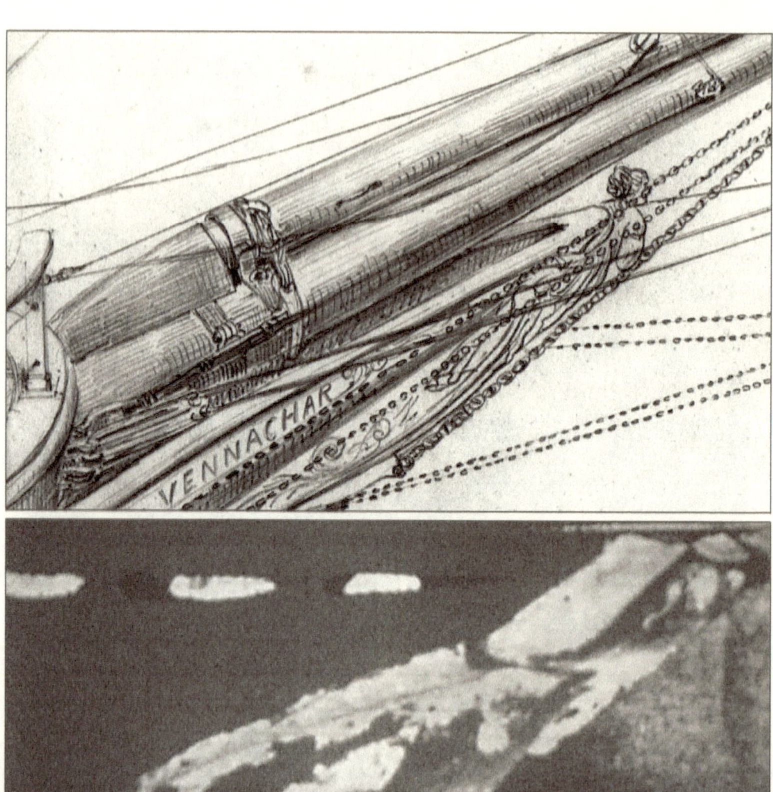

Sketch of figurehead by Henry H. Kemp and a photograph of the bottom third of the Loch Vennachar's figurehead, sheared off during the collision with the cliff and later found washed up at Cape Hart, Dudley Peninsula, Kangaroo Island.

Observer 7th October 1905.

A pile of wreckage from the Loch Vennachar washed up the creek at West Bay.
Observer 10th February 1906.

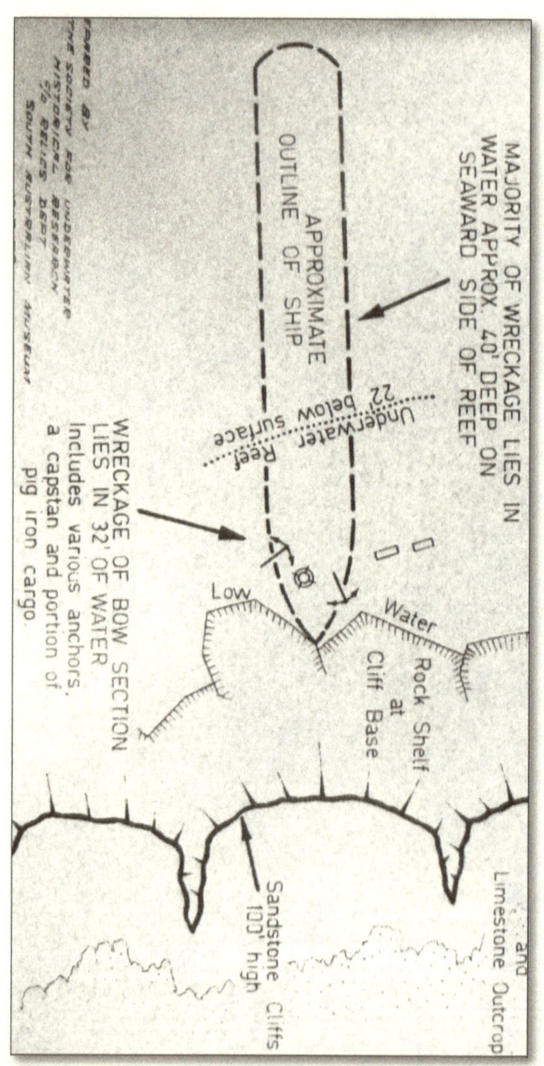

Detailed map of wreck site and approximate location of the bow as it lies across the reef at the base of a wave pounded rock shelf The stern section was later discovered by diver Steven Reynoldst to the south of the bow section broken up into many shattered pieces.
SUHR, Loch Vennachar Expedition Report, 1977.

Vennachar Point. The site of the wreck. Circa 1977.
Photograph supplied by Terry Drew.

Vennachar Point, the site of the wreck of the Loch Vennachar, with West Bay in the background.

down to just a few hundred yards, or just a few dozen feet during the frequent thunder squalls that lashed the ship and her hapless crew.

The clipper was designed to take such brutal punishment and ploughed through the heaving seas unaffected by the stormy conditions. Sometime between two and four in the morning, long after the pale sliver of a moon had set, the Loch Vennachar passed west of Cape Bedout on a starboard tack as conditions began to slowly moderate.

Less than an hour later, travelling at a brisk 10 or 11 knots, the ship's forward lookouts cried out, *"Breakers ahead! Put your helm hard down!"* The watch was called to raise headsails and staysails in an attempt to bring the ship about.

The officer of the watch instructed the helmsman to put the ship hard over to starboard in an attempt to put the clipper about. Other sailors attempted to deploy the spanker so as to force the vessel sharply around. The clipper heaved over, making a rapid arc to the right.

But it was too late to deploy the bower anchors, too late to tack to port. The Loch Vennachar approached her doom as, heading west at the top of her turn under full sail, she ran up onto a rock shelf at the base of a 100-foot cliff. The impact smashed in her bow and killed those unfortunate sailors still within the forecastle.

The ship quickly flooded her forward compartment and then the hold, and settled down by the bow upon the rock shelf. As she foundered, the clipper was thrust forward by a giant roller, her nose wedged in hard against the cliff in a bow-shaped crevice. The huge waves swung the vessel around to be slammed sideways into the northern face of the bluff she was jammed up against.

The same waves then dragged the hulk back and, with the spine broken, the ship broke in two. The bow stayed almost intact against the rock wall below the cliff, while the larger stern section sank into 40 feet of water on the far side of the jagged reef that had snapped the Loch Vennachar's keel. Thus came the end of the Loch Vennachar and her crew: suddenly, violently, fatally. As she disappeared beneath the pounding surf, she passed from history and into the depths of maritime legend.

There were those who perhaps knew of her final resting place. However, because of their perfidy, they were unwilling to reveal the ship's location for fear of revealing their part in the looting of the wreck and the bounty her demise threw upon the isolated shores of Kangaroo Island.

Many were the amateur historians and adventurers who searched out the Loch Vennachar's final resting place. But with the passage of time, memories faded and those who knew the truth joined the lost in their silence. Soon, only newspaper clippings, personal accounts, and long-diluted oral histories were all that remained to point the way to the lost ship Loch Vennachar.

In February 1976, two teams of divers and amateur archaeologists, one a group of divers from Kangaroo Island led by Peter Telfer, a local identity and fisherman, and another group from Adelaide made up of members of the Society for Underwater Historical Research: Donna and Brian Marfleet, Doug Seton, Terry Smith, and Linda Jones, were searching again for the wreck.

The two groups had studied maps, aerial photographs, and old newspaper accounts and reports for several years, and were certain that the ship lay close to the mouth of West Bay. As the groups searched, the weather closed in, making diving impossible, so the divers from SUHR decided to continue their search on foot. Scouring the cliffs searching for signs of the wreck, the three men searched north of West Bay.

In a moment of relative quiet between rollers, Brian Marfleet glanced down and there, in the crystal clear waters, was the faint outline of a ship. Uncertain as to what they had actually seen, the trio climbed down the 30-metre cliff at low tide to gain a closer look at the anomaly and to search the rocky ledge for signs of a wrecked vessel.

Convinced they were onto something, the men's excitement bubbled over when Terry Smith found a water-worn clay brick in a pool of water at the very base of the cliff. Despite

70 years of pounding by the surf, the word 'Glasgow' was clearly legible in the brick. The Loch Vennachar had several thousand fired clay bricks as ballast and also embedded in the core of her cemented waterproof collision bulkhead. The position of the brick indicated that it had come from the bulkhead. Such an occurrence hinted at the violence of the collision that ended the Loch Vennachar and her crew. Further searching found iron and brass fragments embedded in the cliff face at the point of impact and in the northern side of the bluff.

Brass Porthole recovered from wreck for future preservation.
Terry Drew, 1977.

A few days after the tantalising finds had been made, the team climbed down the cliff and dived upon the area they thought the wreck lay in. By dive's end, they had identified the bow section of the missing ship, including two of her bower anchors, still locked inboard where they had been stowed when

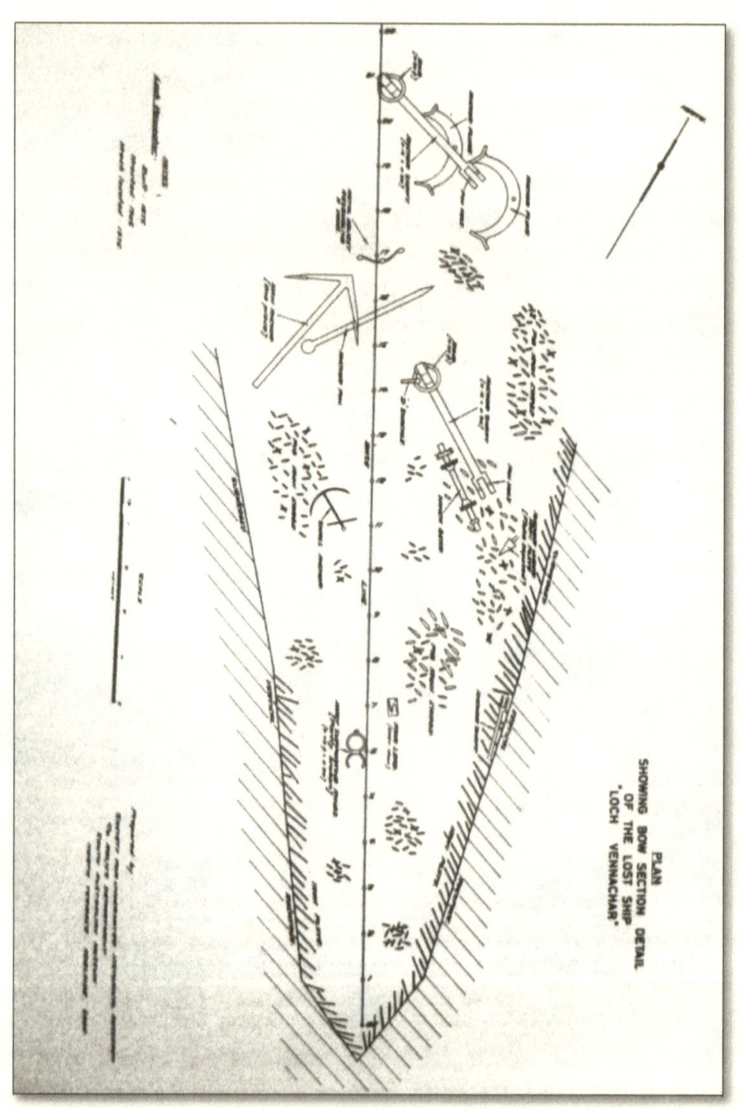

Survey map of the bow section deep in crevice at base of cliff, located here are the ships 7 anchors, the forward windlass, foremast collar, ballast scatterings of pig-iron & firebricks, hull strakes and a fairlead.
SUHR, Loch Vennachar Expedition Report, 1977. supplied by Terry Drew.

Wreck site from sea level showing the steep gorge at the ships' impact point. SUHR, members at the cliff base giving an idea of the height of the cliffs into which the ship ploughed.

Terry Drew, 1977.

Sea floor covered in wreckage, pig-iron, iron spars, frames, hull strakes, cabling and other debris.
Terry Drew, 1977.

Former SAPOL diver Jim Webb holding the windlass gear recovered
from the wreck site of the Loch Vennachar.

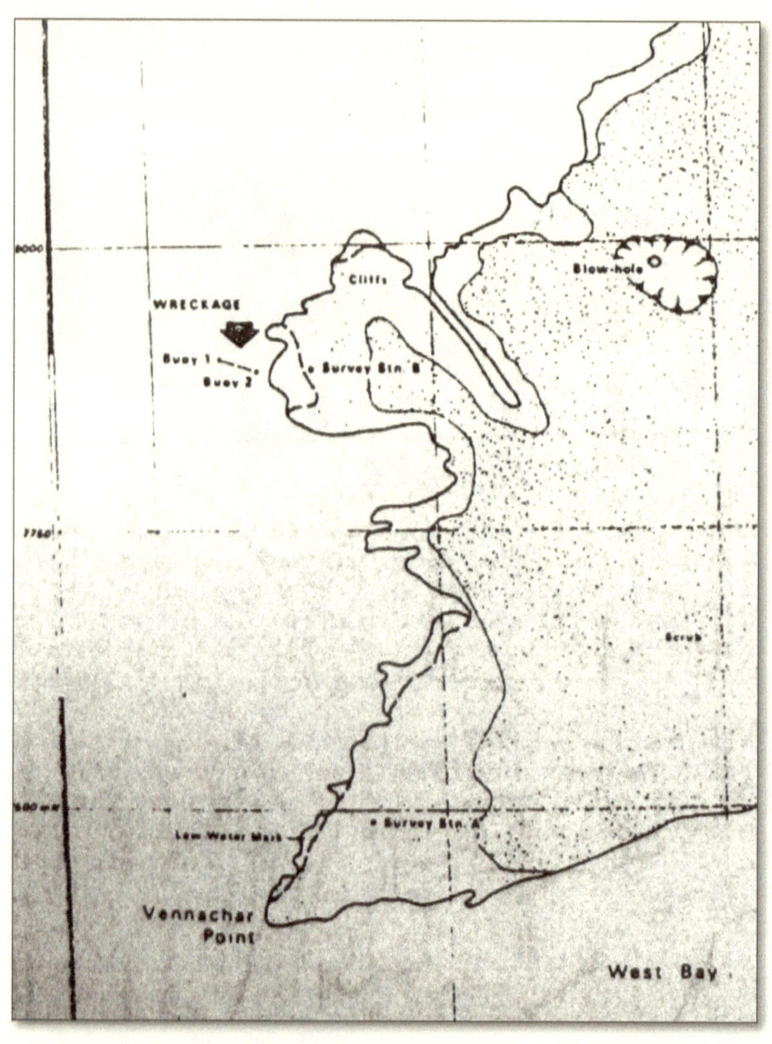

Geospatial survey of Vennachar Point wreck site.
SUHR, Loch Vennachar Expedition Report, 1977, supplied by Terry Drew.

the ship came to grief. Upon seeing the submerged wreck, Doug Seton said of the experience:

"I was looking into the open grave of the Loch Vennachar. Seventy years before, the beautiful ship had sailed into this rocky coffin and our diving party were now the first people to see her again. It was a moment of awe..."

Sunday Mail, 12th December 1976, pg 134.

Soon after arriving back in Adelaide, the SUHR informed state and federal maritime authorities about the find. The wreck's location was kept secret, and local divers were warned off diving upon the site until it had been properly surveyed.

A concerned Peter Telfer wrote to the Islander, expressing his concern that the opportunity to dive upon the Loch Vennachar would be lost to people from Kangaroo Island if the authorities got in first and banned access to the site. The SUHR was afraid that if word got out about the wreck's location, then looters or illegal salvagers would raid the wreck, destroying a valuable heritage site and maritime grave.

Despite the society's best efforts and those of the South Australian Museum Department of Relics, word was leaked to locals on Kangaroo Island who then dived on the wreck and looted it of several objects, including portholes and other relics of historical importance.

Within a year, the wreck site of the Loch Vennachar was being officially surveyed by the SUHR and the South Australian Museum with assistance from the South Australian Police Underwater Recovery Unit. The wind and waves that had protected the Loch Vennachar's final resting place for the last 70 years also made surveying the wreck site extremely hazardous. The grandchildren of Richard 'Dickie' Simpson heard about the find of the ship and, after contacting the SUHR, agreed to donate some funds to help get the project underway. The area around the wreck was declared a historic reserve by the State Government of South Australia and later was protected by Federal Government legislation restricting access to the wreck without a permit.

The 1977 expedition attempted to survey the entire wreck site, but atrocious weather conditions prevented them from doing more than a cursory sampling of the large stern section. A great many photographs were taken and several small artefacts were removed for identification and preservation purposes. With limited time, the team focussed upon the bow section, which was still largely intact.

Iron hull plates from the bow were scattered all across the location being surveyed. Some lay flat, some twisted and bent, and others still upright and attached to their frames that lay protected in layers of sand and debris. Pig-iron ballast lay all about amongst the more obvious and well-preserved relics. Portholes from the fo'c'sle were strewn about along with the base of the foremast, still where it had been stepped into the bow in 1901 when the ship had been completely refitted.

Granite plaque marking the wrecksite.
Photograph supplied by Terry Drew.

The most telling and damning relics were the coils of unused anchor chain still within the remains of the chain lockers. The hull strakes may have corroded away, but the solid coils of chain remained as they had when the bow settled upon the sea floor in 1905.

The social highlight of the Loch Line Captains' season was their attendance at the Ships Boat Race Regatta on the Yarra in December 1905. All the masters and their crews were there but one, William S. Hawkins.

State Library of Victoria.

The saddest finds amongst the wreckage were the seven anchors located in place, indicating that they had never been deployed when the ship foundered. The two main bower anchors, the smaller replacement anchor, and the kedging and streaming anchors were found in the much deteriorated but basically complete bow section of the ship.

The bow has settled in 32 feet of turbulent water, wedged into a crevice between the rock wall and the reef that had snapped the Loch Vennachar's keel. The more heavily damaged and much larger stern section lay outside the reef in 40 feet of water, its plates and contents scattered over a much wider area of the sea floor.

The survey team raised several items from the site. These included portholes, pig-iron ingots, brick ballast, iron strakes, a fairlead, and a rigging windlass for the foremast. The items were taken back to the South Australian Museum for preservation.

Later, in 1979, the society, with help from Kangaroo Island fishermen and divers, recovered one of the bower anchors for 12 months of preservation. After spending time at the Art Gallery of South Australia, and later at the visitors' car park outside the Information Centre at Flinders Chase, the anchor was removed for further preservation work before being moved to stand above West Bay as a monument to the sailors who lost their lives when the Loch Vennachar came to her grisly end on the 7th of September 1905.

As the sun set on the final day of the expedition to survey the wreck site of the Loch Vennachar, the dive team took one last moment to remember those who had lost their lives seventy years before.

High atop the windswept cliffs, Terry Drew mounted a simple dark grey granite plaque dedicated to the ship and her crew. After a few moments of mournful silence, the team picked up their gear and traipsed back along the ragged cliff top to their camp, hidden in the shelter of the very headland that had claimed the Loch Vennachar so long ago.

The final resting place had been discovered, but more questions than answers had been raised and a story finally that needed to be told. This book has been that telling.

XXII

Artefacts from the Shipwreck.

Ship's Bell

A portion of a ships bell was recovered during the 1977 expedition to the Loch Vennachar by the Society of Underwater Historical Research. This portion of the ship's bell, was one of two on the Loch Vennachar, this one coming from the forward end of the ship. The fact that the bell was shattered would suggest something of the force of the impact of the ship against the cliffs.

Specification

Material: High-quality bell metal (approx. 80% copper, 20% tin).

Mouth Diameter: 15 – 16 inches (38–40 cm). This is slightly larger than a standard merchant bell due to the ship's size.

Height: 14 – 15 inches (35–38 cm).

Inscription: Typically cast in raised lettering: **LOCH VENNACHAR** (top arc) and **GLASGOW 1875** (bottom).

Weight: Approximately **60 – 80 lbs** (27–36 kg).

Stave of a ship's firebucket

The wooden stave from a ship's firebucket on the right came from a fire bucket similar in appearance to the contextual image of a fire bucket on the left. Ten firebuckets were placed atop the break of the poop behind the chicken coops, as indicated in the sketch.

Firebuckets on the Loch Vennachar as drawn by Henry Kemp in 1886.

Originally painted white, the mast cap—or truck—from atop the main mast served as the fitting at the very top of the mast. It protected the masthead and provided secure attachment points for rigging, such as halyards and ropes. The truck included sheaves, or pulleys, for the lines and functioned to prevent water from entering and damaging the mast's wood. By shielding the end grain, it kept the mast structurally sound and water-resistant.

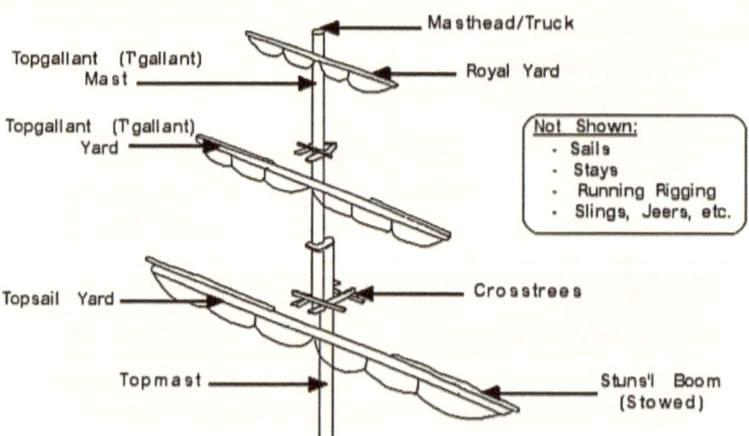

Layout of the top of the mainmast.

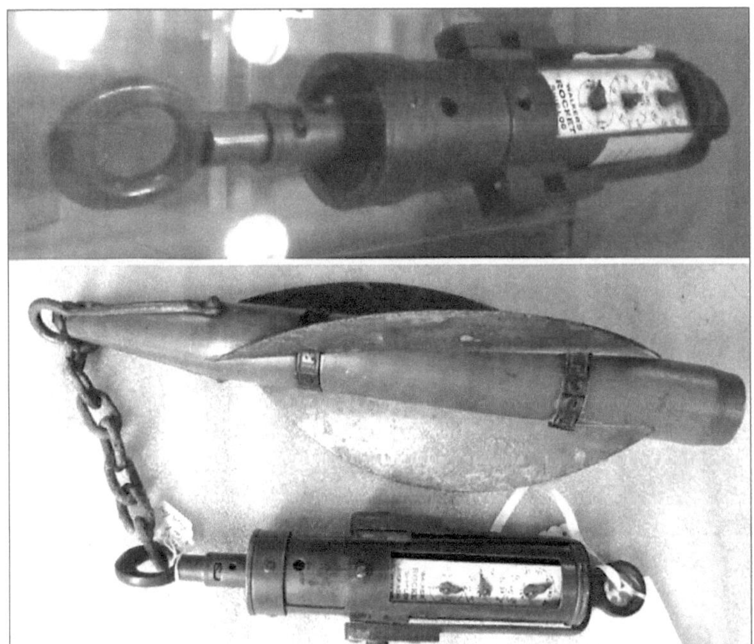

Walker's "Rocket" Ship-Log from the wreck of the Loch Vennachar on the left, and a complete outfit from the Maritime Museum at Greenwich, London.

- Top Dial: Measures fractional miles (1/10ths).
- Middle Dial: Measures single miles (1–10).
- Bottom Dial: Measures tens of miles (10–100).

The Rocket log, developed from the patent log system by Thomas Walker & Son of Birmingham, measured a ship's distance travelled through the water. A finned brass rotor was towed behind the vessel on a long, stiff line; as the ship moved, water flow spun the rotor, and this rotation was transmitted along the line to a register unit. Inside the register, gears converted the rotor's revolutions into distance, which was displayed on three dials showing fractional miles, single miles, and tens of miles. In some versions, the entire mechanism was towed behind the ship as an outrigger-style log.

Scuttles (Porthole Assemblies)

Ship's Porthole Assemblies from the Loch Vennachar.

The object on the right consists of a fixed outer mounting frame and an inner swinging glass sidelight assembly. The outer ring, shown in the photo on the beach at West Bay, was bolted directly to the ship's hull or superstructure and is heavily encrusted and rusted due to long exposure to the elements and the seafloor. This frame includes a hinge point and a butterfly or wing nut at the top, which secured the glass unit tightly to create a watertight seal. The inner swing arms, visible in the first photo, hold the glass sidelights and are hinged to the frame so they could be opened for ventilation or clamped shut against a rubber gasket to keep water out. These parts are in better condition, retaining much of their original brass or bronze finish. Some of the pieces also appear to be deadlights—solid metal covers that could be swung over the glass for protection during heavy weather.

An old capstan bar from the Loch Vennachar, found at West Bay in 2012.

The wooden bars were inserted into the head of the capstan, and one or more sailors would then walk around it, pushing on the bars to raise the anchor or haul in heavy rigging lines, such as those used to lift a yard.

Half-Hull Model of a sailing ship.

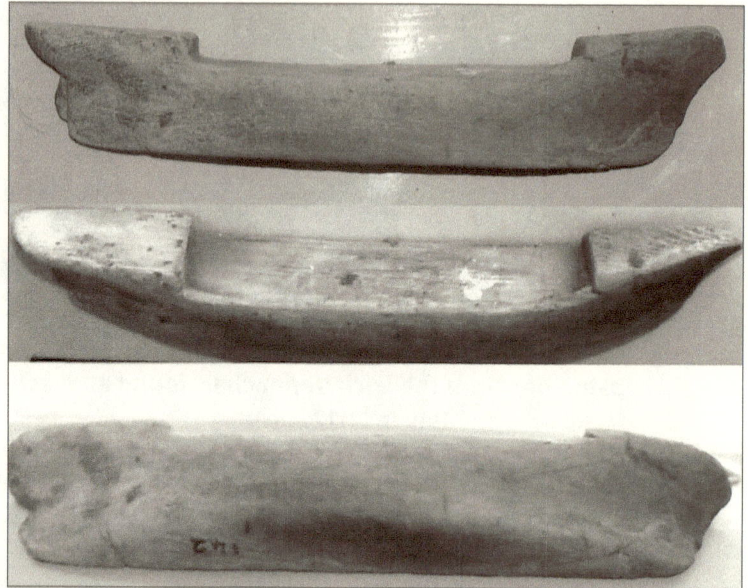

A half-model of sailing ship washed up and was found on the beach at West Bay. Historically, ship half-models (or half-hulls) were used by shipwrights to design, plan, and visualize a vessel's hull shape, ensuring symmetry and serving as templates for construction.

Piece of Swail Cloth

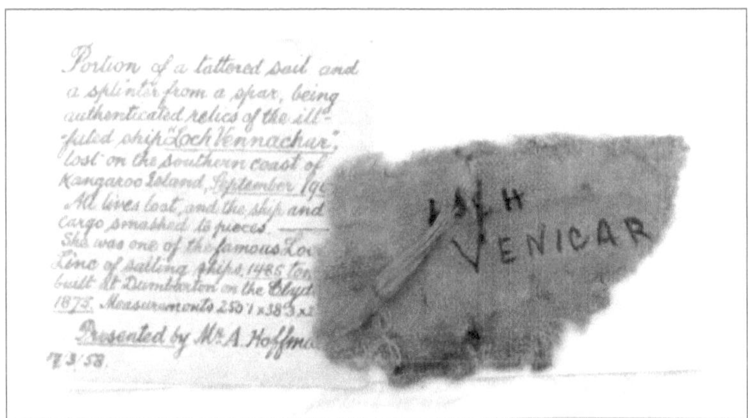

Portion of a tattered sail and a splinter from a spar, being authenticated relics of the ill- fated ship "Loch Vennachar", lost on the southern coast of Kangaroo Island, September 1905. All lives lost, and the ship and cargo smashed to pieces. —— She was one of the famous Loch Line of sailing ships, 1485 tons, built at Dumbarton on the Clyde, 1875. Measurements 250'1 x 38'3 x 22'4 Presented by Mr A. Hoffmann. 17/3/58.

Much of the sail cloth was salvaged by locals and reused as it was expensive and extremely strong and heavy canvas cloth. It made great tents, tarpaulins, inner walls for huts and homes, and covers for carts.

Clinometer

A ship's clinometer from the Loch Vennachar, also called an inclinometer, was a crucial instrument that measured the vessel's angle of heel (tilt) to port or starboard, indicating its stability and balance, essential for safety, especially during rough seas or cargo loading. Using gravity, these devices often featured a pendulum or bubble with a damped liquid-filled tube, providing clear, real-time readings of how much a ship is leaning, helping navigators adjust for uneven weight distribution or rough conditions. The clinometer was often placed within the column of the binnacle to help the helmsman and master judge the vessel's angle of tilt of its centre axis.

Conclusion

The loss of Loch Vennachar remains, in many respects, unresolved. Despite continued interest, the exact circumstances of her final voyage are uncertain. With no survivors to testify and the wreck undiscovered for decades, the 1906 Marine Board could only conclude that she likely foundered against cliffs near West Bay after straying significantly off course. Beyond this, the details of Captain Hawkins' final navigation and the ship's fate remain open to interpretation.

What survives is a combination of recorded fact, informed speculation, and the broader context of the late nineteenth-century maritime trade in which she sailed. Like many vessels of her kind, Loch Vennachar operated within a system reliant on both design and seafaring experience, where losses, though not uncommon, carried profound human and material consequences. Each disappearance marked not just a failed voyage, but lives unaccounted for and stories left incomplete.

Efforts to understand her fate have enriched the historical record, even if they have not produced definitive answers. In this sense, Loch Vennachar reflects a wider pattern of maritime loss, illustrating the challenges of reconstructing events at sea without direct evidence.

Her legacy, however, extends beyond uncertainty. The disaster, followed closely by the wreck of the Montebello, prompted long-delayed action on coastal safety. The construction of the Cape Du Couedic Lighthouse between 1907 and 1909 provided a lasting safeguard along that hazardous coastline, its presence effectively preventing further major losses in the area for decades.

Though the wreck itself was not located until 1976, Loch Vennachar had already left a permanent mark. Vennachar Point on Kangaroo Island stands as a geographical memorial, linking the ship to the region's history. As a vessel that bridged the transition from the clipper era to the age of windjammers, she occupies a distinct place in maritime history.

Remembering Loch Vennachar does not depend on resolving every uncertainty. It rests instead on acknowledging her role within a broader historical narrative, one shaped by risk, progress, and the enduring challenges of the sea.

References

Alam, M. M., Hossain, M. A., & Shafee, S. (2003). Frequency of Bay of Bengal cyclonic storms and depressions crossing different coastal zones. *International Journal of Climatology*, *23*(9), 1119–1125. https://doi.org/10.1002/joc.927

Allen's Indian Mail and Official Gazette. (1843–1870). Wm. H. Allen and Co.

Allen's Indian Mail and Official Gazette. (1871). (Vol. 29). Wm. H. Allen and Co.

Ancestry. (2019). *Ancestry.co.uk*. https://www.ancestry.co.uk/

Anderson, D. E. (1918). *The epidemics of Mauritius: With a descriptive and historical account of the island*. H. K. Lewis & Co. Ltd.

Apollonio, S. (Ed.). (2000). *The last of the Cape Horners*. Brassey's Inc.

Banerjee, A. P., Majumder, A., & Dutta, S. (2013). A study on the ever changing physical regime of the inner estuary of the River Hooghly. *ARPN Journal of Engineering and Applied Sciences*, *8*(12), 1071–1080.

Barr, J. H. (2014). *Distant destiny: The history of Aitken and Lilburn's Loch Line of Glasgow 1867-1912*. James H Barr.

Barr, J. H. (2015). *Distant destiny: The story of Aitken, Lilburn & Co. and the Loch Line of Glasgow 1867 1912*. Star Printing.

Caws, S. J. (1886). *Diary of the voyage of the Loch Sloy*. Empire Printing & Publishing Co.

Chapman, G. (2007). *Kangaroo Island shipwrecks*. Hyde Park Press.

Charlwood, D. (2000). *Wrecks & reputations*. Burgewood Books.

Christopher, P. (1990). *South Australian shipwrecks: A database 1802–1989*. Society for Underwater Historical Research.

Course, A. G. (1969). *Windjammers of the Horn*. Adlard Coles.

Crew List Index Project. (2025). *Crewlist.org.uk*. https://www.crewlist.org.uk/

Dana, R. H. (1840). *Two years before the mast*. T. Nelson & Sons.

Darby, J. (1899). *Loss of the British barque 'Loch Sloy'*. South Australian Marine Board, South Australian Government Printer.

Dixon, C. H. (1981). *Seamen and the law: An examination of the impact of legislation on the British merchant seaman's lot, 1588-1918* [Doctoral thesis, University College London]. UCL Discovery.

FamilySearch. (2015). *Familysearch.org*. https://www.familysearch.org/en/australia/

Findlay, A. G. (1866). *A directory for the navigation of the Indian Ocean, with descriptions of its coasts, islands, etc.*. Richard Holmes Laurie.

Findmypast. (n.d.). *Trace your family tree online*. https://www.findmypast.com

Guthrie, G. (Comp.). (1906). *A digest of cases decided in the Sheriff Courts of Scotland prior to 31st December, 1904*. William Hodge & Company.

Harvey, E. G. (1875). *Mullyon: Its history, scenery and antiquities*. W. Lake; Simpkin, Marshall, & Co.

Hong Kong Public Libraries. (2025). *Old Hong Kong newspapers*. https://sls.hkpl.gov.hk/digital-collection/tc/collection_old-hk-newspapers.html

Lloyd's Register Foundation. (2025). *Lloyd's Register of ships online*. https://hec.lrfoundation.org.uk/archive-library/lloyds-register-of-ships-online

Lloyds Shipping Register 1860–1998. (n.d.). Lloyds of London.

Loney, J. (1993). *The Loch Ard disaster*. Marine History Publications.

Lubbock, A. B. (1902). *Round the Horn before the mast*. John Murray.

Lubbock, A. B. (1914). *The China clippers*. Brown, Son and Ferguson.

Lubbock, A. B. (1921). *The colonial clippers*. Brown, Son and Ferguson.

Lubbock, A. B. (1922). *The Blackwall frigates*. James Brown and Son.

Lubbock, A. B. (1927). *The last of the windjammers* (Vol. 1). James Brown and Son.

Lubbock, A. B. (1932). *The nitrate clippers*. Brown, Son and Ferguson.

Lubbock, A. B. (1933). *The best of sail: The romance of the clipper ships* (A. Campbell, Ed.). The Macmillan Company.

Lubbock, A. B. (1935). *The last of the windjammers* (Vol. 2). James Brown and Son.

Lubbock, A. B. (1983). *The Down Easters*. Dover Publications. (Original work published 1929)

Maury, M. F. (1854). *Explanations and sailing directions to accompany the wind and current charts* (6th ed.). E. C. and J. Biddle.

Maury, M. F. (1855). *The physical geography of the sea*. Harper & Brothers.

Memorial University of Newfoundland. (2025). *Welcome | More than a list of crew*. https://mha.mun.ca/mha/mlc/index.php

Mudie, I. (1966). *Wreck of the Admella*. Rigby Limited.

National Library of Australia. (2019). *Trove*. https://trove.nla.gov.au/

New Zealand Government. (2022). *Papers Past*.
https://paperspast.natlib.govt.nz/newspapers

Newby, E. (1983). *The last grain race*. Granada Publishing.

Old Fulton New York Post Cards. (n.d.). *fultonhistory.com*.
https://fultonhistory.com/Fulton.html

Osterstock, A. (1979). *The Duncow report*. Austaprint.

Phayre, A. P. (1841). Account of Arakan. *Journal of the Asiatic Society of Bengal, 10*(116), 679–712.

Provincial Archives of New Brunswick. (2025). *Archives2.gnb.ca.*
https://archives2.gnb.ca/Search/Hamilton/DMB/SearchResults.aspx

Rosser, W. H., & Imray, J. F. (1867). *Indian Ocean directory: The seaman's guide to the navigation of the Indian Ocean and China Sea*. James Imray and Son.

S., E. H. (1961). Journal of the Hong Kong Branch of the Royal Asiatic Society, Vol. I (1960-61). *Journal of the American Oriental Society, 81*(4), 463.
https://doi.org/10.2307/595750

Simpson, P. W. (2016a). *Windjammer*. Clippership Press.

Simpson, P. W. (2016b). *Windjammer: Tales of the clipper ship Loch Soy: 1878-1899*. Clippership Press.

Simpson, P. W. (2020). *Star of Greece - For profit and glory*. Clippership Press.

Simpson, P. W. (2021). *The missing: Tales of those who never came home*. Lulu.com.

Simpson, P. W. (2025). *Fleurieu shipwrecks*. Clippership Press.

Stark, W. F. (2003). *The last time around Cape Horn*. Carroll & Graf.

State Library Victoria. (2019). *Search & discover*. https://www.slv.vic.gov.au/search-discover

Underhill, H. A. (1988). *Deep-water sail*. Brown, Son and Ferguson.

Vernon-Harcourt, L. F. (1897). *Report on the River Hugli*. Caledonian Steam Printing Works.

Villiers, A. (1972). *Falmouth for orders*. Charles Scribner's Sons.

Wade, J. (1967). Farewell Loch Sloy. *The Compass*. Mobile Oil Company.

Weiss, N. (1875). *Personal recollections of the wreck of the Ville-du-Havre and the Loch-Earn* (N. Weiss, Trans.). A. D. F. Randolph & Co.

Winter, C. (2012, April 23). *Kangaroo Island reveals some of its history and mystery* [Radio broadcast transcript]. Australian Broadcasting Corporation.

Index